TARGUM ONKELOS
TO DEUTERONOMY

TARGUM ONKELOS TO DEUTERONOMY

An English Translation of the Text
With Analysis and Commentary

(Based on A. Sperber's Edition)

by

Israel Drazin

Ktav Publishing House, Inc.

COPYRIGHT © 1982
ISRAEL DRAZIN

Library of Congress Cataloging in Publication Data

Bible. O.T. Deuteronomy. Aramaic. Onḳelos. 1982.
    Targum Onkelos to Deuteronomy.

    Aramaic and English.
    Bibliography: p.
    Includes index.
    1. Bible. O.T. Deuteronomy. Aramaic. Onḳelos
—Translation into English.   I. Onḳelos.
II. Sperber, Alexander, 1897–   .III. Drazin,
Israel, 1935–   . IV. Bible. O.T. Deuteronomy.
English. Drazin. 1982.   V. Title.
BS1274.A7054   1982   222'.15042   82–4596
ISBN 0–87068–755–7

MANUFACTURED IN THE UNITED STATES OF AMERICA

Dedicated
in love and in gratitude
to my dear wife

DINA DRAZIN

ʾttʾ kšrtʾ mnw yškḥ
yqyrʾ hyʾ

Targum, Proverbs 31:10

and to
father and mother
RABBI DR. NATHAN DRAZIN *zṭl*
MRS. CELIA HOENIG DRAZIN

CONTENTS

ACKNOWLEDGMENTS

This commentary was submitted to St. Mary's University, Baltimore, Maryland, together with a companion piece, *Targumic Studies*. As a result of these works and other requirements, the author received the degree of Doctor of Philosophy with honors. He is deeply indebted to Dr. Moses Aberbach, who introduced him to Targumic studies on the Master's level, and to Drs. Samuel Rosenblatt, Jacob B. Agus, and David Altshuler, who accepted this work as partial fulfillment of the Ph.D. requirements. Each gave invaluable suggestions which are greatly appreciated.

The commentary is based on the Targum text of Alexander Sperber, *The Bible in Aramaic* (E.J. Brill, 1959). However, because of the Sperber copyright, the Aramaic text printed in the published edition of this study is that of A. Berliner (Berlin, 1884). Neither text is free of the many errors that have crept into the extant Onkelos texts.

The author is very grateful to his wife, Dina, for her patience during the years he worked on the Targums. He also thanks her, his mother, and those of his children who helped with proofreading.

ABBREVIATIONS

ARN	Aboth de Rabbi Nathan
b.	Babli or Babylonian (indicating that the tractate is from the Babylonian Talmud)
B.	Targum Onkelos text by Dr. A. Berliner (Sabioneta Text of 1557)
B.B.	Baba Bathra
Bek.	Bekoroth
Ber.	Berakoth
Bez.	Beẓah
B.K.	Baba Kama
B.M.	Baba Mezia
BO	*Biure Onkelos,* by S. B. Schefftel (Munich, 1888)
CGT	Cairo Geniza Targum Fragments. These translations are found on many Pentateuchal verses, but only 5:19–26 of Deut
CS	*Chalifot Semalot,* by B. Z. J. Berkowitz (Wilna, 1874)
Deut	Deuteronomy
Exod	Exodus
FT	Fragmentary Targum. In this volume; the reference is to the Bomberg fragments, unless otherwise indicated
Gen	Genesis
Git.	Gittin
Hag.	Ḥagigah
Hul.	Ḥullin
Ket.	Ketuboth
Kid.	Kiddushin
Lam	Lamentations
Lev	Leviticus
LV	*Lechem Vesimla,* by B. Z. J. Berkowitz(Wilna, 1843)
LXX	Septuagint
m.	Mishnah

Meg.	Megillah
Mek.	Mekilta
Men.	Menaḥoth
Mid.	Middoth
MT	Massoretic Text
N	*Targum to the Pentateuch, Codex Vatican, Neofiti I* (Jerusalem: Makor Publishing Ltd.). This is a copy of the original manuscript.
Naz.	Nazir
Ned.	Nedarim
NL	*Netina Lager,* by Nathan Adler (Wilna, 1886)
Num	Numbers
Ohol.	Oholoth
Pes.	Pesaḥim
Pesh.	Peshitta
Ps-Jon	Tagum Pseudo-Jonathan. The text in the Rabbinic Bible was used unless otherwise indicated.
PT	Palestinian Targums: N, FT, and Ps-Jon
R.	Rabbi, Rab
-R.	Rabbah (indicating a volume of Midrash Rabbah)
R.H.	Rosh Hashanah
Sam. Pent.	Samaritan Pentateuch
Sanh.	Sanhedrin
Shab.	Shabbath
Sheb.	Shebuoth
Shek.	Shekalim
Sot.	Sotah
Suk.	Sukkah
t.	Tosephta
Taan.	Taanith
Tam.	Tamid
TJ	Targum Jonathan (to the prophets)
TO	Targum Onkelos
Vulg.	Vulgate
y.	Yerushalmi or Jerusalem (indicating that the tractate is from the Jerusalem Talmud)
Yad.	Yadayim
Yeb.	Yebamot
Yom.	Yoma
Zeb.	Zebaḥim

Transliterations

א	=	ʾ
ב	=	*b*
ג	=	*g*
ד	=	*d*
ה	=	*h*
ו	=	*w*
ז	=	*z*
ח	=	*ḥ*
ט	=	*ṭ*
י	=	*y*
כ ך	=	*k*
ל	=	*l*
מ ם	=	*m*
נ ן	=	*n*
ס	=	*s*
ע	=	ʿ
פ ף	=	*p*
צ ץ	=	*ṣ*
ק	=	*q*
ר	=	*r*
שׁ	=	*š*
שׂ	=	*ś*
ת	=	*t*

INTRODUCTION

1. Contents of This Commentary

Targum Onkelos (henceforth TO) is the most literal of all Targumim, yet it includes thousands of clear and subtle deviations from the Massoretic text (MT). Nearly all Targumic deviations are meaningful and not just accidental. Yet, only the most careful scrutiny of the Targum text—taking into consideration TO's principles of deviation, the renderings of the other extant Targums, and the relevant rabbinic and critical commentaries and studies—can disclose the reasons for the deviations.

This book presents such a study of Targum Onkelos to Deuteronomy. The Targum is translated and over 1,600 Targumic deviations from the MT are noted and discussed. Each is compared with the renderings of the other available Aramaic Targums, Pseudo-Jonathan (Ps-Jon), Neofiti (N), and the fragmented Targums (FT). Where appropriate, attention is given to the comments contained in Talmudic and Midrashic literature as well as to ancient and modern critical commentaries.

2. The Targums

The word Targum is Aramaic and means "translation." There are extant three complete Aramaic Targums to the Pentateuch: (1) TO; (2) Ps-Jon, which is also called Targum Jerushalmi and Palestinian Targum; and (3) N, which is also recognized as incorporating Palestinian traditions. There are also fragmentary texts of Targums; Tosephta Targums to some Pentateuchal books (but not Deut); as well as the "sectarian" Peshitta, the Syropalestinian Aramaic translation, and the Samaritan Targum.

TO is for the most part a literal translation: MT's Hebrew is generally rendered by its Aramaic equivalent word for word. When the Aramaic permits, the Targumist translates every letter. (See, for example, the notes to the Ten Commandments, 5:6–18). When TO is not literal, the deviation is frequently very subtle. There may be, among other things, just a change in number, from singular to plural, or in the use of an apparent synonym for the customary Aramaic rendering, which does not mean exactly what the Hebrew apparently intends. The Targumist may also add a word. Rarely is there more than that. The other Targums are more expansive, frequently paraphrasing and adding interpretations that are not even implied in the MT.

Tradition ascribes the authorship of TO to the proselyte Onkelos, a second-century contemporary of R. Akiba and a pupil of R. Eliezer b. Hyrcanus and R. Joshua b. Hananiah.[1] The Babylonian Talmud (Meg. 3a) states that he translated the Pentateuch under the guidance of R. Eliezer and R. Joshua.[2]

Tradition also recognizes that Targums preceded TO. During the second commonwealth and probably since the time of Ezra (ca. 440 B.C.E.),[3] when the masses of the Judeans in the land of Israel and in Babylonia spoke Aramaic, the Torah was read to the people in the synagogue, first in Hebrew and then in Aramaic translation, so that the people could understand it and be guided by it. Each translator (or *Meturgeman*) rendered the Bible in the vernacular, either briefly or expansively, according to his own knowledge and style.[4] As Targums proliferated with unacceptable translations, TO was composed by Onkelos for the masses and was accepted by the rabbis as the authorized Targum.[5] Jews were told to read the Torah portion each week, twice in Hebrew and once in the official Targum, TO.[6]

Modern scholars disagree concerning TO's origin and its relationship to the extant unofficial Targums and rabbinic literature. In fact, there are virtually as many views on the subject as there are scholars that address it.

In 1832, Leopold Zunz (*Die Gottesdienstlichen Voträge der Juden*) argued that TO was composed at the beginning of the third century of the common era before the Talmuds and Midrashim. He notes many passages in the Talmuds and Midrashim that he feels are dependent upon TO. He recognizes that a freer, expanded Aramaic translation of the Bible, or parts of it, existed prior to TO and was used since the generation of Ezra. However, the extant unofficial Targums, Ps-Jon and FT, which contain some obviously late readings, were not composed until the later part of the seventh century C.E. Hermann Seligsohn (*MGWJ*, 1857, pp. 138–149; *Die Duabus Hierosolymitana Pentateuchi Paraphrasibus*, 1838) is in general agreement with Zunz. He argues that TO was followed by FT, which is a series of glosses to TO based on a then existing PT. Ps-Jon is an expanded version of FT, but it is also dependent upon TO. W. Bacher (*J.E.*, 1906) expresses a similar view. A PT that no longer exists preceded TO. TO was followed by FT during the Babylonian period and by Ps-Jon in the Islamic era.

Contrary positions concerning the order of the Targums were taken by other scholars. For example, in 1841 Z. Frankel (*Vorstudien zur Septuaginta*) pointed to Greek words in the existing PT texts. He feels that these words support an earlier date, at least for these passages, during the Hellenistic period. Thus, FT was not comments on TO, but was originally a complete version of the PT.[7] Abraham Geiger (*Hamikra Vetargumov*, 1857) agrees with Frankel, but argues that FT was always fragmented. He feels that TO is a Babylonian edited version of the PT. Geiger was the first modern scholar to study apparent variants in the vorlage of Ps-Jon and FT from the MT. He found about 100 texts which he felt were evidences of a *pre-Massoretic* Hebrew text. He also pointed out many PT verses which contained divergent explanations from the interpretations contained in rabbinic literature. These explanations, he felt, must predate the rabbinic period, when such divergences could not have been tolerated. He pointed to incidences where, in his view, TO shows literary dependence on Ps-Jon and FT. Theodor Nöldeke (*Die Alttestamentliche Literatur in einer Reihe von Aufsätzen dargestellt von T. Nöldeke*, 1868) also agrees with Frankel. Addressing the problem of late PT readings, Nöldeke argues that these are additions to an early text that had not been fixed.

The first systematic study of the PT language was published in 1894 by Gustav Dalman (*Grammatik des Jüdisch-Palästinischen Aramäisch*). Dalman agrees with Zunz. In contrast to Geiger, he demonstrates that the PT show reliance on TO. He writes that TO is the best representative of the Aramaic spoken in the first century of the common era because the PT were composed no earlier than the fifth century C.E.

In 1930, Paul Kahle published fragmentary PT manuscripts from the Cairo Geniza (*Masoreten des Westerns II*). In *The Cairo Geniza* (1959, pp. 191–208), Kahle posits that the Cairo Geniza fragments (CGT) are the relics of a PT which preceded TO. The PT lacked a fixed text. It developed over centuries from free Biblical interpretations rendered during synagogue services. CGT contains the spoken language of the land of Israel. TO was written in Babylon in the artificial language of Babylonian scholars. Kahle set a third-century date for TO's composition since there are Nehardea readings in the Masora to TO, and the Talmudic Academy

of Nehardea was destroyed in the third century. Ps-Jon, according to
Kahle, is a combination of TO and PT. FT is a collection of "Midrashic
material from the Palestinian Targum which people did not want to lose
after the Targum Onkelos had become the authoritative Targum in Palestine in the ninth or tenth century."[8] Kahle dates the PT to pre-Christian
times because of a reference to John Hyrcanus (Deut 32:11) and a translation of Exod 22:4 which is contrary to the Mishnaic interpretation of the
verse. Kahle states that TO, in contrast, contains no "old parts," although
TJ to the Prophets has them. The "midrashic element is almost entirely
lacking in the Targum Onkelos, which contains only a word-for-word
translation of the Hebrew text of the Torah, reproducing exactly . . . the
interpretation presupposed in Mishna and Talmud." As we shall see, this
study does not support most of Kahle's conclusions.

Kahle's principal opponent was H. Albeck (*Jubilee Volume to B. M.
Lewin*, 1940, pp. 93–104). Albeck points out that the Targums reflect only
the personal views of the translators (*Meturgeman*). He notes that rabbinic tradition has always tolerated dissident opinions as to the *peshat*, the
literal sense of the text. Furthermore, there is no rabbinic statement indicating that every Targumic verse has halakhic authority (*Einleitung und
Register zu Bereshit Rabba*, vol. 3, 1965, pp. 44–54). Albeck reminds us
that anti-halakhic Biblical interpretations are also found in the Midrashim, Talmuds, and Philo. The rabbis never forbade different interpretations of the Torah, but only those teachings which encourage *behavior*
contrary to halakhah (b. Ked. 49a, b. Meg. 25a, y. Ber. 5:3, and Gen R.
70:17). Even famous and accepted rabbinical commentators who knew the
halakhah, like Rashi, Rashbam, Ibn Ezra, and Nachmanides, sometimes
chose to interpret the Torah in a text-faithful manner, contrary to
halakhah.

Y. J. Weinberg ("On the History of the Targumim," *The Abraham
Weiss Jubilee Volume*, 1964, pp. 361–376) suggests that the early Targumists followed the method of aggadists, the popular speakers who were
the first to interpret the Torah for the people. It was only later that
scholarly halakhists attempted to explain verses according to the halakhah.
P. Churgin ("The Halakhah in Targum Onkelos," *Horeb* 9, 1946, pp.
79–93) states that TO's halakhic elements were added over a period of
many generations, by many hands, without an overall plan or concern for
consistency. They represent subjective attempts to lessen confusion and to
clarify texts: the primary purpose was not to teach correct halakhah.

Most scholars, however, agree with Geiger's and Kahle's approach to determining the age of Targumic material by whether it diverges from the accepted rabbinical interpretation. For example, Renee Block (*Revue des Études Juives*, 1955) analyzed Gen 38:1–30 and concluded that Ps-Jon is an edited TO version containing ancient PT traditions. A. Diez Macho (*Neophyti I. Targum Palestinese*, 1968) pointed to other anti-Mishnaic Targumic renderings, such as Ps-Jon to Lev 22:28 being contrary to y. Ber. 5:3 (9c). M. Ahana (*VT*, 1974, pp. 385–389) argues that the rabbis would never have countenanced Targums with anti-halakhic opinions. J. Faur (*JQR*, 1975, 6, pp. 19–26) concludes that the Jerusalem Talmud must have considered the Targums authoritative since the *Meturgeman* who deviated from the halakhah was censured. J. Heinemann (*Tarbiz*, 1968, 9) emphasizes that the Targums were used during the synagogue service, and, therefore, had to conform to rabbinical teachings. Matthew Black (*An Aramaic*, 1954) emphasizes the importance of PT's early date and states that they are the best source for the Aramaic spoken during the time of Jesus.

In 1956, Alejandro Diez Macho notified the world of his discovery in the Vatican of a full PT, the codex of N, and added a new subject to the discussion. In 1959 (*VT*, pp. 222–245), he argued that N, even in its present recension, belongs to the first or second century c.e., but that it is based on a pre-Christian textual tradition. Diez Macho based his conclusion primarily on (a) anti-halakhic Targumic material, (b) early geographical and historical items, (c) New Testament parallels, and (d) Greek and Latin terms. Diez Macho also relied on some supposedly pre-Massoretic Hebrew vorlage, for which he was criticized by P. Wienberg-Møller (*VT*, 1962).

In 1966, M. McNamara (*RSO*, pp. 1–15) showed parallels between N and the Talmud. He concluded that the rabbis used N. Later in the same year (*Analecta Biblica*, pp. 270–272), he supported an early dating of N by showing more New Testament parallels to the Targum.

In 1958, D. Reider (*Tarbiz* 38, pp. 81–86) pointed out that N is incomplete and faulty. The original translator was not learned and translated many words incorrectly. The copyist was careless in his work. He skipped parts of sentences and frequently missed whole passages. The document's censor increased the errors by his deletions because he frequently did not understand the text. The marginal (M) and interlineal additions are an attempt to correct the text, but they too have errors. Many of these additions may have been borrowed from an existing Targum(s)—other additions are pure speculative interpretations or corrections—but they do not attempt to place a complete fragmented Targum in the margin. Reider warns users of N to be very cautions. G. J. Cowling (*The Palestinian Targum*, 1968) and J. A. Foster (*The Language and Text of Codex Neofiti I*, 1969) conclude that errors exist in N because it is a late translation from the Greek. They feel that M, on the other hand, preserves a very early and valuable Aramaic translation from the Hebrew MT.

The present study of Targum Onkelos to Deuteronomy shows that, contrary to the view of Kahle and others (*The Cairo Geniza*, p. 197), there are many Talmudic and Midrashic parallels to TO. It reveals that TO renders the text according to its *peshat*, although the PT use *derash*. It contains many interpretations that are contrary to rabbinic tradition recorded in the Midrashim and Talmuds (Kahle, pp. 196, 205–208), including translations which are contrary to accepted rabbinic halakhah. The latter finding supports Albeck's view that rabbinic tradition tolerated dissident opinions regarding the *peshat* of the Biblical text. This study also reveals close parallels between TO and the PT and the rather remarkable reliance by TO on the Sifre, a fourth-century composition. Thus, TO was, in all probability, also composed or redacted in the land of Israel, but after the Sifre, in the late fourth or early fifth century.

3. The Present Translation

An English translation of TO was published in 1862 by J. W. Etheridge. It is in archaic English and contains many errors.[9] It does not note deviations or explain them. An English rendering of N is contained in A. Diez Macho's *Neophyti I. Targum Palestinense*, vols. 1–5 (Madrid, 1968–78). The translators do not note the deviations of N from the MT. Furthermore, a large number are paraphrased. Thus, many of N's Biblical interpretations are lost. This series contains selected translations of Ps-Jon (by E. Levine), and the Etheridge volume has a complete translation of Ps-Jon and FT with the same problems.

The present study is a modern, generally literal rendering of the original Aramaic. Freer translations are used only when they do not interfere with an understanding of TO deviations. Every deviation (except for additions such as *d* "of," implied in Hebrew grammer, but necessary in Aramaic) is noted. Whenever TO deviates, the renderings by N, FT and

Ps-Jon are noted and compared, and the Targums are explained with references to relevant scholarly literature.

4. The Value of Targumic Statistics

This study also contains a statistical analysis with notes, tabulating, categorizing, and explaining the different types of TO deviations. (A similar statistical study of TO to Genesis is contained in the author's *Targumic Studies*. These are the first Targumic statistical studies.) It will be shown that, although many call TO a literal rendering, TO to Deut contains an average of three deviations for every two verses. Thus TO can only be styled literal in comparison with the other, more expansive Targums.

Once the pattern of TO deviations is understood, it will become evident that many scholars drew erroneous conclusions from deviations. They supposed, for example, that the Targumist deviates in certain verses to teach halakhah or a theological lesson. However, most if not all of these renderings were for other purposes, usually to clarify the text.

By focusing on deviations and comparing TO's deviations with those of the PT, the close family relationship between the Targums is also clarified.

Until now, studies have usually compared the general Targumic ideas or concentrated on their language. The studies found differences and only minor agreements. Thus, for example, as we noted earlier, Geiger and Kahle cited the differences and argued that TO is based on a Babylonian tradition. G. J. Kuiper (*The Ps-Jon Targum and Its Relationship to TO*, 1972) did likewise. He speaks of only "minor agreements" as is "indicated by the fact that the general rendering of the PT and Ps-Jon is not found in TO."

These scholars did not note and tabulate TO's deviations and compare them with those of N and Ps-Jon to determine whether the PT also renders in the same way; thus they failed to see the frequent Targumic agreements. Ps-Jon to Deut has the same (or similar) interpretations as TO 84 percent of the times that TO deviates, and N 69 percent of the times. (The PT also has deviations not in TO.) Thus, it should be clear that while the PT is more expansive than TO and has a different translation philosophy that allows for such expansions, the three Targums are generally based on the same interpretative tradition. Since PT reflects rabbinic material of the land of Israel, so too must TO. (Needless to say, while the Targums share the same tradition, they sometimes present it differently. These differences are noted and explained in the statistical study and in the commentary to the translation.)[10]

5. Sifre

Note 29 to the "Statistics" tabulates the close to 300 instances where TO's deviations from the MT parallel teachings in Midrash Sifre and the Jerusalem and Babylonian Talmuds. There are 201 parallels between TO and Sifre.

Sifre comments on less than half of Deut. TO's deviations in Deut reflect Sifre's interpretation in about a third of the verses where there is extant Midrash.

More significant than the number and percentage is the remarkable fact that TO contains virtually all, if not all, of the non-aggadic Sifre material. To put it differently, TO incorporates Sifre material that interprets the Biblical verses according to the *peshat*, the simple or literal meaning of the text, and not those that are *derash*, interpretations trying to disclose the hidden meaning of the text. Furthermore, TO does not explain the text differently than Sifre except where Sifre has a *derash* (or what the Targumist felt was a *derash*) or where TO has a scribal error (see note 29 for examples).

A few statistics will make this clear. There are, for example, 489 verses in the first 17 chapters, the first half, of Deut. Only 186 of these verses, about 38 percent, have comments by Sifre. TO parallels Sifre in 56 verses (in 60 instances) or about 30 percent. The passages where TO does not reflect the Sifre are all instances where Sifre's comments, either halakhic or aggadic, are *derash*. These are discussed in note 29.

These statistics for the first half of Deut reflect the situation in the remainder of the book. Two words of caution, however, are in order. First, a reader may decide that a particular Sifre verse is *peshat* and wonder why TO does not include it. If he recalls that commentators differ on whether a particular interpretation is *peshat* or *derash*, his problem vanishes. The Targumist was human and had to make human decisions. Furthermore, while there is a remarkable parallelism between TO and the *peshat* of Sifre, it is reasonable to conclude that the Targumist did not feel the need to deviate and incorporate every Sifre interpretation. Second, while the statistics analyzed concern verses, there is frequently more than one interpretation in every Sifre passage, even as there is frequently more than one deviation in every TO verse.

That the parallelism between TO and Sifre are consistent throughout all of Deut is important for establishing the age of the Targum's composition. Sifre is a collection of many rabbinic views from different generations. Also, some of the Sifre material may have been added after the original collection was organized. These facts, with others discussed below, suggest that TO drew from Sifre and not the reverse.

The parallelism between TO and Sifre can be summarized with five points: (1) There are over 200 instances where TO's translation reflects a Sifre interpretation. This number represents about a third of the verses where there are Sifre comments. (2) TO never explains Deut contrary to Sifre. (3) TO uses all, or virtually all, Sifre interpretations that are *peshat*. (4) The reverse is not true: TO has deviations for clarification that are not in Sifre. (5) Thus, TO is reflecting a tradition of the land of Israel also contained in the Sifre. TO, therefore, like Sifre, may have been composed in Eretz Israel, although it may have been edited later in Babylon.

As to which composition, Sifre or TO, came first, there are four possibilities. First, Sifre was composed after TO and follows an interpretative, tradition that originated with or was incorporated into the Targum. This is possible, but in view of the subtle, concise, and often ambiguous nature of TO's deviations, it is doubtful that the editor of Sifre sat down, examined every deviation, found a reason for it, and then wrote an expansion of it, proving his point by the opinion of tannaitic sages who lived over a period of many generations. Furthermore, this would fail to explain Sifre's *derash*, the material in TO not included in Sifre, the collection of divergent tannaitic views, etc.

The second possibility is that both Sifre and TO were composed during several generations, by a series of authors, with mutual borrowings, both basing their interpretations on the same rabbinic tradition, which was transmitted orally or which was written but is no longer extant.

Thirdly, it is similarly possible that both Sifre and TO are based on an earlier, more expansive Targum that is no longer extant. While both (2) and (3) are possible, they are unlikely because of the remarkable and consistent parallels between the two documents and for the other reasons mentioned above. Furthermore, if Sifre drew from a Targum, one would expect some mention of a Targum among the many other sources that are cited, but there is none in Sifre.

The fourth possibility is that Sifre preceded TO and the author(s) of the Targum translated with "one finger in the MT and another in Sifre." (The Talmuds were used, along with oral and no longer extant Midrashim, and perhaps other Targums, as a supplement.) This would explain the remarkable parallelism and the additional material in TO.

This conclusion is similar to the finding of H. Albeck in his study of TO to Gen. Dr. Albeck ("Mekoroth Ha-Bereshet Rabba," *Einleitung und Register zu Berechit Rabba*, vol. 3 [Jerusalem, 1965], pp. 44–54) believes that while the author(s) of Gen R. may have drawn some material from an old written or oral Targum (from which TO and the remaining extant Targums also drew material), Gen R.'s source was not TO. The language of Gen R. is sometimes very close to but is not always identical to TO's. There are about three dozen subjects that both add, but they do so in different language and Gen R. does not cite TO as its source. There are instances where the author(s) of Gen R. has difficulty interpreting a verse which is explained by TO, and Gen R. does not turn to TO for help. Furthermore, an incident is cited in Gen R. where rabbis wanted to know the Aramaic rendering of a word and had to travel to a place where Aramaic was spoken, and they did not look at TO where the word is explained. Gen R. is believed to have been composed in the fourth century. Albeck's statistics of parallels between TO to Gen and Gen R. are supplemented in Israel Drazin's study on TO to Gen in *Targumic Studies*.

The two indications of an earlier date for TO (b. Meg. 3a and Kahle's argument about the Nehardea Masora) do not present a problem. The Babylonian Talmud (Meg. 3a) states that Onkelos translated the Pentateuch into Aramaic before R. Eliezer and R. Joshua. As noted earlier, there is virtually unanimous acceptance that the Talmud is referring to the Greek translation of Aquila. P. Kahle (*The Cairo Geniza*, 1959, pp. 191–208) sets a third-century date for the composition of TO since it is known from the Masora to the Targum that there were Nehardea readings of TO. The Talmudic Academy of Nehardea was destroyed in the third century. However, we also know that the Nehardean scholars went to Pumpedita, where many of them studied apart and continued to produce Nehardean traditions.

6. Halakhah

Because it is apparent to all that TO does not teach every halakhah (from the Hebrew *halakh*, "to go" or "to walk"—meaning "rabbinic law"), various views have been developed to explain when TO adds halakhah.

Z. Hirsch Chajes (*Imre Binah*, Zolkiew, 1850), Solomon I. Rapoport (*Letters of S. I. Rapoport*, Przemyśl, 1885), Nathan Adler (*Netina Lager*, Wilna, 1886), and others argue that TO adds halakhah when:

1. people might be confused, to help them avoid making mistakes in halakhah;

2. teaching a law which concerns the masses, who are generally unfamiliar with the halakhah, but not a law addressed to the court, whose members are expected to know the halakhah;

3. the addition fits in with the plain meaning of the verse;

4. sects disputed the halakhah;

5. there was a tannaitic dispute on the halakhah and TO informs us of the rabbinic view; or

6. teaching proper behavior.

P. Churgin ("Halakhah in Targum Onkelos," *Horeb*, 1946, pp. 79–93), M. Herskovics ("For Whom was Targum Onkelos Written," *Hadarom* 30, 32, 1969–1970, pp. 164–171, 155–170), and others take a different approach. Churgin, as mentioned earlier, argues that the original author(s) of TO did not deviate to teach halakhah. Halakhic elements were added during later periods by copyists and scribes without any overall plan. Herskovics writes that the Targums were originally recited by *Meturgeman* who added oral aggadic material to capture the attention of the congregation. They did not attempt to teach halakhah, which the populace could learn from their spiritual leaders, scholars who were legal experts. Any halakhah found in the Targums was, as Churgin noted, added later over many generations.

Notes 39 and 40 of the "Statistics" to this study discuss some four dozen supposedly halakhic and anti-halakhic elements in TO to Deut. The details of notes 39 and 40 are summarized below. The discussion supports the view expressed by Churgin and Herscovics. There are many verses where a reader might be confused, where there is a tannaitic halakhic dispute, where there are chances to teach an ethical lesson, and other bases for deviating to present a halakhah. Ps-Jon and N frequently render these verses to teach the halakhah, but TO does not do so. Furthermore, most, if not all, Aramaic renderings that various scholars consider "halakhic" may not be so.

As noted earlier, TO rarely adds words, and the deviations are subtle and concise. There is no explicit halakhah, as one finds in N and Ps-Jon (see note 41). It is impossible to be sure that a deviation intends to teach halakhah. It is more reasonable to conclude that the deviation was made simply to clarify the text or for some similar reason.

In analyzing the some four dozen "halakhic" teachings detailed in notes 39 and 40, it is possible to summarize the bases used by the scholars for concluding that they are "halakhic." There are nine bases, but none can serve as a sufficient foundation to support the "halakhic" conclusion.

1. TO is literal and the commentator indicates that the Targum fails to deviate in order to teach a halakhah.

This is an argument from silence. As noted already, TO is a literal translation, and, therefore, nothing should be concluded from the Targum's failure to deviate as long as the Biblical text is clear. If this were done consistently, tens of thousands of questionable "teachings" would be found throughout the Pentateuch. On the contrary, it is only when TO deviates from a literal rendering that one has good reason for asking why.

2. The Aramaic translation contains a Hebrew word similar to or exactly the same as the MT.

TO frequently includes Hebrew words. These words were either in the original translation (see the many Hebraisms in the Sperber apparatus of the textual variants), or they are later scribal additions. The Hebrew wording is the result of a conscious or unconscious attempt to conform the translation to the Biblical original. (Hebraisms, one might note, are even more frequent in N.) Again, if consistent conclusions were drawn from this Targumic practice, there should be hundreds of halakhic teachings, and not just the few that some commentators have found. Furthermore, and this applies to most of the other supposed bases discussed below, if the Targumist wanted to teach halakhah to the general population for the reasons the scholars give, the halakhic teachings should have been stated explicitly. As we noted, this explicit practice is followed by N and Ps-Jon.

3. The commentator relies on a textual reading not found in all TO texts.

A vorlage not found in all texts is suspect as being a late addition, either added purposely or by mistake.

4. The scholar depends on a second rendering in the TO text, a conflation or doublet.

Again, these doublets are suspect of being late additions. Many are clearly the result of combined Targumic texts. N and Ps-Jon usually have only one rendering in these instances. (See note 5 of the "Statistics.")

5. TO has one of several valid translations of a word. There is a rabbinic dispute as to the meaning and TO reflects one view.

If the *peshat* allows more than one translation, the Targumist must choose between them. If the Aramaic always reflects the halakhah, this basis might be considered sound. However, the Targumist also translates contrary to the halakhah (see note 40). Furthermore, simply rendering a word according to its halakhic interpretation does not teach the law, for the word or phrase is generally as unexplicit in TO as it is in the MT. The only thing we can say with any sense of surety is that when faced with the problem of how to translate a word, the Targumist generally tried to give a clear rendering in accordance with the rabbinic tradition. However, the primary interest of the Targumist was the *peshat*, not the halakhah.

6. A word or phrase is added in TO which while not commenting on the halakhah explicitly is seen to imply it.

Most of the points outlined above apply here. An objective analysis of these verses will reveal that these additions can almost always, if not always, be explained as being made for the sake of clarity.

7. An uncharacteristic word is used in the translation.

Frequently, a commentator unfamiliar with the details of the Targumic style will conclude that because TO has a different word than the one used previously in the section, the change hints at a halakhah. However, TO's style is to avoid redundant usages. Again, consistent application of this rule for halakhic investigations shows that it is inappropriate.

8. The halakhic conclusion is based on a characteristic deviation (for example, "accept" for "hear") or a typical addition (such as *qdm* or *dḥl*).

Needless to say, when it is realized that the deviation is characteristic and indeed frequent, it also can be seen that there is no basis for the halakhic conclusion.

9. TO translates with a word that the rabbis use for a halakhah (for example *mezuzah*).

There are many problems with this conclusion. It should suffice to mention two. In the example cited, *mezuzah* is also in the MT. Secondly, the word was well known to the general population and was, therefore, excellent for use in the translation. In contrast, TO does not have *ṭiṭit*, but a Greek word (22:12). If the Targumist adopted the practice of using rabbinic halakhic words, he would have surely done so here.

In sum, this study of some four dozen instances in Deut where commentators have found either halakhic or anti-halakhic elements has revealed no verse where TO deviates in a clear fashion to teach a halakhah. In contrast, the more expansive Targums, N and Ps-Jon, do so.

The most that can be safely said about TO's use of halakhah is that this Targum may have been composed or edited to reflect halakhah in a subtle and inconsistent manner. The teachings, it should be added, are usually undiscoverable by the general lay reader. The halakhot, assuming they exist, are generally found only after careful probing using the tools of *derash,* something the Targumist himself avoids. However, even accepting this approach, care must be taken to discard those halakhic conclusions that clearly have no basis. Thus, at the most, one is left with less than a dozen debatable verses where *it is possible* that our extant Targum texts deviate to reflect halakhah.[11]

A better approach is to recognize that TO, in contrast to N and Ps-Jon, is neither an aggadic nor a halakhic document. There are deviations in TO, designed either to clarify the text or otherwise, that do not intend to highlight halakhah, yet reflect it. There are also deviations that render the plain meaning of the text (the *peshat*) without apparent concern for the halakha or are contrary to it. TO is primarily a translation. The translator(s) was concerned with being faithful to the Biblical text and not with conforming to technical halakhic details. Yet, when the Targumist felt a need to deviate from the MT, and it was not against the *peshat* to do so, he paralleled rabbinic teachings in the Talmuds and Midrashim.[12] TO is a rabbinic document, but one that renders according to the *peshat.*[13]

---

[1] The Talmud (see list in *The Jewish Encyclopedia,* IX, 405) contains references to about a dozen identical or similar stories concerning Onkelos and Aquila. The latter is said to have translated the Hebrew Bible into Greek. The incidents recorded in the Babylonian Talmud and the Tosefta are ascribed to Onkelos, and those in the Jerusalem Talmud and Palestinian Midrashim to Aquila. Some scholars (such as A. E. Silverstone, *Aquila and Onkelos,* Manchester University

Press, 1970) believe that the two are identical persons. Others (such as S. D. Luzzatto, *Briefen*, 1882, No. 71) disagree. In all probability, the Babylonian Talmud, like the Jerusalem Talmud, is referring to the Greek, not the Aramaic, translation. In any event, it is clear that we are unable to identify the Targumist from the Talmud.

[2] The parallel passage in the Jerusalem Talmud (Meg. 1:11, 71c) refers to the translation by Aquila of the Bible into Greek. A. Berliner (*Targum Onkelos*, Berlin, 1884, pp. 108, 245) ascribes TO's translation philosophy to the school of R. Akiba.

[3] See Neh 8:8 and 13:24, and b. Meg. 3a. There are references to written Targums before the common era of Job, Esther, and Psalms. See t. Shab. 14, b. Shab. 115a, y. Shab. 15c. See also W. Bachar, *J.E.*, p. 58, and G. F. Moore, *Judaism* I, pp. 174 f. Among the Dead Sea finds are fragmented Targums to part of one chapter of Lev and many chapters of Job.

[4] Nathan Drazin, *History of Jewish Education from 515 B.C.E. to 220 C.E.* (Baltimore, 1940), p. 84. A. D. York, "The Targum in the Synagogue and in the School," *JSJ* 10, 1979, pp. 74–86.

P. Churgin, "The Targum and the Septuagint," *AJSL* 50, 1933, pp. 41–65, points out that the LXX was based on the Targums. Egyptian Jews visited the land of Israel and heard the Targum rendering in the synagogue.

[5] Rashi and Tosaphot on b. Ked. 49a and Maharsha on b. Ned. 37b write that the TO Targumist did not add original interpretations but that TO's teachings were given on Mount Sinai; cf. b. Meg. 3a. Rashi on b. Meg. 21b states that the Targum was designed for the general population that did not know Hebrew. Maimonides (*Hilkhot Tefilah* 12:10) states that the *Meturgeman* was used from the time he was first introduced by Ezra until Aramaic was no longer the vernacular, so that people would understand the Torah. S. D. Luzzatto (*Oheb Ger*, Cracow, 1895, pp. V–IX) notes that the PT describes Hebrew as the language of the Temple because the average Judean did not speak the language.

The Babylonian Talmud, Meg. 32a, states that Biblical interpretations, the Oral Law, must be read orally to impress upon the people that the interpretations are different from the sacred text.

Luzzatto concludes that TO was originally transmitted orally in accordance with this principle. He suggests that the hypothesis of an oral transmission can also account for some of the variant TO texts. N. M. Adler (*Netina Lager*, Wilna, 1886, Introduction) disagrees. He feels that TO was allowed to be written even when it was first composed because of the need for an exact translation. J. Faur ("The Massorah of Targum Onkelos," *Sinai* 60, 1, 1966–67, pp. 14–27) argues that this need for exactness was resolved by writing a Massorah to the more important verses, but that TO was not set to writing until later.

[6] b. Ber. 8a, b. Tosaphot to b. Ber. 8b states that this requirement could be ful-

filled by reading the PT, but TO is preferred because it is more literal.

The requirement to read the Targum weekly was probably designed to keep the knowledge of Aramaic alive since the Babylonian Talmud and other parts of the Oral Law are written in Aramaic.

European Jewry, except in Spain, did not usually follow the practice of reading the Torah with the Targum. They did so only on Passover and Shavuoth. See *Machzor Vitri*, pp. 103–171, 304, 305, 310, and Y. Komlosh, "Targumic Manuscript," *Sini Jubilee Volume*, 1948, pp. 466–481.

⁷ An interesting recent study on the FT is David Reider's "On The Targum Yerushalmi known as The Fragmentary Targum," *Tarbiz* 39, 1969, pp. 93–95. Rieder argues that the FT existed originally as a complete PT. When Ps-Jon appeared, the scribes preferred to copy this Targum since it contains many additional explanations and legends that did not exist in the earlier PT. The FT fragments are supplements to Ps-Jon, extracts from the PT where it differs from Ps-Jon. Ps-Jon and FT were later frequently altered to conform to each other's readings; hence, the numerous instances where it is noted that Ps-Jon and FT are the same.

⁸ The ninth- or tenth-century date is based upon the curious view that only one Targum could have been accepted in the land of Israel at one time. Since the CGT fragments were not condemned to oblivion in the Cairo Geniza until the ninth or tenth century, TO, it is argued, could not have been widely known in the land of Israel before that time. It is also based on our lack of evidence of any Palestinian source having any real acquaintance with TO before that time.

⁹ J. W. Etheridge, *The Targums of Onkelos and Jonathan Ben Uzziel on the Pentateuch* (New York, 1968). There are six reviews of Etheridge's translation:

Buchanan, George W. *CBQ 31* (1969): 565–566
Emerton, John E., *Bk List* (1970): 25
Fitzmyer, Joseph A., *TS* 30 (1969): 370
Fohrer, Georg, *ZAW* 81 (1969): 417
Greenfield, Jonas C., *JBL* 89 (1970): 238–239
Prijis, Leo, *BZ* n.s. 15 (1971): 303–304

¹⁰ G. Vermes (*The Annual of Leeds University Oriental Society* III, 1961, 2, pp. 81–114, esp. p. 106) points out, without statistical support, that TO is fundamentally a Palestinian Targum, as is evidenced by "an important amount of haggadic material" which "is almost always identical with, or at least similar to that included in the so-called Palestinian Targums."

¹¹ The author's study of TO to Gen (in *Targumic Studies*) reveals only one deviation which some argue reflects halakhah, and this rendering is not according to the accepted law (Gen 9:6).

¹² If one accepts the view that the bases for the halakhic conclusions are well founded, it follows that the bases for the anti-halakhic conclusions (note 40 of the

"Statistics") are similarly valid. Thus, TO must be said to have both halakhic and anti-halakhic elements. Since it is well accepted that TO is post-Mishnaic (a conclusion this study also comes to in the analysis of TO's relationship to Sifre), the view of Geiger, Kahle, et al. that anti-halakha means pre-Mishnaic is shown to be unsupportable.

[13] The fact that TO is a Targum *peshati* and that PT are Targums *derashi* is evidenced both in this study — by analyzing many supposed *derashic* elements in TO — and in the author's *Targumic Studies.*

STATISTICS

Although TO is the most literal of all Aramaic translations of the Bible, it nevertheless includes a large number of deliberate deviations[1] from the literal meaning of the words of the MT.

There are altogether 1,601 such deviations in Deuteronomy, and since this book contains 955 verses, there is an average of more than one and one-half changes from the literal meaning of the Hebrew text for every verse. This in itself adequately proves that TO's reputation for literalness is justified only in comparison with the other, homiletical Targumim, but not in absolute terms.

About half of the deviations, 805, were made primarily to clarify the meaning of the MT.[2] Apart from chapters 32 and 33—where the poetical and often obscure language of the original Hebrew necessitates an extensive interpretation in the translation—all but about a dozen of these deviations are accomplished by a change in, or addition of, only one or two words.[3] The translation frequently clarifies apparent ambiguities; figurative language is generally rendered concretely; many questions, negative statements, and exaggerations are avoided; direct, forceful, and vivid language is preferred over the indirect and passive; the original Hebrew of the MT is sometimes maintained for further clarity; words are not translated literally when the Aramaic idiom requires a deviation; and the translation may refer to other verses. Occasionally, tenses are changed,[4] and two translations from two TO texts are retained in the Targum.[5] Sometimes the Targumist renders opposite from the MT,[6] reads letters different than the MT,[7] and omits words.[8] TO does not clarify every text, even though another Targum may do so. There are 39 cases where the names of Biblical nations or historic sites are changed to those in use during the Talmudic age,[9] and 13 where ethnic and place names are translated as if they were not names.[10] The Targumist does not change[11] or translate[12] every name. In three instances Hebrew words are translated into Greek.[13]

About a quarter of the deviations, 426 in all, are designed to convey a

more respectful concept of God than the literal language of the MT would
indicate. The Targumist avoids anthropomorphisms and anthropopathisms and otherwise deviates for God's honor 118 times.[14] In 46
instances,[15] Memra (word) is used to indicate God's command or to clarify
a metaphor; it also prevents representing God performing such acts as
turning, breaking, fighting, making, consuming, and helping, and generally avoids showing a close physical relationship between God and
humans, creatures, and inanimate objects. Once yqr' (glory) is added[16]
avoiding depicting God as appearing. Shekinah (divine presence) is
included 25 times[17] when God is shown as dwelling. In addition, qdm
(before) is added 141 times[18] as a sign of respect, and dhl (fear) is included
in 27 instances[19] precluding the depiction of man forgetting or approaching God, or substituting dhl for idol. In 10 instances[20] the name Elohim is
changed to the Tetragrammaton. In 58 passages a form of $'l$ (God) is translated as "idol" or "fear."[21] There are many examples where TO does not
avoid anthropomorphisms and anthropopathisms.[22] TO does not always
add Memra,[23] Shekinah,[24] qdm,[25] and dhl[26] when other Targums do so.
Similarly, Elohim is also not always rendered by the Tetragrammaton.
This occurs in four instances.[27]

Twenty-one deviations were made for the sake of preserving the honor
of Israel's ancestors.[28] Many statements of a derogatory nature regarding
their behavior are deleted, radically changed, or at least softened. Israel's
ancestors' attitudes and reactions are depicted with great delicacy, and
sometimes even the remotest suggestion of any wrongdoing on their part
is avoided.

Some 266 of TO's deviations in Deuteronomy are also found in the
Sifre (201) and the Talmuds (65).[29] There are only 18 references to a Targum in the Babylonian Talmud,[30] four from Deuteronomy; and there are
17 references to a Targum in the Midrashim,[31] three from Deuteronomy. It
is likely that the Targumist drew many interpretations from Sifre, and this
would give this Targum a later date than is commonly supposed.[29] As with
other types of deviations, the Targumist in such cases does not always
translate the same as the Talmuds. Indeed, sometimes the rendering is
contrary to the rabbinic teaching.[32] However, the Targum generally gives
the interpretation found in Sifre except where the latter's interpretation is
derash or the extant text of TO is faulty.

In twelve instances TO translates six words as sly, "prayer," even
though these words do not mean prayer, either to elevate the concept of

prayer or the activity of the person mentioned in the verse.[33] The other Targums have even more deviations of this sort.[34] Sixteen deviations are (according to some scholars) designed to teach theological lessons[35] and six to avoid theological difficulties.[36] The scholars recognize that TO does not include all theological teachings[37] and avoid all theological difficulties.[38]

According to some commentators, the Targumist translates some verses to teach mitzvot (Biblical commandments) and halakhot (rabbinical laws),[39] but translates on occasion contrary to the halakhah.[40] However, virtually all, if not all, of these interpretations do not have a sound basis. It is more likely that the Targum simply explains the text. The unofficial Targums deviate frequently to include halakhot.[41]

In summary, while there is more than one TO deviation for every Deuteronomic verse, about half of them are designed to explain a word or a phrase, and a quarter involve the addition or the changing of a word to remove an anthropomorphism, an anthropopathism, or a possibly unseemly misconception of God. These categories represent 80 percent of all the changes. There is no perfect consistency in any of the methods of deviation, and other Targums deviate where TO fails to do so. This may be due to TO being the work of several translators and redactors, or individuals who added to the original translation, who agreed on general principles but not necessarily in every single instance; the well-known truism that no one is perfectly consistent; the errors of copyists; or that the Targumist is following principles of deviation that occasionally only appear to be, but are not, inconsistent. Most probably, the apparent inconsistencies are the result of a combination of these four things.

---

[1] A deviation is any departure in TO from the Hebrew of the MT that cannot be accounted for by characteristics of the Aramaic language. Quantitatively, a deviation is generally made by the addition of a word or two, occasionally by a phrase, and, rarely, by adding or changing an entire sentence. More than one reason can be given for many deviations, and scholars may differ as to the principal reason in certain cases. Some may even consider that there could be more than one

principal reason. Nevertheless, for the sake of computation, this study places each deviation in only one category.

The following are some examples of where TO deviates to clarify the MT and some statistics:

a) *Clarity and precision*

	Verses	MT	TO
1.	1:22	"dig"	"reconnoiter"
2.	1:28	"exalted"	"stronger"
3.	2:30	"passing by him"	"passing through his border"
4.	3:12	"Reuben"	"tribe of Reuben"
5.	20: 8	"melted heart"	"broken heart"
6.	32:22	"burning"	"destroyed"
7.	32:22	"consume"	"to make an end"
8.	32:22	"set on fire"	"destroy"
9.	32:24	"animals"	"wild beasts"
10.	32:43	"Cause to shout"	"Give praise"
11.	33:11	"them that hate him"	"enemies"
12.	33:19	"suck"	"eat"
13.	33:20	"tears"	"kills"
14.	33:21	"lawgiver"	"Moses"

b) *Figurative language*

	Verses	MT	TO
1.	4:11	"heart of the sky"	"towards the sky"
2.	25: 2	"son of flogging"	"one who is obliged to be flogged"
3.	25:18	"cut off a tail"	"killed"
4.	29:17	"a root that is fruitful in poisonous herb and wormwood"	"a man who reflects on sins of inadvertence or a sin of presumption"
5.	29:18	"to add drunkenness to the thirst"	"add sins of inadvertance to those of presumption"
6.	30: 6	"circumcise"	"remove"
7.	33: 2	"beamed"	"revealed His power"
8.	33:16	"crown of the head"	"man"
9.	33:20	"arm with crown of the head"	"sultans with kings"
10.	33:22	"Dan is a lion's whelp"	"Dan is strong as a lion's whelp"
11.	33:29	"tread upon their high places"	"tread upon the necks of their kings"

c) *Questions changed to positive declarations*

The Targumists change questions and negative statements to positive declarations when they may be misunderstood as the opposite of their intended meaning. (Comp. TJ to II Kings 1:16: MT's "Is not God in Israel?" which might be misunderstood as "God is not in Israel!" is rendered: "Behold God exists, His Shekinah dwells in Israel." The Peshitta, on the other hand, frequently changes a positive statement into a negative one; as, for example, 29:11: MT's "you should enter the covenant of the Lord" is rendered "you should not transgress the covenant of the Lord." See also Peshitta to Jud 21:16, Job 31:1, and Ps 60:6, for other examples.)

	Verses	MT	TO
1.	3:24	"for what God is there in heaven or in earth that can do according to Your works and according to Your might?"	"there is none in heaven or the earth who can do according to Your works and according to Your might"
2.	20:19	"are trees of the field like a man to come against you during a siege?"	"trees of the field are not like a man to come against you during a siege"
3.	33:29	"who is like unto You?"	"none is like unto You"

However, see, for example, 11:30, where TO fails to deviate from "Are they not on the other side of the Jordan . . . ?"

d) *Hyperbole*

Verses	MT	TO
9:1	"fortified in the heaven"	"fortified towards the heaven"

e) *Active language*

Verse	MT	TO
18:7	"stand there before the Lord"	"serve there before the Lord"

f) *Avoiding indelicacy*

	Verses	MT	TO
1.	13:7	"wife of your bosom"	"wife of your covenant"
2.	23:2	"testes" and "sexual member"	TO deletes these words. See also note 28.

g) *Retaining Hebrew word*

1.	2: 6	Lowenstein believes that TO retains the Hebrew to avoid a repetition of terms when there were two synonyms in the Hebrew and the Targumist was only able to find one Aramaic equivalent.
2.	7: 9	*ḥsd* is not rendered in the Aramaic, as happens on occasions.
3.	12:27	TO does not translate *špk*, "pour," into Aramaic, according to the Patshegen and Luzzatto, to emphasize that the pouring had a purpose.
4.	16: 3	Adler believes that *ʿny*, "distress," is not translated to emphasize the many rabbinical teachings derived from the Hebrew word.
5.	20:6	*ḥl*, "non-holy," is said to have been retained in the Targum to emphasize a Talmudic teaching.

h) *Word added because of Aramaic idiom*

The Hebrew of 4:18 does not require or have *ʾšr*, "that," but TO has *dy*, "that," common in Aramaic.

i) *Reference to another verse*

TO and Ps-Jon have an additional word in 19:21 found in Exod 21:23 and Lev 24:18.

j) *Changing virtually the entire verse*

1.	1: 1	The second part of the verse in the MT can be translated: "in the desert, in the wilderness over against the Suph, between Paran, and Tophel, and Laban, and Hazeroth, and Dizahab." TO has: "reproving them on account of their wrong conduct in the desert and because they had angered (viz. God) in the plain, opposite Yam Suf in Paran where they slandered the manna, and in Hazeroth where they angered (God) concerning the meat and because they served the golden calf."
2.	3:24	MT reads in the second part of the verse: "You whose powerful deeds no god in heaven or earth can equal." TO translates: "You are the God whose Shekinah is in heaven above and rules on earth, and there is none who can do like Your works, and like Your might."

3.   7:10   MT reads: "but who instantly requites with destruction
                        those who rejects Him—never slow with those who reject
                        Him, but requiting them instantly." TO renders: "never
                        slow to give good recompense to those that hate Him for
                        the good they do before Him, during their lifetime He
                        pays them."

k) *TO does not clarify every Biblical verse. The PT deviates more often to*
clarify the MT. The following are examples of TO's failure to clarify the MT:

	Verses	MT	Targum
1.	1:14	"defeated"	N has "kill"
2.	11:10	"watered by your foot"	Ps-Jon has "watered by yourself"
3.	12: 4	"do not do"	Ps-Jon gives the usual Targum translation, "you do not have permission"
4.	33: 9	"and guarded Your covenant"	Uncharacteristically, TO translates a positive statement with a negative: "And did not alter Your covenant"
5.	33:15	"from the everlasting hills"	TO changes adjectives and renders the positive statement negatively: "from the unfailing hills"

6.   MT's "nor did your feet swell" (8:4) is rendered in TO
                        "nor did your shoes rub down," a phrase which fails to
                        clarify the meaning of the text. There is probably a
                        scribal error here, and TO should read "nor did your feet
                        go naked."

7.   Verses 4 and 11 of chapter 15 seem to contradict each
                        other and are explained in rabbinic literature. Verse 4
                        indicates "There shall be no needy among you" while
                        verse 11 states "For there will never cease to be needy
                        ones in your land." TO does not deviate to explain the
                        apparent contradiction, but N and Ps-Jon do so.

² Statistics

There are 805 deviations in TO to Deut made for clarity. There are 499 times that a word, or words, is changed for clarity (other statistics on clarity are in notes 3, 4, 5, 6, 7, and 8):

Chapter	Verses	Total
1	1, 1, 1, 5, 7, 7, 8, 12, 14, 17, 21, 22, 27, 28, 28, 28, 28, 29, 30, 41, 43, 44	22
2	6, 6, 7, 8, 9, 10, 11, 11, 21, 24, 25, 26, 31, 33, 34, 34	16
3	6, 6, 6, 6, 11, 17, 17, 25, 26, 26	10
4	9, 9, 10, 11, 12, 16, 19, 19, 19, 23, 25, 27, 28, 29, 30, 34, 34, 35, 36, 49, 49	21
5	1, 2, 3, 6, 11, 11, 11, 14, 14, 15, 17, 17, 17, 19, 24, 25	16
6	3, 3, 7, 12, 18, 19, 25	7
7	1, 2, 4, 5, 6, 8, 12, 13, 13, 13, 13, 15, 16, 19, 19, 21, 23, 26	19
8	3, 3, 4, 5, 5, 14, 17, 19, 20	9
9	2, 2, 2, 3, 4, 4, 5, 6, 26, 29	10
10	6, 17, 17, 18, 19	5
11	2, 6, 24, 27, 28, 29, 29	7
12	2, 3, 6, 11, 17, 17, 17, 18, 21, 28	10
13	4, 6, 7, 7, 9, 11, 14, 16, 16, 19	10
14	2, 11, 21, 21, 29	5
15	3, 5, 7, 9, 12, 12, 13, 14, 18, 22	10
16	5, 5, 7, 8, 11, 11, 14, 14, 18, 18, 19, 20, 20, 22	14
17	2, 6, 6, 8, 8, 8, 8, 12, 12, 15, 18	11
18	2, 6, 8, 11, 15, 15, 16, 19, 22	9
19	4, 5, 6, 10, 11, 14, 17, 19	8
20	1, 3, 3, 3, 3, 4, 5, 5, 6, 7, 8, 8, 9, 19, 19, 20	16
21	1, 5, 16, 17, 17, 18, 18, 18, 18, 18, 18, 19, 20, 20, 22, 23	16
22	3, 3, 8, 19, 22, 25, 29, 29	8
23	5, 6, 8, 8, 8, 17, 20, 20, 20, 20, 20, 21, 21, 21	13
24	1, 4, 4, 5, 7, 7, 13, 14, 17, 20, 21	11
25	1, 8, 9, 15, 15, 15, 16, 17, 18	9
26	2, 4, 5, 7, 9, 11, 12, 13, 14, 14, 15, 17, 18, 18	14
27	3, 7, 9, 10, 12, 17, 19, 25, 26	9
28	1, 2, 2, 4, 4, 4, 4, 5, 5, 11, 11, 13, 13, 13, 15, 15, 17, 17, 18, 18, 18, 20, 26, 26, 27, 30, 32, 37, 43, 44, 44, 45, 45, 47, 49, 51, 51, 51, 52, 52, 52, 53, 54, 56, 57, 57, 59, 59, 60, 61, 62, 62, 65	52
29	2, 4, 5, 9, 9, 9, 10, 10, 10, 11, 13, 15, 17, 17, 18, 18, 18, 19, 19, 21, 25, 25	22
30	2, 3, 3, 6, 8, 9, 9, 10, 11, 16, 17, 20, 20	13
31	8, 11, 12, 14, 14, 15, 18, 20, 28, 30	10

32	2, 3, 4, 5, 6, 6, 6, 6, 11, 13, 15, 16, 17, 17, 18, 18, 18, 20, 21, 22, 23, 24, 24, 24, 24, 27, 30, 30, 30, 31, 31, 32, 32, 32, 33, 33, 35, 35, 36, 36, 37, 37, 39, 41, 41, 42, 42, 43, 43, 43, 45, 48	52
33	1, 2, 2, 2, 3, 3, 3, 3, 5, 7, 11, 11, 11, 11, 13, 14, 14, 15, 15, 16, 16, 16, 17, 17, 17, 19, 20, 20, 20, 21, 21, 21, 21, 21, 21, 22, 25, 27, 28, 29, 29	41
34	2, 3, 9, 12	4

[3] Two hundred instances where a word, or words, is needed for clarity:

Chapter	Verses	Total
1	1, 2, 5, 33, 33, 33	6
2	9, 19, 24, 30, 30	5
3	9, 12, 12, 13, 16, 16,	6
4	3, 17, 37, 43, 43, 43	6
5	9, 9, 9, 10, 17	5
6	12, 22	2
7	4	1
8	6, 7, 7, 8, 8, 8, 9, 15, 15, 19	10
9	1, 7, 8, 28	4
10	7, 9, 17	3
11	6, 6, 28, 29, 29	5
12	5, 6, 7, 9, 11, 15, 22, 26, 27	9
13	6, 7, 11, 17	4
14	26	1
15	16, 17, 18, 20, 22	5
16	2, 2, 2	3
17	5, 6, 7, 8, 12, 16	6
18	7, 8, 18	3
19	10, 19, 21	3
20	5, 10, 19	3
21	5, 8, 8, 8, 9, 19, 21, 23	8
22	8, 19, 21, 22, 24, 26, 29	7
23	9, 15, 16, 16, 19, 19	6
24	7, 9	2
25	2, 4, 11, 17	4
26	5, 11	2
27	3	1
28	23, 26, 52	3
29	7, 7, 17	3

30	6, 6	2
31	8, 18, 28	3
32	3, 4, 4, 5, 5, 6, 6, 6, 10, 10, 11, 12, 13, 14, 14, 17, 18, 24, 26, 27, 32, 32, 32, 33, 34, 35, 35, 36, 37, 38, 41, 42, 43, 43, 43	35
33	2, 2, 3, 4, 6, 6, 7, 7, 7, 8, 8, 8, 9, 9, 10, 10, 11, 13, 13, 17, 17, 17, 19, 19, 21, 22, 24, 25, 26, 28, 28, 29	34

[4] Eighty-seven instances where the number or tense is changed (such as a participle to perfect, an infinitive to imperfect, imperative to imperfect, singular to plural, etc.):

1:8	5:30	11:27	15:22	18:22	23:4	28:25	31:16	33:2
2:7	8:7	11:28	16:5	19:5	23:17	28:48	31:26	33:3
2:20	8:7	12:15	16:7	19:15	24:9	28:52	32:5	33:8
4:3	8:17	12:17	16:11	20:20	24:14	28:52	32:7	33:19
4:7	8:20	12:18	16:14	21:4	25:8	28:55	32:10	33:22
4:7	9:2	12:21	16:18	21:9	25:15	28:57	32:15	33:3
4:29	9:7	13:1	17:2	21:10	25:17	29:4	32:25	34:7
5:5	11:7	13:1	17:8	21:11	25:19	29:18	32:27	
5:12	11:26	15:2	17:9	22:2	27:1	29:19	32:38	
5:14	11:26	15:7	18:6	23:4	28:20	31:12	32:38	

[5] Scholars differ as to whether doublets appeared in the original TO text and represent alternative translations or whether one of the doublets is a later addition, a pious attempt to add a teaching, halakhah, theology, or for a similar purpose. (See, for example, N. Adler, NL, Introduction.)

Commentators have noted seven doublets in TO to Deut (see the commentary to the translation for details):

1.	4:17	*bšmym* in TO as *rqyᶜ* and *šmyᵓ*.
2.	18:3	*mšpt* in TO as *dyn* and *dtzy*.
3.	21:17	*mšpt* in TO as *ḥzyᵓ* and *dynᵓ*.
4.	32:14	TO adds both *mlkyhwn* and *šlytyhwn*.
5.	32:26	TO adds both *ᵓḥwl rgzy* and *ᵓšznwn*.
6.	32:42	*ᵓwyb* in TO as *snᵓy* and *bᶜly dbby*.
7.	33:13	*wmthwm* in TO as *wthwmyn* and *mᶜmky*.

[6] Converse translations

In a study of converse translations ("Converse Translation: A Targumic Technique," *Biblica* 57, 1976), M. L. Klein gives five examples where N renders contrary to the MT. In all of these instances, except the last, TO is literal.

1.	2:28	N adds: "even though we are not lacking anything" to supply a reason.
2.	5:21	N states: "It is impossible from before the Lord to speak with man and he should live" to deny the possibility of direct communication with God.
3.	7:4	N includes "lest" twice: "lest they serve other idols . . . lest He destroy you quickly" to ward off the most drastic of the predictions, Israel serving idols and Israel's destruction.
4.	15:11	N has: "For if the Israelites keep the teachings of the Torah and fulfill its commandments, there will not be any poor among them in the land." This resolves the apparent contradiction with 15:4.
5.	20:19	All the Targums add "not" to change the rhetorical question to a positive statement. (See also note 1(c).)

[7] It is a well-known rabbinic technique to base aggadic and halakhic interpretations on textual readings *as if* there were letter or vowel changes, letter metathesis, acronyms, as well as reading the Hebrew *as if* it were Aramaic or another language (see, for example, Y. Heinemann, *Darke Haagadah* [Jerusalem, 1954], pp. 96 ff.).

There are at least ten examples in TO to Deut where the Targum translates as if the MT had a different vorlage.

	Verse	*MT*	*Reading*
1.	5:19	*ysp*	*swp*
2.	24:7	*yhbl*	*thbl*
3.	31:7	*tbw'*	*tby'*
4.	32:2	*y'rp*	*y'rb*
5.	33:2	*lmw*	*lnw*
6.	33:2	*w'th*	*w'mw*
7.	33:2	*qdš mymynw*	*qdš šm ymynw*
8.	33:2	*lmw*	*lnw*
9.	33:19	*ymym*	*'mym*
10.	33:22	*yznq*	*yynq*

For studies on the Targums and a pre-MT, see especially: A. Geiger, *Hamikra Vetargumov (Urschrift)* (Jerusalem, 1948); A. Sperber, "The Targum Onkelos in Its Relation to the Massoretic Hebrew Text," *PAAJR* 6 (1934), 5, pp. 309–351; A. Diez Macho, "The recently Discovered Palestinian Targum: Its Antiquity, and

Relationship with the Other Targums," *VT Supp.* 7 (1959), pp. 222 ff.; S. R. Isenberg, "Studies in the Jewish Aramaic Translations of the Pentateuch" (Ph. D. thesis, Harvard University, 1969).

[8] The Targums rarely omit translating words or phrases. For example, the Targums to Ruth and Lamentations miss only one phrase each: "and they went on the way to return to the land of Judah" (1:7), "and we have sustained their punishment after them" (5:7). These lines were apparently accidentally skipped by a copyist.

TO to Deut has two omissions. MT to 33:9 is "neither did he acknowledge his brothers nor know his sons." TO does not repeat the verbs "acknowledge" and "know," but has "regards not the persons of his brothers and sons." This may have been done to avoid redundancy. However, in view of the rarity of such a practice (and, besides, TO could have used words which were not redundant), it is possible that this text suffers from a copyist's error. Comp., for example, TO to Num 11:5, where *yt* is omitted twice although it is in the other Targums.

TO to 23:2 omits "testes" and "sexual member" for delicacy.

[9] Pinchas Churgin ("The Origin of Targumic Formulas," *Horeb* 7 [1943], pp. 103–109) notes that the translation device of changing the names of nations and places to the names known when the translation or commentary is written is also used by LXX, Jubilees, Josephus, and other early Jewish writings. Churgin believes that this innovation was introduced slowly. Therefore, LXX has the least amount of these changes and Ps-Jon has more than TO.

There are 14 names that are changed in Deuteronomy 39 times.

1:2	Kadesh Barnea	3:1	Bashan	3:14	Argov District
1:4	Bashan	3:3	Bashan	3:17	Kinnereth
1:19	Kadesh Barnea	3:4	Bashan	3:47	Bashan
1:46	Kadesh	3:4	Argov District	4:43	Bashan
2:9	Ar	3:9	Senir	4:47	Bashan
2:14	Kadesh Barnea	3:10	Bashan	9:22	Taberah
2:18	Ar	3:10	Bashan	9:22	Massah
2:20	Zamzumim	3:11	Bashan	9:22	Kibroth Hattaavah
2:23	Chatzerim	3:13	Bashan	9:23	Kadesh Barnea
2:23	Caphtorim	3:13	Bashan	23:5	Naharaim
2:23	Caphtorim	3:13	Argov District	29:6	Bashan
2:29	Ar	3:14	Maachathi	32:51	Meribath Kadesh
3:1	Bashan	3:14	Bashan	33:22	Bashan

[10] Ethnic and place names translated as if they were not a name (13 times):

Verses	MT	TO
2:10,11, 11, 20, 20, 21	Anakim and Rephaim	warriors
3:17, 27; 4:49; 34:1	Pisgah	heights

| 6:16; 33:8 | Massah | trials |
| 33:8 | Meribah | contention |

[11] Examples of TO's failure to change a name although N does so:

Verses	MT	N
1:2, 44; 2:1, 5, 6, 12, 22	Seir	Gabla
1:24	Eshcol	Segulah
2:8	Ezion Geber	Fort Tarnegolah (lit. the fort of the cock. N may be a translation of the Hebrew *geber* = cock.)
3:10	Salecah	Seleucia

[12] Examples of TO's failure to translate a place name as if it were not a name although N does so:

Verses	MT	N
1:44	Hormah	destruction
3:9	Sirion	the mount which corrupts its fruit

[13] TO contains three Greek words:

20:20	palisade	*krqwmyn*
22:12	tassel	*krwspdyn*
32:48	time	*bkrn ywm' hdyn*

Silverstone (*Aquila and Onkelos*, 1931, p. 152) notes that the "fact that Onkelos used Greek words, and did not think it necessary to employ pure Aramaic words, is indisputable evidence that he wrote at a period when Greek was still understood by the masses." Berliner (*Targum Onkelos*, p. 104) points out that the word *krwspdyn* in 22:12 was used in pre-Mishnaic times before *tzitzit* became the accepted term. See the commentary to the three verses for more details. Greek words are also found in the Talmud. Thus, the usage is not indicative of an early date.

[14] Besides adding Memra, *yqr'*, Shekinah, *qdm*, and *dḥl* (see the following notes), the Targums avoid certain unseemly anthropomorphisms and anthropopathisms. For example, they substitute the passive form for the active when God is the subject of verbs such as "seeing," "hearing," "knowing," and "remembering." Also, verbs denoting physical activity, such as "go down," "go forth," and "come," are translated "revealed Himself" or "was revealed" avoiding a suggestion of movement.

The Targums do not shun all anthropomorphisms and anthropopathisms, but only those which might give the populace an unseemly conception of God. TO has fewer deviations of this sort than the PT. However, it has more than the LXX and Vulgate. Recent investigations of anthropomorphisms and anthropopathisms in the LXX and Vulgate have revealed that most of them were translated literally by Greek and Latin translators. (See books listed for Orlinsky, Soffer, and Lehman in the Bibliography.)

There are 118 instances where TO deviates to avoid anthropomorphisms, anthropopathisms, or otherwise has changed wording for the honor of God.

1:8	(swear)		7:12	(swear)
1:33	(spy)		7:13	(swear)
1:34	(swear)		7:25	(abhor)
1:45	(listening)		7:26	(abhor)
1:45	(listening)		7:26	(abhor)
2:7	(knew)		8:1	(swear)
2:14	(swear)		8:18	(swear)
3:24	(limit God)		9:5	(swear)
3:26	(listening)		9:13	(seeing)
4:4	(holding)		9:19	(listening)
4:12	(speaking)		9:23	(God's mouth)
4:20	(taking)		10:9	(giving)
4:21	(swear)		10:10	(listening)
4:25	(God's eye)		10:11	(swear)
4:30	(turn to God)		10:12	(demanding)
4:31	(forgetting)		10:12	(walk in God's
4:31	(swear)			way)
4:34	(coming)		10:20	(cleave)
4:39	(present)		11:9	(swear)
5:4	(speaking)		11:21	(swear)
5:7	(God's face)		11:22	(cleave)
5:7	(polytheism)		12:25	(sight)
5:9	(remembering)		12:28	(sight)
5:25	(hear)		12:31	(abhor)
5:25	(hear)		13:5	(cleave)
6:10	(swear)		13:5	(listening)
6:13	(swear)		13:18	(swear)
6:18	(swear)		13:19	(sight)
6:23	(swear)		14:3	(abhor)
7:8	(swear)		16:22	(hate)
7:8	(swear)		17:1	(abhor)

17:2	(sight)		31:18	(hide)
18:2	(being the		31:21	(know)
	inheritance of		31:23	(help)
	priests)		31:23	(swear)
18:12	(abhor)		32:10	(finding)
18:18	(God's words)		32:18	(forgetting)
18:22	(swear)		32:19	(seeing)
19:8	(swear)		32:20	(hide)
19:9	(walk in God's		32:20	(seeing)
	ways)		32:22	(fiery anger)
20:1	(with God)		32:23	(destroy)
21:9	(sight)		32:27	(wrought by
22:5	(abhor)			God)
23:19	(abhor)		32:36	(seeing)
24:4	(abhor)		32:36	(changing His
25:16	(abhor)			mind)
26:3	(swear)		32:41	(vengeance)
26:7	(seeing)		33:2	(came)
26:15	(swear)		33:2	(shone)
26:17	(God's ways)		33:2	(came)
27:15	(abhor)		33:2	(beamed)
28:9	(God's ways)		33:3	(hand)
28:9	(swear)		33:8	(strive)
28:11	(swear)		33:10	(nostrils)
29:12	(swear)		33:12	(cover)
30:16	(walk in God's		33:16	(revealed)
	ways)		33:26	(ride)
30:20	(swear)		33:27	(God is a dwelling
31:7	(swear)			place)
31:15	(seeing)		33:29	(God's shield)
31:20	(swear)		34:4	(swear)
31:17	(hide)		34:10	(know God)

[15] Memra, literally, "word," is not a substitute for God. G. F. Moore ("Intermediaries in Jewish Theology," *HTR* 15 [1922], pp. 41–61) wrote that Memra should be translated "command," "will," "teaching," "inspiration," "power," "protection," and the like, as the context of the verse may require. As with anthropomorphisms and anthropopathisms generally, we should add, Memra might be used to clarify a metaphor or synechdoche (like "mouth" and "voice"). It is also used, on occasion, for humans. Memra was left untranslated in this English ren-

dering of TO to highlight the deviation. However, as mentioned, the retention of the Aramaic should not lead anyone to suppose that Memra is a supernatural being.

TO uses Memra very restrictively where *dḥl*, Shekinah, or *yqr'* is inappropriate. The PT, on the other hand, add it without any apparent consistency. Probably many of the PT additions were insertions by later copyists, as was done in the marginal notes of N. Some of the Memra usages in TO are also scribal errors. There are occasions where TO has the word with a certain verb in one or two places, but not elsewhere where the action occurs again. See Israel Drazin's *Targumic Studies* for more details.

Memra is found 46 times in TO to Deut in relation to God.

Instead of "mouth" or "voice"				*Added to "voice"*
(N does not substitute Memra for "mouth," but adds it.)				
1:26	13:5	28:1	30:8	4:33
1:43	13:19	28:2	30:10	4:36
4:30	15:5	28:15	30:20	5:21
8:20	26:14	28:45	34:5	5:22
9:23	26:17	28:62		5:23
9:23	27:10	30:2		18:16

God fighting	*God moving*	*Demand*
1:30	31:6	18:19
3:22		
20:4		

God's charge
11:1

God being a consuming fire	*Help*
4:24	2:7
9:3	20:1
	23:15
	31:8
	31:23

Taking
4:37

Relationship to people or things	*Broke faith with*
5:5	32:51

Belief in God	*Made the world*
1:32	33:27

Example where Memra is used in reference to humans or simply to translate MT's "word":

21:18   MT refers to "the voice of his father and the voice of his mother."
21:20   Again, MT speaks of "our (the parents') voice."
32:2   MT has "my (Moses') word."

[16] While the PT's usage of *yqr*², "glory," is more extensive, TO restricts its use to reflect the impact that God's presence makes upon humans. It is found once in TO to Deut 33:2, "brightness of His glory appeared."

[17] Shekinah, from *škn*, "dwell," is used by the author(s) of TO only to depict God dwelling with Israel or in heaven. N generally adds "glory of the Shekinah," the reverse, or just "glory." Ps-Jon is also inconsistent. The PT also use the word to describe God moving. See Israel Drazin's *Targumic Studies* for details. There are 25 instances in Deut where TO adds Shekinah.

1:42   (with Israel)
3:24   (in heaven)
4:39   (in heaven)
6:15   (with Israel)
7:21   (with Israel)
12:5   (with Israel)
12:5   (with Israel)
12:11   (with Israel)
12:21   (with Israel)
14:23   (with Israel)
14:24   (with Israel)
16:2   (with Israel)
16:6   (with Israel)
16:11   (with Israel)
23:15   (with Israel)
26:2   (with Israel)
31:17   (with Israel)
31:17   (with Israel)
31:18   (with Israel)
32:10   (with Israel)
32:20   (with Israel)
32:40   (in heaven)
33:12   (with Israel)
33:16   (in heaven)
33:26   (in heaven)

[18] The use of *qdm*, "before," by the Targums was commonly supposed to be an evasive technique to avoid an anthropomorphic portrayal of a close proximity

between man and God. However, this explanation overlooked, among other things, that the Targums also add *qdm* for humans (for example, 20:5 for officers and 21:10 for judges).

By analyzing the usage of *qdm* in Daniel and elsewhere in the Bible for humans, M. L. Klein ("The Preposition *qdm* (Before): A Pseudo-Anti-Anthropomorphism in the Targums," *JTS* [1979], pp. 502–507) concludes that its use is "out of deference to high office or nobility, and (it is) not related to the nature of the Deity. It is used as an expression of respect. . . . It also occurs as a natural result of the idiomatic variance between biblical Hebrew and Targumic Aramaic, or simply, as the translation of a biblical phrase that was understood figuratively. All of these usages apply equally in reference to man or God."

There are 141 instances in Deut, when God is mentioned, where *qdm* is added or where it replaces a Hebrew word or letter.

1:17	(face)	8:6	(walk)
1:34	(hear)	9:7	(*?t*)
1:37	(anger)	9:7	(*ʿm*)
1:41	(*l*)	9:8	(*?t*)
2:15	(blast)	9:13	(revealed)
3:23	(*?l*)	9:14	(*mmny*)
3:26	(*?ly*)	9:16	(*l*)
3:26	(anger)	9:18	(anger)
4:7	(*?lyw*)	9:18	(*ʿyny*)
4:10	(*ly*)	9:20	(anger)
4:10	(*?ty*)	9:22	(*?t*)
4:21	(anger)	9:24	(*ʿm*)
4:25	(*ʿyny*)	9:26	(*?l*)
4:25	(anger)	9:28	(ability)
4:29	(seek)	10:1	(*?ly*)
5:14	(*l*)	10:12	(*?t*)
5:25	(hear)	10:12	(ways)
5:25	(hear)	10:12	(*?t*)
5:26	(*?ty*)	10:20	(*?tw*)
5:28	(*ʿmdy*)	11:13	(serve)
6:2	(*?t*)	11:22	(walk)
6:13	(*?tw*)	12:4	(*l*)
6:18	(*ʿyny*)	12:11	(*l*)
6:24	(*?t*)	12:25	(*ʿyny*)
7:6	(*l*)	12:28	(*ʿyny*)
7:25	(abhorrent)	12:31	(*l*)
8:3	(mouth)	12:31	(abhorrent)

13:5	(voice)	26:19	(*l*)
13:17	(*l*)	27:5	(*l*)
13:19	(ʿ*yny*)	27:6	(*l*)
14:1	(*l*)	27:9	(*l*)
14:2	(*l*)	27:15	(abhorrent)
14:21	(*l*)	28:9	(walk)
14:23	(ʾ*t*)	28:9	(ʿ*lw*)
15:2	(*l*)	28:47	(ʾ*t*)
15:9	(ʾ*l*)	29:12	(*lw*)
15:19	(*l*)	29:28	(*l*)
15:21	(*l*)	30:16	(walk)
16:1	(observe)	31:6	(ʿ*mk*)
16:2	(*l*)	31:11	(*pny*)
16:8	(*l*)	31:12	(ʾ*t*)
16:10	(*l*)	31:13	(ʾ*t*)
16:12	(*l*)	31:19	(*ly*)
16:15	(*l*)	31:20	(anger)
16:16	(face)	31:21	(revealed)
16:16	(face)	31:27	(ʿ*m*)
17:1	(*l*)	31:28	(ears)
17:1	(abhorrent)	31:29	(ʿ*yny*)
17:2	(ʿ*yny*)	31:29	(anger)
17:12	(ʾ*t*)	31:30	(ʾ*zny*)
17:19	(ʾ*t*)	32:3	(*l*)
18:12	(dispossess)	32:4	(iniquity)
18:16	(*mʿm*)	32:6	(*l*)
19:9	(paths)	31:12	(ʿ*mw*)
20:4	(ʿ*mkm*)	32:16	(provoke)
20:18	(*l*)	32:16	(anger)
21:9	(ʿ*yny*)	32:19	(revealed)
21:23	(guilty)	32:19	(anger)
22:5	(abhorrent)	32:20	(revealed)
23:19	(abhorrent)	32:21	(jealousy)
23:22	(*l*)	32:21	(anger)
23:24	(*l*)	32:22	(fury)
24:15	(ʾ*l*)	32:27	(act happening)
25:16	(abhorrent)	32:34	(*ly*)
25:18	(afraid)	32:35	(*ly*)
26:3	(*l*)	32:36	(revealed)
26:7	(ʾ*l*)	32:44	(ears)
26:7	(revealed)	33:8	(connection to pious man)

33:10   (אפך)   33:23   (connection to
33:13   (connection to   blessings)
         land)   33:29   (*b*)
33:21   (execute
         righteousness)

[19] The word *dḥl* means "fear" or "service." When added by TO in relation to the Israelites, the word connotes a higher level of fear; perhaps even the philosophical level that Maimonides spoke of when he wrote that Scripture teaches us that "God is angry with those who disobey Him, for it leads to the fear and dread of disobedience and then to love and proper service" (*Guide* 3:28).

The word is also used by TO as a respectful substitute for the Biblical "idol."

There are 27 instances in Deut where *dḥl* was added, including four times as a replacement for "idol."

1:36	"followed completely the fear of the Lord"
4:4	"cleave to the fear of the Lord"
4:20	"brought near to the fear of the Lord"
4:23	"forget the fear that the Lord your God concluded with you"
4:29	"seek the fear of the Lord"
4:30	"return to the fear of the Lord"
6:12	"forget the fear of the Lord"
7:4	"err away from my fear"
8:11	"forget the fear of the Lord"
8:14	"forget the fear of the Lord"
10:20	"you must approach His fear"
11:22	"come near to His fear"
13:5	"After the fear of the Lord . . . shall you walk"
13:5	"and Him you shall fear"
13:11	"he wanted to cause you to err from the fear of the Lord"
18:13	"You must be wholehearted in the fear of the Lord"
28:20	"forsaking My fear"
29:17	"whose heart is turning . . . from the fear of the Lord"
29:25	"they turned to the service of the idols of the nations and worshipped fearful things" (idol)
30:2	"return to the fear of the Lord"
30:10	"return to the fear of the Lord"
30:20	"accepting His Memra and keeping close to His fear"
31:16	"they will forsake My fear"
32:17	"They sacrificed to . . . fearful things" (idol)

32:18   "You forgot the fear of the Mighty One"
32:21   "caused jealousy . . . with which is not fearful" (idol)
32:37   "where is their fear" (idol)

[20] The Hebrew Elohim is spelled with the respectful, majestic plural. The uneducated or confused may believe that it implies polytheism. TO avoids this mistake by rendering Elohim by the Tetragrammaton. This is done 10 times in Deut.

1:17	4:33	9:10
4:28	4:34	21:23
4:32	5:21	25:18
	5:23	

[21] Fifty-eight instances where TO deviates translating a form of the word ʾl, "god," as ṭʿwt, "idol," thereby avoiding the implication that the idol is actually a god:

1:19	6:19	10:20	12:30	13:11	28:14	31:18
4:4	7:4	11:16	12:30	13:14	28:36	31:20
4:20	7:5	11:17	12:31	13:15	28:64	32:5
4:28	7:16	11:22	12:31	16:3	29:16	32:12
4:29	7:21	11:25	13:3	17:3	29:17	32:16
4:30	7:25	11:28	13:5	18:13	29:25	32:17
6:8	8:19	12:2	13:7	18:20	30:17	32:21
6:14	8:25	12:3	13:8	20:18	31:16	32:21
6:14						32:37

When ʾl means God—that is, The Lord—it is rendered ʾlhʾ by all the Targums except the Targum to Job which uses tqypʾ, "strength." The latter rendering is also found occasionally in the Targum to Psalms: 50:1, 63:2, 68:20, 68:21. It is also in Ps-Jon to Deut 7:9. When ʾl is connected to another word, TO retains the ʾl and does not render ʾlhʾ, as in Gen 14:18, 20:22, 46:3, 14; Exod 20:5, 34:14; Num 16:22; Deut 4:24, 5:9, 6:15. N and Ps-Jon do not always render like TO in these verses.

[22] Examples of TO's failure to avoid anthropomorphisms and anthropopathisms:

Maimonides (*Guide for the Perplexed*, I, 48) notes the inconsistency in TO's rendering of "to see" in reference to God and suggests that "in these passages there is a mistake which has crept into the copies of the Targum, since we do not possess the Targum in the original manuscript of Onkelos. . . . " The reader should not be hasty in dismissing all apparent inconsistencies, for as Maimonides also noted, there are many instances where seeming inconsistencies are explainable, frequently by reference to the rabbinic interpretation of the verse.

1. 1:21   Give
2. 2:7   Supply
3. 3:21   Work
4. 4:24   Zealous
5. 5:30   Divine paths
6. 7:7   Desire
7. 7:19   Mighty hand
8. 9:10   Finger of God
9. 11:2   Uplifted arm
10. 11:12   Eyes
11. 13:18   Anger
12. 32:41   Hand
13. 34:10   Face to face

[23] Examples of TO's failure to add Memra:

1. Ps-Jon adds Memra to "goes" (1:30).
2. TO includes *dḥl*, "fear," in "followed completely after the Lord" (1:33), but N uses Memra instead.
3. N and Ps-Jon: the "Memra of the Lord" wipes out the worship of Baal-peor (4:3).
4. N: the "Memra of the Lord" is "close at hand" (4:7).
5. N: "you heard . . . nothing but the voice of the Memra" (4:12). Ps-Jon does not add Memra here.
6. N and Ps-Jon: "the Memra of the Lord took" (4:20).
7. N: the Memra "concludes" a covenant (4:23).
8. N: the Memra "enjoins" the people (4:23).
9. N: the Memra "breaks," "brought," and "dispossesses" (9:4).
10. N: "anger before the Memra of the Lord" (9:7).
11. N: "After the service of the Memra of the Lord" (13:5).
12. Ps-Jon: "The Memra of the Lord . . . will prepare them" (32:12).
13. N: "My Memra will join evil" (32:23).
14. N uses Memra in a verse which speaks of God giving help (33:7). The phrase "God giving help" is not in TO, therefore Memra is not needed.
15. FT has the Memra "say" (1:1, 3:2) and perform mighty deeds (1:1) and miracles (4:34).

[24] Examples of TO's failure to add Shekinah:

1. N: the "glory of the Shekinah goes" before the people (1:30).

2. Ps-Jon has the Shekinah "carry" (1:31),
3. "walk" (1:42),
4. and "dwell" (3:25). The latter word is not in TO, therefore the addition is not necessary.
5. N and Ps-Jon add Shekinah to 9:3: "the Lord your God who is passing at your head."
6. Ps-Jon includes Shekinah in 31:3: "The Lord your God Himself who is passing at your head."

[25] Examples of TO's failure to add *qdm*:

1. 1:17   N and Ps-Jon use "before" in "judgment is the Lord's."
2. 10:20   N and Ps-Jon add "before" to "revere the Lord."
3. 13:5   N includes "before" in "Him shall you worship." It is in some TO texts.
4. 6:13   Ps-Jon adds "before," as do some TO texts, to "revere only the Lord."

[26] Examples of TO's failure to use *dḥl*:

1. Ps-Jon uses *dḥl* for idol in 4:7, a use TO prefers to minimize.
2. "not being god" (32:17) is translated "no need." *dḥl* probably is not added in this phrase since it is in the next.
3. *dḥl* is not used with "forsake" in 32:51. Memra is added instead since the verse does not imply that Moses forsook God's service (one meaning of *dḥl*), but refers to his breaking faith with God's command or word, to speak to the rock so that it gush water.

[27] TO's failure to use the Tetragrammaton: There are four instances where TO fails to translate Elohim with the Tetragrammaton because the generic "god" is more appropriate in the verse. Nevertheless, the Targum changes the plural form to the singular to avoid a misconception of polytheism.

1. 4:7   "For what nation is so great, that has a god so close at hand"
2. 5:7   "You shall not have another god"
3. 29:12   "He will be your god"
4. 32:39   "there is no god beside Me"

[28] Twenty-four instances where TO deviates for the honor of Israel's ancestors (three are included in the 21 following paragraphs):
P. Churgin (*Horeb* 7 [1943], pp. 103–109) states that Ps-Jon has fewer changes than TO that are designed to protect the honor of Israelite ancestors. Actually, the reverse is true. In Israel Drazin's *Targumic Studies*, for example, over 100 such TO deviations in Genesis are noted as well as more, not fewer, such changes in the PT.

This tendency is also found in the LXX, Jubilees, Josephus, as well as other early Jewish writings.

1. The word "Memra" is added to 1:32, "you have no faith in the Memra of the Lord," as if to say the people denied God's Memra, but continued to have faith in God Himself.

2. Similarly, Memra is included in "you flouted the word (lit. mouth) of the Lord" (1:43). It is arguable that Memra here only substitutes for "mouth." Both of these deviations also protect God's honor.

3. An expression describing an Israelite defeat, "and they smote" (1:44), is toned down to "they troubled you."

4. Moses did not yearn for "that good mountain and the Lebanon" (3:25) but matters more spiritual, "that good mountain and the Temple." Lebanon, which was not incorporated into the Holy Land, is synonymous with the Temple in rabbinic literature, cf., for example, b. Yoma 39a.

5. MT's "there you will serve man-made gods" (4:28) is rendered "there you will serve people who serve idols" to avoid the degrading depiction of the Israelites worshipping idols. Verses 28:36 and 64 are similar.

6. TO deletes "bosom" from the phrase "wife of your bosom" (13:7) and has "wife of your covenant" so as not to depict the Israelites in an indelicate manner.

7. Following the Massoretic *ktb* rather than *qry*, TO replaces "hemorrhoids" (28:27) with "dysentery" so that language considered indecent would not be applied to the Israelites. Hemorrhoids is the disease with which the Philistines were smitten after they seized the Ark (I Sam 5:6 ff., 6:4 f.).

8. Similarly, "concubine" (28:30) is rendered "lie with her."

9. For the same reason, "between her legs" (28:57) is changed to "which issues from her."

10. Moses' criticism of the Israelites, "This people will prostitute themselves" (31:16), is softened to "will go astray."

11. The criticism, "will break My covenant" (31:16), suggesting a serious rebellion, is replaced with "will change My covenant."

12. God's reaction, "I will abandon them" (31:17), implying that God will leave the people altogether, is weakened, "will drive them far away."

13. The derogatory description of Israel, "grow fat" (31:20 and 32:15), is rendered "luxurious."

14. The critical phrase, "a perverse and crooked generation" (32:5), is softened by TO to "a generation that changes its work and has itself become changed."

15. The disparagement "gross and coarse" (32:15) is changed to "grew strong and acquired possessions."

16. "forsook God" (32:15) becomes "forgot the worship (*plḥn*) of God," avoiding the idea that the Israelites can forget God completely. Cf. note 19 on *dḥl*, which also serves this purpose.

17. "He scorned them" (32:19), implying God shunning the Israelites, is toned down to "anger was kindled."
18. "a generation that turns things upside down" (32:20) is softened to "that changes."
19. TO adds Memra instead of *dḥl* to 32:51 to weaken the criticism of Moses. TO has: "you broke faith with My Memra." *dḥl* means both "fear" and "service." The Targum does not tell us that Moses forsook God's "service" but only His "command" or "word" that he should speak to the rock.
20. It is possible that the Targum adds "he was upright" and "he was faithful," in reference to Aaron, to emphasize that despite his involvement in the episode of the golden calf, Aaron was "upright" and faithful" (33:8).
21. The reference to Moses, "nor had his sap fled" (34:7), is rendered delicately, "the splendor of the glory of his countenance was unchanged."

[29] This study shows a very close relationship between TO to Deut and Sifre to Deut:

(a) Although Sifre does not exist for the entire book of Deut, TO deviates 201 times reflecting interpretations contained in the Sifre. It is estimated (see Introduction) that TO parallels about 30 percent of Sifre's interpretations. These large numbers can hardly be the result of happenstance.

(b) There are many other instances where TO translates paralleling what is implied in the Sifre. For example, TO adds "lawsuit" to 25:1 to teach that the verse concerns a controversy decided by a court. Although this is not explicitly stated in the Sifre to the verse, it is implied in the Sifre to verse 3, which continues the discussion of the same matter. There are also many instances where Sifre explains a word (as in 15:1) according to the generally accepted understanding of the term ($qz = swp$), and this is not noted as a TO deviation (although TO uses the identical word, *swp*, found in Sifre). Thus, the number 201 is really an understatement.

(c) TO includes most, if not all, of the non-*derash* material in Sifre.

As noted earlier, there are, for example, 186 verses in the first 17 chapters of Deut with comments by Sifre. The Targum clearly uses the interpretations recorded in the Sifre in a third of these verses (60 instances in 56 verses). In those verses where TO does not parallel Sifre, it is because Sifre's comments—either halakhic or aggadic—are *derash*.

The following are examples of Midrashim not utilized by TO:

Sifre to 1:6 tells about some of the gifts given by God to the Israelites. Commenting on verses 1:9–15, Sifre expands upon the incidences recorded in the Biblical text to show how difficult Moses' task was in leading the Israelites. Verse 1:18 contains an explanation not apparent in the MT or necessary for the plain understanding of its meaning (the distinction between monetary and capital crimes). Verses 1:19–26 tell of the difficulties of the Israelites during their travels. Verse

3:24 informs us of the favors God did for the Israelites. Verse 3:28 explains why Joshua needed to lead the people and divide the land. Verse 3:29 informs us of some history about Beth Peor. Verse 6:7 gives a metaphorical explanation to a term, thereby deducing a lesson not in the text.

Sifre to 11:13 derives from MT's "if you shall hearken diligently to my commands" that one must study all the commandments, even those he is not obliged to obey. From "I will" (11:14) is derived "but not by an angel." *bnykm*, "sons," (11:19) is interpreted to exclude daughters and that a father should speak to his son in Hebrew as soon as the boy is able to talk. Verse 11:21 tells of the Messianic Age. "Turn aside . . . to go after other gods" (11:28) is said to teach that he who affirms idol worship is like one who denies the entire Torah, but he who denies idol worship is like one who affirms the entire Torah. "Statutes" (12:1) is interpreted as *midrashot*. "You shall eat there" (12:7) is said to mean "with a *meḥezah* and "households" is interpreted as "wives." Verse 12:19 is explained as including the sabbatical and jubilee years under the law of not forsaking the Levite. "You shall stone him with stones" (13:11) means more than one but yet not many. Verses 12:28 and 13:19 teach that if a man makes the effort to listen a little, he will end up being able to hear a lot.

Sifre to 14:27 derives from "you should not forsake him" that a Levite should be given either second tithes, the tithes of the poor, *shelamim*, or charity, in that order. From "God will bless you in all that you do" (15:18), Sifre concludes that one is not blessed if he does not work. Finally, Sifre adds to "the land which the Lord your God gives you" (17:14) "because of your *zachuth* (merit)."

In sum, these many examples have been cited to show the kinds of aggadic interpretations that TO avoids. None of the above interpretations or the others that TO avoids are *peshat*, an explanation according to the simple meaning of the Biblical text. Conversely, when Sifre does explain according to the *peshat*, TO parallels the Midrash's teaching with remarkable consistency.

(d) There is no instance where TO differs with Sifre, except when Sifre contains *derash* or TO has a scribal error (see note 32).

(e) The 201 deviations where TO reflects Sifre interpretations are:

Chapter	Verses	Total
1	1, 1, 3, 4, 5, 7, 8, 12, 16, 17, 27	11
3	23, 26, 26	3
4	34	1
6	4, 5, 8, 9	4
7	10	1
8	6	1
10	12, 21	2
11	10, 18, 20, 22, 22, 22, 24, 26	8

12	3, 4, 5, 9, 17, 21	6
13	5, 5, 5, 6, 7, 14	6
14	2, 5, 11, 21	4
15	2, 9, 18	3
16	1, 2, 3, 8, 9, 19, 22	7
17	3, 6, 7, 8, 12	5
18	3, 7, 8, 9	4
19	5, 9, 12, 13, 14, 16, 17	7
20	3, 3, 5, 8	4
21	1, 1, 4, 7, 8, 9, 12, 16, 17, 17, 20, 21, 23	13
22	3, 5, 9, 11, 15, 17, 18, 21, 22, 24, 29	11
23	2, 2, 2, 3, 3, 4, 4, 4, 4, 6, 13, 14, 15, 16, 19, 20, 20, 20, 20, 20, 21, 21, 25, 26	24
24	1, 6, 7, 12, 14, 14, 15, 15, 16, 16	10
25	1, 7, 11, 17, 18	5
26	5, 8, 13, 14, 14, 17, 18	7
28	9	1
30	16	1
32	2, 2, 3, 5, 6, 6, 7, 9, 10, 10, 11, 12, 12, 14, 15, 19, 20, 20, 22, 23, 23, 24, 25, 26, 27, 31, 36, 40	28
33	2, 2, 3, 3, 8, 8, 9, 10, 11, 12, 14, 15, 17, 17, 18, 18, 19, 19, 21, 21, 23, 23, 24, 28	24

(f) There are also 65 deviations which parallel interpretations in the Jerusalem and Babylonian Talmuds. (Verses already counted in the Sifre listing are not repeated although the teaching is also in the Talmuds):

Chapter	Verses	Total
1	17, 28, 44	3
3	25	1
4	4, 7, 9, 19, 25, 30, 41	7
5	11, 11, 11, 17, 17, 17, 19	7
6	4, 5, 8, 9, 12, 16	6
7	2, 10	2
9	14	1
11	6, 10, 18, 20, 22, 22	6
12	4, 21	2
13	5	1
14	5, 18	2
17	5, 16, 18	3
18	13	1

20	6	1
21	11, 17, 17, 19	4
22	3	1
23	18	1
24	1, 3, 6	3
25	2, 7	2
26	17, 18	2
28	23, 40, 42	3
29	8, 27	2
30	20	1
31	11	1
32	19	1
33	22	1

(g) Examples of instances where TO deviates and translates a verse with an interpretation also contained in the Sifre or Talmuds:

While TO parallels the Midrash and Talmuds, it does so for the sake of clarity, not to teach a lesson. For example, in verse 1:17, TO adds "words of the" to the phrase: "hear the (words of the) small as those of the great." Some argue the deviation emphasizes the teaching that the judge should decide nothing until he hears a complete presentation of all the "words" of each litigant. This teaching is contained in the Sifre to 1:17, b. Shav. 30b, and b. Sanh. 6b. However, the Targumist added "words of the" simply to clarify the ellipses in the text, for "words of the" is implied.

(1) *npš*, "person," (5:17) is added by TO, like b. Sanh. 86a, to clarify that the Biblical command concerns murder, or because of the Aramaic idiom.

(2) TO renders the last word of "You shall love the Lord your God with all your . . . might" (6:5) "possessions." Sifre, b. Ber. 54a, and 61b, advise us not to be overly attached to our possessions.

(3) The Babylonian Talmud, Hul. 80a, indicates: "The rabbis maintain since the Targum renders (*t²w* as) 'the wild ox' (14:5) it is certainly a species of cattle."

(4) MT's "A woman must not put on a man's apparel" (22:5) becomes ". . . a man's armament" in TO. The Babylonian Talmud, Naz. 59a, states that a woman may not join the army to go to war.

(5) In translating "Parents shall not be put to death for (*ʿl*) children" (24:16) as "because of children," TO, like Sifre, may be clarifying that the testimony of relatives may not be accepted in a criminal or civil case. N has ". . . because of the crime of the children." Ps-Jon has both ideas: ". . . either by the testimony or the sin of the children." However, Churgin (*Halakhah*, p. 93), without taking note of N or Ps-Jon, argues that TO

probably has "because of" since it is implied in the text and not to inform us of the halakhah.

(6) The Babylonian Talmud, B.K. 116b, proves the correctness of its translation of a word by referring to the spelling in the Targum to 28:42.

[30] A Targum is mentioned 18 times in the Babylonian Talmud, four citations are to Deut. (See M.M. Kasher, *Torah Shelemah* 24 [Jerusalem, 1974], pp. 155–161, and J. Reifman, *Sedeh Aram* [Berlin, 1875], pp. 8–10).

7:9	25:18
14:5	28:42

[31] A Targum is mentioned 17 times in Midrashim; three are references to Deut. (See Kasher, *op.cit.* pp. 225–238, and Reifman *op.cit.* pp. 12–14).

29:9
32:14
32:24

[32]Examples where TO does not render like a Midrash or Talmud (see also note 40):

1. Adler (NL to 12:26) points out that TO's addition of *maaser*, which is contrary to Sifre and b. Ber. 14b, is a mistaken addition by a copyist.

2. Rashi (to 17:5) feels that the TO texts that add "court" are faulty, for this would be contrary to the halakhah.

3. Ps-Jon, Sifre, and b. Sanh. 65a explain *ydʿny* (18:11) as one who puts a bone of an animal named *ydwʿ* into his mouth and the bone speaks by way of sorcery. TO translates *zkwrw*, "a necromantic apparition." Maharsha, a Talmudic commentary, asks: "how can TO differ with a Tanna?" He responds: "TO is also a Tanna and can therefore differ." TO may not be differing but may be avoiding the specific explanation because it is esoteric and would require the use of at least several words. The Targumist may prefer, instead, the general expression that is more easily understood by the average reader.

4. In translating the figurative "they did not precede you with food" (23:5) as ". . . not meet. . . ," TO and Ps-Jon do not include the teaching in b. Yeb. 73a and b. Sanh. 103b which is derived from a literal reading. The Targums generally prefer to explain figurative expressions; however, N is literal here.

[33] There are various lists of synonyms for "prayer." In Deut R. 2:1, for example, R. Joḥanan cites ten words: (1) *tʿqh* and (2) *šwʿh* (based on Exod 2:23—"and the children of Israel sighed by reason of the bondage, and they cried [*wytʿqw*], and their cry [*šwʿtm*] came up to god"); (3) *nʾqh* (Exod 2:24—"and God heard their groaning [*nʾqtm*]"); (4) *rnh* and (5) *pgyʿh* (Jer 7:16—"neither lift up a cry [*rnh*] for them, neither make intercession [*tpg*]"); (6) *bytwr* and (7) *qryʾh* (Ps 18:6—"in

my distress [*bṭr*] I called [*ʾqrʾ*] upon the Lord"); (8) *npwl* (Deut 9:18—"I fell down [*npwl*] before the Lord"); (9) *plwl* (Ps 106:30—"then Phinehas stood up and executed judgment [*wypll*]"); (10) *tḥnwnym* (Deut 3:23—"I besought [*wʾtḥnn*] the Lord").

Sifre to *wʾtḥnn* has this passage, but 12 synonyms for prayer are mentioned. Yalkut and Tanḥuma on the same verse have 13 and 9 respectively.

TO uses 16 synonyms for prayer. There are 12 instances in Deut where TO replaces the Biblical word with *ṣly*, "prayer." Listed below are the words TO renders as *ṣly*, including those in other Pentateuchal books:

pll	9:20, 9:26
krʾ	4:7, 32:3
ḥnn	3:23
tʿq	26:7
mth	27:19
ʿtr	none
ʿmd	none
rwm	none
ʿnh	none
ptl	none
šwḥ	none
šmʿ	1:45, 9:19, 10:10, 26:7, 33:7
ṭbʾ	none
prš	none
brk	none
ḥlh	none

In addition, TO adds "to accept their prayers in times of trouble" as a gloss to 4:7.

The other Targums also add "prayer" frequently. Comp., for example, TJ to I Kings 8:30 and Isa 1:15, and see the next note.

[34] Examples of where TO fails to use *ṣly* although another Pentateuchal Targum does so:

1. Ps-Jon has "accept my prayer" in 3:26.

2. N translates "and you search there for the Lord" (4:29) and "as you pray there."

3. Ps-Jon adds to 28:32, "in your hand there will be no good work by which you prevail in prayer before the Lord."

[35] Various scholars have found what they consider to be references to theological teachings in TO to Deut. However, as is clarified in the notes to the cited verses, in each instance there are good reasons for concluding that the Targum, in

contrast to N and Ps-Jon, does not really intend to add a theological lesson. Sixteen instances are listed below.

When we attempt to disclose the philosophical underpinnings of the translation, the only things that we can say with any degree of certainty are that TO is sensitive to avoid unseemly depictions of God and Israelite ancestors, its author(s) desires to emphasize the concept of prayer (in contrast to "crying," "calling," "standing," etc.) and he (they) presents a rather literal translation of the MT paralleling, within the constraints of *peshat*, the rabbinical teachings also found in the Midrashim and Talmuds. It is generally recognized that rabbinical Judaism of the early centuries of the common era did not attempt to formulate an organized written Jewish philosophy. This situation is reflected in TO.

All the Targums give preeminence to the interpretation of the Torah text over theology and philosophy. Even the PT, which does address theological issues on occasions, does so only randomly, sometimes inconsistently, solely as the interpretation or the extension of the verse it is paraphrasing. G.F. Moore, *Judaism in the First Centuries of the Christian Era* (Cambridge, 1927), p. 248, speaks of the "atomistic exegesis (of the Targum), which interprets sentences . . . and even single words" in an independent fashion. (See also P. Humbert, "Le Messie dans le Targum des Prophètes," *Rd TEd P* 44 [1911], pp. 5–46). D. Patte ("Early Jewish Hermeneutic in Palestine," *SBL Dissertation Series* 22 [1975]: 49–86) writes that the Targumic hermeneutic method is characterized by (a) "the phenomenon of the interpretation of Scripture by Scripture"—i.e., explaining one Torah verse by another or by the teachings of the Oral Law and (b) "the concurrent phenomenon of the actualization of Scripture," i.e., new conditions of life and moral teachings were read into the Biblical text.

The 16 instances are:

1. 4:19   Jews should teach the non-Jewish world.
2. 5:9   Children are not punished for their parents' sin.
3. 7:10   God rewards the wicked in this world and the righteous in the world-to-come. Cf. Tg to Lam 3:28.
4. 8:6   Evil does not come from God; it is a human creation.
5. 9:4   Jews have a special right to the land of Israel.
6. 9:10   The Torah is divine.
7. 11:12   God watches over the land of Israel.
8. 29:28   People are not punished for sins committed unknowingly.
9. 30:3   God or, more precisely, His Shekinah, accompanies Israel into their exile and dwells with them in their misery.
10. 32:12   There will be a resurrection.
11. 32:33   Whoever desecrates God in secret will be punished openly.
12. 32:34   There will be a Day of Judgment.
13. 33:4   God transmitted an Oral Law.

14. 33:6   The righteous can expect everlasting life.
15. 33:6   The wicked, however, will be punished with a "second death."
16. 34:10   Moses was the greatest of the prophets.

[36] Some commentators argue that TO deviates from the MT to Deut six times to avoid theological difficulties. Others, and the author is among the latter group, feel that the deviations were designed simply to clarify the Biblical text. See the notes to the verses for details.

1. TO may have added to "and make for yourselves a sculptured image of . . . the form of any winged bird" (4:17) the phrase "that flies in the air" to keep away from a misunderstanding that the verse refers to sacred, mystical birds that fly in the heaven itself.

2. A literal reading of 4:19 might give the impression that God allows non-Jewish nations to worship the heaven ("to worship them and serve them, which the Lord your God alloted to other people everywhere under heaven"). TO uses "prepared" ("which the Lord your God prepared") weakening this implication. Comp. b. Meg. 9b and b. Ab. Zar. 55a.

3. According to Adler, TO replaces "in all His ways" with "in all the ways that are right before Him" (11:22 and elsewhere) to avoid the conception that evil emerges from God and that it may therefore be imitated.

4. TO substitutes MT's "terebinth of Moab" (11:30) with "plains of Moab" to remove any misconception that Judaism, even in its early stages, was associated with pagan centers of tree worship.

5. "Belial" (13:14, 15:9), found but twice in the Pentateuch, may have been translated "bad fellows" to get away from the masses accepting the sectarian idea that the word refers to Satan. "Belial," for example, occurs many times in Qumran literature as well as II Cor 6:15.

6. It is arguable that TO renders "the dead" in "I have not deposited any of it with the dead" (26:14 in some texts) as referring back to the words "I have not eaten thereof in my mourning (for the dead)" to avoid the impression of an allusion to the sectarian practice of placing food in the grave with the dead for the use of the departed spirit on its journey to the underworld (Tobit 4:18; Ben Sirah 30:18).

[37] Failure to include theological teachings:
There are two instances where Ps-Jon to Deut mentions the Messiah, although TO and N do not.

Ps-Jon to 25:19 renders MT's "you must not forget" as "even unto the days of the king messiah, you shall not forget," clarifying that the command to destroy Amalek applies even until the days of the messiah.

Ps-Jon to 30:4 interprets MT's two expressions of ingathering, "the Lord will gather you and from there He will take you," as events accomplished by Elijah and the messiah: "the Memra of the Lord your God shall gather you by the hand of Elijah, the High Priest, and from there He shall bring you near by the hand of the king messiah."

Our extant TO text mentions the messiah twice: Gen 49:10 and Num 24:17. See the author's *Targumic Studies*.

[38] Failure to address theological difficulties (see the comments on the text for details):

1. The Talmud notes two instances (4:19 and 17:3) where the LXX deviates from the MT to sidestep theological difficulties. TO, however, does not clearly resolve these difficulties.

2. TO fails to paraphrase 18:15-18 to avoid the messianic interpretation read into the verses by Acts 3:22 f. and 7:37 f. that the verses refer to Jesus. This could have been accomplished by using the plural "prophets" like the Sifre and Rashi. N, Ps-Jon, and Saadya also do not deviate.

3. TO does not highlight the Pharisaic teaching in the dispute with the Sadducees on 19:19.

[39] Examples of verses which some scholars, hoping to find a pedagogical basis to the Targum, argue are translated by the TO Targumist to teach a halakhah (see the commentary to the cited text for more details):

1. *ṭwṭpt* (6:8, 11:18) is rendered "tefillin" in TO (reflecting Sifre, m. Ber. 3:3, m. Meg. 1:8, etc.) to clarify the obscure word (see Rashbam) with a word in common usage. However, Adler (NL) argues that the Targumist highlights the halakhah to wear tefillin.

2. According to the MT, divine words are to be inscribed "on the doorpost of your house and on your gates" (6:9, 11:20). Adler states that TO informs us that we should not write on the doorpost or gate itself but on a parchment that we should place in a mezuzah cylinder. The Targumist, according to Adler, teaches (like b. Men. 34a and elsewhere) that the mezuzah, in turn, should be fixed to the doorpost or gate by adding "fix" (them to the doorpost . . .). However, it is also possible that the addition of the single word was intended merely to clarify an ambiguous text or to supply a word that the translator(s) felt was implied.

3. Basing his interpretation on a characteristic Aramaic rendering (*tkws*) of the Heberw *zbḥ* (one of two frequently used synonyms, the other is *nsk*), Adler (NL to Lev 12:21) implies that TO to Deut. 12:21 teaches that God did not restrict the Israelites during their wilderness sojourn as to how animals were killed for food. This interpretation results in a finding that TO contradicts itself in Lev 17:5 where the Targum has a different word.

4. TO generally renders MT's *škr* as *ḥmr*, but does not do so in Lev 10:9. Adler (NL to Deut 14:26) states that the Lev translation (*mrwy*) parallels the halakhah in b. Kerithoth 13b that drinking a quantity of wine that causes intoxication is forbidden. However, according to Adler, TO's rendering of verses such as

Num 6:3 and Deut 14:26 implies that, in the situations described in these verses, any quantity of wine is prohibited. Jastrow translates *ḥmr* (p. 480) "wine" and *mrwy* (p. 838) "intoxicating drink." Needless to say, the simple meaning of the single word *mrwy* does not imply all of this without *derash*, an exegetical interpretation: the word for "intoxicating drink" does not imply intoxication more than the word "wine."

5. Sifre and b. Kid. 15a interpret MT's "he has given you double service" (15:18) that a Hebrew servant may do service both by day and by night. His night service consists of his master giving him a Canaanite maid-servant to raise children who will belong to the master. TO's "he has been doubly worth" seems to weaken this teaching and certainly does not state it explicitly. Yet Adler argues that the deviation was made to inform us of this halakhah.

6. Kasher (*Torah Shelemah* XXVI, pp. 43–44) points out that TO's addition of "sacred sacrifices" to 16:2 (a characteristic rendering for *shelamim*) reflects the halakhah of R. Akiba (y. Pes. 6:1, Sifre, and elsewhere) that a lamb is used for the paschal sacrifice, but an ox is used for the *ḥagigah*.

7. Adler believes that TO may have retained the Hebrew *'ny* (16:3) to suggest various rabbinic teachings that were drawn from the Hebrew in Sifre and b. Pes. 36a.

8. Adler argues that TO's literal rendering of 16:4 reflects the view of those who interpret the verse as referring to the sixteenth of Nissan and not the fifteenth.

9. TO adds "for himself" after "to add horses" (17:16). Adler suggests that the addition either clarifies the ellipsis in the MT by using the same phrase found earlier in the verse or it refers to the Talmudic teaching (y. Sanh. 10:9) that business was permitted with the Egyptians, even to buy horses; but the Israelites were forbidden to settle in Egypt.

10. TO replaces MT's plural "cheeks" with the singular form (18:3) since the remaining objects in the verse are singular, a characteristic practice (see note on tense and number changes). However, Herskovics (*Halakhah*) derives the halakhah from this that only the bottom cheek is given to the priest.

11. TO has the typical addition "fear" in "You must be wholehearted (in the fear of) the Lord." The Aramaic rendering replaces "with the Lord" and removes an unseemly anthropomorphism. However, Patshegen, Shefftel, Nachmanides, et al., explain that the addition teaches the command to fear God and use his *Urim* and *Tumim*, and not try to predict the future through magic and similar means.

12. TO characteristically substitutes the prosaic "word" for MT's figurative "mouth." However, Wertheimer (*Or*) sees a reflection of the rabbinical ordinance in 19:15 that judges must hear oral and not written testimony.

13. Some, but not all, TO texts to 21:4 have the future tense. Adler concludes that this suggests the law that when the body of a slain person is found cast upon the field, the ground may not be tilled in perpetuity.

14. TO's interpretation of MT's *w'sth* as "grow long" (21:12) could parallel R. Akiba's view. R. Eliezer, on the other hand, states that the MT means "cut." However, Berkowitz (LV) suggests that the Targumist is not teaching halakhah, but is simply clarifying an ambiguity, for *w'sth* literally means "make."

15. TO's use of "separate" rather than the MT's "recognize" (21:17) led the commentators to opposite conclusions. For example, Adler interprets TO as paralleling the halakhah of R. Judah in b. Ked. 74a and elsewhere that a father does not need to inform others of his firstborn son's right to a double portion of all his possessions. In contrast, Patshegen and Lowenstein argue the opposite.

16. TO replaces MT's *py šnym* (which could be translated "two-thirds") with "a double portion" (21:17) either to reflect the halakhah that the first-born gets a double portion of his father's inheritance and not two-thirds of it, or, simply, to clarify the term.

17. Lowenstein (NH) interprets *dyn' hzy'* (in some TO texts to 21:17), two synonyms meaning "right," "proper," or "lawful," as reflecting Sifre's statement that the court has jurisdiction to give a firstborn a double portion if the rest of his family deny it to him. It is likelier that the wording is a joining of two TO versions, alternative translations of a single MT word. N has only one of the synonyms, and Ps-Jon only the other. Sperber's TO text has only *dyn'*.

18. MT to 22:5 has *kly*. The three Targums have *tqwn zyn*, meaning "armament." It can be argued that they are translating according to the opinion of R. Eliezer b. Yaakov in the Sifre and b. Nazir 59a: "a woman may not go to war in armor, nor may she dress as a man generally." However, the Hebrew word is a very general term and is also translated "armament" in Gen 27:3.

19. TO's use of *w'lyt* instead of the equally appropriate *wqrybt* for MT's *w'qrb* (22:14) led Adler (NL) and Shefftel (BO) to contrary conclusions about the wife who is discovered not to have been a virgin. The former interprets TO as teaching that the law applies only if the husband discovers this fact during sexual intercourse. The latter argues the opposite.

20. TO to 22:17 is literal: "And they shall spread out the cloth before the elders of the town." Nevertheless, Adler and Shefftel differ in their views of the Targum's intent. The former believes that TO parallels the halakhah of R. Akiba that the father proves his daughter's virginity by spreading out the bridal bed sheet. Conversely, Shefftel feels that TO is literal so as not to contradict R. Ishmael's opinion that the words are figurative: the father can use any means to make the matter "as white (clear) as a sheet."

21. TO to 22:28 ("who is not betrothed") is also literal. Kasher (*Torah Shelemah* XXVI, p. 51) states that the Targumist parallels R. Akiba's view: When a man violates a girl who was betrothed and then divorced, she is entitled to receive a fine from him. R. Jose disagrees and says that she may not receive compensation.

22. TO adds a single word to 23:2, 3, 3, 4, 4, 9, "privileged." It is implied in

the Biblical text and has no apparent halakhic connotation. However, Shefftel (BO) feels it was added to teach the law that the only thing that is forbidden a eunuch, *mamzer*, Ammonite, Moabite, Edomite, or Egyptian is marriage with an Israelite. Not only is this teaching lacking in a simple reading of the Pentateuchal Targum, but the Targum to Ruth (1:10) uses the same word concerning Ammon and Moab, and in context there, the verse is clearly not referring to marriage but to foreigners entering the assembly.

23. The word "nations" is a characteristic TO addition to clarify an MT ellipsis. Nonetheless, Shefftel argues that it is added to 23:16 to teach that the rule concerns an Israelite slave of a non-Israelite master who escapes to the land of Israel from another country. Besides the obvious fact that "nation" does not state explicitly what Shefftel reads into it, TO does not even imply that the slave is an Israelite, and Ps-Jon, on the contrary, states that he is a non-Israelite.

24. Patshegen is similarly overly resourceful. TO frequently adds *qdm*, "before," in place of words such as "with" and "to" in front of the "Lord" or a human official as a sign of respect (see note on *qdm*). Nevertheless, commenting on 23:16, Patshegen argues that TO's replacement of *m'm* by *qdm* implies a halakhah: the verse concerns a slave who entered the land of Israel but who did not escape from his master. As a result of his interpretation, Patshegen derives a different law than Shefftel. Patshegen's reliance for a halakhah on the typical *qdm* is similar to Nachmanides' dependence on the characteristic *lšmh* for his interpretation of Lev 16:8.

25. As we noted previously, TO's rendering is frequently so brief and ambiguous that it is unlikely that it is designed to teach halakhah to the relatively uninformed population. TO's replacement of MT's "No Israelite woman shall be a cult prostitute" (23:18) with "A woman of the daughters of Israel shall not become the wife of a slave and no man of Israel shall marry a bondwoman" is an example of this problem. The Aramaic has various interpretations. Nachmanides argues that it teaches the rule prohibiting prostitution and betrothal to a slave. Aberbach and Grossfeld state that it implies that the issue of intercourse with a heathen or slave is a *mamzer*. In contrast, Churgin and Melammed feel that the translation does not teach halakhah. The former suggests that the verse is a censuring of the Hasmonean family, and the latter that it is reflecting a lost Midrash.

26. Maimonides (*Commandments*) relies on TO's substitution for "When you come into your neighbor's (field)" (23:25, 26) with "When you hire yourself" for the 267th negative command, which concerns a field laborer. MT's wording is ambiguous, and it is characteristic of TO to clarify ambiguities. It is, therefore, more than likely that the Targumist simply intends to clarify the ambiguity. It is possible that once having felt the need to clarify the verse, the translator(s) chose a rendering that parallels the halakhah. However, the contrary is not true. The Targumist was not prompted to the translation by a need to teach this halakhah.

27. Some, but not all, TO texts render MT's ground for divorce, "he finds some nakedness" (24:1), as "he finds some transgression." These texts are obviously explaining the figurative language. Yet some scholars argue that they reflect halakhah, although they differ as to the intent. Some feel that the Aramaic states that something unseemly is necessary before the divorce can be granted, as taught by the conservative School of Shammai. Others say that TO, like the more liberal School of Hillel, allows any ground for the divorce. Still others believe the Targumist found a middle path between both views.

28. TO probably replaces MT's "writ of separation" (24:1, 2) with "deed of dismissal" because the parties are not only separated by the divorce, but, more to the point, the wife is dismissed from the home, as indicated later in the Biblical verses. TO has the same word as TJ to Isa 50:1 and Jer 3:8. Kasher argues that the Targumist is informing us of the language of the divorce decree.

29. Because TO uses a synonym (*mskn*) rather than the usual word for "needy man" (*'ny'*) (24:12), Adler concludes that the Targum tells us, like Sifre and b. B.M. 114b, that the law applies to one who is not totally destitute. Yet some TO texts have the customary word, TO generally prefers using synonyms to avoid redundant usages, and the word is also found in vv. 14 and 15, where no halakhah is derived from its use.

30. As noted by Churgin (*Halakhah*, p. 93), TO changes MT's *l*, "for" to *l pwm*, "by the mouth of" because it is implied: "Parents shall not be put to death by the mouth of children" (24:16). This is characteristic, and the usage is found, for example, in 25:4. Yet some commentators indicate that TO deviates in 24:16 to instruct that the testimony of relatives is unacceptable in a criminal or civil case.

31. TO's *šry*, "untie," instead of the literal *šlp*, "loosen" or "pull," is said by Melammed (*Bible Commentators*, p. 191) to parallel the halakhic procedure that untying the shoe of the brother-in-law before taking it off is an important aspect of the *ḥaliẓah* procedure (25:9).

32. Relying on a single letter found in only some TO texts, Shefftel argues that TO to 26:14 parallels the teaching of R. Akiba that second tithes may not be sold or bartered.

33. Lowenstein (NH) bases his conclusion that TO includes the rabbinical command to make a blessing before fulfilling a *mitzvah* upon the Targum's substitution of a synonym instead of a characteristic usage (32:3). The MT has *gwdl*, "greatness," and TO *rbwt'* and not *sgy*.

34. Examples where TO's interpretation of the MT is said to be like R. Akiba's include: 2:33, 6:13, 21:12, 23:14, 24:16, and 33:2.

Although some scholars argue that TO's use of *yt* supports the view that it followed the school of R. Akiba, who emphasized the importance of every MT letter, *yt* was found in the Aramaic letters of Bar Kochba written shortly before 135 c. e. It is also in the PT. Thus, it was common usage. (See A. Diez Macho, *Oriens*

Antiquus II [1963]: 95–132 and E. Y. Kutscher, *Leshonenu* XXV [1961]: 117–133. TO to Num 11:5 omits *yt* twice, but this is probably a copyist's error.)

40 Examples of verses which some scholars believe are rendered contrary to the halakhah:

1. TO may understand 12:26 to refer to *maaser* (the tenth of the produce) contrary to the Sifre and b. Temurah 17b, which indicate that this halakhah includes Temurah and *nt^c rb^cy*. This TO text may be the result of a scribal error, see the note to the verse.

2. By rendering "an everlasting ruin of destruction" (13:17), TO could be following the view of R. Jose (in b. Sanh. 111b), who said the burnt town must remain a heap forever. In contrast, R. Akiba said it may be converted into gardens and orchards.

3. TO translates each reference to seething a kid in its mother's milk (14:21, Exod 23:19 and 34:26) as, "You shall not eat flesh with milk," despite the Talmud's explanation (b. Sanh. 4b, and elsewhere) that different lessons are learned from each verse: a prohibition against eating, enjoying, and cooking.

4. TO generally adds "court" to "gate" and does so in 17:5 even though, according to the halakhah, "gate" here refers to the site of the crime, the place where an idol was worshipped. Komlosh (*Hamikra*) states that this verse is an example where the Targum translates according to the plain meaning of the text and not the halakhah. Adler (NL), on the contrary, feels that TO is reflecting the halakhah of a special situation where the majority of the city's inhabitants are non-Jews. In this instance, the death sentence is executed at the door of the court.

5. The *lex talionis*, "life for life," etc., is translated literally and is not paraphrased to reflect the rabbinic teaching that the punishment is monetary (19:21).

6. TO translates the Hebrew word *tt^cmr* (21:14), which is of doubtful origin and meaning, as "you must not trade with her." While this is simply a clarification, Lowenstein (NH) states that the Aramaic reflects the view of R. Judah (which is not the halakhah) that a man cannot sell a female captive for money, but he may give her as a gift or barter.

7. TO's replacement of MT's "enslave" (21:14) with "trade with her" seems to mean that the soldier may not sell the captive woman whom he had intended to marry, but he may give her as a gift or barter. This is contrary to the halakhah contained in b. Sanh. 85b. Ps-Jon is like TO, but N has the halakhah: "you shall surely not sell her for money nor trade with her."

8. The Targums render MT's "chasten" (21:18) according to the *peshat*, "instruct," implying exhortation but not corporal punishment. This is contrary to the halakhah (Sifre and b. Sanh. 71a) which allows a court to order capital punishment for a "perverse and defiant son."

9. TO to 25:5, "son," is literal even though the halakhah states that the law of the levir applies even if the brother leaves no daughter.

10. Similarly, TO to 25:6 "the first son that she bears shall succeed in the name of his brother who is dead" is literal, although the halakhah is that the son need not be called by the name of the dead brother. The MT is interpreted in rabbinic literature to mean that the levir inherits from his dead brother.

11. Herskovics (*Halakhah*) notes that TO translates MT's *bpnyw*, "in his face" (25:9), literally, *'npwhy* rather than *qdmwy*, a word used in Num 12:14 and Deut 7:24. He concludes that this is contrary to the halakhah that the sister-in-law only spits before him, but not in his face. Melammed (*Bible Commentators*, p. 208) notes that *'npwhy* is synonymous with *qdmwy* and also means "before him."

12. Herskovics also feels that TO's literal rendering of "you shall cut off her hand" (25:12) is contrary to the halakhah that the woman only pays monetary damages.

[41] B. Revel (*Ner Maaravi* 2, 5685) and E. Levine ("British Museum Aramaic Additional MS 27031," *Manuscripta* 16 [1972], pp. 3–13) state that Ps-Jon and FT are identical in their approach to halakhah in three ways: (1) Reliance upon the Jerusalem Talmud rather than the Babylonian. (2) When the legal discussion has no bearing upon current practices, the Targums use the literal scriptural meaning, despite the current or subsequent rabbinic understanding. (3) They parallel the teachings of R. Yohannan. Dr. Revel also points out that Ps-Jon includes halakhah upon which Karaites disputed with the Rabbanites in order to clarify the halakhah for the people. M. M. Brauer ("Studies in Targum Jonathan ben Uzziel to the Torah," Ph.D. thesis, Yeshiva University, 1950, p. 114) cites sources showing that this was the reason the Karaites did not want the Targum read.

Without commenting on items (1) and (3), Israel Drazin's *Targumic Studies* demonstrates that the PT includes renderings that are *derash*, what the translators felt the MT implies. In contrast, TO is restricted to a translation according to the *peshat*, the explicit meaning of the text. The present study, *Targum Onkelos to Deuteronomy*, describes many instances where commentators erroneously supposed that TO includes *derash*.

Chapter I

1. These are the words which Moses spoke with all the Israelites beyond the Jordan reproving them on account of their wrong conduct in the desert and because they had angered (viz. God) in the plain, opposite Yam Suf in Paran where they slandered the manna, and in Hazeroth where they angered (God) concerning the meat and because they served the golden calf.[1]

---

[1] The second part of the verse in the MT is: "in the desert, in the wilderness over against the Suph, between Paran, and Tophel, and Laban, and Hazeroth, and Dizahab." This statement is unclear. Contrary to what is indicated, the Israelites were not then in the wilderness, or near the Red Sea, but in the plains of Moab (cf. Num 36:13 and *infra* verse 5). Also, Tophel and Laban are not mentioned elsewhere in the Bible (cf. b. Arachin 15a). In fact, none of the six sites can be identified with certainty.

TO deviates irregularly (comp. 5:9 and 15:4) to resolve conflicts that the translator(s) felt would disturb the Targum's audience. The Targumist inserted the interpretation also found in Sifre (as well as Josephus, Ant. IV, 8; Pseudo-Philo, Ant. XIX, 1–5; Midrash Leqaḥ Tob; ARN I 34; m. Aboth 5:4; and elsewhere).

Sifre notes that whereas it says: "These are the words that Moses addressed to all Israel," these were certainly not *all* the words. Therefore, Moses' introduction is represented as a rebuke. Deuteronomy is Moses' review of the Torah. He explains many of the commandments that pertain to the Land of Israel to the generation that is about to enter the land. He starts by reproving them, reminding them of their mistakes so that they would not revert to their former behavior (Nachmanides). (A similar interpretation is given by TJ to Amos 1:1, Jer 30:1, II Sam 23:1, and by the Aramaic version of Koheleth 1:1.)

Tophel is rendered "slander," and *Laban* is understood as "white," a reference to Num 21:5: "And our soul loathes this light bread."

I

1. אילין פיתגמיא דמליל משה עם כל בני ישראל בעיברא דירדנא אוכח יתהון על
דחבו במדברא ועל דארגיזו במישרא ליקביל ים סוף בפרן איתפלו על מנא
ובחצרות ארגיזו על ביסרא ועל דעבדו עיגל דדהב:

Dizahab is taken in the sense of "sufficiency of gold." This agrees with Sifre
and b. Ber. 32a, where we are told that Moses reproved the Israelites on account of
the golden calf which they had made with their overabundance of gold. Hosea said
(2:10): "And silver did I give them in abundance and gold; they, however, made it
unto a Baal."

B. Z. J. Berkowitz (LV) notes that TO considers the Jordan the site of the rebuke
and not a place where the Israelites acted improperly. This is because there is no
need for a change since there is no contradiction. This parallels the Midrash Rabbah but not Sifre (cf. Rashi and Mizrachi). In CS, Berkowitz translates the introduction as "These are the *matters* that Moses addressed . . ." instead of "words."

N. M. Adler (NL) questions how TO can indicate that the Israelites demanded
meat at Hazeroth when it happened at Kivroth Hataavah. He suggests that
Hazeroth was an earlier name of the place.

S. B. Schefftel (BO) feels that the sites were named after and because of what
occurred there. He explains that it is characteristic of TO to inform what names
allude to. Thus, this is another basis for the overall deviation. He notes that TO uses
lqbyl ym swp for *mwl swp* instead of *ym' dswp* since TO follows the MT very
closely, and when the MT abbreviates, so, too, does TO. Yet TO adds *ym.* for clarity.

N, Ps-Jon, and FT interpret the verse similar to TO. These Targums add that
God gave the law in the desert, explained it in the plains, and performed miracles
at the sea. N and FT lack the interpretation of *Tophel* and *Laban*.

TO and N add *bny*, "children." Ps-Jon and FT, as well as some TO texts, do not.

The Targums frequently add *d,* "of," required by the Aramaic language but
not by Hebrew grammar. See, for example, M. Z. Kadari, "The Use of the *d*
Clauses in the Language of Targum Onkelos," *Textus* 3 (1963): 36–59. These additions will not be noted in this study.

2. It is an eleven day journey[2] from Horeb by the Mount Seir route to Rekam Geah.[3]

3. It was in the fortieth year, in the eleventh month, on the first day of the month, that Moses spoke with the Israelites in accordance with all that the Lord had commanded him for them,

4. after he smote[4] Sihon king of the Amorites who dwelt in Heshbon, and Og king of Matnan[5] who dwelt at Ashtaroth in Edrei.

5. Beyond the Jordan, in the land of Moab, Moses began[6] to explain the instruction[7] of this Torah, saying:

6. "The Lord our God spoke with us at Horeb, saying: 'You have dwelt long enough at this mountain.

7. Turn, and make your way, and come to the hill country of the Amorites and to all their neighbors in the plain,[8] the hill country, and the Shephelah, and the South,[9] and the seacoast, the land of the Canaanites and the Lebanon, as far as the Great River, the river Euphrates.

8. See,[10] I set the land before you. Come, take possession[11] of the land

---

[2] MT does not include the word "journey" although it is implied. It was apparently added by TO for clarity. Cf. Exod 3:18. N and Ps-Jon, continuing the theme of the first passage, have this verse specify God's punishment of the people: "It is (only) an eleven-day journey from (N, Mount) Horeb by the way of Mount Gebal (N, from Seir) to Rekam Geah; but because you sinned and caused anger before the Lord (N has instead, before Him), you have been detained (N, and traveled) forty years." See also Sifre on 1:1, Sifre Num 10:33, and b. Taan. 29a.

[3] MT: "Kadesh Barnea." Cf. N, Ps-Jon, and Targums to Num 34:4; Josh 15:3, etc. Also Sifre and Yalkut to this verse. The Targums identify the current name of the site.

[4] TO does not use the more explicit "defeated." The Targum may be paralleling Sifre, which indicates that Moses chastised the Israelites after they showed sufficient strength to smite (not only defeat) Sihon. Thus, they were strong enough to bear Moses' chastisement. However, it is more reasonable to conclude that TO's failure to deviate suggests nothing since the Targum is generally literal. Ps-Jon is like TO, but N has "kill."

[5] MT: "Bashan." This is a typical Targumic reading designed to update the place name. Cf. N, Ps-Jon, Targums to Num 21:33, Josh 12:4; I Chron 5:12 and elsewhere.

2. מהלך חד עשר יומין מחורב אורח טורא דסעיר עד רקם גיאה:

3. והוה בארבעין שנין בחד עשר ירחין בחד לירחא מליל משה עם בני ישראל ככל
דפקיד יי יתיה לותהון:

4. בתר דמחא ית סיחון מלכא אימוראה דיתיב בחשבון וית עוג מלכא דמתנן דיתיב
בעשתרות באדרעי:

5. בעיברא דירדנא בארעא דמואב שרי משה פריש ית אולפן אוריתא הדא למימר:

6. יי אלהנא מליל עימנא בחורב למימר סגי לכון דיתיבתון בטורא הדין:

7. אתפנו וטולו לכון ועולו לטורא דאימוראה ולכל מגירוהי במישרא בטורא
ובשפלתא ובדרומא ובספר ימא ארע כנענאה וליבנן עד נהרא רבא נהרא פרת:

8. חזו דיהבית קדמיכון ית ארעא עולו ואחסינו ית ארעא דקיים יי לאבהתכון
לאברהם ליצחק וליעקב למיתן להון ולבניהון בתריהון:

<hr />

[6] Sifre notes that MT can be translated as "beginning" or "swear." TO, N, and Ps-Jon have the first interpretation, the ICC the later. Nachmanides, who frequently disagrees with TO, translates: "wished."

[7] TO adds "instruction." Schefftel (BO) feels that TO refers to the entire Torah as indicated by "all" in verse 3: "Torah" by itself can imply a single commandment; hence the necessity for the gloss. N adds "book" and Ps-Jon "words." Each uses a word that could be implied.

[8] MT: "Arabah." The three Pentateuchal Targums and Sifre identify the location of the site.

[9] MT: "the Negev." N and Ps-Jon also have "South."

[10] MT: *r'h*, in the singular. Scholars differ on whether our TO text is correct here and whether the word should be plural in the Targum. Patshegen, Adler (NL), and Schefftel (BO) feel the word should be in the plural form. Schefftel explains that this verse should be plural and verse 21 singular because of the plural and singular language which follow the verbs. The plural form in verse 8 parallels Sifre. Sifre explains that whenever the plural form is used, Moses is addressing the Israelites separately, telling each his individual responsibility. Here, each person was to see and reflect individually. In verse 21, Moses talks to the people as a single nation. See also Rashi; ICC, p. 14, note 8; and Patshegen on 4:1. The plural form is found in the Samaritan Bible, LXX, N, Ps-Jon, and the Peshitta. See 11:26, another verse containing this problem.

[11] TO translates MT's *yrš* as *'ḥsyn* rather than *'rs*. Schefftel (BO) believes that this refers to the Aggadah in Sifre that if the Israelites had trusted in God's promise and not sent spies, no one would have contested their right to Canaan and they would not have needed to conquer the land. They could have entered their inheritance

that the Lord confirmed[12] to your fathers, Abraham, Isaac, and Jacob, to give to them and to their offspring after them.'"

9. I spoke to you, at that time, saying: "I cannot bear the burden of you by myself.

10. The Lord your God has multiplied you until you are today as numerous as the stars in the sky.

11. ((May) the Lord, the God of your fathers, increase your numbers a thousandfold, and bless you as He spoke to you.)

12. How can I bear unaided the trouble of you, and your striving, and your judgments![13]

13. Pick wise and discerning men, those known among your tribes, and I will appoint them rulers over you."

14. You answered me and said, "The thing you propose to do is right."[14]

15. So I took your tribal rulers, wise and known men, and appointed them rulers over you: chiefs over thousands, chiefs over hundreds, chiefs over fifties, and chiefs over tens, and officers for your tribes.

16. I charged your judges at that time saying, "Hear out your fellow men, and decide justly between a man and his brother and between a proselyte.[15]

17. You shall not be partial in judgment: hear the words [16] of the small as well as the great. Have no fear[17] before any man, for judgment is the

easily and immediately. Comp. Rashi. Sifte Hachamin derives this lesson from a prior MT word: "go." Ps-Jon translates like TO and adds a gloss "nor shall you need to carry arms." N has *yrtw* (equivalent to *rš*). Schefftel's interpretation is unlikely. TO is only explaining a metaphor ("inherit" in this context means "seize").

[12] The Targums use "confirmed" instead of "swore" to avoid the idea of binding God by an oath.

[13] MT: *rybkm* "bickering." The Targums render like Sifre; N like TO, but Ps-Jon parallels another Sifre interpretation.

[14] There are seventy three instances where the MT of the Pentateuch has *ṭob*. TO translates each *ṭab* (or *yṭb* four times) except (1) where the word means "beautiful" (Gen 24:16, 26:7, Deut 8:12, TO has *šappira*), (2) "right" (Gen 2:18, 19:8, 20:15, Exod 18:17, Num 3:6, Deut 1:14, TO has *taqyn*) and (3) "honestly" (Gen 40:16, TO has *yaʾut*).

N has *špr* here, but Ps-Jon is like TO.

[15] Some TO texts have "his proselyte," like the MT. See the rabbinical works, Sifre, b. Yebamoth 46b, b. B.B. 154b and b. Sanh. 7b, where various lessons are

9. ואמרית לכון בעידנא ההוא למימר לית אנא יכיל בלחודי לסוברא יתכון:
10. יי אלהכון אסגי יתכון והא איתיכון יומא דין ככוכבי שמיא ליסגי:
11. יי אלהא דאבהתכון יוסף עליכון כותכון אלף זימנין ויברך יתכון כמא דמליל לכון:
12. איכדין איסובר בלחודי טורחכון ועסקיכון ודיניכון:
13. הבו לכון גברין חכימין וסוכלתנין ומדען לשבטיכון ואימנינון רישין עליכון:
14. ואתיבתון יתי ואמרתון תקין פיתגמא דמלילתא למעבד:
15. ודברית ית רישי שבטיכון גברין חכימין ומדען ומניתי יתהון רישין עליכון בני אלפי ורבני מאותא ורבני חמשין ורבני עיסוריתא וסרכין לשבטיכון:
16. ופקידית ית דיניכון בעידנא ההוא למימר שמעו בין אחיכון ותדינון קושטא בין גברא ובין אחוהי ובין גיורא:
17. לא תשתמודעון אפי בדינא כמלי זעירא כרבא תשמעון לא תדחלון מן קדם גברא ארי דינא דיי הוא ופתגמא דיקשי מנכון תקרבון לותי ואשמעיניה:

learned from these words. Comp. Exod 20:10 for the same phrase. S. D. Luzzatto (OG) feels the adjective "his" is strange since a proselyte cannot belong to another person. Schefftel argues that the terminology teaches that one must show respect to every proselyte, for the Torah treats all Jews equally. Hartum explains the word "his" as meaning the proselyte with whom one comes in contact in business. N translates "his stranger." Ps-Jon understands gr as ʾgr, "hire," and translates: "he who hires words of litigation." This is like b. Sanh. 7b.

[16] MT: "hear out low and high alike." The Targums add "words," which is implied."Words" is in Sifre and the Talmud (b. Shav. 30b and b. Sanh. 6b). Sifre explains: "You should not say: This is a poor man and his fellow (opponent) is rich, and is in any case bidden to support him; I will find in favor of the poor man, and he will consequently obtain some support in a respectable fashion." A second explanation in Sifre is: "that you should not say, How can I offend against the honor of this rich man because of one dinar? I will for the moment decide in his favor, and when he leaves the court I will say to him, give it to him because in fact you owe it to him. Thus, you should decide nothing until you hear the *words* of each." Patshegan explains that this means that each litigant should have a full say.

Adler (NL) cites another interpretation of MT: "Ye shall listen to a small matter as to a great." He notes that one cannot read this interpretation into TO since *mly* does not mean "matter." Adler is probably referring to b. Sanhedrin 8a: "You should be concerned about a judgment of a peruta (penny) as of a manna (dollar)."

[17] The Targums, paralleling b. Sanh. 6b, translate *tgwrw*, "fear." Rashi, however, explains it as "you shall not hold back your words because of any man," on the analogy of "gather in" found in Prov 10:5. The Targums render MT's "face" as "before."

Lord's.[18] And any matter that is too difficult for you, you shall bring to me and I will hear it."

18. Thus I instructed you at that time about the things that you should do.

19. We set out from Horeb and traveled the entire great and terrible wilderness that you saw, along the road to the hill country of the Amorites, as the Lord our God had commanded us. We reached Rekam Geah.[19]

20. I said to you, "You have reached the hill country of the Amorites which the Lord our God is giving to us.

21. See, the Lord your God has placed the land before you. Go up, take possession, as the Lord, the God of your fathers, told you. Fear not and be not broken."[20])

22. Then all of you came to me and said, "Let us send men ahead to reconnoiter[21] the land for us and bring back word on the route we shall follow and the cities we shall come to."

23. The thing was pleasing in my eyes, and so I selected twelve of your men, one man from each tribe.

24. They turned and went up to the hill country, came to wadi Eshcol, and spied it out.

25. They took in their hand some of the fruit of the land and brought it down to us. And they gave us this report and said, "It is a good land that the Lord our God is giving to us."

26. Yet you would not go up, and flouted the Memra[22] of the Lord your God.

27. You murmured[23] in your tents and said, "It is because the Lord hates us that He brought us out of the land of Egypt to hand us over to the Amorites to destroy us.

---

[18] The Targums do not use Elohim and prefer the Tetragrammaton, thus avoiding a plural form which could be misconstrued as referring to a plurality of gods. See Introduction for a full discussion of Elohim.

N and Ps-Jon add "before" prior to "Lord." See the Introduction for a commentary on the Targumic usage of "before."

[19] MT: "Kadesh Barnea." Cf. verse 2.

[20] MT: *tḥt*. TO and Ps-Jon retain the metaphor. The word is also found in TO,

18. ופקדית יתכון בעידנא ההוא ית כל פתגמיא דתעבדון:
19. ונטלנא מחורב והליכנא ית כל מדברא רבה ודחילא ההוא דחזיתון אורח טורא דאימוראה כמא דפקיד יי אלהנא יתנא ואתינא עד רקם גיאה:
20. ואמרית לכון אתיתון עד טורא דאימוראה דיי אלהנא יהיב לנא:
21. חזי דיהב יי אלהך קדמך ית ארעא סק אחסין כמא דמליל יי אלהא דאבהתך לך לא תידחל ולא תיתבר:
22. וקריבתון לותי כולכון ואמרתון נשלח גברין קדמנא ויאללון לנא ית ארעא ויתיבון יתנא פיתגמא ית אורחא דניסק בה וית קרויא דניעול להין:
23. ושפר בעיני פתגמא ודברית מנכון תרי עשר גברין גברא חד לשבטא:
24. ואתפניאו וסליקו לטורא ואתו עד נחלא דאתכלא ואלילו יתה:
25. ונסיבו בידהון מאיבא דארעא ואחיתו לנא ואתיבו יתנא פתגמא ואמרו טבא ארעא דיי אלהנא יהיב לנא:
26. ולא אביתון למיסק וסריבתון על מימרא דיי אלהכון:
27. ואתרעמתון במשכניכון ואמרתון בדסני יי יתנא אפקנא מארעא דמצרים למימסר יתנא בידא דאימוראה לשיציותנא:

---

verses 28 and 29. N has "be not frightened." The *Genesis Apocryphon* uses *tbr*, "broken," for "defeat" in 22:9; *ʾtbr* is found in 21:32. J. A. Fitzmyer (*The Genesis Apocryphon of Qumran Cave I*, Rome, 1966, p. 149) states: "The expression undoubtedly refers to the scattering of the troops."

The word "see" in this verse is in the singular, comp. v. 8.

[21] TO frequently fails to distinguish between various apparent synonyms, even when the Midrash derives lessons from the different usages. The MT of verses 22 and 24 have *hpr* and *rgl*, respectively, for "reconnoiter" or "spy out." Both words are translated by TO as *ʾll*. N and Ps-Jon also use the same words in both verses.

[22] TO and Ps-Jon characteristically render "God's mouth" and "voice" by Memra. Memra (word) is used here and in some other verses (for example: 1:43, 8:3, 9:23, and 34:5) in place of a metaphor or synecdoche and to avoid what was considered to be a disrespectful anthropomorphism. N does not substitute, but adds Memra. See Introduction for other uses of Memra.

[23] MT's meaning is uncertain. TO, N, and LXX are like Sifre. B. Sheb. 47b, finding the word *twr*, "spy," in *wtrgnw*, indicates: "you have espied (the land) and found fault with God's tent (tabernacle)." Ps-Jon, Tanh. *šlh* 11, and Yalk. Num 743 render *wtrgnw* as *rgn*, "to cry." Others, including Sifre, translate it as "sympathize." Yalk. Num 732, 805 has: "they sat in their tent and spoke words like sympathizers."

28. Where shall we go up? Our kinsmen have broken[24] our heart saying, 'The people are greater[25] and stronger[26] than we are, the cities are great and fortified towards[27] the sky, and we have seen the sons of the warrior[28] there.'"

29. I said to you, "You should not (let yourselves) be broken[29] nor fear them.

30. The Lord your God, who goes before you, His Memra[30] will fight[31] for you, just as He did for you in Egypt before your eyes,

31. and in the wilderness, where you saw how the Lord your God carried you, as a man carries his son, all the way you traveled until you came to this place.

32. Yet in this thing, you have no faith in the Memra[30] of the Lord your God,

33. who goes before you on the way, to prepare[32] for you a place, a lodging to rest,[33] with a pillar [34] of fire by night to see the way you are to follow and a pillar[34] of cloud by day."

---

[24] MT: "melted," which is a metaphor and as a rule avoided by TO. TO uses the same word *tbr* in verses 21 and 29 for *ths* and *t'rṣwn*. TO is apparently paralleling the Midrash (Num R. s. 17), where the word is interpreted: "they divided our hearts." In y. Maasroth 1:2 there is a dispute as to the meaning of the word. TO translates it in accordance with the accepted ruling (*Torah Tememah*). N and Ps-Jon are literal.

[25] MT: "large."

[26] MT: "exalted." The Targums are more concrete. Cf. 2:10 and 9:2.

[27] TO's rendering is due to the impossibility of the literal meaning of the MT. The MT has: "*in* heaven" or "*up* to heaven."

Scriptural texts sometimes speak in exaggerated terms (Sifre on 1:28, Sifre on Lev 8:2, Mek. on Exod 14:6, Rashi on Exod 14:6 and 50:21, Gen R. 45:3, Gen R. 80:7, Num R. 18:2, b. B. Mez. 56b, and b. Hul. 90b). See also 4:11 and 9:1.

The expression "sky-high" is a stereotyped Mesopotamian phrase (*Understanding Genesis*, by N. H. Sarna, New York, p. 73). N and Ps-Jon are like TO.

[28] MT: "Anakim." Anak means "neck" and is generally understood to imply tall people. Patshegen explains that TO's "warrior" is singular to inform us that all were children of one man. This is consistent with the other Targums. N has "sons of Anak, the warrior," and Ps-Jon has "sons of Ephron, the warrior." TJ, on Josh 11:21, 12:4, and elsewhere, translates like TO.

[29] MT: *t'rṣwm*. TO uses the same Aramaic word *tbr*, "broken," in verse 21 for *tht*

28. לאן אנחנא סלקין אחנא תברו ית ליבנא למימר עם רב ותקיף מיננא קרוין רברבן
וכריכן עד צית שמיא ואף בני גיברא חזינא תמן:

29. ואמרית לכון לא תתברון ולא תדחלון מנהון:

30. יי אלהכון דמדבר קדמיכון מימריה יגיח לכון ככל דעבד עמכון במצרים לעיניכון:

31. ובמדברא דחזיתא דסוברך יי אלהך כמא דמסובר גברא ית בריה בכל אורחא
דהליכתון עד מיתיכון עד אתרא הדין:

32. ובפתגמא הדין ליתיכון מהימנין במימרא דיי אלהכון:

33. דמדבר קדמיכון באורחא לאתקנא לכון אתר בית מישרי לאשריותכון בעמודא
דאישתא בליליא לאחזיותכון באורחא דתהכון בה ובעמודא דעננא ביממא:

and 28 for *hmsw*. *ʿrṣ* is a Hebrew expression generally used only in poetry. Rashi and Ibn Ezra explain: "break the heart because of fear." Ps-Jon translates like to, but N has "be not frightened" as in verse 21.

[30] To and Ps-Jon use Memra, "word," here to obviate the unseemly anthropomorphism, God fighting. The Targums vary in their use of Memra in this verse. Ps-Jon has it at the beginning: the Memra "goes." N does not introduce the Memra here but, instead, has the "glory of the Shekinah" go before the people. See the Introduction for an explanation of Memra and Shekinah.

In the following verse, Memra is added, not to avoid an anthropomorphism, but to maintain respect for God and the people. As rendered by the Targums, the people did not believe in God's Memra, but continued to have faith in God Himself. In verse 32, all three Targums have Memra, although N adds "name of."

[31] Shefftel (BO) explains that to has *ygyh* for "waging battle," while the expression is generally *ygyh qrb*. *qrb* denotes a full-fledged battle against armed troops, an inappropriate activity for God. Patshegen argues that the use of the single word implies that God did much more than involve himself in the outcome of the war. Berkowitz (LV) feels that to's use of the Memra, which he believes connotes God watching over mankind, implies that God will cause the Israelites to be successful through their own efforts. Thus, there is no need to avoid the use of the second word, *qrb*. This is one example among many where scholars read overmuch into and present contrary interpretations of to renderings. The word is found elsewhere where it cannot have these meanings. Ps-Jon translates like to, but N includes *qrb*.

The *Genesis Apocryphon* has the one word *qrb* in 21:24 (= Gen 14:2), 21:25 (=14:3), 21:31 (=14:8), and 22:6 (a paraphrase of 14:14–15).

[32] MT: *ltwr*, "spy." The Targums deviate to maintain God's honor, as does the Peshitta.

[33] To and Ps-Jon add "to rest," which is inferred, for clarity; N does not.

[34] The Targums add "pillar" twice for clarity.

34. When the sound of your words were heard before the Lord, then He was angry and he confirmed, saying:[35]
35. "Not one of these men of this evil generation shall see that good land, which I confirmed[35] to give to your fathers,
36. none except Caleb son of Jephunneh; he shall see it, and to him will I give the land on which he set foot and to his descendants, because he (followed) completely after the fear of the Lord."[36]
37. Also there was anger from before the Lord[37] with me because of you, and He said: "You shall not enter it either.
38. Joshua, son of Nun, who attends you, he shall enter it. Imbue him with strength, for he shall cause Israel to inherit it.
39. Moreover, your little ones who you said would be prey, your children who on this day did know good from bad, they shall enter it; to them will I give it and they shall possess it.
40. As for you, turn about and journey into the wilderness toward the Sea of Suf."

[35] MT: "And the Lord heard the voice of your words and was angry, and swore, saying."

TO maintains the MT's broad spectrum of communications between man and God showing that God is cognizant of people and concerned about them. There is only a slight change in TO and Ps-Jon. They sometimes use the passive voice and add "before." This change avoids a direct connection between the complaints and God, gives the Diety a more transcendental aspect, adds formality to the communication, and prevents having the human function of hearing attributed to God. N, here, does not add "before." For other examples see 5:28, 10:10, etc. as well as the Introduction.

The Targums generally do not change the anthropopathism "anger." Anthropopathisms and anthropomorphisms which were used frequently during the age of the composition of the Targum and which were not considered disrespectful by the populace or likely to lead to erroneous conceptions of God were *not* avoided by the Targums. The Midrash (Yalk. and Esth R. to 1:18) explains: "to them it appears as anger, but to Myself what does anger mean? I . . . reconsider."

The Targums render MT's "swore" as "confirmed" to replace the unseemly concept that God binds himself to humans.

TO renders the MT according to its *peshat*. The terms *peshat* and *derash* (which originated in the period of the Amoraim) are generally understood today as objective and subjective interpretations, respectively. Yet the two, *peshat* and *derash*

34. ושמיע קדם יי ית קל פתגמיכון ורגיז וקיים למימר:
35. אם יחזי גבר בגבריא האילין דרא בישא הדין ית ארעא טבתא דקיימית למיתן
    לאבהתהון:
36. אילהין כלב בר יפנה הוא יחזינה וליה איתין ית ארעא דדריך בה ולבנוהי חלף
    דאשלים בתר דחלתא דיי:
37. אף עלי הוה רגז מן קדם יי בדילכון למימר אף את לא תיעול לתמן:
38. יהושע בר נון דקאים קדמך הוא יעול לתמן יתיה תקיף ארי הוא יחסנינה לישראל:
39. וטפלכון דאמרתון לביזא יהא ובניכון דלא ידעו יומא דין וביש טב וביש אינון ייעלון
    לתמן ולהון איתנינה ואינון יירתונה:
40. ואתון אתפנו לכון וטולו למדברא אורח ימא דסוף:

have both elements. *Peshat* does not demand a mechanical literalness. It explains the text as it unfolds from the meaning of the words and the context of the entire text. *Peshat* may require the addition of material because of what is stated in another Biblical passage, especially when the other passage presents an apparent contradiction to the interpreter. Scholars can disagree concerning the *peshat*, although much less often than the *derash*. Many factors influence how one sees the *peshat*, including one's theological views and environment. *Derash* is influenced by the same factors, but will go beyond the context. Among other things, it frequently attempts to give Biblical support to rabbinical halakhah and theology.

TO does not deviate to teach theology or halakhah; therefore, the Targumist had no need for *derash*. Each verse is rendered according to the *peshat* as the Targumist saw it. When it is consistent with the *peshat* and allowed by Aramaic usage, the MT is translated literally, word for word, letter for letter. The Targum contains deviations to clarify; avoid some, but not all, apparent conflicts; and show what was felt to be proper honor to God and Israelite ancestors. The deviations almost always reflect rabbinic understandings. Generally, the only time that the two differ is when the latter uses *derash* to defend a rabbinic teaching. Although, as in any human communication, one can "detect" certain theological inclinations in TO, there is nothing in any verse beyond what the individual translated phrase meant, in context, to the translator.

[36] TO and Ps-Jon add *dhlt'*, meaning "fear" or "service," showing respect for God: people cannot follow God. Adler notes that *dhlt'* and *pwlhn'* are synonymous, but the first refers to thought or intention and the second to actual conduct or worship. See Introduction 4:4, 4:19, 4:20, and many other places for this word. N adds Memra instead of "fear," for the same purpose.

[37] MT: "the Lord was angry with me." The Targums recast this verse in the passive form and add "before." This may have been done for Moses' honor, to soften the idea that God was angry with him. Comp. 4:21.

41. You replied and said to me: "We stand guilty before[38] the Lord. We will go up and fight, just as the Lord our God commanded us." And each man girded his weapons of war and began[39] to go up into the hill.

42. But the Lord said to me: "Say to them, do not go up and do not wage battle since my Shekinah[40] is not in your midst, lest you be broken[20] before your enemies."

43. I spoke with you, but you would not accept[41] it; you flouted the Memra[42] of the Lord and were presumptuous and went up into the hill.

44. Then the Amorites who lived in those hills came out against you and chased you as bees swarm,[43] and they troubled[44] you in Seir as far as Horma.

45. You returned and wept before the Lord; but the Lord would not accept your prayer or listen to your words.[45]

46. So you abode in Rekam[46] many days, according to the days that you abode there.

Chapter II

1. We turned and journeyed (back) into the wilderness, by way of Yam Suf, as the Lord had spoken with me, and skirted Mount Seir a long time.

---

[38] The Targums add "before" instead of *l*, "to." See Introduction.

[39] MT: *wthynw*. The meaning of this word is uncertain. Adler (NL) feels that TO follows the reasoning of Rashbam and Rashi that the expression is derived from the word *hnnw* (Num 14:40): "Here we are and we will go up to the place." N has the same interpretation as Ibn Ezra, "join."

[40] The characteristic gloss avoids an unfavorable anthropomorphism. N and Ps-Jon add "go:" "My Shekinah does not go in your midst." See Introduction for the different usages of Shekinah by TO and the unofficial Targums.

[41] MT: "hear." Rashi (on Gen 37:27) writes that whenever the word *šmᶜ* in the MT means "hear," TO uses *šmᶜ*, but when it means "accept," TO had *qbl*, "accept." Ps-Jon follows TO's practice, but N, the Qumran Targum to Job, and Targum Sheni to Esther do not render *šmᶜ* as *qbl*. Maimonides (*Guide* 1:48) has a similar observation.

[42] MT: literally, "you flouted the mouth (word) of the Lord." TO and Ps-Jon delete "mouth" and add Memra. Characteristically, N does not drop "mouth" but

41. ואתיבתון ואמרתון לי חבנא קדם יי אנחנא ניסק ונגיח קרב ככל דפקדנא יי אלהנא
וזריזתון גבר ית מני קרביה ושריתון למיסק לטורא:

42. ואמר יי לי אימר להון לא תיסקון ולא תגיחון קרב ארי לית שכינתי ביניכון ולא
תיתברון קדם בעלי דבביכון:

43. ומללית עמכון ולא קבילתון וסריבתון על מימרא דיי וארשעתון וסליקתון לטורא:

44. ונפק אימוראה דיתיב בטורא ההוא לקדמותכון ורדפו יתכון כמא דנתזן דבריתא
וטרדו יתכון בסעיר עד חרמה:

45. ותבתון ובכיתון קדם יי ולא קביל יי צלותכון ולא אציח למילכון:

46. ויתיבתון ברקם יומין סגיאין כיומיא דיתיבתון:

II

1. ואתפנינא ונטלנא למדברא אורח ימא דסוף כמא דמליל יי עמי ואקיפנא ית טורא
דסעיר יומין סגיאין:

translates: "you flouted the mouth (word) of the decree of the Memra of the Lord."

[43] TO has *ntzn* instead of MT's "doings" or "acts of." Adler (NL) translates it as cutting or chopping. Schefftel (BO) translates it as "pour" or "swarming." The latter rendering is in accordance with the Targum attributed to R. Shesheth: "when the bees spring forth and fly in the heights of the world and collect honey from the herbage on the mountains" (b. Sotah 48b). If TO means "swarming" and parallels the longer Targum, this is a classic example of its restraint in that it did not elaborate at length as did R. Shesheth. Komlosh (*Hamikra*, p. 146) understands that TO wants to suggest the enemy's speed. The *Encyclopedia Mekorit* (vol. II, p. 587) indicates that the Amorites are compared to bees because the prior swarmed from the mountains and the latter from the rocks. N has: "like hornets and bees are chased." Ps-Jon has: "as they drive away and destroy hornets."

[44] MT: "and they smote." TO either (1) tones down the incident to avoid a harsh and severe expression of defeat for the Israelites, or (2) continues the simile of the bees, or (3) understands the phrases like Rashi, that the enemy will annoy the Israelites like bees, which die shortly after they bite. N and Ps-Jon have "smote" and FT has "kill."

[45] MT: "Listen to your cry or give ear to you." TO and Ps-Jon remove the anthropomorphism "ear," elevate "cry" to "prayer" and change "to you" to the explicit "your words." As in verse 43, TO and Ps-Jon also replace "hear" and are more explicit by rendering "accept." Num R. 17 indicates that it was the conduct of the Israelites that caused God not to "accept" their petition.

[46] MT: "Kadesh," see verse 2.

2. Then the Lord said to me as follows:

3. "You have been skirting this mountain long enough; now turn north.

4. And charge the people as follows: You will be passing through the territory of your kinsmen, the descendants of Esau, who live in Seir. Though they will be afraid of you, be very careful.

5. Do not provoke them. For I will not give you of their land so much as a foot can tread on; I have given Mount Seir as a possession to Esau.

6. You may buy[1] food from them for money to eat and you may buy[1] yourselves water from them for money to drink."

7. Indeed, the Lord your God has blessed you in all the acts[2] of your hands. He supplied your needs[3] during your wanderings through the great wilderness for forty years, the Memra[4] of the Lord your God has helped you, you have lacked nothing.

8. We then moved away from our kinsmen the descendants of Esau, who live in Seir, away from the road of the plain,[5] away from Elath and Ezion-geber; and we turned and moved in the direction of the wilderness of Moab.

9. Then the Lord said to me: "Do not besiege the Moabites or provoke them to engage in a fight.[6] For I will not give you any of their land as a possession; I have given Lechayath[7] as a possession to the descendants of Lot."

10. (It was formerly inhabited by the Emim, a great and numerous people, and strong[8] as a warrior.[9]

11. They are considered a warrior,[10] they are like a warrior,[10] and the Moabites call them Emim.

---

[1] MT: *tšbrw* and *tkrw*. The meaning of the second term is unclear. It occurs also in Hos 3:2, Job 6:27 and 40:30. TO texts vary. Some have a word which explains *tkrw* as "buy" and others as "dig." Adler (NL) notes that the proper Aramaic text should be *tzbnn* and *tkrwn*, both meaning "buy," the first referring to dry goods and the second to liquids. Cf. Rashi on Gen 50:5. Lowenstein (NH) explains that TO uses Hebrew for the second purchase because it prefers avoiding a repetition of terms and it was unable to find an Aramaic synonym for *tzbnn*. N and Ps-Jon have the root *zbn* in both instances as do the Sperber and B texts.

[2] TO renders "acts" in the plural although MT has the singular.

2. ואמר יי לי למימר:
3. סגי לכון דאקיפתון ית טורא הדין אתפנו לכון לציפונא:
4. וית עמא פקיד למימר אתון עברין בתחום אחיכון בני עשו דיתבין בסעיר וידחלון מנכון ותסתמרון לחדא:
5. לא תתגרין בהון ארי לא אתין לכון מארעהון עד מדרך פרסת רגל ארי ירותא לעשו יהבית ית טורא דסעיר:
6. עיבורא תזבנון מנהון בכספא ותיכלון ואף מיא תזבנון מנהון בכספא ותשתון:
7. ארי יי אלהך ברכך בכל עובדי ידך סופיק לך צורכך במהכך ית מדברא רבה הדין דנן ארבעין שנין מימרא דיי אלהך בסעדך לא חסרת מידעם:
8. ועברנא מלות אחנא בני עשו דיתבין בסעיר מאורח מישרא מאילת ומעציון גבר ואתפנינא ועברנא אורח מדברא דמואב:
9. ואמר יי לי לא תצור על מואבאי ולא תתגרי למעבד עמהון קרב ארי לא אתין לך מארעהון ירותא ארי לבני לוט יהבית ית לחית ירותא:
10. אימתני מלקדמין יתיבו בה עם רב וסגי ותקיף כגבריא:
11. גבריא מתחשבין אף אינון כגבריא ומואבאי קרן להון אימתני:

---

[3] MT: "He knew your ways." TO and Ps-Jon translate in the same way and replace one anthropomorphic phrase with another. N gives the characteristic deviation for "knew:" "your ways were revealed before God." TO and Ps-Jon interpret according to the context of the verse.

[4] MT: "the Lord your God has been with you." TO and Ps-Jon remove the anthropomorphism by (a) adding Memra and (b) having it "help" rather than "be with." N has only the last change.

[5] MT: "Arabah.' N also has this characteristic deviation, but Ps-Jon lacks the entire phrase.

[6] The Targums add "to engage him" for clarity. See also verses 19 and 24.

[7] MT: "Ar." See 2:18. N and Ps-Jon translate like TO.

[8] TO renders MT's "exalted" as "strong." LXX is similar to TO here but is literal in 9:2.

[9] MT: *'nqym*, TO and Ps-Jon: *gbry'*. See note on 1:28. The word also appears twice in verse 11. In each instance the Targums are explaining the meaning of an obscure term. N has "sons of Anak, the warrior." Comp. Gen 6:4, where MT's *npylym* is rendered "warriors" by the Targums.

[10] MT has *rp'ym* and *'nqym*. *rp'ym* means "shades," in the sense of a dead or extinct race. TO and Ps-Jon translate each word as "warrior." N paraphrases the second as "sons of Anak, the warrior."

12. Similarly, Seir was formerly inhabited by the Horites; but the descendants of Esau dispossessed them, wiping them out and settling in their place, just as Israel did in the land of his possession, which the Lord had given them.)

13. "Now rise up, cross wadi Zered." So we crossed wadi Zered.

14. The time we spent in travel from Rekam Geah[11] until we crossed wadi Zered was thirty eight years, until that whole generation of warriors had perished from the camp, as the Lord had confirmed[12] to them.

15. Indeed, a blast (went out) from before[13] the Lord against them, to root them out from the camp, until the last.

16. When all the warriors among the people had died off,

17. the Lord spoke to me, saying:

18. "You are this day passing through the border of Moab, through Lachayath.[14]

19. You will then be close to the Ammonites; do not besiege them or provoke them to engage in a fight[15] with you. For I will not give any part of the land of the Ammonites to you as a possession; I have given it as a possession to the descendants of Lot."

20. (It, too, is considered warrior[16] country. It was formerly inhabited by warriors,[17] whom the Ammonites call Heshbani,[18]

21. a people great and numerous and as strong[19] as the warrior.[20] The Lord wiped them out from before them, and they dispossessed them and settled in their place,

22. as He did for the descendants of Esau who live in Seir, when He wiped out the Horites before them, so that they dispossessed them and settled in their place, even unto this day.

23. So, too, with the Avvim who dwelt in Rafiah[21] as far as Gaza: the Cappadocians,[22] who came from Cappadocia,[22] wiped them out and settled in their place.)

---

[11] MT: "Kadesh Barnea." See 1:2. N and Ps-Jon are like TO.

[12] MT: "swore." See note to 1:8.

[13] MT: "The hand of the Lord struck them." The Targums add a gloss avoiding the anthropomorphism.

TO generally retains the image of God's benevolence and statements concerning His punishing sins and wicked acts. E. T. Rasmussen, "Relationship of God and Man According to a Text and Targum of Deuteronomy," unpublished thesis, 1967. Comp. 4:3, 25–27; 5:9; 7:9–10; 11:2, 26–28; 24:8–9; ch. 28 and 29 *passim*.

[14] MT: "Ar." See 2:9.

‏12. ובסעיר יתיבו חוראי מלקדמין ובני עשו תריכונון ושיציאונון מן קדמיהון ויתיבו
באתריהון כמא דעבד ישראל לארע ירותתיה דיהב יי להון:
‏13. כען קומו ועיברו לכון ית נחלא דזרד ועברנא ית נחלא דזרד:
‏14. ויומיא דהליכנא מרקם גיאה עד דעברנא ית נחלא דזרד תלתין ותמני שנין עד דסף
כל דרא גברי מגיחי קרבא מגו משריתא כמא דקיים יי להון:
‏15. ואף מחא מן קדם יי הות בהון לשיציותהון מגו משריתא עד דשלימו:
‏16. והוה כד שלימו כל גברי מגיחי קרבא לממת מגו עמא:
‏17. ומליל יי עמי למימר:
‏18. את עבר יומא דין ית תחום מואב ית לחית:
‏19. ותתקרב לקביל בני עמון לא תצור עליהון ולא תתגרי למעבד עמהון קרב ארי לא
אתין מארע בני עמון לך ירותא ארי לבני לוט יהבתה ירותא:
‏20. ארע גיבריא מתחשבא אף היא גיברין יתיבו בה מלקדמין ועמונאי קרן להון
חשבני:
‏21. עם רב וסגי ותקיף כגיבריא ושיצינון יי מן קדמיהון ותריכונון ויתיבו באתרהון:
‏22. כמא דעבד לבני עשו דיתבין בסעיר דשיצי ית חוראי מן קדמיהון ותריכונון ויתיבו
באתרהון עד יומא הדין:
‏23. ועואי דיתבין בדפיח עד עזה קפוטקאי דנפקו מקפוטקיא שיציאונון ויתיבו
באתרהון:

---

[15] The Targums add "to engage in a fight" for clarity. The Targums also add
"to engage in" in verses 9 and 24, but here "a fight" is also added.

[16] MT has plural *rp'ym*, which TO and Ps-Jon render in the singular. N has "warriors." See notes on vv. 10 and 11.

[17] MT: *rp'ym*. TO and N have the plural "warriors" but Ps-Jon has the singular.

[18] MT: *zamzumin*. TO's rendering presumably means inhabitants of Heshbon.
Adler notes that some understand both the Hebrew and Aramaic as "thoughtful
ones"; *ḥšb* means "think." Perhaps TO relies on Gen R. s. 26, which translates *zamzumin* as "magistrates." The *zuzim* in Gen 14:5 may be identical with the *zamzumin*. N and Ps-Jon have *zimtaneh*.

[19] MT: *rm*, "high or exalted." The Targums clarify the term.

[20] See verses 10 and 11. Ps-Jon translates like TO, but N has "as the sons of
Anak, the warrior."

[21] MT: "Chatzerim." Adler (NL) notes that both the Hebrew and Aramaic
mean "open spaces." If Rafiah is a name, it is another example of a geographic
identification by TO, cf. Amos 9:7. The Berliner text has *Deaphiach*. N and Ps-Jon
have another name.

[22] MT: "Caftorim." The Targums have "Cappadocia," a province in Asia
Minor. The place is similarly identified by LXX, the Vulgate, and the Peshitta. It
was known by the name Cappadocia at least from the Hasmonean period

24. "Up! Set out across wadi Arnon! See, I give unto your hand Sihon, king of Heshbon, the Amorite, and his land. Begin the dispossession:[23] provoke him so as to engage him[24] in a fight.

25. This day I begin to put the dread and fear of you upon the people everywhere under heaven, who shall hear report of you, and shall tremble and break[25] before you."

26. Then I sent messengers from the wilderness of Kedemoth[26] to Sihon king of Heshbon with words of peace, as follows:

27. "Let me pass through your country. I will keep strictly to the highway. I will neither turn to the right nor to the left.

28. You will sell me food for money, that I may eat, and give me water for money that I may drink: only let me pass through by foot

29. (as the descendants of Esau who dwell in Seir did for me, and the Moabites who dwell in Lachayath)[27] until I cross the Jordan into the land that the Lord our God is giving us."

30. But Sihon king of Heshbon would not give us permission to pass through his border,[28] because the Lord had stiffened his spirit and hardened his heart in order to deliver him into your hands—as (is apparent) this day.

31. Then the Lord said to me: "See, I begin to place Sihon and his land before you. Begin the dispossession,[23] to take possession of his land."

32. Then Sihon came out against us, he and all his men, to fight at Jahaz.

33. But the Lord our God delivered him up before us and we defeated him and his sons[29] and all his people.

34. We captured all his towns at that time, and we destroyed[30] every town—men,[31] women, and children—leaving no survivor.

35. We retained as booty only the cattle and the spoil of the cities that we captured.

36. From Aroer on the edge of the Arnon valley, including the town in the valley, to Gilead, not a city was too mighty for us; the Lord our God delivered everything to us.

(Komlosh, p. 224). See TO to Gen 10:14, TJ to Jer 47:4 and Ez 27:11, b. Ber. 56b and Gen R. 37. LXX is like TO here but not in Gen.

[23] MT: *rš*, "inherit." TO uses a word which connotes driving out rather than inheritance. Perhaps TO did so because the land of Sihon was not originally planned as an inheritance. If Sihon had harkened to Moses' request for peace, the

24. קוּמוּ טוּלוּ וְעִיבַרוּ יָת נַחְלָא דְאַרְנוֹן חֲזִי דְמַסְרִית בִּידָךְ יָת סִיחוֹן מַלְכָּא דְחֶשְׁבּוֹן
אֱמוֹרָאָה וְיָת אַרְעֵיהּ שָׁרִי לְתָרָכוּתֵיהּ וְאִתְגָּרִי לְמֶעְבַּד עִמֵּיהּ קְרָב:

25. יוֹמָא הָדֵין אֵישָׁרֵי לְמִיתַּן זוּעֲתָךְ וּדְחַלְתָּךְ עַל אַפֵּי עַמְמַיָּא דִּתְחוֹת כָּל שְׁמַיָּא דְיִשְׁמְעוּן
שָׁמְעָךְ וִיזוּעוּן וִידְחֲלוּן מִן קְדָמָךְ:

26. וּשְׁלַחִית אִיזְגַּדִּין מִמַּדְבַּר קְדָמוֹת לְוָת סִיחוֹן מַלְכָּא דְחֶשְׁבּוֹן פִּתְגָּמֵי שְׁלָמָא לְמֵימַר:

27. אֵיעִיבַר בְּאַרְעָךְ בְּאוֹרְחָא בְּאוֹרְחָא אֵיזֵיל לָא אִיסְטֵי לִימִינָא וְלִסְמָלָא:

28. עִיבוּרָא בְּכַסְפָּא תְזַבֵּין לִי וְאֵיכוֹל וּמַיָּא בְּכַסְפָּא תִּתֵּין לִי וְאֵישְׁתֵּי לְחוֹד אֵיעִיבַר
בְּרַגְלָי:

29. כְּמָא דְעַבַדוּ לִי בְּנֵי עֵשָׂו דְּיָתְבִין בְּשֵׂעִיר וּמוֹאֲבָאֵי דְּיָתְבִין בִּלְחִית עַד דְּאֵיעִיבַר יָת
יַרְדְּנָא לְאַרְעָא דַּיְיָ אֱלָהָנָא יָהֵיב לָנָא:

30. וְלָא אַבָא סִיחוֹן מַלְכָּא דְחֶשְׁבּוֹן לְמִשְׁבְּקַנָא לְמֶעְבַּר בִּתְחוּמֵיהּ אֲרֵי אַקְשִׁי יְיָ אֱלָהָךְ
יָת רוּחֵיהּ וְתַקֵּיף יָת לִיבֵּיהּ בְּדִיל לְמִמְסְרֵיהּ בִּידָךְ כְּיוֹמָא הָדֵין:

31. וַאֲמַר יְיָ לִי חֲזִי דְשָׁרֵיתִי לְמִמְסַר קְדָמָךְ יָת סִיחוֹן וְיָת אַרְעֵיהּ שָׁרִי לְתָרָכוּתֵיהּ לְמֵירַת
יָת אַרְעֵיהּ:

32. וּנְפַק סִיחוֹן לִקְדָמוּתָנָא הוּא וְכָל עַמֵּיהּ לְאַגָחָא קְרָבָא לְיָהַץ:

33. וּמַסְרֵיהּ יְיָ אֱלָהָנָא קֳדָמָנָא וּמְחֵינָא יָתֵיהּ וְיָת בְּנוֹהִי וְיָת כָּל עַמֵּיהּ:

34. וּכְבַשְׁנָא יָת כָּל קִרְווֹהִי בְּעִידָנָא הַהוּא וְגַמַּרְנָא יָת כָּל קִרְוַיָּא גַּבְרַיָּא וּנְשַׁיָּא וְטַפְלָא לָא
אַשְׁאַרְנָא מְשֵׁיזֵיב:

35. לְחוֹד בְּעִירָא בַּזְנָא לָנָא וַעֲדִי קִרְוַיָּא דְּכַבֵּשְׁנָא:

36. מֵעֲרֹעֵר דְּעַל כֵּיף נַחְלָה דְאַרְנוֹן וְקַרְתָּא דִּבְנַחְלָא וְעַד גִּלְעָד לָא הֲוַת קַרְתָּא דִּתְקֵיפַת
מִינָּנָא יָת כּוֹלָא מְסַר יְיָ אֱלָהָנָא קֳדָמָנָא:

Israelites would not have touched his land. However, see note on 1:8. Ps-Jon translates like TO, but N has "inherit."

24 The Targums add "to engage him" as in verses 9 and 19.

25 MT: *ḥlw*, "tremble." B has "be fearful."

26 N and some TO texts have *dqdmwt*, clearly understanding the word as a noun,
not like Rashi.

27 MT: "Ar." N and Ps-Jon are like TO.

28 The Targums add "permission" and "border," implied in the text, to clarify
the meaning of the verse.

29 MT: *bnyw* and *bnw*, the singular form is the *Ketiv* and the plural is the *Keri*.
TO has the plural form in accordance with the *Keri*. (See Tanchuma end of *ḥwkt*.)
Ps-Jon also has the plural. N has a copyist's error; the word is missing.

30 MT: *ḥerem*. The Targums clarify the meaning of this term.

31 MT has a word, *mtm*, whose meaning is unclear. TO and Ps-Jon translate
"men" like Sifre and Ibn Ezra. See 3:6, 4:27, and Isa 5:13. N has "fortified towns,
women and children."

37. Only to the land of the children of Ammon you did not come near; the entire side of the wadi Jabbok, and the cities of the hill country, and wherever the Lord our God forbade us.

Chapter III

1. We turned and made our way up the road toward Mathnan,[1] and Og king of Mathnan[1] came out against us, he and all his people, to battle at Edrei.
2. But the Lord said to me: "Do not fear him, for into your hand I am delivering him and all his men and his country, and you will do to him as you did to Sihon king of the Amorites, who dwelt in Heshbon."
3. So the Lord our God delivered into our hand also Og king of Mathnan,[1] with all his people, and we smote him until none was left to him remaining.
4. We captured all his towns at that time. There was not a town that we did not take from them: sixty towns, the whole district of Trachonitis,[2] the kingdom of Og in Mathnan.[1]
5. All these towns were fortified with high walls, gates, and bars—apart from a great number of unwalled towns.
6. We doomed[3] them as we had done to Sihon king of Heshbon; we doomed[3] all the towns[4]—men,[5] women, and children.
7. But all the cattle and spoil of the towns we took as booty to ourselves.
8. Thus we seized the country, at that time, from the two Amorite kings, which is beyond the Jordan, from the wadi Arnon to Mount Hermon.
9. (Sidonians call Hermon Sirion, and Amorites call it Mount Talga.[6])
10. All the towns of the plains and the whole of Gilead and Mathnan[1] as far as Salach and Edrei, the towns of Og's kingdom in Mathnan.[1]
11. (Only Og king of Mathnan[1] was left, a remnant of the warrior.[7] His bedstead, an iron bedstead, is it not in Rabbah of the Ammonites? It is nine cubits long and four cubits wide by the king's cubit.[8])

---

[1] MT: "Bashan." Ps-Jon translates like TO, but N has "Botniin."

[2] MT: "Hebel Argob." The Targums read Trachonitis, an area in N.E. Israel identified by this name in Josephus' *Wars of the Jews*. TO's rendering of *ḥbl* by *plk*

37. לחוד לארע בני עמון לא קריבתא כל כיף נחל יובקא וקרוי טורא וכל דפקיד יי
אלהנא:

III

1. ואתפנינא וסליקנא לאורח מתנן ונפק עוד מלכא דמתנן לקדמותנא הוא וכל עמיה
לאגחא קרבא לאידרעי:
2. ואמר יי לי לא תדחל מניה ארי בידך מסרית יתיה וית כל עמיה וית ארעיה ותעביד
ליה כמא דעבדתא לסיחון מלכא אימוראה דיתיב בחשבון:
3. ומסר יי אלהנא בידנא אף ית עוג מלכא דמתנן וית כל עמיה ומחינהי עד דלא
אשתאר ליה משיזיב:
4. וכבשנא ית כל קרווהי בעידנא ההוא לא הות קרתא דלא נסיבנא מינהון שיתין
קרוין כל בית פלך טרכונא מלכותיה דעוג במתנן:
5. כל אילין קרויא כריכן מקפן שור רם דילהון דשין ועברין בר מקרוי פצחיא
דסגיאן לחדא:
6. וגמרנא יתהון כמא דעבדנא לסיחון מלכא דחשבון גמרנא כל קרויא גבריא נשיא
וטפלא:
7. וכל בעירא ועדי קרויא בזנא לנא:
8. ונסיבנא בעידנא ההוא ית ארעא מיד תרין מלכי אימוראה דבעיברא דירדנא
מנחלא דארנון עד טורא דחרמון:
9. צידונאי קרן לחרמון סריון ואימוראי קרן ליה טור תלגא:
10. כל קרוי מישרא וכל גלעד וכל מתנן עד סלך ואדרעי קרוי מלכותה דעוג במתנן:
11. ארי לחוד עוג מלכא דמתנן אשתאר משאר גיבריא הא ערסיה ערסא דברזלא הלא
היא ברבת בני עמון תשע אמין אורכה ואמין וארבע אמין פותיה באמת מלך:

---

captures the double meaning of the Hebrew: "district" (Neh 3:9) and "a portion
or allotment" (Jos 17:14 and 19:9). Argob is also mentioned in I Kings 4:13. Ps-Jon
also has *plk* and N has a synonym *thwm*.

[3] MT: *ḥrm*, which the Targums explain.

[4] TO has the plural "towns" although the MT has the singular.

[5] See note on 2:34.

[6] MT: "Senir." TO and Ps-Jon add "Mount" and call it "Talga," an Aramaic
word meaning "snow." Rashi and Adler (NL) note that the Hebrew "Senir" means
"snow." Ps-Jon adds a gloss: "because the snow never ceases from it either in sum-
mer or winter." See Dan 7:9 and b. Shab. 154a. N calls Mount Hermon in verses 8
and 9 Mount Talga, but retains the Hebrew in this verse, Senir.

[7] MT: "Rephaim." See 2:11.

[8] MT: "a man's cubit." Berkowitz (LV) and Adler (NL) suggest that TO reflects

12. And this is the land which we possessed at that time: (The part) from Aroer along the wadi Arnon, with half of Mount Gilead and its towns, I gave to the tribe[9] of Reuben and to the tribe[9] of Gad.

13. The rest of Gilead, and all of Mathnan,[1] the kingdom of Og, I gave to the half-tribe[9] of Manasseh, the whole district of Trachonitis,[2] with all of Mathnan[1] which is called warrior[7] country.

14. Jair son of Manasseh received the whole district of Trachonitis[2] as far as the boundary of the Geshurites and the Epichaeros,[10] and named it after himself, that is Mathnan,[1] village of Jair, until this day.

15. To Machir I gave Gilead.

16. And to the tribe[9] of Reuben and to the tribe[9] of Gad I gave (the part) from Gilead down to the wadi Arnon, the middle of the wadi being the boundary, and up to the wadi Jabbok, the boundary of the Ammonites.

17. And the plain,[11] and the Jordan, and the adjoining land, from Genosar[12] even unto the sea of the plain,[11] the Salt Sea, from under the slopes of the heights[13] eastward.

18. I charged you at that time saying, "The Lord your God has given you this country to possess. You must go armed, before your Israelite kinsmen, every armed[14] warrior.

19. Only your wives, children, and livestock—I know that you have much livestock—shall be left in the towns that I gave to you,

20. until the Lord has granted your kinsmen rest such as you have, and they too have taken possession of the land that the Lord your God is giving them, beyond the Jordan. Then each man may return each to the possession that I gave you."

21. I also charged Joshua at that time, saying, "You have seen with your own eyes all that the Lord your God has done to these two kings; so shall the Lord do to all the kingdoms into which you shall cross over.

22. Do not fear them, for the Lord your God, His Memra[15] will battle for you."

the common practice that measurements are established by the government. Nachmanides explains that TO interprets the Hebrew as if it read: "the cubit of *the* man," indicating a specific or important man. It happens rather frequently that verses should be translated as if "the" is implied. N and Ibn Ezra are like TO. Ps-

12. וית ארעא הדא ירתנא בעידנא ההוא מערוער דעל נחלא דארנון ופלגות טורא
דגלעד וקרווהי יהבית לשיבט ראובן ולשיבט גד:

13. ושאר גלעד וכל מתנן מלכותיה דעוג יהבית לפלגות שבטא דמנשה כל בית פלך
טרכונא לכל מתנן ההוא מתקרי ארע גבריא:

14. יאיר בר מנשה נסיב ית כל בית פלך טרכונא עד תחום גישוראה ואפקירוס וקרא
יתהין על שמיה ית מתנן כפרני יאיר עד יומא הדין:

15. ולמכיר יהבית ית גלעד:

16. ולשיבט ראובן ולשיבט גד יהבית מן גלעד ועד נחלא דארנון גו נחלא ותחומיה ועד
יובקא נחלא תחומא דבני עמון:

17. ומישרא וירדנא ותחומיה מגיניסר ועד ימא דמישרא ימא דמילחא תחות משפך
מרמתא מדנחא:

18. ופקידית יתכון בעידנא ההוא למימר יי אלהכון יהב לכון ית ארעא הדא למירתה
מזרזין תעברון קדם אחיכון בני ישראל כל מזרזי חילא:

19. לחוד נשיכון וטפלכון ובעירכון ידענא ארי בעיר סגי לכון יתבון בקרויכון דיהבית
לכון:

20. עד דיניח יי לאחיכון כותכון ויירתון אף אינון ית ארעא דיי אלהכון יהיב להון
בעיברא דירדנא ותתובון גבר לירותתיה דיהבית לכון:

21. וית יהושוע פקידית בעידנא ההוא למימר עינך חזאה ית כל דעבד יי אלהכון לתרין
מלכיא האילין כן יעביד יי לכל מלכותא דאת עבר לתמן:

22. לא תדחלון מנהון ארי יי אלהכון מימריה מגיח לכון:

Jon has "in his own cubit" which *Perush Jonathan* explains refers to the cubit of
King Og.

[9] TO adds "tribe," which is implied in MT for clarity. N and Ps-Jon translate like
TO. TJ makes the same deviation. For example, see Josh 12:6.

[10] MT: "Maakhaty." N is like TO, but Ps-Jon has "Entichaeros," which is probably a scribal error.

[11] MT: "the Arabah." See 1:17.

[12] MT: "Kinnereth." N and Ps-Jon subtitute like TO, as does TJ to Josh 11:2 and
elsewhere.

[13] MT: "slopes of Pisgah." See Num 21:20 and v. 27. N, Ps-Jon, and TJ (to Josh
12:3 and elsewhere) translate like TO.

[14] MT: *bny ḥyl*. The Targums replace *bny* with "armed."

[15] TO, characteristically, adds Memra, not wanting to indicate that God engages
in war. See also Exod 14:25. Ps-Jon is like TO. N does not add Memra, but has: "He
will make a successful arrangement of your battle for you."

23. I prayed[16] before[17] the Lord at that time, saying,
24. "Lord God,[18] You have begun to let Your servant see Your greatness and Your mighty hand. You are the God whose Shekinah is in heaven above and who rules on earth, and there is none who can do like Your works, and like Your might.[19]
25. I pray, let me cross over and see the good land beyond the Jordan, that good mountain,[20] and the Temple.[21]
26. But there was anger[22] from before[23] the Lord with me on your account and He would not accept[24] from me. The Lord said to me, "Enough![25] Never speak before[26] Me of this matter again!
27. Go up to the top of the heights[27] and lift your eyes to the west, and to the north, and to the south, and to the east. See with your eyes, for you shall not go across yonder Jordan.

[16] TO parallels Sifre, that the word means prayer. N translates like TO. Ps-Jon has: "I sought mercy"; comp. Exod 33:19.

[17] The Targums replace "to" with "before."

[18] Because of the use of two words for God, TO does not follow its usual practice of replacing Elohim with the Tetragrammaton. See also Gen 2:7, 8, 9, 15, 16, and 15:2, 8. Ps-Jon reads like TO, but N does not have Elohim.

[19] TO revises the latter part of this sentence. MT reads: "for what God is there in heaven or in earth that can do according to Your works, and according to Your might?" TO avoids any thought of limiting God's power and all references to idols. TO follows Exod 15:11, see TO *ad loc*. Berkowitz (LV) notes that MT is phrased as a question, a style that TO avoids. N and Ps-Jon translate differently, but like TO add the Shekinah as dwelling in heaven.

[20] TO retains the singular, which the Midrash (Sifre on Num 27:12) and Talmud (b. Ber. 48b) interpret as Jerusalem (see NL). N translates like TO, and Ps-Jon indicates specifically: "that good mountain on which is built the city of Jerusalem."

[21] MT: "and the Lebanon." TO changes "Lebanon" to "Temple" deriving the interpretation from the root of the word Lebanon, *laban*, which means "white." White, in turn, implies "purity," a Temple function (cf. Isa 1:18). This is also in Sifre. In addition, there is association with the Temple because it was made of the cedars of Lebanon (cf. Isa 10:34 and b. Git. 56b).

In 1:7 and 11:24, TO is literal, retaining Lebanon. Perhaps this is because those verses only list the boundaries of the land. Here, however, Moses is understood by TO as being concerned with matters more spiritual. Lebanon was considered by the

23. וצליתי קדם יי בעידנא ההוא למימר:
24. יי אלהים את שריתא לאחזאה ית עבדך ית רבותך וית ידך תקיפתא דאת הוא
    אלהא דשכנתך בשמיא מלעילא ושליט בארעא לית דיעביד כעובדך וכגבורותך:
25. איעיבר כען ואיחזי ית ארעא טבתא דבעיברא דירדנא טורא טבא הדין ובית
    מקדשא:
26. והוה רגז מן קדם יי עלי בדילכון ולא קביל מיני ואמר יי לי סגי לך לא תוסיף
    למללא קדמי עוד בפיתגמא הדין:
27. סק לריש רמתא וזקוף עינך למערבא ולציפונא ולדרומא ולמדנחא וחזי בעינך ארי
    לא תיעיבר ית ירדנא הדין:

pagans to be a holy mountain. It is mentioned in lists of gods given in Hittite trea-
ties of the second millennium B.C.E. The Psalmist also describes how God appro-
priated the mountains formerly consecrated to old gods: He made Lebanon and
Siryon leap like young calves (Ps 29:6). Furthermore, Lebanon was never incorporated into Israel, not even by King Solomon. Thus, the targumist may have thought
it improper to have Moses yearn for Lebanon and, with the significance of Lebanon as symbolizing the Temple in mind, may have considered Moses' interest as
being for the "true" holy site.

The other Targums to this verse understand the word in the same sense. N
translates "Temple mountain" and Ps-Jon has "Mount Lebanon where the
Shekinah will dwell in the future."

In *Scripture and Tradition in Judaism*, Geza Vermes follows the "new synthe-
sis" developed by Renée Bloch and analyzes, among other subjects, the historical
development of the use of Lebanon in the Targums. The word Lebanon is found in
about 60 MT verses, half of which are understood metaphorically by the Targums.
Vermes shows that the word generally served in the Targums as a symbol for the
king, the rich, the nations, Jerusalem, or the Temple. Vermes considers the Targumic rendering of this verse (Lebanon = Temple) to be the basic text for the development of the symbol.

[22] MT: *wyt῾br*. The Targums translate like Sifre, Tanh. *w῾thnn* and Yalkut Deut
820. LXX has: "But the Lord overlooked me."

[23] TO adds "before," but N and Ps-Jon do not.

[24] MT: "hear." Characteristically, TO and Ps-Jon use "accept" but N has
"hear." N and Ps-Jon add "my prayer."

[25] MT: *rb*, "much." TO, N and Ps-Jon clarify the meaning, as does the Sifre.

[26] The Targums replace "to Me" with "before Me."

[27] MT: "Pisgah." See verse 17 and Num 27:12. N and Ps-Jon are like TO. See N
on 4:49, which translates different words in the MT like the MT here.

28. Charge Joshua, encourage him and strengthen him, for he shall go before this people and he shall allot to them the land that you may see."
29. And we dwelt in the valley opposite Beth-peor.

Chapter IV

1. And now, Israel, give heed to the laws and rules which I am instructing you to observe, so that you may live to enter and take possession of the land that the Lord, the God of your fathers, is giving to you.
2. You shall not add to the word that I command you or take anything from it, but keep the commandments of the Lord your God that I enjoin upon you.
3. Your eyes have seen what the Lord did in regard to the worship[1] of Baal-peor, that the Lord your God destroyed from among you every person who followed Baal-peor.
4. But you, who held fast to the fear of[2] the Lord your God, all are alive today.
5. See, I have taught to you laws and rules, as the Lord my God has commanded me, for you to abide by in the land which you are about to enter to take possession of it.
6. Observe them and do them, for that will be (proof of) your wisdom and discernment in the eyes of other peoples, who on hearing all of these laws will say, "Surely, that great nation is a wise and discerning people."
7. For what nation is so great, that has a god[3] so close[4] to accept their prayers in times of trouble,[5] as (does) the Lord our God at all times that we pray before him.[6]

---

[1] Some TO texts add "worship", like N and Ps-Jon, to clarify the text. The Targums may have also wanted to avoid anyone thinking that the idol was a reality. The Targums tolerate no implication that other gods exist. N and Ps-Jon have the Memra do the act. MT has the participle *hrʾwt*, TO has the perfect.

[2] TO and Ps-Jon add "fear," to replace an unseemly anthropomorphic phrase or mystical connotation. See note on 1:36. They do not drop the phrase "held fast" altogether. This may be in agreement with b. Ket.111b, where this phrase is inter-

28. ופקיד ית יהושע ותקיפהי ועלימהי ארי הוא יעיבר קדם עמא הדין והוא יחסין
יתהון ית ארעא דתחזי:
29. ויתיבנא בחילתא לקביל בית פעור:

IV

1. וכען ישראל שמע לקימיא ולדיניא דאנא מליף יתכון למעבד בדיל דתיחון ותיעלון
ותירתון ית ארעא דיי אלהא דאבהתכון יהיב לכון:
2. לא תוספון על פיתגמא דאנא מפקיד יתכון ולא תמנעון מניה למיטר ית פיקודיא
דיי אלהכון דאנא מפקיד יתכון:
3. עיניכון חזאה ית דעבד יי בפלחי בעלא פעור ארי כל גברא דהליך בתר בעלא פעור
שיצייה יי אלהך מבינך:
4. ואתון דאידביקתון בדחלתא דיי אלהכון קימין כולכון יומא דין:
5. חזו דאליפית יתכון קימין ודינין כמא דפקדני יי אלהי למעבד כן בגו ארעא דאתון
עלין לתמן למירתה:
6. ותיטרון ותעבדון ארי היא חכמתכון וסוכלתנותכון לעיני עממיא דישמעון ית כל
קימיא האלין ויימרון לחוד עם חכים וסוכלתן עמא רבא הדין:
7. ארי מן עם רב דליה אילה קריב ליה לקבלא צלותיה בעידן עקתיה כיי אלהנא בכל
עדן דאנחנא מצלן קדמוהי:

preted as meaning "hold fast to God's commandments," and Sifre, where it means
"hold fast to the wise." It may also have been retained because it was considered to
be an easily understood metaphor. N has: "While you, because you held fast to the
teaching of the Torah of the Lord your God, therefore are all alive and enduring
today."
[3] MT has Elohim, "God," in the plural form, which TO renders in the singular.
TO does not change it to the Tetragrammaton as is done customarily since the general term "god" is more appropriate for the verse. Nevertheless, the Targum
changes the plural form to the singular to avoid the concept of polytheism. See also
4:3, 5:7, and 32:39. B. Sanh. 38b understands this verse to refer to God, but y. Ber.
9:11 explains that it means an idol.
[4] MT has the plural form for "close." The Targums place it in the singular to
conform to the singular "god."
[5] TO glosses: "to accept their prayers in times of trouble." This rendering
evades the impression of God's physical proximity. N has: "For what nation and
kingdom has a god so close at hand as the Memra of the Lord our God, at all times
that we pray before Him, He answers us." Ps-Jon has a long gloss.
[6] MT: "whenever we call to Him." See above note.

8. Or what great nation has laws and rules as truthful as all this Torah that I set before you this day?

9. But take heed[7] and guard[7] yourself scrupulously, so that you do not forget the things that your eyes have seen and so that they do not depart from your heart as long as you live. And make them known to your children and to your children's children:

10. The day you stood before the Lord your God at Horeb, when the Lord said to me, "Gather the people before[8] Me that I may let them hear My words, in order that they may learn[9] to fear before[8] Me as long as they live on earth, and may so teach their children."

11. You came forward and stood at the foot of the mountain. The mountain was ablaze with flames towards the sky,[10] dark, cloud, and thick darkness.

12. The Lord spoke with you[11] out of the fire; you heard the sound of words but perceived no shape—nothing but a voice.

13. He declared to you the covenant which He commanded you to observe, Ten Commandments;[12] and He inscribed them on the two tablets of stone.

14. The Lord commanded me at the same time to teach to you laws and rules for you to observe in the land which you are about to cross into to possess.

15. Be most careful of yourselves, since you saw no shape on the day that the Lord your God spoke with[11] you at Horeb out of the fire,

16. not to act corruptly and make for yourselves a sculptured image in any likeness whatever: the form of a man or woman,

17. the form of any beast on earth, the form of any winged bird that flies[13] in the air of the sky[14] of the heaven,

18. the form of anything that creeps on the ground, the form of any fish that is in the waters below the earth.

---

[7] MT uses the word *šmr*, "watch," twice. TO renders the first *'stmr*, "take heed," and the second *ṭr*, "guard." This was apparently done to explain the tautology of MT. Hence, the first is taken in the negative sense, take heed *not* to do extra things (cf. b. Shav. 36a); while the second is taken in the positive sense of observing, guarding, etc. N and Ps-Jon read similarly.

[8] MT: *ly* and *'ty*, which TO and Ps-Jon replace with "before Me" escaping the anthropomorphic thought of direct contact. N does not.

[9] Rashi explains that TO's use of *ylpyn*, "they may learn," clarifies that the word

8. ומן עם רב דליה קימין ודינין קשיטין ככל אוריתא הדא דאנא יהיב קדמיכון יומא דין:

9. לחוד איסתמר לך וטר נפשך לחדא דילמא תיתנשי ית פיתגמיא דחזאה עינך ודילמא יעידון מליבך כל יומי חיך ותהודעינון לבנך ולבני בנך:

10. יומא דקמתא קדם יי אלהך בחרב כד אמר יי לי כנוש קדמי ית עמא ואשמעינון ית פיתגמי דיילפון למידחל קדמי כל יומיא דאינון קימין על ארעא וית בניהון ילפון:

11. וקריבתון וקמתון בשיפולי טורא וטורא בער באישתא עד ציח שמיא חשוכא עננא ואמטתא:

12. ומליל יי עימכון מגו אישתא קל פגתמין אתון שמעין ודמו ליתיכון חזן אילהין קלא:

13. וחוי לכון ית קימיה דפקיד יתכון למעבד עשרה פתגמין וכתבינון על תרין לוחי אבניא:

14. ויתי פקיד יי בעידנא ההוא לאלפא יתכון קימין ודינין למעבדכון יתהון בארעא דאתון עברין לתמן למירתה:

15. ותיסתמרון לחדא לנפשתכון ארי לא חזיתון כל דמו ביומא דמליל יי עמכון בחורב מגו אישתא:

16. דילמא תחבלון ותעבדון לכון צילמא דמות כל צורא דמות דכר או נוקבא:

17. דמות כל בעירא דבארעא דמות כל ציפר גפא דפרח באויר רקיע שמיא:

18. דמות כל ריחשא דבארעא דמות כל נוני דבמיא מלרע לארעא:

---

ylmdwn in the MT means that the people should teach themselves. N and Ps-Jon translate the word like TO.

[10] MT: "heart of." The Targums replace the metaphor. See also 1:28.

[11] MT: literally, "to you." The Targums render according to Aramaic usage. Comp. 5:24; opposite is 5:25, in one phrase: "the Lord said to me." N concludes the verse: "the voice of His Memra."

[12] Literally "Ten Words" in both MT and the Targums. MT has the word "the" before "Ten Words" but not before "two tablets of stone." TO reverses this. Berkowitz (CS) suggests that TO follows MT's use of "the" in Exodus since the text in Exodus is describing the earlier generation which heard the command from God; thus, the commandments are emphasized there. Here, the new generation learned of the commandments from the stones; thus, the emphasis is placed on the stones. N has "the" before both phrases. Ps-Jon has "the" before the first and describes the second as "sapphire tablets."

[13] Some TO texts have a doublet for "flies:" *dprh* and *dty'wp*.

[14] TO and Ps-Jon add the gloss "in the air of the sky," which is implied, preventing a misunderstanding that the verse refers to birds of a mystical character flying in heaven itself. N is similar.

19. And perhaps you may lift your eyes to the sky and behold the sun, moon, and stars, the whole heavenly host, you may err[15] and bow down to them and serve them[16]—(namely) these which the Lord your God prepared for[17] other people under the whole heaven—

[15] MT: *wndḥt.* TO uses the word *wṭṭʿy* for greater clarity. N and Ps-Jon translate similarly.

[16] MT: *wʿbdtm.* TO, N, and Ps-Jon have: *tblḥynwn.* See note on 1:36. The *Masorah of Targum Onkelos* indicates that *tblḥynwn* is used for *wʿbdtm* in three places, this verse, 5:9, and Exod 20:5; in other verses *tplḥynyn* is to be used (J. Faur, *Sinai 60–61,* [1966–67], 17–27).

[17] MT: *ḥlq,* "divided." TO: *zmym,* "prepared."

b. Meg. 9a, b records (see also y. Meg. 1:19, Sopherim 1:8–9, Mek. *pshḥ* 14 and Mek. *ʿmlq* 1) eighteen variants in the LXX from the MT, two of which are in Deut: 4:19 and 17:3. (a) 4:19 reads "which the Lord your God set aside to give light unto the entire world;" (b) 17:3 reads "worship other gods . . . I never commanded to serve them."

Epstein, in *Torah Tememah ad loc.,* states that the LXX reading wishes to preclude anyone from deriving from our verse that national gods are acknowledged by the Torah and that non-Jews may worship them. (See *The Interpreter's Bible,* where this teaching is derived from this verse.) It is therefore possible (but unlikely, see below) that TO deviates here to weaken this impression.

Adler (NL) feels that TO's language allows two rabbinic views to be deduced: (1) that Jews should give light (i.e., teach) the non-Jewish world (b. Meg. 9b). (This teaching could be the positive impetus underlying the LXX deviation: to elevate the "Jewish role" rather than belittle non-Jews, as implied in the next interpretation.) (2) God allowed non-Jews to go astray and worship idols so that He can drive them from the world (b. Ab. Zar. 55a). In giving this interpretation, Adler is following his view that TO deviates on occasion to address theological and philosophical issues. These two teachings, however, are not apparent in TO. The first teaching could be read into N and Ps-Jon, but there is no certainty that this was the original intention.

N and Ps-Jon translate *ḥlq* literally but add a gloss to explain the meaning of the verse. N has: "and the Lord your God will distribute you among all peoples everywhere under heaven." Ps-Jon has: "for the Lord your God has distributed through them knowledge of all the peoples that are everywhere under heaven." The Targums may be reflecting the first teaching or a third: that the nations learned through God's works—through observing nature—while Israel had direct contact with God (see next verse) and received His revelation.

Some TO texts alter the next-to-the-last clause in this verse to read "which the

19. ודילמא תזקוף עינך לשמיא ותיחזי ית שימשא וית סיהרא וית כוכביא כל חילי
שמיא ותיטעי ותסגוד להון ותפלחינון דזמין ײ אלהך יתהון לכל עממיא דתחות כל
שמיא:

Lord your God *did not* appoint unto all the people which are under all the
heavens." (Emphasis added by E. T. Rasmussen, "Relationships of God and Man
According to a Text and Targum of Deuteronomy," unpublished thesis, 1967, p.
14, who adds: "The negation removes the implication which might otherwise be
seen that [God] appointed the sun, moon, and stars unto some peoples as objects as
worship.")

Komlosh (HBH, p. 148), referring to 29:25, where the word "divided" is used
in reference to the Israelites and is not translated as it is here, interprets the verse
non-theologically. He argues that the Targumic change was made for the honor of
God. Apparently, he means that God does not need to "divide," since division
implies that the original creation was not perfect.

Another interpretation seems more likely. TO deviates here simply because the
heavenly host was not "divided" (an imprecise figure of speech that the Targum
generally prefers to avoid), but "prepared." TO characteristically uses *zmm* for
"prepare," cf. Exodus 19:10, 14.

This verse is one of many where some scholars incorrectly read philosophical or
theological interpretations into TO. It is unlikely that the single word *zmym* can
stop people from believing that the Bible recognizes the existence of national gods.
Nor does the word clearly imply the two rabbinical interpretations. N and Ps-Jon
add glosses to interpret the verse, but these glosses do not reflect either of the rabbinic interpretations definitely and, furthermore, neither Targum changes *ḥlq* to
zmym. Thus no proof can be derived from them that *zmym* implies these teachings. Further indication that TO does not involve itself in the theological problem
addressed by LXX, the Talmud, and Midrash is that it does not deviate to translate
17:3, the other Deut verse mentioned in rabbinic literature as a LXX deviation
prompted by theological difficulties.

It is the author's view (*Targumic Studies*) that TO does not deviate to teach
theological and philosophical matters. This is supported by Maimonides (*Guide*
1:28): TO is not involved in "every profound matter, the understanding of which is
not a fundamental element in our faith, and the comprehension of which is not
easy for the common people."

There are instances (2:30, 33, 41; 3:45; and elsewhere) where Maimonides
seems to imply that by translating with a particular word instead of another, TO is
expressing a philosophical view. However, these instances concern the honor of
God. Furthermore, it is likely that what Maimonides means is that TO was not written to answer philosophical questions, but that the author(s) had a view which may

20. but you the Lord brought near to the fear of Him[18] and brought you out of Egypt, that iron blast furnace, to be to Him a people of inheritance, as this day.

21. Now from before the Lord there was anger against me[19] because of your words and He affirmed[20] that I should not cross the Jordan and enter the good land that the Lord your God is giving you as a heritage.

22. For I must die in this land; I shall not cross the Jordan. But you will cross and take possession of that good land.

23. Take care not to change the fear[21] that the Lord your God concluded[22] with you, and not to make for yourselves a sculptured image in any likeness, against which the Lord your God has enjoined you.

24. For the Lord your God, His Memra[23] is a consuming fire, a zealous God.

25. When you will beget children and children's children and you will be ancient[24] in the land, act wickedly and make for yourselves a sculptured image in any likeliness, and do what is evil before[25] the Lord your God to make displeasure before[25] Him.

26. I call heaven and earth this day to witness against you that you shall quickly perish from the land which you are crossing the Jordan to take possession of it; you shall not long endure in it, but shall be utterly wiped out.

27. The Lord will scatter[26] you among the peoples, and you shall be left as only a small people[27] among the nations to which the Lord will lead you.

be inferred occasionally from the manner of the translation. Maimonides would recognize, however, that these inferences are speculations which do not have clear textual bases. See also the notes to 32:12 and 33:6 in this study for other attempts to derive theological principles from TO.

[18] MT: "the Lord took." The Targums recast this unseemly anthropomorphism. TO: "brought near to the fear of Him," N: "the Memra of the Lord separated," Ps-Jon: "the Memra of the Lord took for His portion."

[19] MT: "Now the Lord was angry with me." Although the Targums do not always replace the anthropopathism, and ascribe anger directly to God, they may have done so here to soften the concept that God was angry with Moses. Comp. 1:37.

[20] The Targums change "swore" to "affirmed."

20. ויתכון קריב יי לדחלתיה ואפיק יתכון מכורא דברזלא דבמצרים למיהוי ליה לעם
אחסנא כיומא הדין:

21. ומן קדם יי הוה רגז עלי על פתגמיכון וקיים בדיל דלא למיעברי ית ירדנא ובדיל
דלא למיעל לארעא טבתא דיי אלהך יהיב לך אחסנא:

22. ארי אנא מאית בארעא הדא לית אנא עבר ית ירדנא ואתון עברין ותירתון ית
ארעא טבתא הדא:

23. איסתמרו לכון דילמא תתנשון ית קימא דיי אלהכון דיגזר עמכון ותעבדון לכון
צילם דמות כולא דפקדך יי אלהך:

24. ארי יי אלהך מימריה אישא אכלא הוא אל קנא:

25. ארי תולדון בנין ובני בנין ותתעתקון בארעא ותחבלון ותעבדון צילם דמות כולא
ותעבדון דביש קדם יי אלהך לארגזא קדמוהי:

26. אסהידית בכון יומא דין ית שמיא וית ארעא ארי מיבד תיבדון בפריע מעל ארעא
דאתון עברין ית ירדנא לתמן למירתה לא תורכון יומין עלה ארי אשתיצאה
תשתיצון:

27. ויבדר יי יתכון ביני עממיא ותשתארון עם דמנין בעממיא דידבר יי יתכון לתמן:

---

[21] The Sperber text has "fear" instead of "covenant," but other TO texts, B, N, and Ps-Jon are literal.

[22] MT has *krt*, a Hebrew term for establishing (literally: cutting) a covenant. The Targums render the word with the Aramaic idiom, *gzr*. N has the Memra of the Lord perform the two acts mentioned in the verse. Ps-Jon does not.

[23] TO and Ps-Jon add Memra, but N does not. Both N and Ps-Jon have the fire being zealous, rather than God, avoiding the anthropopathism.

Reifmann (*Sedeh Aram*) feels that TO uses the word אשׁ for fire rather than the characteristic *nwr'*, to show that the fire is spiritual. N and Ps-Jon are like TO.

[24] MT: *wnwštm*, which according to b. Sanh. 38a and b. Git. 88a means a long period exceeding 800 years. The Targums read *wtt'tqwn*, meaning: to be settled a long time (Jastrow, p. 1130b).

[25] The Targums drop the words "eye of" the Lord your God converting the anthropomorphism with "before." See also: 6:18, 9:18; 12:25, 28; 13:19; 17:2; 21:9; and 31:29, the eight other times these words occur in Deut. See note on 12:25 for examples in other books. The Targums also add "before" at the end of the verse.

[26] N has "exile" for clarity, and Ps-Jon adds "to exile" at the end of the verse for the same reason.

[27] MT: *mty mspr*. The Targums clarify the text. See note on 2:34.

28. And there you shall serve people[27a] who serve idols, man made of wood and stone, that cannot see or hear or eat or smell.

29. You will seek[28] there for the fear[29] of the Lord your God, you will find it; if only you seek[30] before[31] Him with all your heart and soul.

30. When you are in distress because all these things have befallen you and, in the end of days, return to the fear[32] of the Lord your God and accept[33] His Memra.[34]

31. For the Lord your God is a compassionate God: He will not forsake you nor will He destroy you; He will not change[35] the covenant which He affirmed[36] to your fathers.

32. Inquire now about the beginning days that came before you, ever since the Lord[37] created man on earth, from one end of heaven to another; has anything as grand as this ever happened, or has its like ever been heard?

33. Has any people heard the voice of the Memra[38] of the Lord[39] speaking out of a fire, as you have, and survived?

[27a]"There you will serve man-made gods," etc. ᴛᴏ replaces ᴍᴛ's "god's" with "idols." Also, instead of serving idols, the people will serve idol-worshippers. The Targum also does not want to berate the people of Israel. Additionally, generally the Israelites did not worship idols when they were exiled. There was also a possibility that people would misunderstand this verse as a command to worship idols when in exile. Furthermore, ᴛᴏ may have wanted to avoid an interpretation of the text given in b. Ketub. 110b that whoever lives outside of Israel is considered as if he worshipped idols.

Adler (NL) explains that ᴛᴏ renders the last phrase "that cannot see," etc., in the feminine gender since, according to ᴛᴏ, this phrase refers to the nations and not the idols. ᴛᴏ uses the feminine gender also in Deut 28:64. I Samuel 26:19 is similarly rendered by ᴛᴊ.

Ps-Jon is like ᴛᴏ but ɴ is almost literal. The most significant change in ɴ is the translation of "god" by "idol."

[28] ᴍᴛ has a plural form which ᴛᴏ converts to in the singular. Schefftel (BO) explains that this was done to conform to the rest of the sentence, which is in the singular form. Ps-Jon is like ᴛᴏ, but ɴ adds "pray."

[29] ᴛᴏ and Ps-Jon add "fear," rejecting a direct anthropomorphic contact between the humans and God. ɴ evades the anthropomorphism by adding "before."

[30] Characteristically, the Targums do not use different words for synonyms con-

28. ותפלחון תמן לעממיא פלחי טעותא עובד ידי אינשא אעא ואבנא דלא חזן ולא
שמעין ולא אכלין ולא מריחין:

29. ותתבע מתמן ית דחלתא דיי אלהך ותשכח ארי תיבעי מן קדמוהי בכל ליבך ובכל
נפשך:

30. כד תיעוק לך וישכחונך כל פתגמיא האילין בסוף יומיא ותתוב לדחלתא דיי אלהך
ותקביל למימריה:

31. ארי אלהא רחמנא יי אלהך לא ישבקינך ולא יחבלינך ולא יתנשי ית קימא
דאבהתך דקיים להון:

32. ארי שאל כען ליומיא קדמאי דהוו קדמך למן יומא דברא יי אדם על ארעא
ולמיסיפי שמיא ועד סיפי שמיא ההוה כפתגמא רבה הדין או האשתמע דכותיה:

33. השמע עמא קל מימרא דיי דממליל מגו אישתא כמא דשמעת את ואתקים:

---

tained in the MT. MT has *drš* and *bgš*, both of which are rendered *tbʿ*, "seek."

[31] TO and Ps-Jon add "before," avoiding an inappropriate direct contact with God. N does not add "before," perhaps because this Targum uses it earlier in the verse.

[32] The Talmud, y. Taanit 1:5, understands the return as repentance. Perhaps this is one reason why TO adds "fear." The addition also replaces the anthropomorphism by having the people return to the "fear" and not God Himself. Ps-Jon has "fear," but N adds "before."

[33] MT: "hear His voice." TO and Ps-Jon change "hear" to "accept," but N does not.

[34] TO and Ps-Jon add Memra instead of "voice," but N has "voice of the Memra of the Lord." Memra is frequently added to "voice" or in place of "voice" as an object of the verb "to hear" to state more precisely what is heard. One does not only hear the "voice" of God, but also his "word." See also 4:33, 36; 5:24, 25, 26; 8:20; 13:5, 19; 15:5; 18:16; 26:14; 27:10; 28:1, 2, 15, 45, 62; 30:2, 8, 10, 20.

[35] MT: "forget." TO prevents the concept of God forgetting, but the other Targums, translating literally, do not.

[36] MT: "swore."

[37] The Targums replace Elohim with the Tetragrammaton.

[38] This time all three Targums add Memra and do not delete "voice." "Voice" is necessary here.

[39] TO and Ps-Jon render this word as if it applies to God (the Tetragrammaton rather than Elohim) instead of an idol since they do not want to refer even to the possibility of powers to idols. N has *Elah*, referring to an idol. (The Torah, JPS ed.; interprets the verse to refer to an idol. *Konteros Hashemoth*, which expresses the rabbinical interpretation, considers this Elohim as the Lord.)

34. Or has the Lord[40] performed[41] miracles[42] to reveal Himself[43] and take for Himself one nation from the midst of another by miracles,[42] by signs and portents, by war, by a mighty hand and uplifted arm[44] and great appearances,[45] like all that the Lord your God did for you in Egypt before your very eyes?

35. It has been shown to you[46] that you may know that the Lord is God; there is none other beside Him.

36. From the heaven He let you hear the voice of His Memra[47] to teach you;[48] on earth He let you see His great fire: and His words you heard from amidst that fire.

37. And because he loved your fathers, He chose their offspring after them; and with His Memra,[49] with great might, brought you out of Egypt,

38. to drive out nations greater and mightier than you from before you, to bring you into their land and give it to you as a heritage, as this day.

39. Know therefore this day and keep it in your heart that the Lord is God, His Shekinah[50] is in heaven above and rules[51] on earth below; there is no other.

40. Observe His laws and commandments, which I enjoin upon you this day, that it may go well with you and your children after you, and that you may long remain in the land that the Lord your God is giving you for all time.

41. Then Moses set aside[52] three cities beyond the Jordan toward the sun-rising,

---

[40] MT: Elohim. TO and N change it to the Tetragrammaton. Ps-Jon and FT have "Memra of the Lord."

[41] The Targums add "performed" for clarity.

[42] The Targums clarify that the word in the MT means "miracles." It is by no means certain that this is the correct rendering. Normally, *nsh* in the MT means "tried" or "attempted." The word is also found in 26:8, 29:2, and 34:12.

[43] MT: "to come," an anthropomorphism. Ps-Jon reads like TO, but N is literal.

[44] The Targums change "outstretched" to "uplifted" but do not attempt to remove the anthropomorphic "arm." See also: 5:15, 7:19, 9:29, 11:2, and 26:8.

[45] The Targums render MT's *mwrᵓym*, "awesome," paralleling Sifre, referring to the appearance of the Shekinah. Schefftel (BO) explains that the deviation avoids the idea of idol worship. Reider (*Deuteronomy* 34:12) explains that TO's rendering is in accordance with the well-known interpretation that "great terror" implies

‫‪.34‬ או נסין עבד יי לאיתגלאה למיפרק ליה עם מגו עם בנסין באתין ובמופתין ובקרבא‬
‫ובידא תקיפתא ובדרעא מרממא ובחזוונין רברבין ככל דעבד לכון יי אלהכון‬
‫במצרים לעיניכון:‬

‫‪.35‬ את אתחזיתא למידע ארי יי הוא אלהים לית עוד בר מניה:‬

‫‪.36‬ מן שמיא אשמעך ית קל מימריה לאלפותך ועל ארעא אחזיך ית אישתיה רבתא‬
‫ופיתגמוהי שמעתא מגו אישתא:‬

‫‪.37‬ וחלף ארי רחים ית אבהתך ואתרעי בבניהון בתריהון ואפקך במימריה בחיליה‬
‫רבא ממצרים:‬

‫‪.38‬ לתרכא עממין רברבין ותקיפין מינך מן קדמך לאעלותך למיתן לך ית ארעהון‬
‫אחסנא כיומא הדין:‬

‫‪.39‬ ותידע יומא דין ותתיב לליבך ארי יי הוא אלהים דשכינתיה בשמיא מלעילא‬
‫ושליט על ארעא מלרע לית עוד:‬

‫‪.40‬ ותיטר ית קימוהי וית פיקודוהי דאנא מפקיד לך יומא דין דייטב לך ולבנך בתרך‬
‫ובדיל דתוריך יומין על ארעא דיי אלהך יהיב לך כל יומיא:‬

‫‪.41‬ בכן אפריש משה תלת קרוין בעיברא דירדנא מדנח שימשא:‬

divine Revelation. Patshegen shows how TO is consistent in employing this terminology. It is used, for example, in regard to the Ten Commandments, Deut 4:34.
See also 26:8 and 34:12. When the word is used in connection with sin, it is translated by TO as "fear." See 11:25.

[46] TO clarifies the MT. Since the Targum has *'ythzyt'* instead of *'hzyt*, Rashi
explains that TO is giving the following interpretation: When the Holy One,
blessed be He, gave the Israelites the Torah, He rent open the heavens so that they
saw that He was alone. Therefore, it is stated: "It has been shown to you that
you may know." Rashi is reading more then is warranted into the Targum.

[47] The Targums add Memra.

[48] MT: "to discipline you." N has "discipline," and Ps-Jon has both "discipline"
and "teach."

[49] TO adds Memra, but N and Ps-Jon do not.

[50] TO and Ps-Jon use Shekinah. N has "glory of His Shekinah."

[51] By adding "rules," the Targums avoid any possible misunderstanding that
God is physically present on earth. See a similar Targum on Joshua 2:11.

[52] The Targums may retain the imperfect form contained in the MT because,
according to the Talmud, Moses wanted to be zealous in this matter—to set the
cities apart at his earliest opportunity. Although the cities were not to serve for
refuge until those in Canaan were assigned that purpose, Moses said: "any duty
that it is possible for me to perform I will perform now" (b. Mac. 10a). However,
there can be no certainty of this since the Targums are literal.

42. to which a manslayer could escape, one who unwittingly slew a fellow man without having been hostile to him in the past; he could flee to one of these cities and live:

43. Bezer, in the wilderness in the plain country, belonging to the tribe[53] of Reuben; Ramoth in Gilead, belonging to the tribe[53] of Gad; and Golan, in Mathnan,[54] belonging to the tribe[53] of Manasseh.

44. This is the Torah that Moses set before the Israelites:

45. these are the testimonies, laws, and rules of which Moses spoke with the people of Israel, after they had left Egypt,

46. beyond the Jordan, in the valley opposite Beth-peor, in the land of Sihon King of the Amorites, who dwelt in Heshbon, whom Moses and the Israelites defeated after they had left Egypt.

47. They had taken possession of his country and that of Og king of Mathnan[54]—the two kings of the Amorites who were beyond the Jordan, toward the sun-rising—

48. from Aroer on the banks of wadi Arnon, as far as Mount Sion, that is, Hermon;

49. also the whole plain[55] beyond the Jordan, in the east, as far as the Sea of the plain[55] from under the slopes of the heights.[56]

Chapter V

1. Moses summoned all the Israelites and said to them: Hear, Israel, the laws and rules that I proclaim before you[1] this day! Study them and observe them and do them!

2. The Lord our God made[2] a covenant with us as Horeb.

3. It was not with our fathers that the Lord made[2] this covenant, but with us,[3] even us every one of us who is here today, all of us living.

4. Speech to speech[4] the Lord spoke with you, at the mountain, out of the fire—

---

[53] The Targums add "tribe" for clarity.
[54] MT: "Bashan." See note on 3:1.
[55] MT: Arabah. Cf. 3:17.
[56] MT: "slopes of Pisgah." See note on 3:17. Ps-Jon is like TO, but N has "top of the heights," translating the MT as if it had "top of the Pisgah," as in 3:27.

42. למיערק לתמן קטולא דיקטול ית חבריה בלא מדעיה והוא לא סני ליה מאיתמלי
ומדקמוהי ויערוק לחדא מן קרויא האלין ויתקים:

43. ית בצר במדברא בארע מישרא לשיבט ראובן וית ראמות בגלעד לשיבט גד וית
גולן במתנן לשיבטא דמנשה:

44. ודא אוריתא דסדר משה קדם בני ישראל:

45. אלין סהידותא וקימיא ודיניא דמליל משה עם בני ישראל במיפקהון ממצרים:

46. בעיברא דירדנא בחילתא לקביל בית פעור בארע סיחון מלכא אימוראה דיתיב
בחשבון דמחא משה ובני ישראל במיפקהון ממצרים:

47. ויריתו ית ארעיה וית ארע עוג מלכא דמתנן תרין מלכי אימוראה דבעיברא
דירדנא מדנח שימשא:

48. מערער דעל כיף נחלא דארנון ועד טורא דסיאון הוא חרמון:

49. וכל מישרא עיברא דירדנא מדינחא ועד ימא דמישרא תחות משפך מרמתא:

V

1. וקרא משה לכל ישראל ואמר להון שמע ישראל ית קימיא וית דיניא דאנא ממליל
קדמיכון יומא דין ותילפון יתהון ותיטרון למעבדהון:

2. יי אלהנא גזר עימנא קים בחורב:

3. לא עם אבהתנא גזר יי ית קימא הדין אילהין עימנא אנחנא אלין בא יומא דין
כלנא קימין:

4. ממלל עם ממלל מליל יי עמכון בטורא מגו אישתא:

[1] MT has a Hebrew idiom, "in your ears." TO and Ps-Jon translate "before you"
to avoid the metaphor. N has "in your hearing." Some TO texts have "ears."

[2] MT: *krt*, a Hebrew idiom used in the creation of covenants, literally "cut."
The Targums explain the word. Comp. 4:23.

[3] The Targums have a word which Schefftel (BO) explains: only with us, but
not with our ancestors. Rashi and Ibn Ezra interpret the MT: "also with us."

[4] MT: "face to face," an anthropomorphism that occurs five times in the Torah,
twice in Deuteronomy. TO renders the phrase "face to face" twice, and "speech to
speech" three times. Lowenstein (NH) explains that the first rendering is made
when the verse refers to a revelation, but TO has "speech to speech" if the verse
infers speaking or hearing. Adler (NL) notes that the same phrase in Deut 34:10 is
rendered "face to face" by TO. He feels that this may be because in Chapter 34 the
reference is made to Moses, who had a greater prophetic experience, while here it
is made to all Israelites.

5. I was standing[5] between the Memra[6] of the Lord and you at that time
to tell you the Lord's words—for you were afraid of the fire and did
not go up the mountain—saying:

6. "I[7] the Lord am your God who brought you out of the land of Egypt,
the house of servitude:[8]

7. You shall have no other god[9] besides Me.[10]

8. You shall not make for yourself a sculptured image, any[11] likeness of
what is in the heaven above, or on the earth below, or in the waters
below the earth.

9. You shall not bow down to them nor serve them. For I the Lord your
God am an impassioned God visiting[12] the guilt of the fathers[13] upon
the rebellious[14] children, upon[15] the third generation[16] and upon the

"Speech to speech" here somewhat parallels a Talmudic statement (b. Ber.
45a) that during the promulgation of the Decalogue the relation between God and
Moses was that of a reciter and an interpreter. The Israelites, who could not ascend
the mountain, heard the voice of God distinctly, but they could not understand the
words and were in need of an interpreter.

There is also, a parallel with the Midrash (Pes. Rabbati) quoted by Rashi: R.
Berechia said; "Thus did Moses, in effect, say: Do not think that I am misleading
you with something which does not exist at all, as an agent does acting between the
vendor and the purchaser; behold the seller (God) Himself is *speaking* to you."
This late Midrash was probably influenced by TO.

[5] MT has the participle *'md*, TO has the participle and *hwh* in the perfect.

[6] The Targums add Memra, avoiding the idea of an anthropomorphic appearance of God.

[7] There are a number of variations between the rendering of the Ten Commandments in Exodus 20:2 ff. and here, both in MT and TO. These differences are
noted below. They show how consistently TO follows the MT.

TO is much more literal in rendering the Ten Commandments than N and
Ps-Jon. Among other things, the latter Targums do not make a distinction between
the lengthy and the concise commandments in the two tablets. The commandments are addressed in the plural to the entire nation, not to each individual
separately. Also the unofficial Targums describe the manner of delivery and give
reasons for the fulfillment. These differences are discussed by Y. Komlosh in "The
Ten Commandments in the Jerusalem Targums," *Sinai* (1962–63) 289–295.

[8] MT, in both versions: "house of slaves," implying a place where slaves are
bred. N renders literally. Ps-Jon and CGT add "servitude": "house of servitude of

5. אנא הויתי קאים בין מימרא דיי וביניכון בעידנא ההוא לחואה לכון ית פתגמיא
דיי ארי דחילתון מן קדם אישתא ולא סליקתון בטורא למימר:

6. אנא יי אלהך דאפיקתך מארעא דמצרים מבית עבדותא:

7. לא יהוי לך אילה אוחרן בר מיני:

8. לא תעביד לך צילם כל דמו דבשמיא מלעילא ודבארעא מלרע ודבמיא מלרע
לארעא:

9. לא תסגוד להון ולא תפלחינון ארי אנא יי אלהך אל קנא מסער חובי אבהן על בנין

slaves." Peshitta: "house of servitude of their work. See also 6:12, 7:8, and 8:14.
FT adds a gloss emphasizing the terrible slavery in Egypt.

⁹ Adler (NL to Exod 20:3) explains that TO cannot translate "idols of the
nations" as it is accustomed to do because God would be compared to an idol. He
believes TO cannot use "other fears" because the Targum wants to reflect the rabbinic teaching that "God" includes parents and teachers.

The Aramaic construction of Elohim is in the singular to weaken the concept of
polytheism.

¹⁰ MT has "before My face" in both versions, an anthropomorphism that TO
generally prefers to avoid. TO's understanding of the Hebrew word *ʿl* in the sense of
"besides" is found in Num 28:15, Gen 28:9 and 31:50. The rendering is in accordance with Jewish law. *Sefer Mitzvot Gadol*, a medieval work, for example, has as
its first precept: "not to imagine that there is any other deity *besides* God." The
translation is also in accordance with Isaiah 44:6, "and besides me there is no god."
N and Ps-Jon also have "besides Me."

¹¹ Both MT and TO have "and any" in Exodus. N and Ps-Jon have the *w*, "and,"
here.

¹² MT: "remembering," an unseemly anthropomorphism that TO prefers to
avoid since it implies that God can forget. N, CGT, and Ps-Jon have "remembering." FT to the Ten Commandments in Exodus adds that God's creatures are
frightened before Him, therefore the Israelites can certainly not serve them as
idols.

¹³ MT: *ʾbt* in Exodus and *ʾbwt* here.

¹⁴ TO adds "rebellious" changing the meaning of the text. See note 17. N and
Ps-Jon have "the guilt of wicked fathers on rebellious children."

¹⁵ MT: *ʿl* in Exodus and *wʿl* in Deuteronomy, adding the word "and." TO has *ʿl*
in both sites. In view of TO's consistent following of the MT, this is probably a textual error. Moreover, N and Ps-Jon do not have the *w*. Comp. TO to Lev 11:19
which has an extra *w*.

¹⁶ The Targums add "generation" three times in verses 9 and 10 for greater
clarity.

fourth generation[16] of those who reject Me, when the children continue to sin as their fathers,[17]

10. but doing kindness to the thousandth generation[16] of those who
love Me and keep My commandments.[18]

11. You shall not swear[19] by the name of the Lord your God in vain;[20] for
the Lord will not clear one who swears falsely[21] by His name.

12. Observe[22] the sabbath day and keep it holy, as the Lord your God has
commanded you.[23]

---

[17] In Exod and here, TO adds the gloss from "when the children" evading the
erroneous view that innocent children are punished for their parents' misdeeds.

The principle of punishing children for their parents' sin is clearly contradicted
by Deut 24:16, Jer 31:29, and Ezek 18:20. These verses teach that each person
suffers for his own iniquity. The Talmud maintains (b. Ber. 7a, b. Sanh. 27b, and
elsewhere; comp. also Mekhilta, ed. Lauterbach, II 246 and Mekhilta de RSBY
106) that the Decalogue refers to children who follow iniquitous practices of their
parents— hence incurring a similar punishment—while the verses that indicate no
punishment apply when children break away from the evil practices and follow the
better dictates of their own conscience. But cf. b. Makkot 24a, where the contradiction between Moses and Ezekiel is acknowledged. Ps-Jon is phrased like TO, and N
renders similarly. Ps-Jon, however, does not make the addition in Exod. Adler (NL
on Exod 20:5) argues that the gloss is a conflation to "those who reject Me." Thus,
this deviation was not made to teach a theological lesson. It intends either to
resolve an apparent contradiction (comp. 1:1), or to explain "those who reject
Me."

[18] MT in Exodus is _mṣwty_. Here it is _mṣwtw_ in the Ketiv and _mṣwty_ in the Kere.
The Targums, as usual, follow the Kere.

In the beginning of the verse, the unofficial Targums render MT's _w ʿwśh ḥsd_ as
nṭyr ḥsd, meaning "guarding" or "observing kindness." This wording may imply
the concept of _Zachuth Aboth_, "merit of the fathers," which is stored and used
when needed by the Israelites. The concept is explicit in many verses in the
unofficial Targums. It is nowhere in TO. See the author's _Targumic Studies_ for a
full discussion of _Zachuth_.

[19] MT has _tśʾ_ and _yśʾ_, "to take up," which TO renders _tymy_ and _ymy_, "to swear,"
in accordance with the Talmud and Midrash; for example, b. Shav. 29a, and
Mekhilta on the Exodus version of the Decalogue, Ps-Jon, M, CGT, and Peshitta
also translate "swear," but N has "take up."

[20] MT has _lśwʾ_ twice in this verse. TO translates the first _lmgnʾ_ meaning
"unnecessarily, falsely" and the second _lśqrʾ_, "falsely." N and Ps-Jon have _ʿl mgn_
twice, meaning "unnecessarily, falsely." Comp. Targum to Eccl 8:2: "Be careful
not to swear in vain, _ʿl mgn_, by the name of the Lord." CGT has two nouns in the

מרדין על דר תליתי ועל דר רביעי לסנאי כד משלמין בניא למיחטי בתר אבהתהון:

10. ועביד טיבו לאלפי דרין לרחמי ולנטרי פיקודי:

11. לא תימי בשמא דיי אלהך למגנא ארי לא יזכי יי ית דיימי בשמיה לשיקרא:

12. טר ית יומא דשבתא לקדשותיה כמא דפקדך יי אלהך:

first instance *šbw῾h dšqr*, "the oath of falsehood," and a verb the second time *wmšqr*, "and is lying." There are other variations in the fragmented Targums.

TO is paralleling the rabbinic interpretation prohibiting, in the first instance, the useless mention of God's name (for example, one who swears that a tree is a tree), but only the false speaking of His name is punished in the second reading.

N and Ps-Jon have the verses read that both empty and false uses of God's name are punished. CGT interprets the MT as prohibiting and punishing a false oath.

[21] This is the second *lšw᾿* which TO translates "falsely." According to the above sources, it refers to one who swears, for example, that a stone is water. Only the second type of oath is punished.

It is also possible that TO is not referring to the rabbinic understanding in its translation but is following its usual procedure that when a word is repeated it changes the word to avoid a redundancy. N and Ps-Jon use the same word as before.

N and Ps-Jon add that it is on the "day of the great judgment," in the world-to-come, that God will "not clear." The PT have many references to the world-to-come. See the author's *Targumic Studies* for a full discussion.

[22] MT in Exodus has *zkwr*, which is rendered *hwy dkyr* by TO, a change from the infinitive to the imperative. The Mekhilta explains that *zkr* is positive and *šmwr* is negative. Adler (NL) questions why TO did not use *hwy*, "continue," in Deuteronomy. TO renders the commandment of remembering as if it is an ongoing process, while the commandment of observing is restricted. He gives two answers: (1) remembering is something that a person has little control over; thus, he should accustom himself continually to remember. For the same reason, TO renders the command "and you should love the Lord your God" with the word *hwy*; that is, you should work on it continually to make it part of your nature. (2) Remembering is by its very essence continual, whereas observance is possible only on occasions. Thus, *hwy* is appropriate for the first but not the second.

Berkowitz feels TO is alluding to a Talmudic injunction: one should give attention *continually* to remember the sabbath. If one sees something during the week which is appropriate for the sabbath, he should set it aside for the sabbath (b. Beẓah 16a). This is unlikely. Ps-Jon adds the word, but N does not.

[23] The second half of this verse is not in Exodus. Here it refers to the Sinai experience.

13. Six days you shall labor and do all your work,
14. but the seventh day is a sabbath[24] before[25] the Lord your God: you shall not do any work—you, your son or your daughter, and[26] your male or female slave, your ox or your ass, and any of your cattle,[27] and the stranger[28] in your settlement,[29] so that your male and female slaves may rest as you do.[30]
15. Remember that you were a slave in the land of Egypt and the Lord your God freed you from there with a mighty hand and an uplifted arm;[31] therefore, the Lord your God has commanded you to observe the sabbath day.[32]
16. Honor your father and your mother, as the Lord your God has commanded you,[33] that you may long endure,[34] and that you may fare well,[35] in the land that the Lord your God is giving you.
17. You shall not murder.[36]

   And[37] you shall not commit adultery.

   And[37] you shall not kidnap.[36]

   And[37] you shall not testify[38] against your neighbor false[39] testimony.[40]

---

[24] While TO renders "sabbath" literally, N, Ps-Jon, and CGT add "and a rest."

[25] The Targums add *qdm*, "before," instead of *l*, "to."

[26] There is no *w*, in Exodus. TO adds the *w* whenever it is added in Deuteronomy, except verse 9.

[27] Exodus does not have *wšwrk wḥmrk wkl bḥmtk* but has *wbmtk*.

[28] The Targums use two words to render *gr*: *gywrʾ* meaning "proselyte" and *dywrʾ*, "resident." LXX has three words. Two imply that the stranger shares with the Israelite or that a privilege is conferred on the stranger. The first word was later used to describe a convert to Judaism. The third word implies exclusion from the Israelite fold. LXX uses the first here, 10:18, 19; 16:14; and elsewhere. The third word is found in 14:21 (see P. Churgin, "The Targum and the Septuagint," *AJSL* 50 [1933]: 47–51).

[29] MT: "gates," which TO explains according to the context. All the Targums except TO have "settlements" in the plural. This is characteristic.

[30] The last part of the verse, from "so that," is not in Exodus.

[31] The Targums do not delete the anthropomorphisms "hand" and "arm" here, see note on 11:2.

[32] This verse is not in Exodus, which has the creation as the rationale for the observance.

Ps-Jon to the Exodus Decalogue has the reward of the world-to-come for

13. שיתה יומין תפלח ותעביד כל עיבידתך:

14. ויומא שביעאה שבתא קדם יי אלהך לא תעביד כל עיבידא את וברך וברתך ועבדך ואמתך ותורך וחמרך וכל בעירך וגיורך דבקרוך בדיל דיינוח עבדך ואמתך כותך:

15. ותידכר ארי עבדא הויתא בארעא דמצרים ואפקך יי אלהך מתמן ביד תקיפא ובדרע מרמם על כן פקדך יי אלהך למעבד ית יומא דשבתא:

16. יקר ית אבוך וית אימך כמא דפקדך יי אלהך בדיל דיירכון יומך ובדיל דייטב לך על ארעא דיי אלהך יהיב לך:

17. לא תקטול נפש:
ולא תגוף:
ולא תיגנוב נפשא:
ולא תסהיד בחברך סהדותא דשיקרא:

honoring the sabbath, "the world that is entirely Sabbath."

[33] The phrase from "as" is not in Exodus.

[34] MT in Exodus has *y'rkwn*, while here it is *y'r'kn*. TO renders them both in the same way.

Ps-Jon to the Exodus Decalogue states that the reward for honoring parents is the world-to-come.

[35] The phrase from "and that" is not in Exodus.

[36] TO adds *npš*, "person," probably referring to the interpretation also found in the Talmud (b. Sanh. 86a) that this concerns murder. Also, perhaps because *l' tqtwl* could, theoretically, mean to any living being, not necessarily human. *npš* usually, but not always, implies a human being. Adler (NL to Exod) states that *qtl* could mean "a blow that does not lead to death," but this is unlikely. Some TO texts add *npš* to "steal" in the next command to show that the command prohibits kidnapping (Mek. Bachodesh 8). Luzzatto (*Oheb Ger*, Exodus 20) states that *npš* was probably first only in the kidnapping phrase. N and Ps-Jon have a long gloss here but do not add *npš*. These Targums explain that the result of stealing is hunger (like b. Shab. 32b).

[37] "And" is not in Exodus. TO parallels the MT.

[38] MT has *l' t'nh*, literally: "you should not answer" (i.e., answer in a law court). N and Ps-Jon understand the text like TO.

[39] MT has *šw'*, "in vain" as in verse 11. The Targums use the word *dšqr*, like the second *šw'* in verse 11. Exodus has *šqr*, "false." Referring to verse 11, Adler (NL) explains that *šw'* means both "in vain" and "falsely."

[40] TO clarifies the meaning of *'d*, which can be translated "witness," or "testimony." TO parallels the Talmud (b. Shav. 31a). N and Ps-Jon have long glosses. N states that the result of false testimony is "wild beasts attack the sons of men," Ps-Jon that it does not rain.

18. And[37] you shall not covet your neighbor's wife.[41]

    And[37] you shall not desire[42] your neighbor's house,[43] or his field, or his male or female slave, his ox,[44] or his ass, or anything that is your neighbor's."

19. These words the Lord spoke with your whole congregation at the mountain, out of the fire, the cloud and the thick darkness, with a mighty voice, and He did not cease.[45] He inscribed them on two tablets of stone, which He gave to me.

20. When you heard the voice out of the darkness, while the mountain was ablaze with fire, you came up to me, all your tribal heads and elders,

21. and said, "The Lord our God has just shown us His glory and His greatness, and we have heard the voice of His Memra[46] out of the fire; this day we have seen that the Lord[47] speaks with man and he lives.

22. Why then should we die, for this great fire will consume us; if we hear the voice of the Memra[48] of the Lord our God any longer, we shall die.

23. For what mortal ever heard the voice of the Memra[48] of the living Lord[49] speak out of the fire, as we did, and lived?

---

[41] Exodus had "house."

[42] Exodus has *thmd*. There are many Talmudic and Midrashic comments on the words *thmd* and *tt'wh*, and some identify differences between the terms. For example: Mekhilta (264) and Maimonides (*Sefer Ha-mitzvot*, commands 9, 10, and 11) treat the words as two different concepts. *Sefer Mitzvot Gadol* (158) treats them as one. Rashi feels that although TO uses different words for each term, they are synonymous, both meaning "desiring." Ps-Jon varies the words like TO, but N has *hmd* in both verses.

[43] Exodus has "wife."

[44] In this instance, it is Exodus that has an additional *w*, "and." Characteristically, TO follows Deuteronomy here and does not include the *w* although, also typically, it is included in translating Exodus. This brief study of the Decalogue versions confirms that where there are no special reasons for deviation, TO is literal. It also reflects the unfortunate situation (verse 9) that errors have become part of the Targumic texts.

[45] MT: "and he added no more." The language of the Targums is paralleled in various rabbinic interpretations. The Talmud (b. Sanh. 17a) states: "Because it is

18. ולא תחמיד איתת חברך ולא תירוג בית חברך חקליה ועבדיה ואמתיה תוריה וחמריה וכל דלחברך:

19. ית פיתגמיא האילין מליל יי עם כל קהלכון בטורא מגו אישתא עננא ואמיטתא קל רב ולא פסק וכתבינון על תרין לוחי אבניא ויהבינון לי:

20. והוה כמשמעכון ית קלא מגו חשוכא וטורא בער באישתא וקריבתון לותי כל רישי שבטיכון וסביכון:

21. ואמרתון הא אחזינא יי אלהנא ית יקריה וית רבותיה וית קל מימריה שמענא מגו אישתא יומא הדין חזינא ארי ממליל יי עם אינשא ומתקים:

22. וכען למא נמות ארי תיכליננא אישתא רבתא הדא אם מוספין אנחנא למשמע ית קל מימרא דיי אלהנא עוד מיתין אנחנא:

23. ארי מן כל ביסרא דשמע קל מימרא דיי קימא דממליל מגו אישתא כותנא ואתקים:

characteristic of human beings that they are unable to utter all their words in one breath, but must make pauses, and it is characteristic of the Holy One, blessed be He, that this is not so, therefore He did not pause, and since He did not pause, He did not have to resume—for His voice is strong and goes on continuously." y. Meg. 1:5 is similar.

R. Yohanan understood that the MT means "cease" and said: "The Prophets and Writings will be suspended in the future, but the Five Books of the Torah will not, because it says 'did not cease'" (y. Megilah 70:4). Komlosh cites (p. 203) another rabbinic statement based upon this understanding: "Every sage that appears in future generations received his (teachings) from Sinai" (Exod R. 23:4).

G. Vermes, in *In Memoriam Paul Kahle*, Berlin, 1968, pp. 236 ff. notes that the interpretation is not derived from MT's *ysp*, but from a variation of the word, the root *swp*. This does not mean that our sources used a pre-Massoretic text. It is a well-known Targumic (as well as Midrashic) technique to base interpretations on such things as change of letters, sound changes, letter metathesis, and acronyms, as well as on reading the Hebrew as if it were Aramaic or another language. Comp. 31:7; 32:2; 33:19, 22. See, for example, Y. Heinemann, *Darke Haaggadah*, Jerusalem 1954, pp. 96 ff.

[46] TO adds Memra. N has an additional Memra, and Ps-Jon has Memra twice and Shekinah once, avoiding other anthropomorphisms.

[47] The Targums replace Elohim with the Tetragrammaton. Some TO texts add "from before" prior to "the Lord," removing the anthropomorphism. N and Ps-Jon do not.

[48] The Targums add Memra.

[49] TO changes Elohim to the Tetragrammaton, but N and Ps-Jon do not.

24. You go closer and hear all that the Lord our God says, and then you tell us everything that the Lord our God tells you, and we will willingly accept it[50] and do it."

25. Now there was heard before[51] the Lord the sound of your words, when you spoke with me, and the Lord said to me, "There was heard before[52] Me the sound of the words that this people spoke with you; all they said has been established.[53]

26. O that there were such heart in them, to fear before[54] Me and keep all My commandments every day, that it may go well with them and with their children forever!

27. Go, say to them, 'Return to your tents.'

28. But you (Moses) stand here before[55] Me, and I will tell you the whole instruction—the laws and the rules—which you shall teach them, that they may observe them in the land that I am giving them to possess."

29. Therefore, be careful to do as the Lord has commanded you. Do not turn aside to the right or to the left:

30. (only) the path that the Lord your God has enjoined[56] upon you, you shall walk,[57] so that you may live and that it may go well with you, and that you may long endure in the land you are to possess.

Chapter VI

1. And this is the instruction—the laws and the rules—that the Lord your God has commanded me to teach you, to be observed in the land which you are about to cross into to take possession of it,

2. so that you fear before[1] the Lord your God and observe all His laws and commandments which I enjoin upon you, you, your son, and your son's son, as long as you live, so that you may long endure.

---

[50] "Hear" is a key word in this section and is repeated often. TO and Ps-Jon this time have "accept," N does not.

[51] MT: "The Lord heard the sound of your words." TO and Ps-Jon render the phrase passively and add "before." N uses Memra. The deviation may have been made to soften the improper Israelite reaction to God. They should have listened to the delivery of the commands.

24. קרב את ושמע ית כל דיימר יי אלהנא ואת תמליל עימנא ית כל דימליל יי אלהנא
עימך ונקביל ונעביד:

25. ושמיע קדם יי ית קל פתגמיכון במללותכון עימי ואמר יי לי שמיע קדמי ית קל
פתגמי עמא הדין דמלילו עימך אתקינו כל דמלילו:

26. לוי דיהי ליבא הדין להון למידחל קדמי ולמיטר ית כל פיקודי כל יומיא בדיל
דייטב להון ולבניהון לעלם:

27. איזיל אימר להון תובו לכון למשכניכון:

28. ואת הכא קום קדמי ואימליל עימך ית כל תפקידתא וקימיא ודיניא דתליפינון
ויעבדון בארעא דאנא יהיב להון למירתה:

29. ותיטרון למעבד כמא דפקיד יי אלהכון יתכון לא תסטון לימינא ולסמאלא:

30. בכל אורחא דפקיד יי אלהכון יתכון תהכון בדיל דתיחון וייטב לכון ותורכון יומין
בארעא דתחסנון:

VI

1. ודא תפקידתא קימיא ודיניא דפקיד יי אלהכון לאלפא יתכון למעבד בארעא
דאתון עברין לתמן למירתה:

2. בדיל דתידחל קדם יי אלהך למיטר ית כל קימוהי ופיקודוהי דאנא מפקיד לך את
וברך ובר ברך כל יומי חיך ובדיל דיורכון יומך:

---

[52] Again the passive is used and "before" is included in TO and Ps-Jon, but not N.

[53] MT: "well said." TO has "established" and Ps-Jon "well said." N has both.

[54] The three Targums have "before Me" instead of *'ty*, "Me."

[55] MT: with Me. The Targums have "before Me."

[56] MT has the imperative *'mr*, some TO texts have the imperfect.

[57] The Targums do not deviate here to remove the concept of "divine paths" upon which humans can walk. As noted earlier, the Targums do not replace every anthropomorphic Biblical phrase (the results of such an effort would be far from a literal translation) but only phrases that the translators felt would show disrespect to God. While it is possible that the literal rendering here is the result of a copyist's error in a proto-Targum from which TO, N, and Ps-Jon drew material, it is more likely that this phrase was not felt to be disrespectful in context. The metaphor "path" has a clear meaning, obvious from the prior passages, and is a substitute word for *mitzva* (instruction) in verse 28 and 6:1.

[1] MT: *'t*. TO and Ps-Jon replace it with "before." N adds Memra.

3. Accept,[2] Israel, observe and do, that it may go well with you and that
   you may increase greatly, as the Lord, the God of your fathers, spoke
   to you, in the land that produces[3] milk and honey.
4. Hear,[4] Israel! The Lord is our God, the Lord is one.
5. You shall love the Lord your God with all your heart and with all your
   soul and with all your possessions.[5]
6. And these words, which I command you this day, shall be on your
   heart.
7. Repeat[6] them to your children. Recite them when you stay at home
   and when you are on the way, when you lie down and when you get
   up.
8. Bind them as a sign on your hand and let them serve as Tefillin[7]
   between your eyes,
9. and write them on Mezuzot[8] and fix[9] them to the doorpost of your
   house and on your gates.

[2]MT: "hear." TO and Ps-Jon have "accept," N "hear."

[3] MT: "flowing." TO replaces the metaphor and has "producing." N and FT
have "produces good fruit, pure as milk, and sweet and tasty as honey." Ps-Jon: "a
land whose fruit are as rich as milk, and sweet as honey."

[4] TO and Ps-Jon generally construe "hear" as "accept." (See note 2 and NL on
this verse.) They may ignore this practice here because, in this instance, the
accepted version of the command is to "hear." *Sefer Mitzvot Gadol* states that the
second positive Biblical command is "to believe and hear." Schefftel (BO) points
out that TO reflects the rabbinical interpretation in b. Ber. 15a, where the command to "hear" is explained. Additionally, b. Ber. 13a and 16a, as well as many
other sources, including Sifre, stress that the word is to be taken literally as "hear."

[5] MT: "with all your might." TO parallels b. Ber. 61b and Sifre. "Some people's
property is dearer to them than their bodies. Therefore the Torah adds 'with all
your possessions.'" TO also reflects the Talmudic explanation: "What is 'with all
your might'? With all your money" (b. Ber. 54a). See also m. Ber. 9:5

Deut 6:5 can be cited as one proof for the argument that all the Targums
depend on a general interpretative tradition. The Targums have different words
which express the same idea. TO (and TJ to II Kings 23:25) have *nksk*, "possessions"; N, FT, and Ps-Jon *mmwnkwn*, "wealth"; Peshitta *qnynk*, "possessions."
M, however, has *hyylykwn*, "your strength."

[6] Schefftel (BO) explains that the Hebrew word in the MT means "repeat in
order to learn." The word is similarly translated in Gen 41:35 and II Sam 20:4. The
Sifre and Talmud (b. Kidd. 30a) understand the Hebrew metaphorically: "to be
sharply impressed." N is like TO. Ps-Jon has "teach."

3. ותקביל ישראל ותיטר למעבד דייטב לך ודתיסגון לחדא כמא דמליל יי אלהא
דאבהתך לך ארע עבדא חלב ודבש:

4. שמע ישראל יי אלהנא יי חד:

5. ותירחם ית יי אלהך בכל ליבך ובכל נפשך וכל ניכסך:

6. ויהון פתגמיא האלין דאנא מפקיד לך יומא דין על ליבך:

7. ותתנינון לבנך ותמליל בהון במיתבך בביתך ובמהכך באורחא ובמשכבך ובמקימך:

8. ותקטרינון לאת על ידך ויהון לתפילין בין עינך:

9. ותכתובנון על מזוזין ותקבעינון בסיפי בתך ובתרעך:

---

[7] MT has *twtpwt*, the etymology of which is uncertain. The Targums render the word "Tefillin" like the Sifre and Talmud (m. Ber. 3:3, Meg. 1:8, etc.). Deut 11:18 and Exod 13:16 are similar. Adler (NL) argues that this is an instance where TO presents the rabbinical teaching on a verse because of the likelihood that some people might differ with the tradition. A still likelier explanation is that the word Tefillin was more commonplace among the people that *twtpwt*.

The Targums use the plural form of Tefillin, even though this part of the verse is only referring to the Tefillin placed on the head. However, *twtwt* is in the plural (b. Sanh. 4b). Adler (NL) thinks this plural form refers to the four sections of the Tefillin. Additionally, the Targums may be referring to the rabbinical teaching: When Tefillin are put on, the hand Tefillin should be put on first. When taken off, the head Tefillin should be taken off first. Since the plural form is used, this teaches that as long as one wears the head Tefillin, he must wear both (b. Men. 37a and 36a). Adler's thesis is improbable since the MT has the plural.

Ps-Jon adds the law, "and you shall bind them as written signs on your left arm, and they shall serve as Tefillin upon your forehead opposite your eyes."

[8] MT has *mazuzot*; literally, "doorposts." Deut 11:20 is similar. Adler (NL) argues that this is another instance (see above note) where TO wants to stress the Oral Torah teaching. Thus, it does not translate the MT "and you shall write on parchment," but has instead the name used for the parchment by the rabbis. It is more likely that the Targumist is using the word because it is in the MT.

[9] MT: "inscribe them on the doorpost of your house and on your gates." The Targumic words prevent the possible misunderstanding that one writes on the doorpost or gate itself and not on a parchment put in a cylinder which is placed on the doorpost or gate. The Targums reflect the rule contained in b. Men. 34a and elsewhere. Sifre (*Vaeschanan* 36) states that one should not imagine that the writing can be on the stones of the doorpost (as is the practice even today among some Near Eastern nations). However, "fix" was added only because it is implied.

Ps-Jon has the law, "and you shall write them on your doorposts, and fix them a third of the distance from the ceiling on the doorpost of your house, on your gates, on the right as you come in."

10. When the Lord your God brings you into the land which He confirmed[10] to your fathers, Abraham, Isaac, and Jacob, to give you great and goodly cities which you did not build,

11. and houses full of all good things which you did not fill, hewn cisterns which you did not hew, vineyards and olive groves which you did not plant—and you eat and be replete—

12. take heed that you do not forget the fear[11] of the Lord who took you from the land of Egypt, the house of servitude.[11]

13. Fear only the Lord your God and worship before[12] Him, and confirm[10] only by His name.

14. Do not follow after the idols[13] of the nations, any of the idols[13] of the nations round about you—

15. for the Lord your God is an impassioned God—His Shekinah[14] is in your midst—lest the anger of the Lord your God blaze forth against you and He wipe you off the face of the earth.

16. Do not try the Lord your God, as you tried Him with tests.[15]

17. Be sure to keep the commandments of the Lord your God and His testimonies and laws which He enjoined upon you.

18. Do what is right and proper[16] before[17] the Lord, that it may go well with you and that you may enter and take possession of the good land which the Lord your God confirmed[10] to your fathers,

19. to break[18] all your enemies before you, as the Lord has spoken.

---

[10] MT: "swore."

[11] TO and Ps-Jon add "fear," to avoid the concept that it is possible to forget God Himself. N adds "the teachings of this law." Comp. TJ to Isa 1:29 "forsake the law of the Lord" and b. Ber. 8a on that verse.

TO renders MT's "house of slaves" as "house of servitude" as in 5:6 and 7:8.

[12] See Patshegen, Lowenstein (NH), and Schefftel (BO) for a discussion on why TO does not add "before" here and in verse 10:20. Nachmanides writes that this verse may allude, as indicated in the Sifre, to sacrifices. The word is placed here in most TO versions instead of *²tw*. It is in Ps-Jon twice as well as Memra. N adds "the glory of the Shekinah."

Silverstone (p. 75) explains why, in his opinion, TO inserted *yt* for *²t*. Onkelos was a disciple of R. Akiba who interpreted every *²t* in the Torah. R. Akiba stated that from this *²t* we deduce that scholars must also be feared and respected. Actually the reason for the translation is that TO is literal. Thus, even when TO

10. ויהי ארי יעילינך יי אלהך לארעא דקיים לאבהתך לאברהם ליצחק וליעקב למיתן
לך קרוין רברבן וטבן דלא בניתא:

11. ובתין מלן כל טוב דלא מליתא וגובין פסילן דלא פסלתא וכרמין וזיתין דלא נצבתא
ותיכול ותיסבע:

12. איסתמר לך דילמא תתנשי ית דחלתא דיי דאפקך מארעא דמצרים מבית עבדותא:

13. ית יי אלהך תדחל וקדמוהי תפלח ובשמיה תקיים:

14. לא תהכון בתר טעות עממיא מטעות עממיא דבסחרניכון:

15. ארי אל קנא יי אלהך שכנתיה בינך דילמא יתקוף רוגזא דיי אלהך בך וישיצינך
מעל אפי ארעא:

16. לא תנסון קדם יי אלהכון כמא דנסיתון בניסיתא:

17. מיטר תטרון ית פיקודיא דיי אלהכון וסהידותיה וקימוהי דפקדך:

18. ותעביד דכשר ודתקין קדם יי בדיל דייטב לך ותיעול ותירת ית ארעא טבתא דקיים
יי לאבהתך:

19. למיתבר ית כל בעלי דבבך מן קדמך כמא דמליל יי:

renders the verse in the passive, when *yt* is not used in Aramaic (the *Genesis Apcryphon*, for example, does not have it), то copies the мт's style.

[13] мт: "Do not follow other gods . . . gods of the nations." Characteristically, то removes any possible misconception that idols are living gods. то generally replaces "other gods" with *ta'awath*, a noun derived from the Aramaic root meaning "to stray." The word signifies "an aberration." There are 21 passages like this one in Deuteronomy. Ps-Jon is like то, both understanding "other" as meaning "of the nations." Characteristically, n reads "other idols," creating a possible misunderstanding that God is an idol.

[14] то and Ps-Jon add "Shekinah." See Introduction. n has "the glory of the Shekinah." The anthropopathisms in the verse are not removed by the Targums.

[15] мт: "at Massah." то, n, and Ps-Jon render the word according to its meaning rather than as a noun as was done in (Exodus 17:7) and later in Deuteronomy (38:8). These Targums do not intentionally parallel the Talmudic teaching (b. Taan. 9a), derived from this verse, that one may not try to test God. See also Aboth 1:3 and Jeremiah 44:17.

[16] мт: "and good." то clarifies the meaning of the text. n and Ps-Jon translate similary.

[17] мт: "in the sight of." The Targums replace the anthropomorphic metaphor.

[18] мт has a rare word (meaning "thrust" or "hurry") found only twice more in the Hebrew Bible (9:4 and Josh 23:5). то gives the meaning of the text, "that the enemy will be destroyed." This verse refers to Exod 23:27. n and Ps-Jon have "thrust," as does LXX. M has "to blot out."

20. When your son asks you tomorrow, as follows: "What mean the testimonies, laws, and rules which the Lord our God has enjoined upon you?"

21. you shall say to your son, "We were slaves to Pharaoh in Egypt and the Lord brought us out from Egypt with a mighty hand.

22. The Lord wrought signs and portents, great and evil, upon Egypt, against Pharaoh and all the people[19] of his house, before our eyes;

23. and us He brought us out from there, that He might bring us in and give us the land that He had confirmed[10] to our fathers.

24. Then the Lord commanded us to observe all these laws, to fear before[20] the Lord our God, for our lasting good and to preserve us alive, as this day.

25. And it shall be accounted meritorious[21] if we observe to do all this instruction before the Lord our God, as He has commanded us."

Chapter VII

1. When the Lord your God brings you to the land that you are about to enter and inherit, and He drives out[1] many nations before you—the Hittites, Girgashites, Amorites, Canaanites, Perizzites, Hivites, and Jebusites, seven nations larger and stronger than you—

2. and the Lord your God delivers them to you and you defeat them, you must utterly destroy them:[2] you shall not make a covenant with them and do not be merciful with them.[3]

3. You shall not intermarry with them: do not give your daughters to their sons or take their daughters for your sons.

4. For they will cause your children to err[4] away from My fear (service)[5]

---

[19] The Targums add "people" to explain the meaning of the passage.

[20] MT: *'t*. The Targums have "before."

[21] MT: *ṭdqh*. See note on 9:5. Ps-Jon has, "and *Zachuth* (merit) shall be stored for us in the world to come." TO ignores the concept of vicarious *Zachuth*. See note on 9:5.

[1] MT has a rather obscure word which TO defines. It is used twice more with reference to human beings: below verse 22 and II Kings 16:6. N and Ps-Jon translate similarly, as does the Targum to II Kings.

‏20. ארי ישאלינך ברך מחר למימר מא סהידותא וקימיא ודיניא דפקיד יי אלהנא יתכון:

‏21. ותימר לברך עבדין הוינא לפרעה במצרים ואפקנא יי ממצרים ביד תקיפא:

‏22. ויהב יי אתין ומופתין רברבין ובישין במצרים בפרעה ובכל אינש ביתיה לעיננא:

‏23. ויתנא אפיק מתמן בדיל לאעלא יתנא למיתן לנא ית ארעא דקיים לאבהתנא:

‏24. ופקדנא יי למעבד ית כל קימיא האלין למידחל קדם יי אלהנא דייטב לנא כל יומיא לקימותנא כיומא הדין:

‏25. וזכותא תהי לנא ארי ניטר למעבד ית כל תפקידתא הדא קדם יי אלהנא כמא דפקדנא:

VII

‏1. ארי יעילינך יי אלהך לארעא דאת עליל לתמן למירתה ויתריך עממין סגיאין מן קדמך חיתאי גרגישאי ואימוראי וכנענאי ופרזאי וחיואי ויבוסאי שבעה עממין סגיאין ותקיפין מינך:

‏2. וימסרינון יי אלהך קדמך ותמחינון גמרא תגמר יתהון לא תיגזר להון קים ולא תרחים עליהון:

‏3. ולא תתחתן בהון ברתך לא תיתין לבריה וברתיה לא תיסב לברך:

‏4. ארי יטעין ית בנך מבתר פולחני ויפלחון לטעות עממיא ויתקף רוגזא דיי בכון וישיצינך בפריע:

[2] MT has the concept of *ḥrm*, a term denoting a mode of separating or secluding anything endangering the religious life of the people and presenting it to the sanctuary, either to be used for lawful purposes or else to be destroyed. This institution was applied particularly for the purpose of wiping out idolatry; hence it was directed against the idolatrous Canaanites, as in the passage before us and 20:16 ff., or against idolatrous Israelites as in 13:13 ff. and Exod 22:19. A similar use is found above in 2:34. It is possible that TO avoids translating this term in accordance with its technical meaning and prefers instead its general intent because the Targum was intended for the average person, who would not understand the concept without an overly lengthy explanation, something contrary to TO's style. See 7:26. Ps-Jon is like TO, but N has "kill them."

[3] MT has a phrase ("show grace" or "give gifts") which has been given various aggadic interpretations (b. Av. Zar. 20a, b. Yeb. 10a, y. Av. Zar. 81:9). The Targums avoid the aggada and render the phrase literally.

[4] MT: "turn." The Targums give this phrase a clearer meaning.

[5] MT: "away from Me." TO prevents the concept that one can turn away from God Himself. The Sperber text has *dḥl*, "fear"; B and Ps-Jon have *plḥn*, "service"; but N has "My Memra," as if to say the Israelites cannot turn away from God, but they can turn from His Memra.

and they will serve the idols of the people,[6] and the anger of the Lord will be strong against you[7] and promptly destroy you.

5. Instead, this is what you shall do to them: you shall tear down their altars,[8] smash their pillars, cut down their sacred posts, and burn their images with fire.

6. For you are a holy people before[9] the Lord your God: the Lord your God chose you to be His beloved[10] people from all peoples on earth.

7. It is not because you are the most numerous of peoples that the Lord desired[7] and chose you—indeed, you are the smallest of peoples;

8. but it was because the Lord loved you and kept the confirmation He confirmed[11] to your fathers that the Lord brought you out with a mighty hand and rescued you from the house of servitude[12] from the hand of Pharaoh king of Egypt.

9. Know, therefore, that only the Lord your God is God, the steadfast God who keeps his covenant and kindness[13] with those who love Him and keep His commandments, to a thousand generations,

10. and he pays to those that hate Him for the good deeds they do before Him during their lifetime, in order to cause them to perish—never slow to give good recompense to those that hate Him for the good they do before Him, during their lifetime He pays them.[14]

---

[6] MT: "to worship other gods." TO and Ps-Jon invariably render this phrase as "idols (literally "error") of the people," to preclude the misconception of polytheism, while N has "other idols."

[7] The Targums do not remove this anthropopathism.

[8] TO, Ps-Jon, and LXX (but not N and the Samaritan Targum) use one word for an idolatrous altar, *'gwy'*, and another for God's altar, *mdgh'*. The former word is used here in Deut and in 12:3. It is a derogatory term implying a "heap." Thus, for example, by using the latter word, the Targums and LXX show that in Exod 32:5 Aaron erected the altar to God, not to the calf. LXX is not as consistent in following this rule as TO and Ps-Jon. See P. Churgin, "The Targum and the Septuagint," *AJSL* 50 (1933): 44–47 and *Horeb* 7 (1943). Churgin notes that TO and Ps-Jon differ in interpreting the sanctity of Baalam's altar (Num 23): TO considers it an altar for God and Ps-Jon for idol worship. LXX is like Ps-Jon, leading Churgin to believe that this verse in Ps-Jon reflects an early interpretation.

[9] MT: "to the Lord." The Targums replace "to" with "before."

[10] MT: *sglh*, meaning "a people of unique value" or "special possession." The Targums' rendering may have been designed to emphasize the concept of divine love for Israel, which both pagans and some sectarians denied. See Exod 19:5. N

5. ארי אם כדין תעבדון להון איגוריהון תתרעון וקמתהון תתברון ואשיריהון תקצצון וצילמיהון תוקדון בנורא:

6. ארי עם קדיש את קדם יי אלהך בך אתרעי יי אלהך למהוי ליה לעם חביב מכל עממיא דעל אפי ארעא:

7. לא מדסגיאין אתון מכל עממיא צבי יי בכון ואתרעי בכון ארי אתון זעירין מכל עממיא:

8. ארי מדרחים יי יתכון ומדנטר ית קימא דקיים לאבהתכון אפיק יי יתכון ביד תקיפא ופרקך מבית עבדותא מידא דפרעה מלכא דמצרים:

9. ותידע ארי יי אלהך הוא אלהים אלהא מהימנא נטר קימא וחיסדא לרחמוהי ולנטרי פיקודוהי לאלף דרין:

10. ומשלם לסנאוהי טבון דאינון עבדין קדמוהי בחייהון לאובודיהון לא מאחר עובד טב לסנאוהי טבון דאינון עבדין קדמוהי בחייהון משלים להון:

---

has "a people beloved like a special possession," retaining MT's *sglh*.

[11] MT: "oath," found twice in the verse.

[12] MT: "slaves." See 5:6, 6:12, and 8:14.

[13] TO generally renders *ḥsd wʾmt* by *ṭybw wqšwt* and *ḥsd* by itself by *ṭybw*, except in Gen 32:11, Deut 7:9 and 12, where the Hebrew *ḥsd* is retained.

[14] MT: "but who instantly requites with destruction those who reject Him— never slow with those who reject Him, but requiting them instantly." TO reflects the interpretation contained in Sifre and the Talmud (m. Peah 1:1, m. Taan. 11:11, b. Erub. 22a). Sifre (*Haazenu* 307) states that God rewards a fully righteous person in the world-to-come for his/her *mitzvahs*, but rewards a fully evil person in this world. He punishes a fully righteous person in this world for his/her misdeeds, but punishes a fully evil person in the world-to-come.

Schefftel (BO) feels that TO is avoiding a theological difficulty with this interpretation: why many evil people live well. TO explains that evildoers live a good life in this world so that there will be no need to pay them for the good they have done in the world-to-come. Good people, on the other hand, may be treated badly in this world, but they will be paid for their good behavior in the world-to-come. Adler (NL) notes that the language in the verse is doubled, as if to say: God not only pays, but He hastens the payment. Both read more into the Targum than is warranted. The Aramaic paraphrase is a reasonable interpretation of the verse's *peshat*. Adler also notes that while MT has the singular form for the second "hater," TO recasts it in the plural in accordance with the Targumic method of matching the end of the sentence with the beginning (the end has the plural "haters").

N has: "and he pays in this world the wages of their good work to those that hate Him, so as to punish them in the world-to-come. He does not delay good wages to those that hate Him while they are in this world; He pays them the wages

11. Therefore, observe faithfully the instruction—the laws and rules—which I command you today to do them.

12. And if as a consequence[15] you do accept[16] these rules and do them, the Lord your God will maintain for you the covenant and the kindness[13] that He confirmed[11] to your fathers:

13. He will love you and bless you and multiply you: He will bless the children[17] of your womb and the produce[17] of your soil, your new grain and wine and oil, the calves[18] of your herd and the lambs[19] of your flock, in the land that He confirmed[11] to your fathers to give you.

14. You shall be blessed above all other peoples: there shall be no sterile male or female among you or among your livestock.

15. The Lord will remove from you all sickness; He will not bring upon you any of the pestilences[20] of Egypt, about which you know, but will inflict them upon all your enemies.

16. You shall destroy[21] all the peoples that the Lord your God delivers to you, your eyes should have no pity on them. And you shall not worship their idols,[6] for that would be a snare to you.

17. Should you say in your heart, "These nations are more numerous than we; how can we dispossess them?"

18. You need have no fear of them. You have but to remember what the Lord your God did to Pharaoh and all the Egyptians:

19. the great miracles[22] that you saw with your own eyes, the signs and the portents, the mighty hand, and the uplifted arm[23] by which the Lord your God liberated you. Thus will the Lord your God do to all the peoples you now fear.

20. The Lord your God will also send a plague against them, until those who are left in hiding perish before you.

---

for the small deeds that are in their hands." Ps-Jon paraphrases similarly. See also Targums to Eccl 8:14 and Lam 3:28.

[15] MT: "heel" or "follow." The Targums clarify the plain meaning of the text. Nachmanides notes that TO is giving the word the meaning it has in Isaiah 40:4 and the Sifre.

[16] TO and Ps-Jon change "hear" to "accept."

[17] MT has the metaphor "fruit," which TO clarifies. N has "fruit of the children of your womb," but Ps-Jon is like TO. N and Ps-Jon have "fruit of your soil" in the next phrase.

11. ותיטר ית תפקידתא וית קימיא וית דיניא דאנא מפקיד לך יומא דין למעבדהון:

12. ויהי חלף דתקבלון ית דיניא האלין ותטרון ותעבדון יתהון ויטר יי אלהך ית קימא וית חיסדא דקיים לאבהתך:

13. וירחמינך ויברכינך ויסגינך ויברך ולדא דמעך ואיבא דארעך עיבורך וחמרך ומישחך מקרי תורך ועדרי ענך על ארעא דקיים לאבהתך למיתן לך:

14. בריך תהי מכל עממיא לא יהוי בך עקר ועקרא ובבעירך:

15. ויעדי יי מינך כל מרעין וכל מכתשי מצרים בישיא דידעתא לא ישוינון בך ויתנינון בכל סנאך:

16. ותגמר ית כל עממיא דיי אלהך יהיב לך לא תחוס עינך עליהון ולא תפלח ית טעותהון ארי לתקלא יהון לך:

17. ארי תימר בליבך סגיאין עממיא האלין מיני איכדין איכול לתרכותהון:

18. לא תדחל מינהון אידכרא תידכר ית דעבד יי אלהך לפרעה ולכל מצראי:

19. ניסין רברבין דחזאה עינך אתיא ומופתיא וידא תקיפתא ודרעא מרממא דאפקך יי אלהך כן יעביד יי אלהך לכל עממיא דאת דחיל מן קדמיהון:

20. ואף ית ערעיתא יגרי יי אלהך בהון עד דייבדון דאישתארו ודאיטמרו מן קדמך:

---

[18] MT has a metaphor meaning "that which is cast out." N and Ps-Jon are like TO. Luzzatto (*Letter 43*) states that TO uses the Syrian word *bqry* to avoid repeating the Aramaic *'dry* used in the next phrase.

[19] MT has a word of doubtful meaning. In b. Hul. 84a, it is taken to mean riches. N and Ps-Jon define it like TO.

[20] MT has a word, *mktšy*, of doubtful meaning. Adler (NL) explains that TO uses an Aramaic word which connotes a plague or disease. The same word is found several times in the Genesis Apocryphon, Chapter 20. J. A. Fitzmyer (*The Genesis Apocryphon of Qumran Cave I*, 1966) and N. Avigad and Y. Yadin (*The Genesis Apocryphon*, 1956) translate it "pestilence." See Fitzmyer, pp. 116, 7, for a full discussion of the word. N and Ps-Jon are like TO. Ps-Jon clarifies the text by adding "that He sent against." The word is singular in the MT, but the Targums use the plural according to the context. Comp. 28:60, 32:24, and Gen 46:1, where the word is found.

[21] MT has a word which literally means "eat" and "destroy" (cf. Lev 26:28; Jer 10:25, 30:16, 50:17; etc.) This word does not have the double meaning in Aramaic. Thus, TO uses another word meaning "destroy" to conform to the Aramaic idiom. Ps-Jon is like TO, but N is literal. TO does not change the metaphor "eyes have pity," since it would cause no confusion among the populas.

[22] MT: "proofs." N and Ps-Jon are like TO.

[23] The Targums do not avoid the anthropomorphic "hand" and "arm," see note on 11:2. Comp. Targum to II Chron 6:40 and 7:15, where "ears" is not replaced. "Outstretched arm" is changed to "uplifted arm."

21. Do not break[24] before them, for the Lord your God, His Shekinah[25] is in your midst, a great and fearful God.

22. The Lord your God will dislodge those peoples before you little by little; you will not be able to put an end to them speedily, else the wild beasts would multiply against you.

23. The Lord your God will deliver them up to you, throwing them into utter confusion[26] until they are destroyed.

24. He will deliver their kings into your hand, and you shall obliterate their name from under the heaven; no man shall stand up to you, until you have destroyed them.

25. You shall consign the images of their idols[6] to the fire; you shall not covet the silver and gold on them and keep it for yourselves, lest you be ensnared thereby; for it is remote[27] before[28] the Lord your God.

26. You must not bring a remote[27] thing into your house, or you will be proscribed[29] like it; you must utterly reject it and you must consider it utterly remote;[27] for it is proscribed.

Chapter VIII

1. You shall observe all the commandments that I enjoin upon you today to do it, that you may live and increase and enter to possess the land which the Lord confirmed[1] for your fathers.

2. Remember all the way that the Lord your God has led you in the wilderness these forty years, that He might humble you and test you, to learn[1a] what was in your hearts: whether you would keep His commandments or not.

3. He humbled you and subjected you to hunger and fed you manna, which neither you nor your fathers had ever known, in order to make

---

[24] MT: "tremble," which the Targums characteristically translate "break."

[25] TO and Ps-Jon add Shekinah. N adds "glory of the Shekinah."

[26] The Hebrew word *mhwmh* is subject to various interpretations (see Rashi) and the Targums clarify its meaning.

[27] MT: "abhorrent." It is arguable that the Aramaic *mrḥq* softens the anthro-

21. לא תיתבר מן קדמיהון ארי יי אלהך שכנתיה ביגך אלהא רבא ודחילא:
22. ויתריך יי אלהך ית עממיא האלין מן קדמך זעיר זעיר לא תיכול לשיציותהון בפריע דילמא תיסגי עלך חית ברא:
23. וימסרינון יי אלהך קדמך וישגישנון שיגוש רב עד דישתיצון:
24. וימסר מלכיהון בידך ותוביד ית שומהון מתחות שמיא לא יתעתד איגש קדמך עד דשתיצי יתהון:
25. צילמי טעותהון תוקדון בנורא לא תחמיד כספא ודהבא דעליהון ותיסב לך דילמא תיתקל ביה ארי מרחק קדם יי אלהך הוא:
26. ולא תעיל דמרחק לביתך ותהי חירמא כותיה שקצא תשקצניה ורחקא תרחקניה ארי חירמא הוא:

VIII

1. כל תפקידתא דאנא מפקיד לך יומא דין תטרון למעבד בדיל דתיחון ותסגון ותיעלון ותירתון ית ארעא דקיים יי לאבהתכון:
2. ותידכר ית כל אורחא דדברך יי אלהך דנן ארבעין שנין במדברא בדיל לעניותך לנסיותך למידע ית דבליבך התיטר פיקודוהי אם לא:
3. ועניך ואכפנך ואוכלך ית מנא דלא ידעתא ולא ידעו אבהתך בדיל להודעותך ארי

popathisms. Therefore, the Targums change "abhorrent" to "remote" when it is used in reference to God. However, *mrhq* is also translated "abhorrent" by Jastrow.

[28] The Targums add "before."

[29] The Hebrew word is *hrm*, which TO renders here similarly, *hrm²*, as in Lev 27:28, and not as "destroy" as was done in 7:2. Adler (NL) explains that the Hebrew has the dual conotation of "proscribe" and "destroy." The Aramaic has the restricted meaning of "proscribe." Thus, TO sometimes has to use a word meaning "destroy." N has: "so that you not be remote like it." Ps-Jon has: "so that you not be accursed like it."

[1] MT: "swore."

[1a] TO is literal. The Targum retains the future tense, implying that God does not have present knowledge of the facts, even though it does deviate on occasions (e.g. 33:20) and use the past tense. It is possible that the Targumist felt that a deviation here (in 13:14 and Gen. 3:21) would lead his audience to imagine they lacked free-will.

known to you that man does not exist[2] by bread alone, but man lives
on all that the Memra brings forth from before[3] the Lord.

4. Your clothes did not wear out on you, nor did your shoes rub down[4]
these forty years.

5. Consider in your heart, that just as a man teaches[5] his son, the Lord
your God teaches you.[5]

6. Therefore, keep the commandments[6] of the Lord your God: walk in
the ways that are right before Him[7] and revere Him.

7. For the Lord your God is bringing you into a good land, a land with
flowing[8] streams, springing[9] wells and fountains issuing from plains
and hills;[10]

8. a land[11] of wheat and barley, of vines, figs, and pomegranates, a land
whose olives produce[12] oil and it[13] produces[12] honey;

---

[2] MT has "live" twice in the verse, but TO translates each differently. Schefftel
(BO) explains that TO generally varies the rendering when words are repeated.
Adler (NL), on the other hand, suggests that TO is teaching a moral lesson. Man
only "survives" on bread but really "lives" on that which God brings forth, that is,
the Torah and *Mitzvot*. Ps-Jon uses the same word twice. N is faulty and does not
have the phrase "live (or exist) by bread," but it is in the margin.

[3] MT: "all that proceeds out of the mouth of the Lord;" an unseemly anthropomorphism that the Targums prefer to avoid. The Targums add Memra and
"before."

Ps-Jon translates "bringing forth" as "created," and N adds "brings forth from
the mouth of the decree of the Memra of the Lord." FT specifies that man does not
live by "manna alone."

[4] MT: "nor did your feet swell." Patshegen explains that TO deviates to match
up the end of the verse to the beginning, which speaks of a body covering.
However, this radical deviation for consistency does not fit TO's style. Other commentators offer other explanations. It is possible that this is an error of a copyist.
The Aramaic word translated "rub down" also means "naked;" the word "shoes"
is not in N or Ps-Jon, which have instead "feet." Thus, all three Targums probably
originally had "nor did your feet go naked." The Targums are explaining that since
the Israelites' feet were covered, they did not swell.

[5] MT: "discipline." TO's rendering precludes the lessons learned by the rabbis
from the word "discipline" (e.g., b. Ber. 5a). The deviation shows a sensitive relationship between God and man to the average Jew. TO, designed as it was for synagogue audiences, wishes to soften words of chastisement and suffering. People
might not take kindly to the idea of a chastising deity, even though the chastisements are chastisements of love. Ps-Jon has *msqr*, which *Perush Jonathan* translates "teaches." N is literal.

לא על לחמא בלחודוהי מתקים אינשא ארי על כל אפקות מימר מן קדם יי חיי
אינשא:

4. כסותך לא בליאת מינך ומסנך לא יחיפו דנן ארבעין שנין:

5. ותידע עם ליבך ארי כמא דמליף גברא ית בריה יי אלהך מליף לך:

6. ותיטר ית פיקודיא דיי אלהך למהך באורחן דתקנן קדמוהי ולמידחל יתיה:

7. ארי יי אלהך מעילך לארעא טבתא ארע נגדא נחלין דמין מבועי עינון ותהומין
נפקין בבקען ובטורין:

8. ארע חטין וסערין וגופנין ותינין ורמונין ארעא דזיתהא עבדין מישחא והיא עבדא
דבש:

[6] The Targums retain MT's possessive, highlighting that the commands are God's.

[7] MT: "walk in His ways." TO adds "right" and "before" to avoid any possible misunderstanding and an unseemly anthropomorphism: God does not have earthly "paths" on which man can walk and literally follow God.

Adler (NL), however, argues that the deviation teaches a theological and moral lesson. One should not think that evil is also ultimately from God and that it too may be imitated. The addition of "right" clarifies that one should only follow those ways that God desires.

The moral lesson is contained in the Sifre and Talmud. B. Sotah 14a states: "What means the text, 'Ye shall walk after the Lord your God'? Is it, then, possible for a human being to walk after the Shekinah, for has it not been said, 'For the Lord your God is a devouring fire' (Deut 4:24)? But the meaning is to walk after the attributes of the Holy One, blessed be He. As He clothed the naked . . . so do thou also clothe the naked. The Holy One, blessed be He, visited the sick . . . so do thou also visit the sick. The Holy One, blessed be He, comforted mourners . . . so do thou also comfort mourners. The Holy One, blessed be He, buried the dead . . . so do thou also bury the dead."

Ps-Jon is like TO, but N has: "walk in His ways and revere before Him."

[8] TO adds "flowing," for clarity. Ps-Jon translates like TO, but N adds "a place of."

[9] TO adds "springing" for clarity. Ps-Jon also makes this addition among others. N has "springing," but not "wells."

[10] TO renders "plains" and "hills" in the plural because of the context.

[11] TO would generally make an addition here as in verse 7, such as "which produces (wheat);" however, since there was a need to make additions twice later in the sentence, TO follows the Hebrew style and does not add (BO). Ps-Jon adds "which produces" here, N does not. The Targums render "wheat" and "barley" in the plural.

[12] MT: "a land of olives, oil, and honey." The Targums add "produce" for clarity. Schefftel (BO) explains that the verse cannot mean olive oil because then the

9. a land where you may eat bread without stint, where you will lack nothing,[14] a land whose rocks are iron and from whose hills you can hew copper.

10. When you have eaten and are replete, give thanks to the Lord your God for the good land which He has given you.

11. Take care lest you forget the fear[15] of the Lord your God and fail to keep His commandments, His rules,and His laws, which I enjoin upon you today.

12. When you have eaten and are replete, and have built beautiful[16] houses and lived in them,

13. and your herds and flocks have multiplied, and your silver and gold have increased, and everything you own has prospered,

14. and your heart is lifted up and you forget the fear[15] of the Lord your God—who brought you from the land of Egypt, the house of servitude;[17]

15. who led you through a great and fearful wilderness, a place[18] of fiery snakes and scorpions[19] and a place of thirst, a place[20] where there was not water, who brought forth water for you from a flinty rock;

16. who fed you in the wilderness with manna, which your fathers had never known, in order to humble and test you, only to benefit you in the end—

17. and you say in your heart, "My own power and the might of my own hand acquired[21] for me these possessions,"[22]

18. remember that it is the Lord your God who gives you advice[23] on how to acquire possessions, in fulfillment of the covenant He confirmed[24] to your fathers, as this day.

---

adjective "olive" should have followed the noun "oil" as is characteristic in Hebrew. N and Ps-Jon explain that the oil is from olives.

[13] TO adds "it" in order to refer back to the land (BO). FT and Ps-Jon have "and from its dates one produces honey," and N "whose dates are sweet as honey."

[14] MT has *kl bh,* a Hebrew idiom which literally means "all in it." The Targums add *md'm* for greater clarity.

[15] TO adds "fear" to avoid the concept that one can forget God Himself. Similarly, TO also adds "fear" whenever MT has "forsake" God. Ps-Jon is like TO, but N adds: "the teachings of the Torah."

[16] See note to 1:14.

9. ארעא דלא במסכינו תיכול בה לחמא לא תיחסר כל מידעם בה ארעא דאבנהא ברזלא ומטורהא תפסול נחשא:

10. ותיכול ותיסבע ותבריך ית יי אלהך על ארעא טבתא דיהב לך:

11. איסתמר לך דילמא תתנשי ית דחלתא דיי אלהך בדיל דלא למיטר פיקודוהי ודינוהי וקימוהי דאנא מפקיד לך יומא דין:

12. דילמא תיכול ותיסבע ובתין שפירין תבני ותיתיב:

13. ותורך וענך יסגון וכספא ודהבא יסגי לך וכל דלך יסגי:

14. וירם ליבך ותיתנשי ית דחלתא דיי אלהך דאפקך מארעא דמצרים מבית עבדותא:

15. דדברך במדברא רבה ודחילא אתר דחיון קלן ועקרבין ובית צחונא אתר דלית מיא דאפיק לכון מיא מטינרא תקיפא:

16. דאוכלך מנא במדברא דלא ידעו אבהתך בדיל לעניותך ובדיל לנסיותך לאיטבא לך בסופך:

17. ותימר בלבך חילי ותקוף ידי קנו לי ית ניכסיא האילין:

18. ותידכר ית יי אלהך ארי הוא בך יהב לך עיצא למיקני ניכסין בדיל לקימא ית קימיה דקיים לאבהתך כיומא הדין:

---

[17] MT: "slaves." See note to 5:6.

[18] TO and Ps-Jon add "place." N has a word literally meaning "house." Ps-Jon indicates that the Lord took the Israelites with love.

[19] The Targums have the plural for "fiery," "snakes," and "scorpions;" the MT has the singular.

[20] TO and Ps-Jon add "place" twice—the first word literally meaning "house" because "thirst" itself it is too abstract. N does not add words here, apparently relying on the previous "place."

[21] MT: literally, "made," the Targums are more explicit.

[22] The Targums render "possessions" in the plural.

[23] TO and Ps-Jon change "who gives you the power to get strength (or wealth)" to advise how to acquire possessions. Adler (NL) explains that TO does not want to leave an implication that God gives strength to acquire wealth through plunder. This would be unseemly. Instead, God gives you counsel on how to act properly. Schefftel (BO) explains that the counsel concerns possession of the land and not war because the acquisition of the land was through miracles, as is indicated in verse 3. Reiffman (*Sedeh Aram*, p. 43) explains that TO is giving general advice to the masses: do not try to attain your goods through physical means; instead, use your minds—for even the weak can succeed by using their minds. N has the Memra give power to acquire possessions.

[24] MT: "swore."

19. If you do completely forget the fear[15] of the Lord your God and follow after idols of the people[25] to serve them or bow down to them, I warn you this day that you shall certainly perish;

20. like the nations that the Lord will cause to perish before you, so shall you perish—because[26] you did not accept the Memra[27] of the Lord your God.

Chapter IX

1. Hear, Israel! You are to cross the Jordan this day to go in to possess nations greater and mightier than you: great cities and fortified towards[1] the sky;

2. a people great and strong,[2] sons of a warrior[3] of whom you have knowledge; for you have heard it said, "Who can[4] stand before sons of a warrior?"[5]

3. Know then this day that it is the Lord your God who is passing at your head, His Memra[6] is a devouring fire. He will destroy them. He will break them[7] before you, that you may dispossess and destroy them quickly, as the Lord told you.

4. Do not say in your heart when the Lord your God has broken them[8] before you: "It is because of my merit[9] that the Lord has brought me

---

[25] MT: "follow other gods." TO and Ps-Jon avoid any reference to other gods, while N has "other idols."

[26] MT has a word meaning "heel" or "follow" as in 7:12. Schefftel (BO) feels that in chapter 7 the word is rendered in the future tense, while here it is in the past tense, to reflect the concept that one is rewarded for a good thought immediately, but punishment is not inflicted until after the deed is accomplished.

[27] MT: "you did not heed the voice of the Lord your God." TO and Ps-Jon change the verb from "heed" to "accept," delete "voice," and add Memra. N has: "did not heed the voice of the Memra of the Lord your God."

MT's *tšmʿwn*, which is in the imperfect, is rendered with the participle and *hwh* in the perfect in some TO texts, but not in N or Ps-Jon.

[1] MT: "in the heaven." See note on 1:28 and 4:11.

[2] TO and N change MT's "tall" to "strong." Ps-Jon has "proud." Comp. 2:10, where LXX is like TO. LXX is literal here.

‫19. ויהי אם איתנשאה תיתנשי ית דחלתא דיי אלהך ותהך בתר טעות עממיא‬
‫ותפלחינון ותסגוד להון אסהידית בכון יומא דין ארי מיבד תיבדון:‬

‫20. כעממיא דיי מובד מן קדמיכון כן תיבדון חלף דלא קבילתון למימרא דיי אלהכון:‬

IX

‫1. שמע ישראל את עבר יומא דין ית ירדנא למיעל למירת עממין רברבין ותקיפין‬
‫מינך קרוין רברבן וכריכן עד צית שמיא:‬

‫2. עם רב ותקיף בני גיבריא דאת ידעתא ואת שמעתא מן יכול למקם קדם בני גברא:‬

‫3. ותידע יומא דין ארי יי אלהך הוא עבר קדמך מימריה אישה אכלא הוא ישיצינון‬
‫והוא יתברינון מן קדמך ותתריכנון ותובידנון בפריע כמא דמליל יי לך:‬

‫4. לא תימר בליבך בדיתבר יי אלהך יתהון מן קדמך למימר בזכותי אעלני יי למירת‬
‫ית ארעא הדא ובחובי עממיא האלין יי מתריך להון מן קדמך:‬

[3] MT: "sons of Anakim." See note on 1:28. N has: "sons of Anak, a warrior." Ps-Jon has: "as a warrior."

[4] MT: "who stands before." Schefftel (BO) explains that TO's rendering is designed to make the phrase clearer. N and Ps-Jon translate likewise.

[5] MT: "sons of Anak." While MT varies the rendering from the singular to the plural form, TO characteristically gives one form. The word "warrior" is used rather than "Anakim," probably to clarify the meaning of the term. Ps-Jon translates here like TO, but N has: "sons of Anak, a warrior."

[6] TO adds Memra. Berkowitz (CS) notes that TO does not use Memra in the previous phrase (God passing). He suggests that TO may have understood the second phrase as an explanation of the first. Therefore, there was no need to include Memra twice. N has "glory of the Shekinah" in the first phrase and no addition in the second. Ps-Jon adds "Shekinah of His glory" to the first phrase and Memra to the second.

[7] TO characteristically changes MT's "subdue them" to "break them." N retains the Hebrew word. Ps-Jon has "arrange them."

[8] MT and Ps-Jon: "thrust out." N: "destroy."

[9] MT: *tdk*, "righteousness." The three Pentateuchal Targums have *zkwt*, merit. There is no implication here of the concept of proxy *Zachuth*, by which one can vicariously tap into the reward owed to others for their righteous acts. One aspect of this concept is *Zachuth Aboth*, whereby Jews were (or, according to some, are) able to reap the rewards of Abraham, Isaac, and Jacob. The unofficial Targums contain many verses reflecting this concept, but it is not found anywhere in TO. The official Targum is simply rendering the Hebrew with an Aramaic equivalent.

to possess this land and because of the guilt[10] of those nations that the Lord is dispossessing them before you."

5. It is not because of your merits[9] and the truthfulness of your heart that you will enter to occupy their country, but because of the guilt[10] of those nations that the Lord your God is driving them out before you, and in order to fulfill the word that the Lord confirmed[11] to your fathers, Abraham, Isaac, and Jacob.

6. Know, then, that it is not for any merit[9] of yours that the Lord your God is giving you this good land to occupy; for you are a stiff-necked people.

7. Remember,[12] do not forget, how you caused anger before[13] the Lord your God in the wilderness: from the day that you left the land of Egypt until you reached this place, you have been rebellious before[13] the Lord.

8. At Horeb you caused anger before[13] the Lord, and anger of the Lord took hold[14] of you to destroy you.

9. When I had ascended the mountain to take the tablets of the stone, the Tablets of the Covenant that the Lord concluded with you and I stayed on the mountain forty days and forty nights, I ate no bread and drank no water.

10. And the Lord gave me the two tablets of stone inscribed by the finger[15] of the Lord,[16] and on them were all the words that the Lord spoke with you on the mountain out of the fire on the day of the Assembly.

11. At the end of those forty days and forty nights, the Lord gave me the two tablets of stone, the Tablets of the Covenant.

12. The Lord said to me, "Arise, go down quickly from here, for your people whom you brought out of Egypt have become corrupt; they have strayed quickly from the path that I enjoined upon them; they have made themselves a molten image."

A full discussion of *Zachuth* is found in the author's *Targumic Studies*.

N adds Memra three times in this verse, attaching it to each verb.

[10] MT: "wickedness." The Targums use a word emphasizing the legal "wrong," i.e., the violation of the Torah laws. The Targums have the plural form although the MT has the singular.

[11] MT: "swore."

5. לא בזכותך ובקשיטות ליבך את עליל למירת ית ארעהון ארי בחובי עממיא האלין
יי אלהך מתריך להון מן קדמך ובדיל לקיימא ית פיגתמא דקיים יי לאבהתך
לאברהם ליצחק וליעקב:

6. ותידע ארי לא בזכותך יי אלהך יהיב לך ית ארעא טבתא הדא למירתה ארי עם
קשי קדל את:

7. הוי דכיר לא תתנשי ית דארגיזתא קדם יי אלהך במדברא למן יומא דנפקתא
מארעא דמצרים עד מיתיכון עד אתרא הדין מסרבין הויתון קדם יי:

8. ובחורב ארגיזתון קדם יי ותקיף רוגזא דיי בכון לשיציאה יתכון:

9. במסקי לטורא למיסב לוחי אבניא לוחי קימא דגזר יי עימכון ויתיבית בטורא
ארבעין יממין וארבעין לילון לחמא לא אכלית ומיא לא אישתיתי:

10. ויהב יי לי ית תרין לוחי אבניא כתיבין באצבעא דיי ועליהון ככל פתגמיא דמליל יי
עימכון בטורא מגו אישתא ביומא דקהלא:

11. והוה מסוף ארבעין יממין וארבעין לילון יהב יי לי ית תרין לוחי אבניא לוחי
קימא:

12. ואמר יי לי קום חות בפריע מיכא ארי חביל עמך דאפיקתא ממצרים סטו בפריע
מן אורחא דפקידתון עבדו להון מתכא:

---

[12] TO and Ps-Jon have *hwy dkyr*. See note on 5:12. N does not.

[13] TO and Ps-Jon have "before" instead of *'t*, *'m*, and *'t*, in this verse and the next. N adds Memra instead of the first "before."

[14] MT: "the Lord was angry with you." TO and N add "took hold," Ps-Jon does not. Ps-Jon adds "before."

[15] Adler (NL) wonders why TO does not avoid an anthropomorphism here as in Exodus 8:15. He suggests that Exodus speaks of punishment and judgment; therefore, TO adds Memra. Here TO wants to emphasize the sanctity and value of the Ten Commandments and therefore relates them directly to the Lord, and to the Lord alone.

Adler's explanation is unlikely. This is another instance where Adler unfoundedly seeks a theological teaching in TO. There are several instances where TO adds Memra in chapter 5, regarding the Ten Commandments. TO does not deviate here because it frequently depicts God with human organs. See note on 11:2.

Ps-Jon translates like TO, but N softens the anthropomorphism in this verse. The stones are inscribed by "the finger of the Almighty from before the Lord." Furthermore, it is not the Lord that "addressed" the people, but "the Memra of the Lord."

[16] MT: "Elohim."

13. The Lord said to me as follows: "It is revealed before Me[17] (concerning) this people; it is a stiff-necked people.

14. Cease your request before Me[18] and I will destroy them and blot out their name from under the heaven, and I will make you a nation mightier and greater then they."

15. I turned and started down the mountain, the mountain was ablaze with fire, the two Tablets of the Covenant in my two hands.

16. I saw how you acted wrongly before[19] the Lord your God: you had made yourselves a molten calf; you strayed quickly from the path that the Lord had enjoined upon you.

17. Thereupon, I gripped the two tablets and flung them away from both my hands, smashing them before your eyes.

18. I threw myself down before the Lord as I had done before: for forty days and forty nights, I ate no bread and drank no water because of all the wrongdoings you had committed, doing that which is bad before the Lord to cause anger before[20] Him.

19. For I was afraid of the anger and hot displeasure with which the Lord was angry with you to wipe you out. But the Lord accepted my prayer[21] at that time also.

20. And concerning Aaron, there was anger from before[22] the Lord enough to have destroyed him; so I also prayed for Aaron at that time.

21. As for that wrong behavior—that you had made the calf—I took it and burned it in the fire; I stamped and ground it thoroughly until it was fine as dust, and I threw its dust into the brook that descended from the mountain.

[17] MT: "I see." The Targums avoid the anthropomorphism. Maimonides (*Guide* 1:48) explains that when "see" in relation to God is connected with wrong, injury, or violence, it is paraphrased "it was revealed before the Lord." Examples of TO's failure to follow this rule are Deut 32:19 and 36. Maimonides states that these renderings are the result of mistakes of copyists.

[18] MT has "Let Me alone." Again, the Targums replace an anthropomorphism. TO translates here as in Exodus 32:10. That Moses prayed is found in the Talmud (b. Ber. 32a). When Israel sinned with the calf, Moses' strength weakened and he

13. ואמר יי לי למימר גלי קדמי עמא הדין והא עם קשי קדל הוא:
14. אגח בעותך מן קדמי ואישיצנון ואימחי ית שומהון מתחות שמיא ואעביד יתך לעם תקיף וסגי מינהון:
15. ואיתפניתי ונחתית מן טורא וטורא בער באישתא ותרין לוחי קימא על תרתין ידי:
16. וחזית והא חבתון קדם יי אלהכון עבדתון לכון עגל מתכא סטיתון בפריע מן אורחא דפקיד יי יתכון:
17. ואחדית בתרין לוחיא ורמיתינון מעל תרתין ידי ותברתינון לעיניכון:
18. ואשתטחית קדם יי כדבקדמיתא ארבעין יממין וארבעין לילון לחמא לא אכלית ומיא לא אשתיתי על כל חובתכון דחבתון למעבד דביש קדם יי לארגזא קדמוהי:
19. ארי דחילית מן קדם רוגזא וחימתא דרגיז יי עליכון לשיצאה יתכון וקביל יי צלותי אף בזימנא ההוא:
20. ועל אהרן הוה רגז מן קדם יי לחדא לשיציותיה וצליתי אף על אהרן בעידנא ההוא:
21. וית חובתכון דעבדתון ית עיגלא נסיבית ואוקידית יתיה בנורא ושפית יתיה בשופינא יאות עד דהוה דקיק לעפרא ורמית ית עפריה לנחלא דנחית מן טורא:

had no strength to speak before God. When he heard God say "Let Me alone," he said, "this matter depends on me." Immediately, he rose, straightened himself, and prayed for mercy. The aggadic statement in b. Ber. 32a shows that the Exodus passage (and by implication the parallel passage here) was recognized by the Talmud as being unseemly anthropomorphic.

[19] MT has a lamed meaning "to" or "against." The Targums change it to "before."

[20] The Targums add "before" twice. They delete MT's "in the eyes of the Lord."

[21] MT: "listened to me." TO and Ps-Jon change this to "my prayer," paraphrasing an anthropomorphism. N has: "heard the sound of my prayer."

Ps-Jon speaks of five destroying angels dispatched from before the Lord. This Targum also speaks of angels in 10:14 and elsewhere. TO generally does not add glosses about angels.

[22] Luzzato (OG) and Adler (NL) note that "before" was added in this verse but not in the preceding one. B has the word in both verses. Sperber's text does not include "before" in the previous verse. Ps-Jon does not remove the anthropomorphism in the preceding verse, but it adds "before" here. N has the Memra being angry both in the preceding verse and this one.

22. At Dalakta (fire),[23] and at Nesata (trials)[24] and at the graves of those who ask (for meat)[25] you caused anger before[26] the Lord.

23. And when the Lord sent[27] you on from Rekam Geah[28] saying, "Go up and occupy the land that I am giving to you," you flouted the Memra[29] of the Lord your God; you did not put your trust in Him and did not accept His Memra.[30]

24. You have been defiant before[31] the Lord as long as I have known you.

25. Thus I lay prostrate before the Lord those forty days and forty nights, I fell down because the Lord had said He would destroy you,

26. and I prayed before[32] the Lord and said, "Lord God, do not annihilate Your people, Your inheritance, whom You redeemed with Your might,[33] whom You freed from Egypt with a mighty hand.

27. Remember[34] Your servants, Abraham, Isaac, and Jacob; pay no heed to the stubbornness of this people, their guilty acts, and their improper conduct.

28. Else the inhabitants[35] of the country from which You brought us out will say, 'It was because there was an inability before[36] the Lord to bring them to the land that He had spoken of to them, and because He hated them, that He brought them out to slay them in the wilderness.'

29. Yet they are Your people and Your inheritance, whom You brought out with your great might and Your uplifted arm."[37]

---

[23] TO changes the names of the three places mentioned in this verse as it does elsewhere. Each name was derived from the misdeed committed by the Israelites at the site (cf. Deut 1:1). TO transposes the Hebrew into an Aramaic equivalent. MT's "Taberah" is rendered "fire." The incident is recorded in Num 11:1 ff. "And he called the name of the place Taberah; because the fire of the Lord had burnt among them" (Num 11:3). N and Ps-Jon have "place of fire."

[24] MT: "Massah," "quarrel," a reference to the incident recorded in Exod 17:2 ff. "And he called the name of the place Massah and Meribah; because of the quarreling of the children of Israel, and because they tempted the Lord . . . ." N and Ps-Jon translate like TO with a word literally meaning "trials."

22. ובדליקתא ובניסיתא ובקברי דמשאלי מרגזין הויתון קדם יי:

23. וכד שלח יי יתכון מרקם גיאה למימר סקו ואחסינו ית ארעא דיהבית לכון וסריבתון על מימרא דיי אלהכון ולא הימנתון ליה ולא קבילתון למימריה:

24. מסרבין הויתון קדם יי מיומא דידעית יתכון:

25. ואשתטחית קדם יי ית ארבעין יממין וית ארבעין לילון דאשתטחית ארי אמר יי לשיצאה יתכון:

26. וצליתי קדם יי ואמרית יי אלהים לא תחביל עמך ואחסנתך דפרקתא בתוקפך דאפיקתא ממצרים ביד תקיפא:

27. אידכר לעבדך לאברהם ליצחק וליעקב לא תתפני לקשיות עמא הדין ולחוביהון ולחטאיהון:

28. דילמא יימרון דיירי ארעא דאפיקתנא מתמן מדלית יוכלא קדם יי לאעלותהון לארעא דמליל להון ומדסני יתהון אפיקינון לקטלותהון במדברא:

29. ואינון עמך ואחסנתך דאפיקתא בחילך רבה ובדרעך מרממא:

---

[25] MT: "Kibroth-hattaavah," "graves of lust," a reference to the incident in Num 11:4 ff. "And the mixed multitude that was among them felt lustful longing . . . ." (Num 11:4). N and Ps-Jon read like TO.

[26] The Targums have "before" instead of 't.

[27] N has the Memra send the people.

[28] MT: "Kadesh-barnea." See note on 1:22. N and Ps-Jon are like TO.

[29] MT has the Hebrew idiom "the word (lit. mouth) of the Lord." TO and Ps-Jon replace "mouth" with Memra. Some TO texts also add "decree" like N.

[30] MT: "and did not hear His voice." Ps-Jon translates like TO. N has: "you did not heed the voice of the Memra of the Lord."

[31] MT: "with," which the Targums change to "before."

[32] MT: "to." N and Ps-Jon also change "to" to "before."

[33] MT: "greatness." The Targums are more specific.

[34] Although TO frequently prefers to avoid the idea that God can forget, it does not always do so, as is evidenced here.

[35] TO, N, and Ps-Jon add "inhabitants" for clarity.

[36] The Targums add "before."

[37] The Targums do not replace the anthropomorphic "arm," see note on 11:2, but change "outstretched" to "uplifted."

Chapter X

1. At that time the Lord said to me, "Carve out two tablets of stone like the first, and come up before[1] Me on the mountain; and make for yourself an ark of wood.

2. I will inscribe on the tablets the words that were on the first tablets which you broke, and you shall place them in the ark."

3. I made an ark of acacia wood and carved out two tablets of stone like the first; I ascended the mountain with the two tablets in my hand.

4. He inscribed on the tablets the same text as on the first, the Ten Commandments (lit., words) that He spoke with you on the mountain out of the fire on the day of the Assembly; and the Lord gave them to me.

5. Then I turned and descended the mountain; I placed the tablets in the ark that I had made, and they have been there as the Lord had commanded me.

6. The Israelites marched from Beeroth-bene-jaakan to Moserah. Aaron died there and was buried there; and his son Eleazar served[2] in his stead.

7. From there they journeyed to Gudgod, and from Gudgod to Jotbath, a region where brooks of water flow.[3]

8. At that time the Lord set apart the tribe of Levi to carry the Ark of the Lord's Covenant, to stand before the Lord, to serve Him and to bless in His name, until this day.

9. That is why Levi has no part or inheritance along with his kinsmen: the gift that the Lord gave him[4] is his portion, as the Lord your God spoke concerning him.

10. I stayed on the mountain, as the first time, forty days and forty nights; and the Lord accepted my prayer[5] that time also; the Lord was not willing to destroy you.

---

[1] The Targums change MT's "to me" to "before."

[2] MT: "became a priest." Ps-Jon translates like TO, but N has "served as high priest." Some commentators (see, for example, NL to Gen 14:18 and Exod 2:16) suppose that TO deviates in rendering MT's "priest" as "serve," in regard to non-

X

1. בעידנא ההוא אמר יי לי פסול לך תרין לוחי אבניא כקדמאי וסק לקדמי לטורא
   ותעביד לך ארונא דאעא:
2. ואכתוב על לוחיא ית פתגמיא דהוו על לוחיא קדמאי דתברתא ותשוינון בארונא:
3. ועבדית ארונא דאעי שטין ופסלית תרין לוחי אבניא כקדמאי וסליקית לטורא
   ותרין לוחיא בידי:
4. וכתב על לוחיא ככתבא קדמאה ית עשרה פתגמין דמליל יי עימכון בטורא מגו
   אישתא ביומא דקהלא ויהבינון יי לי:
5. ואתפניתי ונחתית מן טורא ושויתי ית לוחיא בארונא דעבדית והוו תמן כמא
   דפקדני יי:
6. ובני ישראל נטלו מבירות בני יעקן למוסרה תמן מית אהרן ואתקבר תמן ושמיש
   אלעזר בריה תחותוהי:
7. מתמן נטלו לגודגוד ומן גודגוד ליטבת ארע נגדא נחלין דמין:
8. בעידנא ההוא אפריש יי ית שיבטא דלוי למיטל ית ארון קימא דיי למקם קדם יי
   לשמשותיה ולברכא בשמיה עד יומא הדין:
9. על כן לא הוה ללוי חולק ואחסנא עם אחוהי מתנן דיהב ליה יי אינון אחסנתיה
   כמא דמליל יי אלהך ליה:
10. ואנא הויתי קאים בטורא כיומיא קדמאי ארבעין יממין וארבעין לילון וקביל יי
    צלותי אף בזימנא ההיא לא אבה יי לחבלותך:

Israelites, to avoid the concept that a non-Israelite can function as a priest. The deviation in this verse weakens that conclusion since it is evidence that the change is also made regarding Israelites.

[3] TO adds "flow" for clarity. Ps-Jon is like TO, but N has "a place of," as in 8:7.

[4] MT: "the Lord is their portion." The Sperber text is literal here but B has the addition in the above text. Adler (NL) explains that TO adds to and changes the reading of the text here, as in 18:2 and Num 18:20, out of respect for God. Ps-Jon is like B. While these Targums remove one anthropomorphism, the Lord being "a portion," they produced another, the Lord "giving." This problem is resolved by N, which also has a more concise deviation, the addition of only one word: "the sacrifices of the Lord are their portion" (from Josh 13:14, TJ to Josh 13:33 translates similarly). M is literal. N and Ps-Jon include "tribe of" before levites, a practice that TO also generally follows (see, for example, 4:43), but not here.

[5] MT: "the Lord listened to me," which is anthropomorphic. Ps-Jon is like TO, but N has: "and the voice of the Memra of the Lord heard the voice of my prayer."

11. Then the Lord said to me, "Up, resume the journey before the people, that they may go and occupy the land that I confirmed[6] to their fathers to give them."

12. And now, Israel, what does the Lord your God demand[7] of you? Only this: to fear before[8] the Lord your God, to walk in all the paths that were established[9] before[8] Him, to love Him, and to serve before[8] the Lord your God with all your heart and soul,

13. keeping the Lord's commandments and laws, which I enjoin upon you today, for your good.

14. Mark, the heaven to its uttermost reaches belongs to the Lord your God, the earth and all that is on it!

15. Only the Lord took delight in your fathers to love them, and He chose their descendants that followed them from among all peoples as this day.

16. Remove the foolishness of your hearts[10] and stiffen your necks no more.

17. For the Lord your God is the God of judges[11] and the master of kings,[12] the great, the mighty, and fearful God; there is none before Him who favors persons, and also none who accepts a bribe,[13]

18. but upholds the judgment of the fatherless and the widow, and befriends the proselyte,[14] providing him with food and clothing.

19. You must love the proselyte,[14] for you were dwellers[14] in the land of Egypt.

---

[6] MT: "swore."

[7] MT: "request," which is a disrespectful anthropomorphism, implying weakness. Ps-Jon renders like TO, but N is literal.

[8] The Targums have "before" three times later in the verse.

[9] MT: "to walk only in His paths," which is unfavorably anthropomorphic, implying that God has paths upon which humans can tread behind him. N and Ps-Jon are like TO. N paraphrases "love Him" as "love the teachings of His Torah."

[10] MT: "Circumcise the foreskin of your hearts." As usual, TO avoids the metaphor and explains it. Adler (NL) explains that TO means: "remove the foolishness that entered your hearts, for no man does wrong unless a spirit of folly entered his heart." Cf. b. Succah 3a. B. Succah 52a derives from this verse that Moses called the evil desire "uncircumcised part." Ps-Jon reads like TO. N has: "circumcise the foreskin of the foolishness of your hearts."

11. וַאֲמַר יי לי קוּם אִיזֵיל לְמִטוֹל קֳדָם עַמָּא וְיֵיעֲלוּן וְיֵירְתוּן יָת אַרְעָא דְקַיֵּימִית
לַאֲבָהָתְהוֹן לְמִיתַּן לְהוֹן:

12. וּכְעַן יִשְׂרָאֵל מָה יי אֱלָהָךְ תָּבַע מִינָךְ אֵילָהֵין לְמִידְחַל קֳדָם יי אֱלָהָךְ לִמְהַךְ בְּכָל
אוֹרְחָן דְתַקְנָן קֳדָמוֹהִי וּלְמִירְחַם יָתֵיהּ וּלְמִפְלַח קֳדָם יי אֱלָהָךְ בְּכָל לִבָּךְ וּבְכָל נַפְשָׁךְ:

13. לְמִיטַר יָת פִּיקּוּדַיָּא דַיי וְיָת קְיָמוֹהִי דַּאֲנָא מְפַקֵּיד לָךְ יוֹמָא דֵין דְיֵיטַב לָךְ:

14. הָא דַיי אֱלָהָךְ שְׁמַיָּא וּשְׁמֵי שְׁמַיָּא אַרְעָא וְכָל דְּבַהּ:

15. לְחוֹד בַּאֲבָהָתָךְ צְבִי יי לְמִירְחַם יָתְהוֹן וְאִתְרְעִי בִּבְנֵיהוֹן בַּתְרֵיהוֹן בְּכוֹן מִכָּל עַמְמַיָּא
כְּיוֹמָא הָדֵין:

16. וְתֵעְדּוּן יָת טִפְּשׁוּת לִבְּכוֹן וְקַדְלְכוֹן לָא תַקְשׁוּן עוֹד:

17. אֲרֵי יי אֱלָהָכוֹן הוּא אֱלָהּ דַּיָּינִין וּמָרֵי מַלְכִין אֱלָהָא רַבָּה גִּבָּרָא וּדְחִילָא דְלֵית קֳדָמוֹהִי
מִיסַּב אַפִּין וְאַף לָא לְקַבָּלָא שׁוּחֲדָא:

18. עָבֵיד דִּין דִּין וְיַתַּם וְאַרְמְלָא וְרָחֵים גִּיּוֹרָא לְמִיתַּן לֵיהּ מְזוֹן וּכְסוּ:

19. וּתְרַחֲמוּן יָת גִּיּוֹרָא אֲרֵי דַיָּירִין הֲוֵיתוֹן בְּאַרְעָא דְמִצְרָיִם:

---

[11] This verse has several metaphors which TO alters. The MT could be translated: "For the Lord your God is the God of gods, and the Lord of lords, the great,
the mighty, and the terrible God who has no regard for persons, and takes no
bribe." Characteristically, TO avoids the reference to idols. In the first phrase, the
second word "god" is rendered "judges" in accordance with the Mekhilta (on
Exod 21:6) and elsewhere. See also Dan 2:47, from where the phrase is borrowed.
A literal translation would imply the existence, albeit subordinate, of other gods.
Ps-Jon interprets the verse like TO, but N has: "For the Lord your God is the great
God, the mighty and the awesome, who has no regard for persons in judgment nor
accepts any bribes." There are words missing in N, but added in the margin.

[12] MT has "the Lord of the lords." Schefftel (BO) explains that TO has "kings"
since they are the highest earthly officials. He also notes that TO does not use the
definite "the" for the two phrases about "judges" and "kings." The absence of
"the" implies that God is the Lord of all judges and all kings. TO is also apparently
influenced by the expression *mlk mlky hmlkym*.

[13] MT: "who favors no person and takes no bribe." TO and Ps-Jon add several
words because it would be presumptuous even to say that God does *not* show
favoritism or take bribes. The very association of such wrongdoing with God is
inadmissible, even for the purpose of denying it. N does not make this addition. TO
and Ps-Jon add "also" for the same reason.

[14] Characteristically, the Targums render *ger* as "proselyte." See Deut 1:16.
This third *ger* is not translated "proselyte" because the Israelites were not proselytes in Egypt, but "dwellers." N and Ps-Jon have "proselyte."

20. You must fear the Lord your God: (only) before[15] Him shall you worship, and you should approach his fear,[16] and by His name shall you
confirm.[6]

21. He is your praise and He is your God, who did with you these
great and awesome[17] things which your eyes have seen.

22. Your ancestors went down to Egypt seventy persons; and now the
Lord your God has made you as numerous as the stars of heaven.

Chapter XI

1. Love, therefore, the Lord your God, and keep the charge of His
Memra,[1] His laws, His rules, and His commandments for all time.

2. And you shall know this day that it was not your children, who neither
knew nor saw the teaching of the Lord your God—His greatness, His
mighty hand, and His uplifted[2] arm;

3. and the signs and the deeds that He performed in Egypt for Pharaoh
King of Egypt and all his land;

4. and what He did to Egypt's army, its horses and chariots; how He
overflowed the waters of the Yam Suf upon them when they were pursuing you, thus the Lord destroyed them to this day;

5. what He did for you in the wilderness before you arrived in this place;

6. and what He did to Dathan and Abiram, sons of Eliab son of Reuben,
when the earth opened her mouth and swallowed them, along with
the people[3] of their households, their tents, and all the substance they
had,[4] from amidst all Israel—

---

[15] TO adds "before" once instead of *'tw*, while N and Ps-Jon have it also in the
prior phrase. Some versions do not have the word even here, and it is missing in
verse 6:13.

[16] MT: "to him you should hold fast," an unseemly anthropomorphism that the
Targums prefer to avoid. See 4:4. Ps-Jon is like TO, but N has: "You should hold
fast to the teachings of His Torah," a characteristic deviation.

[17] In verse 4:34, TO renders this word as "appearances," paralleling the teaching in Sifre. Here the prior words "wrought for you" show that the word must refer
to "awesome" deeds (BO). N and Ps-Jon translate similarly.

20. ית יי אלהך תדחל וקדמוהי תפלח ולדחלתיה תתקרב ובשמיה תקיים:

21. הוא תושבחתך והוא אלהך דעבד עימך ית רברבתא וית חסינתא האילין דחזאה עינך:

22. בשבעין נפשן נחתו אבהתך למצרים וכען שויך יי אלהך ככוכבי שמיא לסגי:

XI

1. ותירחם ית יי אלהך ותיטר מטרת מימריה וקימוהי ודינוהי ופיקודוהי כל יומיא:

2. ותדעון יומא דין ארי לא ית בניכון דלא ידעו ודלא חזו ית אולפנא דיי אלהכון ית רבותיה ית ידיה תקיפתא ודרעיה מרממא:

3. וית אתותיה וית עובדוהי דעבד בגו מצרים לפרעה מלכא דמצרים ולכל ארעיה:

4. ודעבד למשרית מצראי לסוסותהון ולרתיכיהון דאטיף ית מי ימא דסוף על אפיהון במרדפהון בתריכון ואבידנון יי עד יומא הדין:

5. ודעבד לכון במדברא עד מיתיכון עד אתרא הדין:

6. ודעבד לדתן ולאבירם בני אליאב בר ראובן דפתחת ארעא ית פומה ובלעתנון וית אינש בתיהון וית משכניהון וית כל יקומא דעימהון בגו כל ישראל:

---

[1] TO and Ps-Jon add Memra. N does not, but has: "You shall love the teaching of the Torah of the Lord your God."

[2] MT: "outstretched arm." The Targums deviate frequently to avoid unseemly anthropomorphisms, but do not do so here or in other places where this phrase occurs: 4:34, 5:15, 7:19, and 26:8. Other verses where TO translates literally God's hand or arm include: Exod 6:6, 13:3, 14:31, 15:6, and Deut 9:29. Deut 9:10 on the "finger" of God and 11:12 on God's "eyes" are similar. N and Ps-Jon translate here like TO. The Targums probably considered these popular phrases to be easily understandable metaphors which would not convey improper anthropomorphic images of God to the general population.

[3] TO, N and Ps-Jon add "the people of" since the MT cannot refer to houses, which did not exist in the desert, or tents, which are mentioned immediately after (Lowenstein, NH). The MT is a synechdoche, a sometimes confusing figure of speech that the Targums prefer to avoid.

[4] MT: "at their feet," an idiomatic expression paraphrased by TO, which the Talmud (b. Sanh. 110a) interprets as referring to money. Ps-Jon deletes this phrase and has: "along with the people of their households, and all tents (or, storehouses; see *Perush Jonathan*) they had, from amidst all Israel." N translates the MT literally.

E. Z. Melammed (*Bible Commentators*, p. 179) notes that TO generally prefers to avoid "feet" and uses a more delicate substitute. Other examples include Exod 11:8 ("feet" = "with them"), Exod 4:25 ("feet" = "before them") and Deut 28:57 ("feet" = "from them").

7. but your eyes saw[5] all the deeds of the mighty Lord, which he did.

8. Keep therefore, all the commands that I enjoin upon you today, so that you may be strong, enter and take possession of the land which you are about to cross into and possess,

9. and that you may long endure upon the soil which the Lord confirmed[6] to your fathers to give to them and to their descendants, a land producing[7] milk and honey.

10. For the land which you are going to enter and possess is not like the land of Egypt from which you have come, where you sowed the grain and watered it by your foot,[8] like a vegetable garden;

11. but the land you are about to cross into to take possession of it, is a land of hills and valleys, it soaks up its water from the rains of heaven.

12. It is a land which the Lord your God seeks, on which the Lord your God always keeps His eyes,[9] from year's beginning to year's end.

13. If, then, you accept[10] the commandments that I enjoin upon you this day, loving the Lord your God and serving before[11] Him with all your heart and soul,

14. I will give the rain of your land in its season, the early rain and the late rain. You shall gather in your new grain and your wine and your oil.

15. I will also provide grass in your field for your cattle—and thus you shall eat and be full.

---

[5] Sperber and B have the singular for "saw," but the plural form is found in variant texts noted by Sperber, N, and Ps-Jon. The plural is correct since "eyes" is plural.

[6] MT: "swore."

[7] MT: "flowing with." TO replaces the metaphor as in 6:3 and elsewhere. N and Ps-Jon avoid the figurative language by adding other words.

[8] While TO frequently removes metaphors, this phrase may be intended to be understood literally. It may refer to the process of distributing the stored-up water of the Nile through the field by many small channels in the soft mud. The mud was removed by the foot of the peasant to allow the water to pass and replaced to divert it (Driver, *Deuteronomy*).

It is unlikely that TO maintains the literal wording to highlight the teaching contained in Sifre and b. Ber. 42a: blessing follows immediately on the entrance of scholars. Sifre uses the word "foot" repeatedly to emphasize the direct connection between the coming in of scholars and the entrance of blessings.

7. ארי עיניכון חזאה ית כל עובדא דיי רבה דעבד:

8. ותיטרון ית כל תפקידתא דאנא מפקיד לך יומא דין בדיל דתתקפון ותיעלון
ותירתון ית ארעא דאתון עברין לתמן למירתה:

9. ובדיל דתורכון יומין על ארעא דקיים יי לאבהתכון למיתן להון ולבניהון ארע
עבדא חלב ודבש:

10. ארי ארעא דאת עליל לתמן למירתה לא כארעא דמצרים היא דנפקתון מתמן
דזרעת ית זרעך ומשקית ליה ברגלך כגינת ירקא:

11. וארעא דאתון עברין לתמן למירתה ארע טורין ובקען למטר שמיא שתיא מיא:

12. ארעא דיי אלהך תבע יתה תדירא עיני יי אלהך בה מרישא דשתא ועד סופה
דשתא:

13. ויהי אם קבלא תקבלון לפיקודי דאנא מפקיד יתכון יומא דין למירחם ית יי
אלהכון ולמיפלח קדמוהי בכל לבכון ובכל נפשכון:

14. ואיתין מטר ארעכון בעידניה בכיר ולקיש ותכנוש עיבורך וחמרך ומישחך:

15. ואיתין עיסבא בחקלך לבעירך ותיכול ותיסבע:

Ps-Jon deletes the metaphor and reads: "to be watered by yourself, like a vegetable garden." N is like TO, but has the plural "feet."

[9] Adler (NL) feels that TO (N and Ps-Jon) renders the verse literally, without
avoiding the anthropomorphism, out of a desire to make clear God's supervision
over all the needs of the Land of Israel. There are many Talmudic references to
God's constant supervision over the Land of Israel, such as b. R.H. 16b and 17b.
Sifre also emphasizes God's watchfulness. Cf. Ps 33:18 and 34:16. Lowenstein
(NH) argues that TO retains the original wording to teach the Talmudic law (b.
Hag. 2b and b. Sanh. 4b) that a person blind in one eye is exempt from the commandment of appearing at the Temple during Pilgrimage Festivals. Just as God
"sees" the land with both "eyes," so must the pilgrim see with both eyes.

Adler's and Lowenstein's views have no basis. TO does not replace all anthropomorphisms, only those that do not show God proper respect. However, TO does frequently deviate to avoid "eyes" when it is applied to God. See, for example, Gen
18:3; 19:19; 30:27; 32:6; 33:8, 10, 15; 34:11; 39:4; 47:25, 29; 50:4; Exod 3:21;
11:3; 12:36; 33:12, 13, 16, 17; 34:9; Num 11:11, 15; 32:5; and Deut 24:1.

Ps-Jon includes Memra in the first part of the verse, "looks after with His
Memra that he may bless it always," but not the end, probably because it is
implied after being mentioned once. N does not include Memra.

[10] MT: "hear." Ps-Jon is like TO. N has "hear." Sifre emphasizes that the command is to act.

[11] TO, like N and Ps-Jon, adds "before."

16. Take care that your heart be not deceived, that you turn aside and serve the idols of the nations[12] and bow to them.[13]

17. For the Lord's anger will flare up against you, and He will shut up the heaven so that there will be no rain and the ground will not yield its produce; and you will soon perish from the good land the Lord is giving you.

18. Now place these My words upon your heart and soul: bind them as a sign on your hand and let them serve as Tefillin[14] between your eyes,

19. and teach them to your children—to speak of them when you stay at home and when you are going on the road, when you lie down and when you get up;

20. and write them on Mezuzot and fix them to[15] the doorposts of your house and on your gate—

21. that your days and the days of your children will be lengthened[16] on the land that the Lord confirmed[6] to your fathers to give them, as the days of heaven upon the earth.

22. If, then, you faithfully keep all of these commandments that I command you to do, loving the Lord your God, walking in all the ways that are right before Him[17] and come near to His fear (or service),[18]

23. the Lord will drive out all these nations before you: you will dispossess nations greater and mightier than you.

24. Every place on which the sole of your foot treads shall be yours: from the wilderness to the Lebanon, from the river, the river Euphrates to the Western Sea,[19] shall be your border.

25. No man shall stand up to you: the fear of you and the dread of you shall be lain by the Lord your God over the whole land in which you set foot, as He spoke to you.

---

[12] MT: "other gods." As usual, TO removes all possible misconceptions of the existence of other gods. See also Gen 35:2, 4; Exod 22:19; 23:13; Deut 6:14; 7:4; 8:19; 11:28; 12:2, 4; 13:1, 7, 14; 17:3; 18:20; 29:25; and elsewhere. An exception to this practice is the Ten Commandments (5:7): "You shall have no other god besides Me." Among other interpretations, Sifre also understands "other" as "nations"; those that consider the idols to be gods.

Ps-Jon translates this verse like TO, but adds one Aramaic word, "led astray by the *inclination* of your hearts." N does not add "inclination." See *Targumic Studies*.

16. אסתמרו לכון דילמא יטעי לבכון ותסטון ותפלחון לטעות עממיא ותסגדון להון:
17. ויתקף רוגזא דיי בכון וייחוד ית שמיא ולא יהי מיטרא וארעא לא תתין ית עללתה ותיבדון בפריע מעל ארעא טבתא דיי יהיב לכון:
18. ותשוון ית פיתגמיא אלין על לבכון ועל נפשכון ותקטרון יתהון לאת על ידכון ויהון לתפלין בין עיניכון:
19. ותלפון יתהון ית בניכון למללא בהון במתבך בביתך ובמהכך באורחא ובמשכבך ובמקימך:
20. ותכתובינון על מזוזין ותקבעינון בסיפי בתך ובתרעך:
21. בדיל דיסגון יומיכון ויומי בניכון על ארעא דקיים יי לאבהתכון למיתן להון כיומי שמיא על ארעא:
22. ארי אם מיטר תטרון ית כל תפקידתא הדא דאנא מפקיד יתכון למעבדה למירחם ית יי אלהכון למהך בכל אורחן דתקנן קדמוהי ולאתקרבא לדחלתיה:
23. ויתריך יי ית כל עממיא האלין מן קדמיכון ותירתון עממין רברבין ותקיפין מינכון:
24. כל אתרא דתדרוך פרסת רגליכון ביה דילכון יהא מן מדברא וליבנן מן נהרא נהרא פרת ועד ימא מערבאה יהי תחומכון:
25. לא יתעתד אינש קדמיכון דחלתכון ואימתכון יתין יי אלהכון על אפי כל ארעא דתדרכון בה כמא דמליל לכון:

---

13 Adler (NL) notes that TO (like N and Ps-Jon) does not deviate from the MT, and translates "to them" in the masculine form, although the word "idols" is feminine, because the Israelites are understood to be serving the people (masculine) and not the idols. This is characteristic of TO, which attempts to remove disparaging statements about the Israelites, such as worshipping idols.

14 MT: *totafot*. See note on 6:8, and Exod 13:16. N and Ps-Jon also have "Tefillin," and Ps-Jon adds a gloss explaining the law.

15 MT: "and write them on the Mezuzot of your house and on your gates." TO and N add words for clarity. Ps-Jon has a teaching about the law of Mezuzot. See note on 6:9.

16 The metaphor "days lengthened" is not removed by the Targums since there is little possibility that it would be misunderstood by the masses.

17 MT: "in all His ways." See note on 8:6.

18 MT: "clinging to Him." See note on 4:4.

19 MT: "the hinder sea." So 34:2, Ezek 47:18, Zech 14:8, and Joel 2:20. M and Ps-Jon translate in the same way. N has "hinder sea," as do some TO texts. The Sifre identifies the sea similarly: to the great sea where the sun sets.

26. See,[20] I set before you this day blessings and curses:[21]
27. blessings[21] if you accept[22] the commandments of the Lord your God which I command you this day;
28. and curses[21] if you do not accept[22] the commandments of the Lord your God, but turn aside from the path which I command you this day, to go after the idols of the nations,[23] whom you have not known.
29. When the Lord your God brings you into the land which you are about to enter to possess it, you shall place those who bless[24] on Mount Gerizim and those who curse[25] on Mount Ebal.
30. Are they not on the other side of the Jordan, after the way of the setting of the sun, which is in the land of the Canaanites who dwell in the plain[26]—opposite Gilgal, beside the plain[27] of Moreh?[28]
31. For you shall cross the Jordan to enter and possess the land which the Lord your God is giving you. You shall possess it and settle in it.
32. Take care to observe all the statutes and laws that I have set before you this day.

[20] As in 1:8, some TO texts have the plural here (as do N and Ps-Jon). See that note. Sifre understands that each individual Israelite is being asked to make a decision. Thus, the plural is appropriate.

[21] MT has the singular form: "blessing and curse." TO's plural may refer to the blessings and curses detailed in chapter 27. TO may not be paralleling Sifre, which understands the verse to refer to "life and death," as in chapter 30. However, MT may be the collective form which the Targums usually render by plurals. Ps-Jon has the singular: "blessing and its contrary," avoiding "curses," which it does not want to associate with the Israelites. M makes the change in v. 29. N is literal.

[22] MT: "hear."

[23] MT: "other gods." TO, as well as Ps-Jon, removes the thought that idols are divine. N has a copyist's error. See note on 11:16.

[24] MT: "put the blessing." TO explains this verse by what is clarified in the MT later. The passage refers to the Levites who were to pronounce the blessing (28:14). Sifre also understands the verse in this way. TO may also be deviating here because the blessing itself (an intangible object) could not be "placed" anywhere. Cf. Gen 6:11, 12:2, and Num 23:21, 23. Ps-Jon has a long gloss in which the problem is avoided: "you shall place six tribes on Mount Gerizim and six tribes on Mount Ebal. They who recite the blessings shall turn their faces towards Mount Gerizim, and they who recite the curses shall turn their faces towards Mount Ebal." N is literal. Ps-Jon does not avoid "curses" here, but M does.

26. חזו דאנא יהיב קדמיכון יומא דין בירכן ולוטין:

27. ית בירכן אם תקבלון לפקודיא דיי אלהכון דאנא מפקיד יתכון יומא דין:

28. ולוטין אם לא תקבלון לפקודיא דיי אלהכון ותסטון מן אורחא דאנא מפקיד יתכון יומא דין למהך בתר טעות עממיא דלא ידעתון:

29. ויהי ארי יעילינך יי אלהך לארעא דאת עליל לתמן למירתה ותיתין ית מברכיא על טורא דגריזין וית מלטטיא על טורא דעיבל:

30. הלא אינון בעיברא דירדנא אחורי אורח מעלני שימשא בארע כנענאה דיתיב במישרא לקביל גלגלא בסטר מישרי מורה:

31. ארי אתון עברין ית ירדנא למיעל למירת ית ארעא דיי אלהכון יהיב לכון ותירתון יתה ותיתבון בה:

32. ותטרון למעבד ית כל קימיא וית דיניא דאנא יהיב קדמיכון יומא דין:

---

[25] MT: "the curse." See above note. Comp. Josh 8:30–35 and Deut 27:1–13, 31:10 ff.

[26] MT: "Arabah." See note on 1:1. N , Ps-Jon and Sifre translate like TO.

[27] MT: "terebinth." TO's rendering may have been designed to remove an association with centers of tree worship. Aberbach and Grossfeld (*Targum Onkelos to Genesis,* on 12:6) explain that TO translates "terebinth of Moreh" as "plain of Moreh" to remove Abraham from any association with centers of tree worship. U. Cassuto (*A Commentary on the Book of Exodus,* Hebrew version, p. 223) suggests that the translation counteracts the Samaritan belief in the holiness of a certain local tree. TO's wording parallels the view of R. Judah in Gen R. 42 and not R. Nehemiah, who translates "palace of Mamre." Its use of the more general "plain" instead of the specific "terebinth" may also reflect Sifre's interpretation that all references to this place are to the city of Shechem.

Ps-Jon has "by the vision of Mamre," and N, "plains of the vision," doing what Cassuto tells us TO wants to avoid. *Perush Jonathan* notes that Ps-Jon translates *ʾlwny mrh* as *ʾlwny mmrʾ,* found in 12:6, 13:18, 14:13, 18:1, and 35:4. Peshitta does likewise.

TJ to Joshua (24:26) and Judges (9:6) deviates like TO, using "plain" in Judges and *ʾlt*ʾ (post, pole, doorpost) in Joshua ("under the doorpost in the Lord's Temple")—the Targum could not render the word "plain" in Joshua since there is obviously no plain in the Temple.

[28] TO frequently replaces rhetorical renderings because they sometimes confuse people who read them as positive statements. See Introduction for examples. The Targum does not deviate here probably because it was not felt that this verse would be misunderstood, and even if it was, it would not lead to an improper idea. In contrast to other rhetorical questions, this verse is not phrased opposite its intended meaning, such as "Are they on *this side* of the Jordan."

Chapter XII

1. These are the laws and rules which you must carefully observe in the land that the Lord, God of your fathers, is giving you to possess, as long as you live on earth.

2. You must utterly destroy all the sites at which the nations you are to dispossess worshipped their idols,[1] in lofty mountains, on hills, or under any luxuriant tree.[2]

3. Tear down their altars,[3] smash their pillars, put their sacred posts to the fire, and cut down the images of their idols,[4] obliterating their name from that site.

4. Do not do so[5] before[6] the Lord your God,

5. but only to the site that the Lord your God will choose amidst all your tribes to establish His Shekinah.[7] There you should seek Him at the house[8] of His Shekinah,[9] there you are to come,

6. and there you are to bring your burnt offerings and sacred[10] sacrifices, your tithes and contributions[11] of your hands, your votive and freewill offerings and the firstlings of your herds and flocks.

7. You shall feast there before the Lord your God, happy in all your undertakings, you and with the people[12] of your households, with which the Lord your God has blessed you.

8. You shall not act at all as we now act here today; every man whatever is right in his own sight,

---

[1] MT: "gods."

[2] The precise meaning of the word in the MT rendered "luxuriant" is unknown (Reider, *Deuteronomy*). Ps-Jon translates "every tree of beautiful form," explaining the MT (*Perush Jonathan*). N has "praiseworthy tree."

[3] TO and Ps-Jon (but not N and the Samaritan Targum) use a derogatory term for altar, meaning "heap," see note on Deut 7:5. Sifre explains that the verse speaks of an altar built originally for idol worship.

[4] MT: "gods."

[5] TO generally paraphrases "do not" as "you do not have permission" but does not do so here. Ps-Jon translates in the latter manner and N renders like TO. See note on 12:17. It is unlikely that TO failed to deviate here to hint at the several

XII

1. אלין קימיא ודיניא דתטרון למעבד בארעא דיהב יי אלהא דאבהתך לך למירתה כל
יומיא דאתון קימין על ארעא:

2. אבדא תאבדון ית כל אתריא דפלחו תמן עממיא דאתון ירתין יתהון ית טעותהון
על טוריא רמיא ועל רמתא ותחות כל אילן עבוף:

3. ותתרעון ית אגוריהון ותתברון ית קמתהון ואשיריהון תוקדון בנורא וצילמי
טעותהון תקצצון ותובדון ית שומהון מן אתרא ההוא:

4. לא תעבדון כן קדם יי אלהכון:

5. אילהין לאתרא דיתרעי יי אלהכון מכל שבטיכון לאשראה שכינתיה תמן לבית
שכינתיה תתבעון ותיתון לתמן:

6. ותיתון לתמן עלותכון וניכסת קודשיכון וית מעסריכון וית אפרשות ידכון ונדריכון
ונדבתכון ובכורי תורכון וענכון:

7. ותיכלון תמן קדם יי אלהכון ותחדון בכל אושטות ידכון ואנש ואיניש בתיכון דברכך
יי אלהך:

8. לא תעבדון ככל דאנחנא עבדין כא יומא דין גבר כל דכשר בעינוהי:

teachings in the Sifre which are derived from the phrase "do not do so." Ps-Jon cites the halakhah of R. Ishmael from the Sifre, b. Shab. 102a, and b. Mac. 22a, that one may not blot out God's name from any writing. This verse is missing in the MS 27031 Ps-Jon text.

[6] TO and N render MT's *l* as "before."

[7] MT: "name." See Introduction for a discussion of the use of Shekinah. Like TO, Ps-Jon has Shekinah twice in the verse, but instead of God in the beginning, Ps-Jon has the Memra of God. N adds Shekinah once.

[8] TO, N and Ps-Jon may have added "house" to refer to the Temple in Jerusalem, as indicated in the Sifre. See 12:9. It is more likely that the Targums added "house" for clarity or to remove a close proximity between the Shekinah and the people.

[9] MT: "after his residence." TO and Ps-Jon add Shekinah. N has "Temple" rather than "Shekinah."

[10] The Targums add "sacred." This is the characteristic rendering of *Shelamim*, "peace offerings." See, for example, Lev 31:1 and 7:11 ff. See also note on v. 21.

[11] MT has *trwmt*, implying elevation. The Targums have a word implying separation.

[12] TO, N and Ps-Jon add "people." This is a characteristic addition; see, for example, 11:6.

9. because you have not yet come to the house[13] of rest and to the inheritance, which the Lord your God is giving you.

10. When you cross the Jordan and settle in the land that the Lord your God is allotting to you, and He gives you rest from all your enemies around you and you live in security,

11. then there shall be a site where the Lord your God will choose to establish his Shekinah,[14] there you shall bring everything that I command you: your burnt offerings and sacred[15] sacrifices, your tithes and the contributions[11] of your hands, and all the choice votive offerings that you vow before[16] the Lord.

12. And you shall rejoice before the Lord your God: you, your sons and daughters, your male and female slaves, along with the Levite of your settlement, for he has no part or inheritance among you.

13. Take care not to sacrifice your burnt offerings in any place you see,

14. but only in the place which the Lord will choose in one of your tribes. There you shall sacrifice your burnt offerings and there you shall observe all that I command you.

15. But with your whole desire, you may slaughter and eat meat, according to the blessing which the Lord your God has granted you, in all your settlement.[17] The unclean and the clean may eat it, as the flesh[18] of the gazelle and the deer.

16. But you must not partake of the blood; you shall pour it out on the ground like water.

17. It is not permissible[19] for you to partake in your settlement[17] of the tithes of your new grain or wine or oil, or of the firstlings of your herds and flocks, or of any of the votive offerings that you vow, or of your freewill offerings, or the contributions[11] of your hands.

18. Rather before the Lord your God you must eat it, in the place that the Lord your God will choose—you and your son and your daughter, your male and female slaves, and the Levite in your settlement[17]— and you shall rejoice before the Lord your God in all your undertakings.

19. Be sure not to neglect the Levite as long as you live in your land.

---

[13]TO and Ps-Jon add "house." They may understand the verse to refer to the Temple in Jerusalem, as does the Sifre (see also b. Zevachim 117a): "rest refers to

9. ארי לא אתיתון עד כען לבית ניחא ולאחסנתא דיי אלהך יהיב לך:

10. ותיעברון ית ירדנא ותיתבון בארעא דיי אלהכון מחסין יתכון ויניח לכון מכל בעלי דבביכון מסחור סחור ותיתבון לרוחצן:

11. ויהי אתרא דיתרעי יי אלהכון ביה לאשראה שכינתיה תמן לתמן תיתון ית כל דאנא מפקיד יתכון עלותכון ונכסת קודשיכון מעסריכון ואפרשות ידכון וכל שפר נדריכון דתדרון קדם יי:

12. ותיחדון קדם יי אלהכון אתון ובניכון ובנתכון ועבדיכון ואמהתכון וליואה דבקרויכון ארי לית ליה חולק ואחסנא עימכון:

13. איסתמר לך דילמא תסיק עלותך בכל אתרא דתיחזי:

14. אילהין באתרא דיתרעי יי בחד מן שבטך תמן תסיק עלותך ותמן תעביד כל דאנא מפקיד לך:

15. לחוד בכל רעות נפשך תיכוס ותיכול ביסרא כברכתא דיי אלהך דיהב לך בכל קרוך מסאבא ודכיא ייכליניה כבסר טביא ואילא:

16. לחוד דמא לא תיכלון על ארעא תישדיניה כמיא:

17. לית לך רשו למיכל בקרוך מעסר עיבורך וחמרך ומשחך ובכורי תורך וענך וכל נידרך דתידר ונדבתך ואפרשות ידך:

18. אילהין קדם יי אלהך תיכליניה באתרא דיתרעי יי אלהך ביה את וברך וברתך ועבדך ואמתך וליואה דבקרוך ותיחדי קדם יי אלהך בכל אושטות ידך:

19. אסתמר לך דילמא תשבוק ית ליואה כל יומך על ארעך:

Jerusalem, inheritance to Shiloh. . . . This is the view of R. Simeon, R. Judah had a contrary understanding." See 12:5 for a similar deviation. N does not have the addition.

[14] MT: "name." Like TO, N adds Shekinah. Ps-Jon also joins the Memra here.

[15] TO, N, and Ps-Jon add "sacred" as in 12:6, 27, and elsewhere.

[16] TO and Ps-Jon include "before" instead of *l*, "to." N has "to the name of the Lord."

[17] MT: "gates."

[18] The Targums add "flesh" for clarity. The deer and the gazelle are animals that may be eaten (cf. 14:5; Lev 11:1 ff.), but not sacrificed (Lev 1:1 ff.).

[19] MT: "you are unable." This is the usual Targumic translation, and all three do so here. See, however, 12:4, where TO does not deviate. Adler (NL) explains that the MT means that it is impossible to perform in this way because of a Torah commandment. Sifre uses the same language as the Targums.

20. When the Lord your God enlarges your territory, as he has promised
    you, and you say, "I shall eat meat," for you have the urge to eat
    meat, you may eat meat with your whole desire.

21. If the place where the Lord has chosen to establish His Shekinah[14] is
    too far from you, you may slaughter[20] your cattle or sheep that the
    Lord gives you, as I have instructed you; and you may eat in your
    settlement[17] with your whole desire.

22. However, as the flesh[21] of the gazelle and the deer is eaten, so you
    shall eat them: the unclean and the clean shall eat (of) them alike.

23. But be strong that you do not eat the blood; for the blood is the life,
    and you must not eat the life with the flesh.

24. You may not eat it; you must pour it out on the ground like water:

25. you must not eat it, so that it may go well with you and with your des-
    cendants after you, so that you may do what is right before[22] the Lord.

26. But your sacred things[23] which you have and votive donations, you
    shall take and go to the site that the Lord will choose.

27. You shall offer your burnt offerings, the flesh and the blood, on the
    altar of the Lord your God; and the blood of your sacred[24] sacrifices,
    shall be poured out[25] on the altar of the Lord your God, then you
    may eat the flesh.

[20] Sifre and b. Hullin 16b and 17a record a dispute between R. Ishmael and R.
Akiba about the interpretation of chapter 17 of Leviticus and chapter 12 of Deuteronomy. R. Ishmael interprets these chapters as teaching that when the Israelites
were in the wilderness, they were forbidden to slaughter and eat flesh at will.
Since, they lived near the sanctuary, animals fit for a sacrifice had to be sacrificed
at the Sanctuary before being eaten. R. Akiba interprets the verses as teaching that
in the wilderness the Israelites were permitted to eat the flesh of an animal no matter how it was killed (even by stabbing), because ritual slaughter was not intended
to be effective until the Israelites had entered the land of Israel.

Adler, NL to Lev 17:5, stating that TO uses *dbḥ* for slaughter not intended for
the Sanctuary and *nkst* for slaughter intended for the Sanctuary, even though the
MT has the same word, believes that TO differentiates to teach that in the wilder-
ness the Israelites could not eat flesh at will but must first bring it as a sacrifice.
(Adler does not note that some TO versions in Lev have the other word. Similarly,
there are different versions in Gen 46:1. N and Ps-Jon have *dbḥ* in Lev.) Thus,
Adler is in effect stating that TO is translating Lev according to the teaching of R.
Ishmael and not according to R. Akiba. (This seems to contradict those [like Ber-
liner] who maintain that TO generally translates according to the school of R.
Akiba. However, it is conceded that there are exceptions to this generality.)

20. ארי יפתי יי אלהך ית תחומך כמא דמליל לך ותימר איכול ביסרא ארי תתרעי
נפשך למיכל ביסרא בכל רעות נפשא תיכול ביסרא:

21. ארי יתרחק מינך אתרא דיתרעי יי אלהך לאשראה שכינתיה תמן ותיכוס מתורך
ומענך דיהב יי לך כמא דפקידתך ותיכול בקרוך בכל רעות נפשך:

22. ברם כמא דמתאכיל בסר טביא ואילא כן תיכליניה מסאבא ודכיא כחדא ייכליניה:

23. לחוד תקף בדיל דלא למיכל דמא ארי דמא הוא נפשא ולא תיכול נפשא עם
ביסרא:

24. לא תיכליניה על ארעא תישדיניה כמיא:

25. לא תיכליניה בדיל דייטב לך ולבנך בתרך ארי תעביד דכשר קדם יי:

26. לחוד קודשך דיהון לך ונידרך תטול ותיתי לאתרא דיתרעי יי:

27. ותעביד עלותך ביסרא ודמא על מדבחא דיי אלהך ודם ניכסת קודשך ישתפיך על
מדבחא דיי אלהך וביסרא תיכול:

Adler does not comment on this issue in Deut and takes no note of the apparently inconsistent translation here. Although this verse contains the same teaching as Lev 17:5, and TO should, therefore, render sacrifice *dbḥ*, TO (N and Ps-Jon) translates *nkst*, which would not be according to the view of R. Ishmael.

E. Z. Melammed (*Bible Commentators*, p. 184) states that TO uses *dbḥ* when the word implies an act connected with sacrifice, but when the sacrifice itself (the killing of the animal) is implied, TO has *nkst*. Thus, although Melammed does not mention it, there is no foundation to Adler's analysis.

See the Introduction for a discussion of the Targums and the halakhah.

21 The Targums add "flesh." See 12:15.

22 MT: "in the eyes of." TO and Ps-Jon avoid the anthropomorphism, which was apparently unseemly to these translators. TO and Ps-Jon generally render "doing right in the eyes of God" in this way. See also Gen 6:8, 38:7; Lev 10:19; Num 23:27, 24:1, 32:13; and note on 4:25. N is slightly different: "what is good and right before the Lord." N adds the extra word contained in the MT of 12:28, "good."

23 Some TO texts (but not Sperber's text or B) add "tenth," indicating that the verse refers to Maaser. This is contrary to Sifre and b. Temurah 17b, where Maaser is specifically excluded. It also contradicts the plain meaning of the verse, which implies sacred gifts dedicated on special occasions (comp. I Kings 7:51, 15:15; II Kings 12:19; II Sam 8:11). The Midrash and Talmud have R. Akiba's view that the reference is to Temurah (exchanges). This is another instance where a TO text apparently translates contrary to R. Akiba's opinion; see note on verse 21.

The addition of "tenth" is probably the result of a copyist's error. Ps-Jon adds "animals which are your sacred tenth," clearly rendering contrary to the halakhah. N is literal.

24 TO, N, and Ps-Jon add "sacred." See 12:6 and 12:11.

25 Patshegen and Luzzatto (OG) believe that TO (like N and Ps-Jon) does not

28. Observe and accept[26] all these words which I command you that it will go well with you and with your descendants after you forever, so that you do what is good and right before[27] the Lord your God.

29. When the Lord your God will destroy the nations, among which you are going, to dispossess them before you, and you will dispossess them and you will settle in their land,

30. take heed that you do not be ensnared[28] to follow them after they are destroyed before you and lest you inquire about their idols,[29] saying, "How did those nations worship their idols?[29] I will do so likewise."

31. You shall not act thus before[30] the Lord your God, for everything that is remote[31] before[32] the Lord, which He hates, they do for their idols,[29] for they even offer up their sons and daughters in fire to their idols.[29]

Chapter XIII

1. Every matter which I command you, observe to do it; you[1] should not add to it nor should you[1] diminish it.

2. If there arises among you a prophet or a dreamer of the dream and he gives you a sign or a wonder,

3. and if the sign or the wonder comes true, whereof he spoke with you as follows: "Let us go after the idols of the nations"[2]—whom you had not known—"and let us serve them,"

---

translate MT's "pour" into Aramaic, although it does so in v. 24, to emphasize the importance of the pouring. The MT does not have "toss" or "throw" as in Lev 3:2, 8, 13, and often. However, some TO versions have an Aramaic translation.

   [26] MT: "hear."

   [27] MT: "in the eyes of." See note on 12:25.

   [28] Rashi states: "Onkelos translates (this word) as 'snare.' However, I (Rashi) say that he was not careful in minutely examining the term." Rashi argues that it means "struck." M. M. Kasher (*Torah Shelemah* XVII, p. 317) explains that there are many instances where rabbinical commentators disagree with TO: TO's opinion

28. טר ותקביל ית כל פתגמיא האילין דאנא מפקיד לך בדיל דייטב לך ולבנך בתרך עד
עלמא ארי תעביד דתקין ודכשר קדם יי אלהך:
29. ארי ישיצי יי אלהך ית עממיא דאת עליל לתמן למירת יתהון מן קדמך ותירת
יתהון ותיתיב בארעהון:
30. איסתמר לך דילמא תיתקיל בתריהון בתר דישתיצון מן קדמך ודילמא תיתבע
לטעותהון למימר איכדין פלחין עממיא האילין ית טעותהון ואעביד כן אף אנא:
31. לא תעביד כן קדם יי אלהך ארי כל דמרחק קדם יי דסני עבדין לטעותהון ארי אף
ית בניהון וית בנתהון מוקדין בנורא לטעותהון:

XIII

1. ית כל פתגמיא דאנא מפקיד יתכון יתיה תטרון למעבד לא תוספון עלוהי ולא
תימינעון מיניה:
2. ארי יקום ביניך נביא או חלים חילמא ויתין לך את או מופת:
3. וייתי אתא ומופתא דמליל עימך למימר נהך בתר טעות עממיא דלא ידעתינין
ונפלחינין:

equals the view of other Tannaim, but commentators can interpret according to
another Tannaitic view. Rashi, however, does not indicate his reliance on the views
of other Tannaim. He based his interpretation upon the meaning of the term in
other verses. See the Introduction to this translation for a discussion of the Targums and halakhah, where the view is presented that TO was not composed to
inform about halakhah, but simply to translate according to the plain sense of the
text.

[29] N and Ps-Jon also substitute MT's "gods" with "idols."

[30] TO and N add "before" instead of *l*, "to." Ps-Jon has: "You shall not perform
such worship to the Lord."

[31] MT: "abhorrent." See note on 7:25.

[32] TO and N add "before," but not Ps-Jon.

[1] Adler (NL) explains that "you" (twice at the end of the verse) is rendered by
TO (N and Ps-Jon) in the plural, although the MT has the singular, for consistency.
The beginning of the verse is addressed to the people in the plural form.

[2] MT: "other gods." Ps-Jon reads like TO, but N has "other idols," which could
imply that God is also an idol.

4. do not accept[3] the words of that prophet or that dreamer of the dream. For the Lord your God is testing you to know whether you really love the Lord your God with all your hearts and with all your souls.

5. After the service[4] of the Lord your God shall you walk, and Him shall you fear; observe His commandments, and accept His Memra;[5] and before[6] Him shall you serve and come near to His fear.[7]

6. As for that prophet or dreamer of the dream, he shall be put to death; for he urged disloyalty to the Lord your God—who freed you from the land of Egypt and who redeemed you from the house of servitude[8]— to make you stray from the path that the Lord your God commanded you to follow. Thus you will sweep out the evildoer[9] from your midst.

7. If your brother, your mother's son, or your son or daughter, or the wife of your covenant,[10] or your closest friend advises[11] you in secret saying, "Come let us worship the idols of the nations"[2]—whom neither you nor your fathers have known—

8. from among the idols[12] of the nations around you, either near to you or distant from you, (anywhere) from one end of the earth to the other end of the earth—

---

[3] MT: "hear." As usual, Ps-Jon is like TO, but N has "hear."
See note on 8:2 regarding "to know."

[4] TO and Ps-Jon add "service," but some TO texts have "fear." See Introduction, b. Sotah 14a and Sifre. The Talmud asks: how can one walk after God? It responds that one should follow His attributes. N has Memra.

[5] MT: "unto His voice shall ye hearken." Sifre explains, "to the voice of His prophets." Adler (NL) states that TO does not include this teaching because it may have in mind the rabbinical statement: if you merit it, you will not need prophets. TO is not reflecting this theology. It renders the *peshat* and includes a characteristic deviation. N has "listen to the voice of His Memra," and Ps-Jon is like TO.

[6] The Targums add "before Him" instead of *ʾtw*.

[7] MT: "and Him shall you serve, and unto Him shall you cleave." See 11:22 and Sifre. Patshegen explains that TO does not add "before" here to avoid a redundancy. It was added in the previous phrase. N has: "and before Him shall you worship with a full heart, and unto the teachings of the Torah shall you cleave." Ps-Jon reads like TO.

[8] MT: "slaves."

4. לא תקביל לפיתגמי נביא ההוא או מן חלים חילמא ההוא ארי מנסי יי אלהכון
יתכון למידע האיתיכון רחמין ית יי אלהכון בכל לבכון ובכל נפשכון:

5. בתר פולחנא דיי אלהכון תהכון ויתיה תדחלון ית פיקודוהי תטרון ולמימריה
תקבלון וקדמוהי תפלחון ובדחלתיה תתקרבון:

6. ונביא ההוא או חלים חילמא ההוא יתקטיל ארי מליל סטיא על יי אלהכון דאפיק
יתכון מארעא דמצרים ודפרקך מבית עבדותא לאטעיותך מן ארחא דפקדך יי
אלהך למהך בה ותפלי עביד דביש מבינך:

7. ארי ימלכינך אחוך בר אימך או ברך או ברתך או איתת קימך או חברך דכנפשך
בסיתרא למימר נהך וניפלח לטעות עממיא דלא ידעתא את ואבהתך:

8. מטעות עממיא דבסחרניכון דקריבין לך או דרחיקין מינך מסיפי ארעא ועד סיפי
ארעא:

---

[9] TO (as N and Ps-Jon) adds "doer." The explanatory addition is also in the Sifre.

[10] MT: "wife of your bosom." The Targums render the phrase here as they do in 28:54, 56, and like TJ to Micah 7:5. E. Z. Melammed (*Bible Commentators*, pp. 178, 9) notes that the Targums took the words "wife of your covenant" from Mal 2:14.

Adler (NL) notes that TO translates the word which has a *yud* in the MT, meaning "bosom," as if it has no *yud* and means "law." Schefftel (BO) explains TO's word as "marriage." Wertheimer (*Or*) explains the word as "loin" or "sustaining." Wertheimer believes that both the MT and TO are emphasizing that because of the closeness of the wife to her husband, there is a greater likelihood of his being misled by her. Komlosh (*Hamikra*, p. 236) states the deviation is one of many examples where TO avoids picturesque language.

These interpretations may not be correct. TO's real motive in rendering *ḥyq* by *qymʾ* may be to avoid an indelicacy. Cf. Gen 16:5, where TO deletes "bosom" from the phrase "I myself gave you my maid-servant into your bosom" because the rabbis were sternly denouncing cohabitation with female servants and TO did not want to depict Abraham as violating this later injunction. Cf. TJ to I Kings 1:2, which likewise avoids an accurate translation of the word "bosom," probably for the same reason. TO renders MT's "bosom" in Exod 4:6,7, as "upper garment," in Num 11:12 as "strength," and in Deut 28:56, 57, as "covenant."

FT has "your wife who sleeps with you"; Ps-Jon and M, "your wife sleeps on your bosom"; and N is literal.

[11] MT: "entices." Adler (NL) explains that TO uses "advice" not "entices" because all enticement comes through advice suggesting that the proposed behavior is good. See Sifre for the same thought. Ps-Jon is like TO but N is literal.

[12] MT: "gods." N is like TO. Ps-Jon has: "idols of the seven nations."

9. do not assent to him or accept[13] from him, nor shall your eye pity him, nor shall you spare, nor shall you conceal him,

10. but surely kill him. Let your hand be the first against him to put him to death, and the hand of the rest of the people thereafter.

11. Stone him with stones, that he die, for he sought to make you go astray from the fear[14] of the Lord your God, who brought you out of the land of Egypt, out of the house of servitude.[8]

12. Thus all Israel will hear and fear, and shall do no more any such evil things in your midst.

13. If you hear in one of your settlements that the Lord your God is giving you to dwell therein as follows:

14. that some bad fellows[15] from among you have gone out and subverted the inhabitants of their town, saying, "Come let us worship the idols of the nations"[2]—whom you have not known—

15. you shall investigate and inquire and interrogate thoroughly. If it is true, the fact is established—that the abhorrent[16] thing was perpetrated in your midst—

16. you should surely smite the inhabitants of that town with the edge[17] of the sword destroying it utterly, and all that is therein, and the cattle thereof, with the edge[17] of the sword;

---

[13] MT: "hear."

[14] TO and Ps-Jon add "fear" (also translated "service"). N has Memra.

[15] *Belial* is found twenty five times in the Hebrew Bible, including twice in the Pentateuch: here and Deut 15:9. The word occurs about forty times in Qumran literature, mostly in the War Scroll (sixteen times) and the Thanksgiving Hymns (thirteen times). It is found once in the NT: II Cor 6:15.

The Targums use different words to explain the concept, but each is similar. TO and TJ (with one exception) have *rs*, "evil." Ps-Jon:*zdnynt*, "insolent." Ps-Jon adds "against the teaching of the sages that are among you," showing that these are people who do not accept the Torah. N to 13:14: *bny ʿyzm byšn*, "bad advice." N to 15:9 *zydnh*, "insolent." TJ to I Sam 25:25: *sty*, "fool." Targum to Prov 16:12 and 27: *ṭlwm*, "wrongdoer."

Sifre explains the term as a composite word: *bly ʿwl*, "without a yoke," for they have removed the yoke of the Omnipresent. *Perush Jonathan* understands Ps-Jon similarly. Bertinoro on b. Sanh. 111b understands it as the composite *bly yʿl*, "those who do not ascend to the future world." Saadya translates 13:15 as "unbelievers" and 15:9 as "foolish." Rashbam explains it as "a thing of evil people." Ibn Ezra comments: "this is a name, but some say it is a composite word,

9. לא תיבי ליה ולא תקביל מיניה ולא תחוס עינך עלוהי ולא תרחים ולא תכסי
עלוהי:

10. ארי מיקטל תקטלניה ידך תהא ביה בקדמיתא למקטלניה וידא כל עמא בבתריתא:

11. ותרגמיניה באבניא וימות ארי בעא לאטעיותך מדחלתא דיי אלהך דאפקך מארעא
דמצרים מבית עבדותא:

12. וכל ישראל ישמעון וידחלון ולא יוספון למעבד כפתגמא בישא הדין בינך:

13. ארי תשמע בחדא מקרוך דיי אלהך יהיב לך למיתב תמן למימר:

14. נפקו גברין בני רישעא מבינך ואטעיו ית יתבי קרתהון למימר נהך וניפלח לטעות
עממיא דלא ידעתון:

15. ותיתבע ותיבדוק ותישאל יאות והא קושטא כיון פתגמא אתעבידת תועיבתא הדא
בינך:

16. מימחא תימחי ית יתבי קרתא ההיא לפתגם דחרב גמר יתה וית כל דבה וית בעירה
לפתגם דחרב:

bly yʿl, "without success." It appears likely that TO is doing no more than explaining the term. It is unlikely that TO is deviating to avoid the idea (hinted at by Ibn Ezra) that the term applies to a supernatural being.

In post-biblical literature, *belial* generally refers to Satan. Evil men are dominated by him or his attendant spirits. See, for example, "Of the Works of Belial" (*The Dead Sea Scriptures*, by T. H. Gaster, Anchor Press, 1976, p. 71), where he is shown as catching men in the snares of lewdness, lucre, and profanity. The sectarian belief in *belial* as the opponent of God probably owes much to Persian dualism, where the eternal antagonists Asha (Right) and Druj (Perversity) are portrayed as destined to engage in a final Armageddon (*Encyclopedia Judaica*, Keter Publishing House, Jerusalem, 1972, cols. 427 f.). See also II Cor 6:15, the sole mention of *belial* in the NT, where the term is synonymous with Satan, and the author's *Targumic Studies* for a discussion of the use of the "evil inclination" by the Targums other than TO.

[16] TO does not deviate here and render *mrḥq*, "remote," since the unseemly feeling of abhorrence is not ascribed explicitly to God. Comp. 18:19.

[17] MT has an idiomatic phrase: "according to the mouth of the sword." The word "mouth" is used for "edge." TO, N, and Ps-Jon translate literally: "the word (or edge) of the sword."

Lowenstein (NH, pp. 7–10) explains the translation as meaning "by the word of prayer"; that is, what is described is the result of prayer. See 19:15 for a similar interpretation. Whereas Lowenstein's understanding of *lpy ḥrb* is not explicit in TO, a somewhat similar interpretation of the two words is found in Ps-Jon to Exod 17:13, "by the word of the Memra of Lord, with death by sword," and Num 21:24 "they killed with the name of the Lord, with the edge of the sword."

17. gather all its spoils into the open square, and burn the town and all its spoil totally before[18] the Lord your God. And it shall remain an everlasting ruin of destruction,[19] it shall not be built again.

18. Let nothing that has been doomed stick to your hand, in order that the Lord may turn from His blazing anger[20] and show you compassion, and have compassion upon you to increase you as He confirmed[21] to your fathers.

19. But you shall accept[13] the Memra[22] of the Lord your God, keeping all His commandments which I order you this day, doing what is right before[23] the Lord your God.

Chapter XIV

1. You are the children before[1] the Lord your God. You shall not gash yourselves[2] nor make a baldness between your eyes because of the dead.

2. For you are a holy people before[1] the Lord your God: the Lord your God chose you to be His beloved[3] people from among all people on earth.

3. You shall not eat anything remote.[4]

4. This (type) of animal you may eat: the ox, the lamb of a sheep and the young of a goat,

---

[18] TO, N, and Ps-Jon add "before" instead of *l*, "to."

[19] TO, like Ps-Jon, adds "destruction." See Josh 6:17, 26. N has "an everlasting ruin," without the addition.

Lowenstein (NH) explains that TO is in effect informing us that in the dispute between R. Akiba and R. Jose (b. Sanh. 111b) the law is according to R. Jose, who said it shall be a heap forever. It may not be converted into gardens and orchards. R. Akiba said it may be converted into gardens and orchards. Sifre also has R. Jose's opinion. However, Lowenstein's interpretation is not certain. TO probably added *hryb* as an explanatory word, since *tl l'lm* or *tl 'lm* would have been difficult to understand (if not meaningless) in Aramaic.

[20] TO and Ps-Jon do not avoid the anthropopathisms. God can become "angry" and can "change His mind." N adds Memra. Probably the two Targums under-

17. וית כל עדאה תכנוש לגו פתאה ותוקיד בנורא ית קרתא וית כל עדאה גמיר קדם יי אלהך ותהי תל חרוב לעלם לא תתבני עוד:

18. ולא ידבק בידך מידעם מן חירמא בדיל דיתוב יי מתקוף רוגזיה ויתין לך רחמין וירחים עלך ויסגינך כמא דקיים לאבהתך:

19. ארי תקביל למימרא דיי אלהך למיטר ית כל פיקודוהי דאנא מפקיד לך יומא דין למעבד דכשר קדם יי אלהך:

XIV

1. בנין אתון קדם יי אלהכון לא תתחממון ולא תשוון מרט בין עיניכון על מית:

2. ארי עם קדיש את קדם יי אלהך ובך איתרעי יי למהוי ליה לעם חביב מכל עממיא דעל אפי ארעא:

3. לא תיכול כל דמרחק:

4. דין בעירא דתיכלון תורין אימרין דרחלין וגדין דעזין:

---

stood the phrases as easily comprehended metaphors. It is also possible that the Targums conceived of anger as being something separated from God. Sifre explains: "as long as idol worship exists there is anger in the world."

[21] MT: "swore."

[22] MT: "voice." Ps-Jon also has Memra. N has "the voice of the Memra."

[23] MT: "in the eyes of." The Targums remove the anthropomorphism. See notes on 4:25 and 12:25. N has "what is good and right before the Lord your God."

[1] TO renders MT's *l* as "before." N and Ps-Jon also add "beloved" (children) from verse 2. Ps-Jon removes the concept of "divine children" by translating: "like beloved children," but N does not.

[2] H. Torczymer ("Toward an Understanding of the Aramaic Translation of the Torah," *Magnes Anniversary Book* [1938]: 143–151) states that TO's *lʾ tthmmwn* is an error. It should be a literal rendering of *lʾ tthmswn*. This is clear from Ps-Jon's literal translation.

[3] MT: *segulah*, "a people of unique value" (Reider, *Deuteronomy*). See 7:6 and compare Eccl 2:8 and I Chron 29:3, where the word is used for a private treasure belonging to kings. Ps-Jon translates like TO, as does the Sifre, but N has "beloved like a special possession."

[4] MT: "abhorrent." This is a characteristic deviation because the unseemly emotion is ascribed to God (v. 2). Comp. 13:15, 17:1, 18:19, etc., which do not have the deviation, since these verses describe human reactions.

5. the deer, the gazelle, the roebuck, the wild goat, the ibex, the wild ox, the mountain goat,[5]

6. and any animal that has cloven hoofs, and that divides the hoof in two parts, (and) chews the cud, among the cattle, such you may eat.

7. But these you shall not eat of those which chew the cud or have cloven hoofs which are cleft through: the camel, the hare, and the coney. Although they chew the cud, they part not the hoof: they are unclean for you.

8. Also the swine—for although it parts the hoof, it does not chew the cud—is unclean for you. You shall not eat of their flesh or touch their carcass.

9. These you may eat of all that are in the water: all that have fins and scales shall you eat.

10. But all that have no fins and scales you may not eat; it is unclean for you.

11. You may eat any clean[6] bird.

12. But these are they of which you may not eat: the eagle, the vulture, the black vulture;

13. the kite, the falcon, and the buzzard of any variety;

14. every variety of raven;

15. the ostrich, the nighthawk, the sea gull, and the hawk of any variety;

16. the little owl, the great owl, and the white owl;

17. the pelican, the bustard, and the cormorant;

18. the stork,[6a] any variety of ibis, the mountain cock,[7] and the bat.

---

[5] A number of these creatures cannot be identified with certainty, especially those TO translates as wild ox and mountain goat.

An Aramaic Targum is mentioned eighteen times in the Babylonian Talmud, four citations of which are from Deuteronomy: 7:9, 14:5, 25:18, and 28:42. There is no certainty that the references are to our TO text. They may refer to a completely different Targum or one upon which TO is based.

On this verse, the Talmud, in b. Hull. 80a, states: "The rabbis maintain, since the Targum renders (*Teo* as) 'the wild ox,' it is certainly a species of cattle, whereas R. Jose felt that since it is reckoned together with the other species of wild animals, it is a species of wild animal." See also m. Kel. 8:6, t. Kel. 1:9, the Sifre, and y. Kel. 8:4.

‏5. אילא וטביא ויחמורא ויעלא ורימא ותורבלא ודיצא:
‏6. וכל בעירא דסדיקא פרסתה ומטלפן טלפין תרתין פרסתה מסקא פישרא בבעירא יתה תיכלון:
‏7. ברם ית דין לא תיכלון ממסקי פישרא ומסדיקי פרסתא מטלפי טילפיא ית גמלא וית ארנבא וית טפזא ארי מסקי פישרא אינון ופרסתהון לא סדיקא מסאבין אינון לכון:
‏8. וית חזירא ארי סדיק פרסתא הוא ולא פשר מסאב הוא לכון מבסרהון לא תיכלון ובנבילתהון לא תקרבון:
‏9. ית דין תיכלון מכל דבמיא כל דליה ציצין וקלפין תיכלון:
‏10. וכל דלית ליה ציצין וקלפין לא תיכלון מסאב הוא לכון:
‏11. כל צפר דכי תיכלון:
‏12. ודין דלא תיכלון מינהון נישרא וער ועוזיא:
‏13. ובת כנפא וטרפיתא ודיתה ליזנה:
‏14. וית כל עורבא ליזניה:
‏15. וית בת נעמיתא וציצא וציפר שחפא ונצא ליזנוהי:
‏16. קדיא וקיפופא ובותא:
‏17. וקתא וירקריתא ושלינונא:
‏18. וחוריתא ואיבו ליזנה ונגר טורא ועטליפא:

TO and Ps-Jon translate like the rabbis, but N renders like R. Jose (Kasher, *Torah Shelemah* XXVI, p. 27).

[6] Some of these creatures cannot be identified with certainty. J. A. Emerton, *JSS* 7 (1962): 204–11, discusses the Targumic renderings of Deut 14:12–18 and Lev 11:13–19. He shows that the Targums differed as to the meaning of the names and that the translators did not know the meaning of some of them. The rabbis also had the same difficulty (b. Hul. 63a–b). The Peshitta resolved the problem of meaning by omitting some of the words.

[6a] *Sefer Hasidim* (sec. 10) defines a hasid (pious person) as one who allows himself to become white (ashamed) without returning insult. His face will shine brightly in the hereafter. The author(s) based his interpretation on TO's rendering of *hasidah* (meaning "stork" and "pious") as *ḥwryt'* (literally, "white one"). This is only a play on words: the stork is called "white" in Aramaic to differentiate it from the heron and ibis which are related birds.

[7] TO parallels the Talmudic translation (b. Hul. 63a). Saadya, Rashi, and others translate it "hoopoe." N and Ps-Jon have the same word as TO here.

19. All winged swarming things are unclean for you: they may not be eaten.

20. You may eat any clean-winged creatures.

21. You shall not eat any carcass (i.e., that which died a natural death); to the uncircumcised sojourners[8] in your settlement[8a] give it to eat, or sell it to a foreigner.[9] For you are a holy people before[10] the Lord your God. You shall not eat flesh with milk.[11]

22. You shall surely tithe all the yield of your sowing that the field brings forth every year.

23. You shall eat before the Lord your God, in the place where He will choose to establish His Shekinah,[12] the tithes of your new grain and wine and oil, and the firstlings of your herd and flock, so that you may learn to revere before[13] the Lord your God forever.

24. Should the distance be too great for you, should you be unable to transport it, because the place is too far from you, where the Lord your God has chosen to establish His Shekinah[12] there, because the Lord your God has blessed you,

25. you may convert them into money. Wrap up the money in your hand and go to the place that the Lord your God will choose,

26. and spend the money on anything you want—cattle, sheep, new and old wine[14]—or on anything you may desire. And you shall feast there before the Lord your God, and you shall rejoice with the people[15] of your household.

27. But do not forsake the Levite in your settlement[8a], for he has no portion or inheritance with you.

---

[8] MT: *ger.* TO, like the Sifre, refers to one who has undertaken not to worship idols but has not converted to Judaism. N has "a sojourner of the nations," and Ps-Jon, "an uncircumcised *ger.*" TO does not render the word as "proselyte" since a proselyte, like any other Jew, is prohibited from eating non-kosher food. See Lev 17:15 for a contrary rule applicable to non-Jews in the desert.

[8a] MT: "gates."

[9] MT: "stranger." TO, N, and Ps-Jon are more explicit, as is the Sifre. The word *nkry* in the MT is not always identical with a non-Israelite, cf. Prov 27:2 and Eccl 6:2. Hence the need for the Targums to use *br ʿmmyn*. The term is also found in Deut 15:3, 23:21, and 29:21.

19. וכל ריחשא דעופא מסאב הוא לכון לא יתאכלון:
20. כל עוף דכי תיכלון:
21. לא תיכלון כל נבילא לתותב ערל דבקרוך תתנינה וייכלינה או תזבנינה לבר עממין ארי עם קדיש את קדם יי אלהך לא תיכלון בסר בחלב:
22. עסרא תעסר ית כל עללת זרעך דיפיק חקלא שנא שנא:
23. ותיכול קדם יי אלהך באתרא דיתרעי לאשראה שכינתיה תמן מעסר עיבורך חמרך ומישחך ובכורי תורך וענך בדיל דתילף למידחל קדם יי אלהך כל יומיא:
24. וארי תסגי מינך ארחא ארי לא תיכול למיטליה ארי יתרחק מינך אתרא דיתרעי יי אלהך לאשראה שכנתיה תמן ארי יברכינך יי אלהך:
25. ותיתין בכספא ותצור כספא בידך ותהך לאתרא דיתרעי יי אלהך ביה:
26. ותיתין כספא בכל דתתרעי נפשך בתורי ובענא ובחמר חדת ועתיק ובכל דתשאלינך נפשך ותיכול תמן קדם יי אלהך ותיחדי את ואינש ביתך:
27. וליואה דבקרוך לא תשבקניה ארי לית ליה חולק ואחסנא עימך:

---

[10] The Targums render "before" instead of *l*, "to."

[11] MT: "You shall not seethe a kid in its mother's milk." Sifre and the Talmud (b. Hul. 113a) note that the prohibition of seething meat in milk is mentioned in the Torah three times (here, Exod 23:19 and 34:26). The wording is the same but different rules are derived from each verse: a prohibition against eating, having benefit, and cooking. TO phrases each verse the same. See also Mekhilta on Exod 23:19, b. Sanh. 46b, b. Hul. 113b, 114a, and 115b. E. Z. Melammed (*Bible Commentators,* p. 184) states that the author(s) of TO only wanted to mention the general commandment and not all of its details. See Introduction for a discussion of TO's failure to explain the halakhah.

Ps-Jon has: "you are not permitted to boil, much less to eat, meat with milk when both are mixed together." N has: "You shall not boil or eat meat with milk mixed together."

[12] MT: "name." N and Ps-Jon also add Shekinah.

[13] TO, N and Ps-Jon render *'t* with "before."

[14] TO translates *shekkar* as "old wine" in all places but Lev 10:9. The context of Lev requires the rendering "intoxicating" because the priests were not obligated to abstain totally. This rendering parallels the halakhah in b. Kerithoth 13b. R. Eleazar taught that *shekkar* in Lev implies the prohibition against drinking a quantity of wine that causes intoxication. However, if one dilutes it with water, one is not guilty. The other verses, such as Num 6:3 and Deut 14:26, are not translated "intoxicating" because these verses refer to any quantity of wine, even less than that which causes intoxication. N and Ps-Jon translate here like TO.

[15] TO (as N and Ps-Jon) adds "people."

28. After a period of three years you shall bring out all the tithe of your field of that year, but leave it within your settlement.

29. Then the Levite shall come, who has no portion or inheritance with you, and the proselyte,[16] the orphan, and the widow in your settlement and eat and be satisfied, so that the Lord your God may bless you in all the enterprises of your hand which you undertake.

Chapter XV

1. At the end of seven years, you shall make a release.

2. This is the nature of the release: every creditor that lends anything to his neighbor[1] shall release it; he shall not claim it of his neighbor or kinsman, for a release is proclaimed before[2] the Lord.

3. Of a foreigner[3] you may claim it, but whatever is yours with your kinsmen your hand shall release.

4. Save when there shall be no needy among you[4]—since the Lord your God will bless you in the land which the Lord your God is giving you as an inheritance to possess it—

5. if only you carefully accept[5] the Memra[6] of the Lord your God to observe and carry out all this commandment that I order you this day.

6. For the Lord your God will bless you as He told you: you will extend loans to many nations, but you will not borrow; you will dominate many nations, but they will not dominate you.

---

[16] Here TO has "proselyte" whereas earlier, in verse 21, as required by the context, the word is translated "stranger." N and Ps-Jon have "stranger." See M. Ohara, VI 23 (1973). 391–394.

[1] MT's "hand," which is not retained in TO, is understood in the accusative. See Neh 10:32. Schefftel (BO on Gen 16:12) understands it as referring to "money," which is implied in TO. Wertheimer (*Or*) understands it as meaning "power." TO's interpretation is also in the Sifre.

MT's infinitive *šmwṭ* is rendered by TO in the imperfect.

Ps-Jon paraphrases the verse as follows: "And this is the indication of the law of Shemittah, every man who controls a loan which was lent to his neighbor, shall not have power to coerce his neighbor in demanding his loan, nor of his brother, a

28. מסוף תלת שנין תפיק ית כל מעסר עללתך בשתא ההיא ותצנע בקירוך:
29. וייתי ליואה ארי לית ליה חולק ואחסנא עימך וגיורא ויתמא וארמלתא דבקרוך וייכלון ויסבעון בדיל דיברכינך יי אלהך בכל עובדי ידך דתעביד:

XV

1. מסוף שבע שנין תעביד שמיטתא:
2. ודין פתגם שמיטתא דישמיט כל גבר מרי רשו דירשי בחבריה ולא יתבע מן חבריה ומן אחוהי ארי קרא שמיטתא קדם יי:
3. מן בר עממין תתבע ודיהי לך עם אחוך תשמיט ידך:
4. לחוד ארי לא יהי בך מסכינא ארי ברכא יברכינך יי בארעא דיי אלהך יהיב לך אחסנא למירתה:
5. לחוד אם קבלא תקביל למימרא דיי אלהך למיטר למעבד ית כל תפקידתא הדא דאנא מפקיד לך יומא דין:
6. ארי יי אלהך ברכך כמא דמליל לך ותוזיף לעממין סגיאין ואת לא תזיף ותשלוט בעממין סגיאין ובך לא ישלטון:

son of Israel, because the *Beth Din* (Court) has proclaimed a Shemittah before the Lord." N has "And this is the law of Shemittah, every man who controls a loan should drop the hand which lent to his neighbor. . . . "

[2] TO and N have "before" instead of MT's *l*. Ps-Jon also adds *Beth Din* as indicated in note 1. This would parallel the halakhah that the Shemittah can only be proclaimed by a *Beth Din*. Since there is no *Beth Din* today, there is no Shemittah (Kasher, *Torah Shelemah* XXVI, p. 187).

TO translates *'t*, which appears twice in the verse as "from," but N is literal.

[3] MT: *nkr*, "stranger." TO, N, and Ps-Jon have *br 'mmyn*, literally, "son of nations." See note on 14:21.

[4] Verses 4 and 11 seem to contradict each other and are explained in rabbinical literature. Verse 4 states, "There shall be no needy among you," while verse 11 indicates, "For there will never cease to be needy ones in your land." TO has no explanatory addition in either verse. However, Ps-Jon resolves the problem by including in the first verse, "if you are involved in doing the Torah commandments," and in the second, "if the Israelites do not obey the Torah commandments." N combines both points in verse 11. The teaching is in the Sifre.

[5] MT: "hear."

[6] MT: "voice." N has "the voice of the Memra."

7. If there is a needy person among you, one of your kinsmen, in any settlement[7] of yours, in your land that the Lord your God is giving you, do not harden your heart nor shut your hand towards your needy kinsman.

8. Rather, you surely must open your hand and surely lend him sufficient for his need, in that which he lacks.

9. Beware lest you harbor in your heart a thought, in wickedness,[8] saying, "The seventh year is approaching, the year of release," so that your eye is evil against your needy kinsman and give him nothing. He will cry against you before[9] the Lord and you will incur guilt.

10. You shall surely give him, and your heart shall not be grieved when you give to him; because for this thing the Lord your God will bless you in all your efforts and in all that you put your hand.

11. For there will never cease to be needy ones in the land, which is why I command you: surely open your hand to your kinsman, to your poor and your needy in your land.

12. If your brother, an Israelite male, or Israelite female, is sold to you, he shall serve you six years, and in the seventh year you shall set him free as a free person[10] from you.

13. When you set him free as a free person[10] from you, do not set him free empty-handed:

14. You shall surely furnish[11] him out of your flock, threshing floor, and vat, with which the Lord your God has blessed you, (that) give to him.

15. Remember that you were a slave in the land of Egypt and the Lord your God redeemed you; therefore I command you this thing today.

16. But should he say to you, "I will not leave you"—for he loves you and the people[12] of your household, because he is happy with you—

17. you shall take an awl and put it through his ear and into the door, and he shall become your slave, serving[13] in perpetuity. Do the same with your female slave.[14]

---

[7] MT: "gates."

[8] MT: *belial*. Verse 13:14 mentions *belial* and TO also translates it there as "evil." See note *ad loc.*

[9] MT: "to." N and Ps-Jon read like TO.

[10] TO and Ps-Jon replace MT's "Hebrew" with "Israelite,"(like Mekilta,

7. ארי יהא בך מסכינא חד מאחך בחדא מקרוך בארעך דיי אלהך יהיב לך לא
תתקיף ית ליבך ולא תקפוץ ית ידך מאחוך מסכינא:

8. ארי מפתח תפתח ית ידך ליה ואוזפא תוזפניה כמיסת חוסרניה דיחסיר ליה:

9. אסתמר לך דילמא יהי פתגמא עם ליבך ברשע למימר קריבת שתא שביעיתא
שתא דשמטתא ותבאש עינך באחוך מסכינא ולא תיתין ליה ויקרי עלך קדם יי ויהי
בך חובא:

10. מיתן תיתין ליה ולא יבאש ליבך במיתנך ליה ארי בדיל פתגמא הדין יברכינך יי
אלהך בכל עובדך ובכל אושטות ידך:

11. ארי לא יפסוק מסכינא מגו ארעא על כן אנא מפקיד לך למימר מפתח תפתח ית
ידך לאחוך לעניך ולמסכינך בארעך:

12. ארי יזדבן לך אחוך בר ישראל או בת ישראל ויפלחינך שית שנין ובשתא
שביעיתא תפטרניה בר חירין מעימך:

13. וארי תפטרניה בר חירין מעימך לא תפטרניה ריקן:

14. אפרשא תפריש ליה מענך ומאידרך וממעצרתך דברכך יי אלהך תיתין ליה:

15. ותידכר ארי עבדא הויתא בארעא דמצרים ופרקך יי אלהך על כן אנא מפקיד לך
ית פתגמא הדין יומא דין:

16. ויהי ארי יימר לך לא איפוק מעימך ארי ריחמך ולאינש ביתך ארי טב ליה עימך:

17. ותיסב ית מרצעא ותיתין באודניה ובדשא ויהי לך עבד פלח לעלם ואף לאמתך
תעביד כן:

Nezikin I) but N retains "Hebrew." TO and Ps-Jon render MT's "free" by words
literally meaning "free man," while N has "freedom." See v. 18.

[11] MT's *ḥʿnq tʿnyq* are unique to this verse. Some understand the words as
meaning something conspicuous or a neck jewel (see Rashi). Wertheimer (*Or*)
notes that this is an instance where TO does not translate words but explains the
subject. N is like TO, but Ps-Jon has "Comfort him."

[12] The Targums characteristically add "people." B. Ked. 22a, Maimonides,
Hilkhoth Avadim 3:5, etc., have the laws for the people of the household.

[13] The Targums add "serving" for clarity. Comp: Exod 21:6. E. Z. Melammed
(*Bible Commentators*, p. 206) suggests that TO does not add the halakhah here
(that the slave only serves until the Jubilee) because slavery did not exist when TO
was composed and there was, therefore, no need to teach the halakhah. The
halakhah is in Ps-Jon, but not N. See the Introduction for a discussion of halakhah
in the Targums.

[14] While TO is literal, Ps-Jon adds a gloss: "And also to your female slave you
should write a document of freedom and give it to her." Ps-Jon to Exod 21:11 is
similar, paralleling the Mekhilta, *loc.cit.*

18. It shall not seem hard to you when you do set him free as a free person[15] from you, because[16] he gave you double the service of a hired man while serving you six years. Moreover, the Lord your God will bless you in all you do.

19. You shall consecrate before[17] the Lord your God all firstling males that are born among your herd and among your flock: you must not work your firstling ox or shear your firstling sheep.

20. Before the Lord your God you shall eat it annually, in the place the Lord will choose, you and the people[18] of your household.

21. But if it has a defect, lameness or blindness, any serious defect, you shall not sacrifice it before[19] the Lord your God.

22. Eat it in your settlement,[20] the unclean among you no less than the clean, just like the flesh[21] of the gazelle and the deer.

23. Only you must not eat its blood; you shall pour it out on the ground like water.

Chapter XVI

1. Observe the month of Abib and make a passover (sacrifice) before[1] the Lord your God, for it was in the month of Abib, that the Lord your God freed you from Egypt and did miracles for you during the night.[2]

2. You shall slaughter the passover (sacrifice) before[1] the Lord your God, from[3] the lamb and sacred sacrifices[4] from [3] your herd, in the place where the Lord will choose to cause his Shekinah[5] to dwell.

---

[15] TO and Ps-Jon add *br*, "person," but N does not.

[16] MT: *ky*. TO: *ʿry ʾl*. N and Ps-Jon: *ʾrwm*.

[17] TO and Ps-Jon change *l* to "before." N has "to the name of the Lord your God."

[18] The Targums add "people."

[19] The Targums render *l* "before."

[20] MT: "gates." TO has the singular.

[21] The Targums add "flesh" as in 12:15, 22.

[1] TO, N, and Ps-Jon have "before" instead of MT's *l*, "to."

[2] TO adds "and did miracles for you." This may have been prompted by the contradiction noted by Sifre and b. Ber. 9a: "But did they not go forth by day, as it

18. לא יקשי בעינך במפטרך יתיה בר חירין מעימך ארי על חד תרין כאגר אגירא
פלחך שית שנין ויברכינך יי אלהך בכל דתעביד:

19. כל בוכרא דיתיליד בתורך ובענך דיכרין תקדיש קדם יי אלהך לא תפלח בבוכרא
דתורך ולא תיגוז בוכרא דענך:

20. קדם יי אלהך תיכליניה שנא בשנא בעתרא דיתרעי יי את ואינש ביתך:

21. וארי יהא ביה מומא חגיר או עויר כל מום ביש לא תכסניה קדם יי אלהך:

22. בקרוך תיבליניה מסאבא ודכיא כחדא כבסר טביא ואילא:

23. לחוד ית דמיה לא תיכול על ארעא תישדיניה כמיא:

XVI

1. טר ית ירחא דאביבא ותעביד פיסחא קדם יי אלהך ארי בירחא דאביבא אפקך יי
אלהך ממצרים ועבד לך ניסין בליליא:

2. ותיכוס פיסחא קדם יי אלהך מן בני ענא וניכסת קודשיא מן תורי באתרא דיתרעי
יי לאשראה שכנתיה תמן:

is said (Num 33:3): 'on the morrow after the passover the children of Israel went out'? But it states that they went out by night, after the miracle of the plague of the firstborn, because Pharaoh gave them permission to go forth by night after the miracles; as it is said (Exod 12:31): 'and he called for Moses and Aaron by night and said, 'Rise up, go forth from among my people.''' See 1:1 and note 4 for other changes prompted by apparent contradictions.

Berkowitz (CS) feels that TO is hinting at two kinds of exoduses. God, in effect, freed the people when he performed the final miracle, but they left Egypt in the morning; Adler (NL) dismisses this interpretation as frivolous: "one cannot say 'God freed the people' until they actually left."

N is similar to TO: "that the Lord your God freed you from Egypt during the night and did miracles and mighty deeds for you." M is like TO. Ps-Jon, in contrast to TO, N, M, and Sifre, resolves the problem by relating the word "night" to the pascal sacrifice which this Targum adds to the verse, "in the month of Abib to perform the pascal sacrifice before the Lord your God . . . you shall eat it therefore during the night."

[3] TO adds "from" twice.

[4] TO adds "sacred sacrifices," the phrase it characteristically used for "Shela-mim."

MT is difficult to understand since the passover offering is not brought from the herd. Thus this verse seems to contradict Exod 12:5.

By its addition, TO is clarifying that only the lamb is used for the pascal sacrifice

3. You shall not eat anything leavened with it. For seven days you shall eat unleavened bread with it, bread of distress[6]—for you departed from the land of Egypt hurriedly—so that you may remember the day of your departure from the land of Egypt as long as you live.

4. There shall not be seen with you leaven in all your territory for seven days, and you shall not leave any of the flesh of what you sacrifice on the evening of the first day[7] until morning.

5. You are not permitted[8] to slaughter the passover (sacrifice) in any (part) of your settlement[9] that the Lord your God is giving you;

6. but at the place where the Lord your God will choose to cause His Shekinah[10] to dwell, there you shall slaughter the passover (sacrifice), in the evening, at sundown, the time when you departed from Egypt.

7. You shall boil it and eat it in the place which the Lord your God will choose; and turn in the morning and go to your settlement.[9]

8. Six days you shall eat unleavened bread, on the seventh day there should be a gathering[11] before[12] the Lord your God, (on which) you shall do no work.

---

but the ox is used for the *ḥagigah*, the festival offering. This interpretation parallels the opinion of R. Akiba, also found in y. Pes. 6:1, Sifre, and b. Pes. 69b–70b: "Oxen thou shalt slaughter as the *ḥagigah*, the festival offering, in addition to the passover offering; for if they have counted themselves formed into too large a company for the passover offering, so that one lamb will not suffice for them, they bring together with it a festival offering and this is eaten first, in order that the passover sacrifice can be eaten after the appetite is satisfied." See also b. Ber. 9a.

Nachmanides disagrees with TO and believes that MT intended that both the flock and the herd are for the *ḥagigah*. See *Mini Targuma* for a lengthy discussion of the controversy.

Kasher (*Torah Shelamah* XXVI, pp. 43–44) notes that while TO reflects the halakhah of R. Akiba, N and Ps-Jon have opposing views. N (like Nachmanides) treats the verse as applying only to the *ḥagigah* sacrifice. Ps-Jon has the view of Tosaphot that the verse refers to the *ḥagigah* sacrifice of the fifteenth day of Nissan and not the fourteenth (which is Rashi's view).

[5] MT: "choose to establish His name." The Targums add Shekinah.

[6] MT: *'ny*. Adler (NL) notes that TO retains the Hebrew word and does not translate it into Aramaic. He speculates that this may have been done to suggest the many rabbinical teachings derived from this word (b. Pes. 36a and Sifre).

3. לא תיכול עלוהי חמיעא שבעה יומין תיכול עלוהי פטיר לחים עני ארי בבהילו
נפקתא מארעא דמצרים בדיל דתידכר ית יום מפקך מארעא דמצרים כל יומי חיך:

4. ולא יתחזי לך חמיר בכל תחומך שבעה יומין ולא יבית מן ביסרא דתיכוס ברמשא
ביומא קדמאה לצפרא:

5. לית לך רשו למיכס ית פיסחא בחדא מקרוך דיי אלהך יהיב לך:

6. אילהין באתרא דיתרעי יי אלהך לאשראה שכנתיה תמן תיכוס ית פיסחא ברמשא
כמיעל שימשא זמן מיפקך ממצרים:

7. ותבשיל ותיכול באתרא דיתרעי יי אלהך ביה ותתפני בצפרא ותהך לקירוך:

8. שיתה יומין תיכול פטירא וביומא שביעאה כניש קדם יי אלהך לא תעביד עיבידא:

Ps-Jon uses a variation of the same word, but N has צֵר, a synonym, which M changes to "bread of distress (the same word as Ps-Jon) of the poor."

Ps-Jon adds *lšmyh*, "to His name," which Kasher (*Torah Shelemah* XXVI, p. 150) understands as the opinion of R. Judah, in y. Pes. 1:4: the Jew is obligated to eat matzah all seven days of passover. The halakhah, contrary to R. Judah, requires eating matzah only on the first night. Kasher's view is unlikely. "To His name" is a characteristic addition of Ps-Jon and N when TO has "before." It is used by PT on occasions to refer to a sacrifice or other Mitzvah. See for example: 12:11 (N), 15:19 (N), and 18:7 (Ps-Jon).

[7] The words "the first day" are used for two different commandments, here and in Exod 12:15. TO renders both literally even though the Talmud teaches that Exodus refers to the day before passover and there is a dispute regarding Deut as to which day it refers to. (See b. Pes. 4b on Exodus and 71b on Deut.) In Exodus, Adler (NL) writes that TO does not deviate unless necessary. Here, Adler states that TO seems to teach according to the opinion asserting that the verse refers to the sixteenth of Nisan. Ps-Jon translates like TO. N has: "on the evening of the holiday, the first day of passover, shall be left until morning." Sifre explains that "the first day" is "the morning of the second," meaning the sixteenth.

[8] MT: "you are unable." See 12:17.

[9] MT: "tents." TO and Ps-Jon generally change the word to "settlement" to clarify its meaning or because when the Israelites entered the land of Israel, they no longer dwelt in tents. N is literal. Some TO texts have "tent" in verse 7.

[10] MT: "name." Ps-Jon adds Shekinah and N, "glory of His Shekinah."

[11] MT: *atzereth*. Sifre indicates that *atzereth* means "restriction" or "gathering." See II Kings 10:20, Jer 9:1, Joel 1:14, and 2:15. While TO renders this phrase according to its plain meaning, N has "a joyous gathering" and Ps-Jon has "you shall gather in praise."

[12] The Targums have "before" instead of MT's *l*, "to."

9. Seven weeks you shall number to you, from (the time) you begin to reap with the sickle the Omer of the wave offering[13] you shall commence to number seven weeks.

10. Then you shall observe the Feast of Weeks before[14] the Lord your God, with a freewill contribution of your hand, according as the Lord your God has blessed you.

11. You shall rejoice before the Lord your God, you, your son and daughter, your male and female slave, the Levite in your settlement,[9] and the proselyte,[15] the orphan, and the widow in your midst, at the place where the Lord your God will choose to cause His Shekinah[16] to dwell.

12. Bear in mind that you were slaves in Egypt; therefore observe and do these laws.

13. You shall observe the Feast of Booths for seven days after you have gathered from your threshing floor and from your vat.

14. You shall rejoice in your festival, you, your son and daughter, your male and female slave, the Levite, the proselyte,[17] the orphan, and the widow in your settlement.[9]

15. Seven days you shall hold a festival before[18] the Lord your God, in the place that the Lord will choose; for the Lord your God will bless you in all your crops and all the work of your hand, and you shall only be happy.

16. Three times a year shall all your males be seen before[19] the Lord your God in the place that He will choose, on the Feast of Unleavened Bread, on the Feast of Weeks, and on the Feast of Booths. They shall not be seen before[19] the Lord empty-handed,

17. each person according to his means, in accordance with the blessing that the Lord your God has bestowed upon you.

18. You shall appoint judges and officials[20] for all your settlement[9] that the Lord your God is giving you throughout your tribe, and they shall judge the people with true[22] justice.

---

[13] MT: "standing grain." TO, N, and Ps-Jon clarify, like the Sifre and b. Men. 65b, 71a, etc., that the counting begins when the Omer has been cut; that is, from

9. שבעה שבועין תימני לך משריות מגלא בחצד עומרא דארמותא תשרי לממני שבעה שבועין:

10. ותעביד חגא דשבועיא קדם יי אלהך מסת נדבת ידך דתיתין כמא דיברכינך יי אלהך:

11. ותיחדי קדם יי אלהך את וברך וברתך ועבדך ואמתך וליואה דבקרוך וגיורא ויתמא וארמלתא דבינך באתרא דיתרעי יי אלהך לאשראה שכנתיה תמן:

12. ותידכר ארי עבדא הויתא במצרים ותיטר ותעביד ית קימיא האילין:

13. חגא דמטליא תעביד לך שבעה יומין במכנשך מאידרך וממעצרתך:

14. ותיחדי בחגך את וברך וברתך ועבדך ואמתך וליואה וגיורא ויתמא וארמלתא דבקרוך:

15. שבעה יומין תיחוג קדם יי אלהך באתרא דיתרעי יי ארי יברכינך יי אלהך בכל עללתך ובכל עובדי ידך ותהי ברם חדי:

16. תלת זימנין בשתא יתחזי כל דכורך קדם יי אלהך באתרא דיתרעי בחגא דפטיריא ובחגא דשבועיא ובחגא דמטליא ולא יתחזון קדם יי ריקנין:

17. גבר כמתנת ידיה כברכתא דיי אלהך דיהב לך:

18. דיינין ופורעניין תמני לך בכל קירוך דיי אלהך יהיב לך לשיבטא וידינון ית עמא דין דקשוט:

---

the sixteenth of Nisan. The Omer is the first produce harvested. See Lev 23:10 and 15.

¹⁴ The Targums have "before" instead of MT's *l*, "to."

¹⁵ MT: *ger*, which TO generally translates "proselyte." Some TO texts have "stranger." N and Ps-Jon have "proselyte."

¹⁶ MT: "name." Ps-Jon also adds Shekinah, and N, "glory of His Shekinah."

¹⁷ MT: *ger*. The three Targums translate this word in the same way.

¹⁸ TO, N, and Ps-Jon render MT's *l* as "before."

¹⁹ MT: literally, "the face."

²⁰ MT: *štrym*. TO has a word meaning "avenger" or "executioner." This is like Sifre, b. Sanh. 8a, 16b, and Hor. 11a: these officials chastise the people at the judges' order, beating the recalcitrant with a stick or a strap until he accepts the judges' sentence. In 1:15, 29:9, and Exod 5:6, TO translates the word differently.

Ps-Jon reads: "upright judges and efficient officials." N and FT have: "judges and officials." Both Targums use the word employed by TO in the other verses.

TO replaces MT's "tribes" with the singular, while N and Ps-Jon retain the plural. Comp. 18:5.

²² MT: "Justice, justice." The Targums are more specific .

19. You shall not judge unfairly: you shall show no partiality; you shall
    not accept bribery, for bribery blinds the eyes of the discerning and
    perverts straight words.[21]
20. Truth, truth[22] shall you pursue, that you may thrive and occupy the
    land that the Lord your God is giving you.
21. You shall not set up an Asherah of any kind of tree, beside the altar of
    the Lord your God that you make for yourself,
22. or erect for yourself a pillar; which is remote[23] to the Lord your God.

Chapter XVII

1. You shall not sacrifice before[1] the Lord your God an ox or a sheep that
   has a defect (or) anything evil, for that is remote[2] before[1] the Lord
   your God.
2. If there is found among you, in a settlement[3] of yours which the Lord
   your God is giving you, a man or woman who does wrong before[4] the
   Lord our God and transgresses His covenant—
3. and has gone and served the idols of the nations[5] and bows down to
   them, to the sun or the moon or any of the heavenly host, something I
   never commanded[6]—

[21] TO translates "straight words" and not "the words of the righteous." This
parallels N, Ps-Jon, and the LXX on 23:8—but not the LXX on this verse, M, and
the Temple Scroll 51:13. Sifre has both interpretations.

[23] MT: *śnʾ*, "hates." TO: "remote." Patshegen and Shefftel (BO) write that TO
parallels Sifre. Although pillars were pleasing to God in the ancestral days (cf. Gen
28:18), now He wants them *removed* because the Cananites used them in idolatrous practices. This comment presupposes that TO's rendering here is unusual.
See, however, 17:1 and elsewhere, where the same word appears and it is clear that
this is a characteristic way of translating the Hebrew "detests" or "abhorrent"
when the emotion is applied to God. Rashi (see *Sifte Hachamin*) and Malbim
derive this lesson from the MT's "hates."

N and Ps-Jon also have "remote," although N adds "hates," and Ps-Jon, "Just
as you are not permitted to erect a pillar so you are not permitted to appoint as a
community leader a willful man who is remote to the Lord your God."

19. לא תצלי דין לא תשתמודע אפין ולא תקביל שוחדא ארי שוחדא מעור עיני
חכימין ומקלקל פתגמין תריצין:

20. קושטא קושטא תרדוף בדיל דתיחי ותירת ית ארעא דיי אלהך יהיב לך:

21. לא תיצוב לך אשירת כל אילן בסטר מדבחא דיי אלהך דתעביד לך:

22. ולא תקים לך קמא דרחיק יי אלהך

XVII

1. לא תיכוס קדם יי אלהך תור ואימר דיהי ביה מומא כל מידעם ביש ארי מרחק קדם
יי אלהך הוא:

2. ארי ישתכח ביניך בחדא מקירוך דיי אלהך יהיב לך גבר או איתא דיעביד ית דביש
קדם יי אלהך למיעיבר על קימיה:

3. ואזל ופלח לטעות עממיא וסגיד להין ולשימשא או לסיהרא או לכל חילי שמיא
דלא פקידית:

[1] TO, N, and Ps-Jon have "before" in place of MT's *l*, "to," and add a second "before" at the end of the verse. Ps-Jon has a gloss to explain the defect: "which is stolen or robbed." This explanation is not found in the Talmud or Sifre.

[2] MT: "abhorrent." This is a characteristic deviation. Comp. 14:3 and 17:4. See v. 4, where TO does not deviate since the "emotion" is not ascribed to God.

[3] MT: "gates."

[4] MT: "do evil in the sight of the Lord your God." See note on 12:5. Ps-Jon is like TO, but N has: "do what is hateful and remote before the Lord your God," adding an anthropopathism.

[5] MT: "other gods." See note on 11:16. N reads like the other Targums, but also adds "before" as if the reference were to God.

[6] This is one of the two instances mentioned in b. Meg. 9a, b, where the LXX text differs from the MT. LXX adds "to serve them" at the end of the verse. Epstein, in *Torah Temimah* on this verse, explains that had "to serve them" not been added, non-Jews might infer from this verse that God had *not commanded* that the heavenly bodies *exist*. Since they do exist, non-Jews might believe that they are gods who created themselves. This may not have been the reason for the addition. It may have been added simply because it is implied in the MT. It is in the Sifre. See 4:19 for the other verse. While the Targums deviate in 4:19 to resolve the problem noted by the LXX, they do not do so here.

Ps-Jon adds "evil inclination" at the beginning of the verse, a concept TO avoids.

4. and you have been informed or have learned of it, then you shall make a thorough inquiry. If it is true, the fact is established, that this abhorrent thing was perpetrated in Israel,

5. you shall take out the man or the woman who did that wicked thing to the gate of your court,[7] man or woman, and you shall stone them to death.—

6. On the testimony[8] of two witnesses or three witnesses; shall a person who is guilty[9] of death be put to death, but do not kill on the testimony[8] of a single witness.—

7. Let the hands of the witnesses be the first against him to put him to death, and the hands of the rest of the people thereafter. Thus you will sweep out an evildoer[10] from your midst.

8. If a case is too baffling for you to decide, between blood and blood, between plea and plea, and between leprosy and leprosy,[11] matters of legal controversy[12] in your settlement,[3] you shall rise and go to the place which the Lord your God shall choose,

9. and come to the priests, the levites, and to the judges[13] who are (in charge) at the time, and inquire, and they shall tell you the verdict in the case,

10. you shall carry out the verdict that is announced to you from that place which the Lord chose, you shall observe to do all that they will instruct you.

11. In accordance with the word of the Torah which they shall teach you and the ruling they shall tell you, you shall do; you must not deviate from the verdict that they announce to you either to the right or to the left.

---

[7] TO and Ps-Jon add "your court" (as in 21:19, 22:15, and 25:7) emphasizing that people should not take justice into their own hands. Cf. TO on Gen 9:6; see also note 9. Rashi believes there is a misprint and the words should not have been added because, according to Sifre and b. Ket. 45a, "gate" refers to the site of the crime, the place where the idol was worshipped. There are TO texts where the words are not added. Komlosh (*Hamikra*) believes the reading is correct and that this verse is an example where TO translates according to the plain meaning of the text and not the halakhah. Adler (NL), on the other hand, believes that the reading

4. ויתחוה לך ותשמע ותיתבע יאות והא קושטא כיון פתגמא אתעבידת תועיבתא
הדא בישראל:

5. ותפיק ית גברא ההוא או איתתא ההיא דעבדו ית פתגמא בישא הדין לתרע בית
דינך ית גברא או ית איתתא ותרגומינון באבניא וימותון:

6. על מימר תרין סהדין או תלתה סהדין יתקטיל דחיב קטלא לא יתקטיל על מימר
סהיד חד:

7. ידא דסהדיא תהי ביה בקדמיתא למקטליה וידא דכל עמא בבתריתא ותפלי עביד
דביש מבינך:

8. ארי יתפרש מינך פתגמא לדינא בין דם לדם בין דין לדין ובין מכתש סגירו למכתש
סגירו פתגמי פלוגת דינא בקירוך ותקום ותיסק לאתרא דיתרעי יי אלהך ביה:

9. ותיתי לות כהניא ליואי ולות דינא דיהי ביומיא האינון ותיתבע ויחוון לך ית
פתגמא דדינא:

10. ותעביד על מימר פתגמא דיחוון לך מן אתרא ההוא דיתרעי יי ותיטר למעבד ככל
דילפונך:

11. על מימר אוריתא דילפונך ועל דינא דיימרון לך תעביד לא תיסטי מן פתגמא
דיחוון לך לימינא ולסמאלא:

---

is correct and TO is referring to the rabbinical teaching (b. Ket. 45b) that in a city
where the majority are non-Jews, the death sentence is carried out at the door of
the court. N does not have "court" and has, instead, "cities."

[8] MT: "mouth."

[9] TO, N, and Ps-Jon add: "is guilty." See note 7. Again, the Targums emphasize
rule by courts of law. The word is implied in the MT and is in the Sifre.

[10] The Targums add "doer," as does the Sifre.

[11] MT: "plague and plague." Lowenstein (NH) believes the words in TO also
mean "plague." Adler (NL) believes the Aramaic words mean "leprosy." They
were added by TO to clarify that we are dealing here with a dispute among the
judges as to whether the plague renders the individual ritually unclean. N, FT, and
Ps-Jon clearly have "leprosy." This understanding is in the Sifre and y. Sanh. 30:1.
Comp. TO to 21:5, Gen. 12:16, Lev. 13:9, etc. for this characteristic deviation.

[12] TO and N add "law" or "legal." See note on verses 5 and 6. Ps-Jon and FT are
literal. M has "matters of controversy in your houses of study." TO retains "controversy" even though in 21:5 "controversy" is substituted by "law," and parallels
Sifre and y. Sanh. 11:2, in highlighting that the issue here is a difference of opinion
and a refusal to change that opinion (see v. 12).

[13] MT: "judge," which some TO texts render in the plural.

12. Should a man act wickedly and not accept[14] from the priest charged with serving there before[15] the Lord your God, or the judge, that man shall be killed.[16] Thus you will sweep out an evildoer[17] from Israel:

13. all the people will hear and be afraid and will not act wickedly again.

14. If, after you have entered the land that the Lord your God has given you, and occupied it and settled in it, you say, "I will set a king over me, like all the nations about me,"

15. you may set a king over yourself, one chosen by the Lord your God, one of your own people shall you set as king over you; you have no permission[18] to set a foreigner over you, one who is not your kinsman.

16. Moreover, he shall not amass for himself horses or send people to Egypt to add horses for himself[19] since the Lord has said to you, "You must not go back that way again."

17. And he shall not have many wives, lest his heart go astray; nor shall he amass silver and gold to excess.

18. When he is seated on his royal throne, he shall write for himself a copy[20] of this Torah on a scroll from (a book) before the priests, the levites.

19. Let it remain with him and let him read in it all his life, so that he may learn to revere before[21] the Lord his God, to observe every word of this Torah as well as these laws, to do them.

20. Thus he will not lift his heart over his fellows, or deviate from the commandment to the right or to the left, to the end that he may prolong his days in his kingdom, he and his descendants in the midst of Israel.

---

[14] MT: "hear."

[15] The Targums have "before" instead of MT's ʾt.

[16] MT: "die."

[17] TO, N, and Ps-Jon add "doer," because of the usual preference for the concrete over the abstract. Sifre has the addition. See also v. 7.

[18] MT: "You are unable," a characteristic deviation. See note on 12:17.

[19] TO and N add "for himself." Adler (NL) believes that this addition clarifies the ellipsis in the MT or it refers to the Talmudic teaching (y. Sanhedrin 10:9) that business was permitted: they may return for business, even to buy horses.

Ps-Jon has: "Moreover, he shall not keep for himself more than two horses, lest his princes ride upon them, and become proud, neglect the words of the Torah, and incur the punishment of Egyptian captivity; since the Lord has warned you; 'You must not go back that way again.'"

12. וגברא דיעביד ברשע בדיל דלא לקבלא מן כהנא דקאים לשמשא תמן קדם יי
אלהך או מן דיניא ויתקטיל גברא ההוא ותפלי עביד דביש מישראל:

13. וכל עמא ישמעון וידחלון ולא ירשעון עוד:

14. ארי תיעול לארעא דיי אלהך יהיב לך ותירתה ותיתיב בה ותימר אימני עלי מלכא
ככל עממיא דבסחרני:

15. מנאה תמני עלך מלכא דיתרעי יי אלהך ביה מגו אחך תמני עלך מלכא לית לך רשו
למנאה עלך גבר נוכרי דלא אחוך הוא:

16. לחוד לא יסגי ליה סוסון ולא יתיב ית עמא למצרים בדיל לאסגאה ליה סוסון ויי
אמר לכון לא תוספון למתב באורחא הדא עוד:

17. ולא יסגי ליה נשין ולא יטעי ליביה וכספא ודהבא לא יסגי ליה לחדא:

18. ויהי כמתביה על כורסי מלכותיה ויכתוב ליה ית פרשגן אוריתא הדא על ספרא מן
קדם כהניא ליואי:

19. ותהי עימיה ויהי קרי ביה כל יומי חיוהי בדיל דיילף למידחל קדם יי אלהיה למיטר
ית כל פתגמי אוריתא הדא וית קימיא האילין למעבדהון:

20. בדיל דלא יירם ליביה מאחוהי ובדיל דלא יסטי מן תפקידתא לימינא ולסמאלא בדיל
דיוריך יומין על מלכותיה הוא ובנוהי בגו ישראל:

---

20 MT: *mishne Torah*, a term found in Josh 8:32. TO (and Peshitta): *parshegen*, a
word which occurs in Esth 3:14 and Ezra 4:11. The Targum to Esther translates
this word *diatagma*, which means "edict" or "ordinance." The Targum to II
Chron 24:17 renders the Hebrew word *midrash* by *parshegen*. This latter sense of
parshegen, as meaning "interpretation," is also contained in Rashi and Ibn Ezra to
Ezra 4:11.

Adler explains that TO interprets *mishne* in the sense of "repeat," as in
weshinnantam (see also Kimhi to Josh 8:32). While making a copy, the scribe
utters (repeats) each word when he is writing it. Adler also feels that it is possible
that the word in TO means "two scrolls" as understood by b. Sanh. 21b. One scroll
was placed in the treasury and the second was used by the king. Lowenstein states
that TO is explaining that the king should not only write the Torah (or have it written for him) but he should be able to "repeat" the Torah orally when asked questions about it, or when he needs to decide a case.

N, translating like b. Sanh. 21b, has "two scrolls of this teaching," and M,
"praiseworthy Torah." Ps-Jon understands the word like the Targum to Chron:
"the elders shall write the interpretation (see Jastrow 1244a) of this Teaching." The
word "elder" is added as in y. Sanh. 2:6 and t. Sanh. 4:7 to inform us that the court
should teach the king.

21 Patshegen notes that TO does not add "before" here instead of MT's *'t*. Sperber's edition of TO has "before," as do B, N and Ps-Jon.

Chapter XVIII

1. The priests, the levites, the whole tribe of Levi, shall have neither portion nor inheritance with Israel: the offerings of the Lord and His inheritance shall they eat.
2. He shall have no inheritance among his brethren: the gifts that the Lord will give him, they are his inheritance,[1] as He said to him.
3. This then shall be the priests' due[2] from the people: everyone who offers a sacrifice, whether an ox or a sheep, must give to the priest the shoulder, the cheek,[3] and the stomach.
4. The first (fruits) of your new grain, your wine and your oil, and the first shearing of your sheep, you shall give to him.
5. For the Lord your God has chosen him and his descendants, out of all your tribe,[3a] to stand to minister in the name of the Lord, he and his sons for all time.
6. If a levite would come, from any settlement[4] of yours throughout Israel where he resides, and come with all the longing of his soul to the place that the Lord has chosen,
7. he may serve in the name of the Lord his God like all his fellow levites who stand there to serve[5] before the Lord.
8. They shall receive equal shares to eat, beside the (allotment of the) division of duty which will come (on) the Sabbath, as established by the fathers.[6]

---

[1] MT: "the Lord is his inheritance." Adler (NL) explains that TO deviates for God's honor. MT's language implies an unseemly, overly close relationship between God and the priests and that God is like property that can be passed on from one generation of priests to another. Lowenstein (NH) feels that TO is teaching about the priestly due. This is explicit in the unofficial Targums. N has: "the offerings of the Lord are their inheritance." M: "the Memra of the Lord shall be his inheritance." Ps-Jon: "The twenty-four gifts of the priesthood which the Lord will give to him are his heritage." A similar deviation is made in 10:19 and Num 18:20. Cf. TJ to Josh 13:14, 33; 18:7; and Ezek 44:28.

[2] Some TO texts have a doublet for "due," literally "law," *dyn dhzy*. This understanding of the word is in the Sifre, b. Hullin 130b, and elsewhere. The rabbis explain that judges can compel delivery of the gifts. The doublet is not in N or Ps-Jon.

[3] MT has the plural "cheeks." M. Herskovics ("Halakhah and Aggadah in

XVIII

1. לא יהי לכהניא ליואי כל שיבטא דלוי חולק ואחסנא עם ישראל קורבניא דיי ואחסנתיה ייכלון:
2. ואחסנא לא תהי ליה בגו אחוהי מתנן דיהב ליה יי אנון אחסנתיה כמא דמליל ליה:
3. ודין יהי דחזי לכהניא מן עמא מן נכסי נכסתא אם תור אם אימר ויתן לכהנא דרעא ולועא וקיבתא:
4. ריש עיבורך חמרך ומשחך וריש גיזת ענך תיתין ליה:
5. ארי ביה איתרעי יי אלהך מכל שיבטך למקם לשמשא בשמא דיי הוא ובנוהי כל יומיא:
6. וארי ייתי ליואה מחדא מן קירוך מכל ישראל דהוא דאר תמן וייתי בכל רעות נפשיה לאתרא דיתרעי יי:
7. וישמיש בשמא דיי אלהיה ככל אחוהי ליואי דמשמשין תמן קדם יי:
8. חולק כוחלק ייכלון בר ממטרתא דיתה שבתא דכין אתקינו אבהתא:

Onkelos," unpublished Ph. D. thesis, Yeshiva University, 1950) argues that TO's rendering reflects the halakhah (also found in Sifre) that only the bottom cheek is given to the priest. However, TO is only rendering words in the same verse in the same tense.

[3a] MT: "tribes." See 16:18.

[4] MT: "gates."

[5] MT: "stand." TO adds "serve," stating explicitly what the MT only implies.

It is questionable whether the author(s) of TO understood verses 6 and 7 to refer to priests (like Sifre) or plain levites (like b. Eruchin 11a). One could argue that "serve" was added to parallel the interpretation of Sifre: one might think that verse 6 speaks of a levite who is not a priest; however, verse 7 adds "serve" showing that priests are intended, for only priests "serve" in the Temple. It is also possible to maintain that TO is reflecting the Talmudic understanding and that "serve" refers to the levitical singing.

Some TO texts have only "serve," as does Ps-Jon; however N has "stand" and "serve." N and Ps-Jon have the service performed in the name of the Memra of the Lord. B has "who serve there before the Lord."

[6] MT is cryptic but can be translated: "beside his sellings according to the fathers."

TO adds words to resolve this difficult phrase. The Targum may be explaining that when priests decide to serve in the Temple on a festival which is not within their assigned rotation, they may share in the hides of the festival burnt offerings and the flesh of the festival sin offerings. They may not participate in the non-festival offerings. These belong to the members of the rota. E. Z. Melammed (*Bible*

9. When you enter the land that the Lord your God is giving you, you shall not learn to do the abhorrent practices[7] of those nations.

10. Let there not be found among you, one who consigns his son or daughter to the fire, or who is an augur, a soothsayer, a diviner, or sorcerer,

11. one who casts spells, or one who consults ghosts or familiar spirits,[8] or one who inquires of the dead.

12. For anyone who does these things is remote before[9] the Lord, and it is because of these abhorrent[9] things that the Lord your God is dispossessing them before you.

13. You must be wholehearted in the fear[10] of the Lord your God.

Commentators, p. 197) believes TO means that they may share in everything equally, but the "show bread" is not divided equally. R. Judah (at the end of b. Succoth) states that those who enter take seven and those who exit take five of the twelve "show breads."

By explaining that the verse refers to the rotations, TO is paralleling Sifre: "What did the fathers sell to each other? (They said to each other:) You take one Sabbath (as your rotation to serve in the Temple) and I will take another."

By retaining "fathers," TO seems to be stating that the rotations were established during Moses' lifetime rather than during the days of David and Samuel as indicated in I Chron 9:22. However, it is possible that TO is reflecting the Talmudic view that Moses only established eight watches, but David and Samuel enlarged it (Sifre, b. Succ. 56a, b. Tan. 27a). It is also possible that TO was not thinking of Moses establishing the rotations at all. TO had to resolve the difficult phrase and did so by predicting a future development.

Maimonides (*The Commandments*, Soncino Press, pp. 46–47) quotes TO and Sifre on this verse in deciding that the functioning of the priests through rotations is a Biblical halakhah (the thirty-sixth positive command). Nachmanides disagrees. He feels that there is no Biblical commandment ordaining assigned rotations.

N translates: "beside the remainder of the offerings which your fathers have given them to inherit." Ps-Jon: "beside the gift of the offerings which the priests eat, which Elazar and Ithamar your fathers have given them to inherit." FT and M: "beside the sales which they sell from their fathers."

[7] TO does not render *twʿbh* as *mrḥq* as it customarily does (see 17:1, 18:2, etc.), although N and Ps-Jon do so. It is unlikely that TO wants to highlight the teachings of the Sifre and b. Sanh. 68a: "you may learn of their practices in order to understand and teach your children how corrupt these practices are so they can avoid them." Had TO used *mrḥq* literally meaning "remote," it would have implied that

9. ארי את עליל לארעא דיי אלהך יהיב לך לא תילף למעבד כתועבת עממיא האינון:
10. לא ישתכח בך מעבר בריה וברתיה בנורא קסים קיסמין מעניין ומנחיש וחרש:
11. ורטין רטן ושאיל בבידין ובזכורו ותבע מן מיתיא:
12. ארי מרחק קדם יי כל עביד אילין ובדיל תועיבתא האילין יי אלהך מתריך יתהון מן קדמך:
13. שלים תהי בדחלתא דיי אלהך:

one has to avoid these practices entirely. While this interpretation is possible, it is more likely that TO (generally more careful in its renderings than the unofficial Targums) only deviates when the unseemly emotion (abhorrence) is ascribed to God, but does not do so (here and other places like 13:15) when the word applies to man.

[8] MT: *yd'ny*. TO: *zkwrw*. Jastrow translates the Aramaic (p. 398a): "necromantic apparition." Adler (NL) understands it as: "familiar spirit." TO renders here as in Lev 20:27, and like FT and N, TJ to II Kings 21:6, 23:24, Isa 8:19, 19:3, and Ps-Jon to Lev 20:27.

Ps-Jon to this verse (like Sifre and b. Sanh. 65a) has "the bone *ydw'*," one who puts a bone of an animal named *ydw'* into his mouth and the bone speaks through sorcery.

While Ps-Jon parallels the rabbinic interpretation, TO (N and FT) does not. Commenting on b. Sanh. 65a, Maharsha asks: how can TO disagree with a Tanna? He responds: TO is also a Tanna and can therefore disagree.

In contrast to Maharsha's view, TO is probably not disagreeing but only presenting a rendering that is more easily comprehensible to most readers. As the word is understood by Jastrow, TO has a more general expression, "necromantic apparition," since it was not expected that the average reader would know the animal *ydw'*. As the word is understood by Adler, TO is informing us that the prior word implies one who calls up any ghost while the latter refers to one who consults only "familiar spirits."

[9] The word "abhorrent" is used twice in the verse, but TO and Ps-Jon render each differently. The first ascribes an unseemly emotion to God and is therefore avoided and "before" is added. The second "abhorrent" is only an adjective. N is not so careful and uses "remote" twice, the first time adding "hateful."

[10] MT: "with the Lord your God." TO and Ps-Jon add "fear" since "with" implies an improper attachment to God. The Targums inform us that the connection is with the "fear" of the Lord and not with God Himself. Some commentators feel that the addition of "fear" instead of "before" has halakhic implications. Patshegan, Shefftel (BO), Nachmanides, etc. explain that "fear" refers to a positive commandment: one should not be deficient in the fear of God. See also b. Pes. 113b. N has: "wholehearted with good deeds with the Lord your God." M corrects N by adding "before."

14. For those nations that you are about to dispossess listen[11] to sooth-
    sayers and augurs; to you, however, the Lord your God has not
    assigned the like.
15. A prophet from the midst of you, of your brethren, like myself,[12] the
    Lord your God will raise up, from him you shall accept.[13]
16. This is just what you asked before[14] the Lord your God at Horeb, on
    the day of the Assembly, saying, "Let me not hear[15] any longer the
    voice of the Memra[16] of the Lord my God or see this great fire any
    more, lest I die."
17. Whereupon the Lord said to me, "They have done well in speaking
    thus.
18. I will raise up a prophet for them from among their brethren, like
    yourself: I will put My words of prophecy[17] in his mouth and he will
    speak with them all that I command him;
19. and if anybody fails to accept[18] the words he speaks in My name, My
    Memra[19] will require it of him.

---

[11] MT: *sm*ᶜ, meaning "hear" or "listen." TO retains this word although it
generally substitutes "accept," as in the next verse. Adler (NL) feels that TO is
warning the people against even listening to soothsayers, etc., even if the listening
is not followed by acceptance. In the following verse, however, TO is indicating
that it is not sufficient to just listen. One must accept the teachings of the prophets.
Shefftel (BO) explains that only "listen" is appropriate for soothsayers, etc. These
individuals give enigmatic oracles subject to various meanings. One does not
"accept" oracles; but only listens. After hearing what is said, one interprets as one
likes and acts accordingly. N is like TO, but Ps-Jon has *ṣyytwn*, "obey."

[12] The Aramaic words meaning "like myself" and "like yourself" are found
here and in verse 18 respectively. Beside the part of the word meaning "my" and
"your," the two words differ in that a *daleth* is added, in most editions, to the word
in verse 15. Shefftel (BO) feels that the *daleth* makes the word refer back to Moses.
Moses, the meekest of men, says that the future prophet will be like him and his
prophecy will be on the same high level. However, when God speaks, the *daleth* is
not added, and the word "like yourself" refers to "among their brethren" and not
to Moses. Thus, the future prophet will be like Moses in being an Israelite, but the
level of his prophecy will not be the same, as indicated in 34:10: "There will not
arise another prophet in Israel like Moses." Ps-Jon translates similarly. N does not

14. ארי עממיא האילין דאת ירית יתהון מן מעניא ומן קסמיא שמעין ואת לא כן יהב
לך יי אלהך:

15. נביא מבינך מאחך דכותי יקים לך יי אלהך מיניה תקבלון:

16. ככל דשאילתא מן קדם יי אלהך בחורב ביומא דקהלא למימר לא אוסיף למישמע
ית קל מימרא דיי אלהי וית אישתא רבתא הדא לא איחזי עוד ולא אימות:

17. ואמר יי לי אתקינו דמלילו:

18. נביא אקים להון מגו אחיהון כותך ואיתין פתגמי נבואתי בפומיה וימליל עימהון
ית כל דאיפקדיניה:

19. ויהי גברא דלא יקביל לפתגמי דימליל בשמי מימרי יתבע מיניה:

---

have the *daleth* in verse 15 or 18, but it is added by M in both these verses. Sper-ber's edition of TO has the *daleth* also in verse 18. B does not.

Ps-Jon adds *rwh gwdš*ᵓ, "holy spirit," in this verse and in 18 to clarify how the prophet is like Moses: "who is like me (in having) the holy spirit."

TO fails to render 18:15–18 to avoid the messianic interpretation read into the verses by John 5:45, 6:14, 7:40; Acts 3:22 and 7:37 (cf. Matt 11:3, 17:5; Luke 7:19, 9:35), that the verses refer to Jesus. This could have been accomplished by using the plural "prophets," such as was done by Sifre and Rashi. N, Ps-Jon, and Saadya also do not deviate.

[13] MT: "to him you shall hearken." N is literal, but Ps-Jon is like TO.

[14] TO, N, and Ps-Jon have "before" instead of MT's *mˁm*.

[15] MT: *šmˁ*. As in verse 14, TO does not substitute "accept." "Hear" is necessary since the verse refers to the Israelite fear when they "heard" the heavenly voice speaking the Ten Commandments. See 9:10 and 10:14. N and Ps-Jon translate like TO.

[16] TO and N add Memra. Ps-Jon does not add Memra, but "hear the voice of the revelation from before the Lord." TO frequently drops the word "voice" when Memra is added (see, for example, 15:5), but not here because of the context.

[17] TO and Ps-Jon add "of prophecy" to remove an unseemly anthropo-morphism and to clarify the text. N does not add a word here.

TJ also occasionally translates *dbr*, "word," as "prophecy." See, for example, TJ to Jer 1:6, 7; 9:21; 26:2; Ezek 2:7 and 14:4.

[18] MT: "hear." See verse 14. While this is a characteristic TO reading, Adler (NL) believes that TO deviates here to include the teaching (also in Sifre and b. Sanh. 89a) that the verse concerns both a prophet who refuses to prophesy and one who does not follow his own prophecy. Adler writes that "accept" includes both interpretations. Ps-Jon renders like TO, but N has "hear."

[19] TO and Ps-Jon use Memra instead of "I." See verse 16. N has: "speaks in the name of My Memra; I, with my Memra, will call him to account."

20. But any prophet who presumes to speak a word in My name which I did not command him to say, or who speaks in the name of idols of the nations, [20] that prophet shall be killed."

21. And if you say in your heart, "How can we know the word the Lord did not speak?"

22. If the prophet speaks in the name of the Lord and the word does not come to pass and it is not confirmed,[21] that is the word that was not spoken by the Lord; the prophet has spoken it presumptuously: do not stand in fear[22] of him.

Chapter XIX

1. When the Lord your God will cut down the nations whose land the Lord your God is giving you, and you will dispossess them and settle in their towns and houses,

2. you shall set aside three cities in your land that the Lord your God is giving you to possess.

3. You shall prepare the way for yourself and divide into three parts the boundary of the land that the Lord your God has allotted to you, so that any murderer may flee there.

4. Now this is the case of the murderer who may flee there and live: one who has killed[1] his fellowman unwittingly, and he did not hate him yesterday or earlier;

5. as when a man goes with his fellowman into a grove to cut wood; as his hand moves[2] the iron to cut down a tree, the iron slips off[3] the wood and happens (to come upon) his fellowman so that he dies, he may flee to one of these cities and live.

---

[20] MT: "other gods." See note on 11:16. Ps-Jon is like TO, but N has "other idols."

[21] MT: "will not come." TO, like Ps-Jon, deviates here because: (1) Not all prophecies "come," for example when the prophet says something will not happen or it will stop (Patshegen). (2) TO wants to be specific, yet not repeat the wording of the prior phrase (Adler). (3) The word "come" in regard to prophecy is generally changed to "confirmed" (Shefftel and Lowenstein). (4) The verse refers to a prophet who is being tested. You say to him: "tell us things that will happen." He

20. ברם נביא דירשע למללא פתגמא בשמי ית דלא פקידתיה למללא ודימליל בשום
טעות עממיא ויתקטיל נביא ההוא:
21. וארי תימר בליבך איכדין נידע ית פתגמא דלא מלליה יי:
22. דימליל נביא בשמא דיי ולא יהי פתגמא ולא יתקיים הוא פתגמא דלא מלליה יי
בירשע מלליה נביא לא תדחלון מניה:

XIX

1. ארי ישיצי יי אלהך ית עממיא דיי אלהך יהיב לך ית ארעהון ותירתינון ותיתיב
בקרויהון ובבתיהון:
2. תלת קרוין תפריש לך בגו ארעך דיי אלהך יהיב לך למירתה:
3. תתקין לך ארחא ותתלית ית תחום ארעך דיחסנינך יי אלהך ויהי למיערק לתמן כל
קטול:
4. ודין פתגם קטולא דיערוק לתמן ויתקים דיקטול ית חבריה בלא מדעיה והוא לא
סני ליה מאיתמלי ומדקמוהי:
5. ודייעול עם חבריה בחורשא למיקץ אעין ותתמריך ידיה בברזלא במיקציה אעא
וישתליף ברזלא מן אעא וישכח ית חבריה וימות הוא יערוק לחדא מן קירויא
האילין ויתקיים:

tells things, and you wait and see if they happen. In order to pass the test, everything foretold by the prophet must occur (Wertheimer). N is literal.

[22] MT: *tgwr*, which Sifre understands to mean "store up." The word in the MT is
in the singular form. TO renders its replacement in the plural form to adjust the
tense to verse 21, which is plural. Some TO texts have the singular, but N and
Ps-Jon have the plural.

TO can be understood as: "do not fear that you may incur punishment on his
account because you contributed to his death" (Rashi), or "do not fear him
because of the Mitzvoth he performed" (*Torah Temimah*). See also 1:17.

[1] MT: "smite." The Targums are more specific.

[2] MT: literally: "his hand is driven by the ax." There are two principal versions
of *wttmryg* in TO. Sperber and B have it ending with a *qof*, meaning "unsteady."
Rashi, Adler, etc., have it with a *gml*, meaning "move." Sifre explains that the
verse concerns one who intends to cut down the tree.

N and Ps-Jon have "push." FT has "made an effort," but this is probably a
transcription error: *wytqwp* for *wtdḥp*. The Sperber text and B have "iron" instead
of "ax."

[3] Adler (NL) notes that "slips off," intransitive in the MT, is recast to the

6. Lest the avenger of the blood pursue the slayer, because his heart is hot, and overtake him, because the way is long, and kill[4] him; yet he does not incur the death penalty, since he did not hate him since yesterday or earlier.

7. That is why I command you saying: "set aside three cities."

8. And when the Lord your God enlarges your territory, as He confirmed[5] to your fathers, and gives you all the land of which He spoke to give your fathers—

9. if you keep all of this commandment which I command you this day to love the Lord your God and to walk in the ways that are right before Him[6] all the days—then you shall add for yourself three more towns to those three.

10. Thus blood of the innocent will not be shed[7] in your land that the Lord your God is giving you for an inheritance, and there be on you the liability of a death sentence.[8]

11. If, however, a man hates his neighbor and lies in wait for him and sets upon him and kills[4] him and he dies, and then flees to one of these towns,

---

passive, meaning that the ax-head fell off the handle. Thus, TO seems to parallel the majority view against Rabbi Judah the Patriarch, who understands that the iron made a splinter which killed someone (b. Mac. 7b and Sifre).

Shefftel (BO) argues that TO deviates to reflect the halakhah when this is necessary. Here, the law is surely as announced by the majority and, therefore, no deviation is necessary. Shefftel, therefore, believes that TO is explaining that both parties interpret the verse that the ax fell on the victim. The majority feel the ax-head fell off the handle, but Rabbi Judah argues that the ax was swung unto the tree where it was attached, but it loosened itself and then fell upon the victim. This is Maimonides' interpretation of the controversy.

Shefftel's analysis is doubtful. It is possible that the Targum preceded the recorded dispute and was formulated when the majority had not yet developed their opinion. It is more likely that TO renders the plain meaning of the text without any intention of clarifying the halakhah. (See the Introduction for a discussion of the Targums and the halakhah.) The passive is used to clarify that the death resulted from an accident.

N and Ps-Jon indicate that the iron separated from the handle and fell upon someone. The Peshitta is like TO.

6. דילמא ירדוף גאל דמא בתר קטולא ארי ייחם ליביה וידבקניה ארי תיסגי ארחא ויקטליניה נפש וליה לית חובת דין דיקטול ארי לא סני הוא ליה מאתמלי ומדקמוהי:

7. על כן אנא מפקיד לך למימר תלת קרוין תפריש לך:

8. ואם יפתי יי אלהך ית תחומך כמא דקיים לאבהתך ויתין לך ית כל ארעא דמליל למיתן לאבהתך:

9. ארי תיטר ית כל תפקידתא הדא למעבדה דאנא מפקיד לך יומא דין למירחם ית יי אלהך ולמהך באורחן דתקנן קדמוהי כל יומיא ותוסיף לך עוד תלת קרוין על תלת איליך:

10. ולא ישתפיך דם זכי בגו ארעך דיי אלהך יהיב לך אחסנא ויהי עלך חובת דין דקטול:

11. וארי יהא גבר סני לחבריה ויכמון ליה ויקום עלוהי ויקטליניה נפש וימות ויעירוק לחדא מן קרויא האילין:

<hr />

See verse 20:19, where the word is translated differently.

[4] MT: "smite." TO (like N and Ps-Jon) is more specific.

[5] MT: "swore."

[6] TO, N, and Ps-Jon use "right before Him" to avoid the unseemly anthropomorphic image of divine pathways upon which humans can follow God. This is a characteristic deviation. See, for example, note to 8:6. M changes "ways" to "way," even though the plural is the customary Targumic rendering, interpreting MT's plural as meaning the Torah Laws.

[7] TO generally translates *špk*, "shed," with *šdy*, as in Gen 9:6 and verse 13 of this chapter, when the word refers to killing, but does not do so here. (N is like TO, but Ps-Jon has a variation of *šdy*.) The word used here (a variation of *špk*) may refer to both the killer and the victim being innocent; the indefinite form implies both persons (Shefftel, BO). The plural form may refer to the many people saved by the institution of the three cities (Wertheimer, *Or*). It may differentiate between the holy (e.g., spilling the blood of sacrifices, Lev 18:3) and the profane (here) (Lowenstein, NH). This explanation, however, does not fit in with verse 13, where TO and Ps-Jon (but not N) have *šdy*. The word may refer to unintentional killing (Adler, NL). It is also possible that the Targum used a different word simply to avoid a redundant usage.

[8] MT: "and blood be upon you." TO's addition, like Ps-Jon's, emphasizes rule of law. See 17:5, 22:8, and Exod 2:1 and 2. Comp. II Sam 21:1. The addition also paraphrases the Biblical idiom. N does not make the addition.

12. the elders of his town shall send and take him from there and shall hand him over to the blood-avenger and he shall die;[9]

13. your eye should not have mercy on him. Thus you will do away with the shedder[10] of innocent blood from Israel, and it will go well with you.

14. You shall not change[11] your neighbor's boundary, set up by previous generations within your possession, which you shall inherit in the land that the Lord your God is giving you to possess.

15. A single witness may not stand up against a person for any wrongs or guilts,[12] for any offense that he may have committed; by the word[13] of two witnesses or the word[13] of three witnesses shall the matter be established.

16. If a false[14] witness stands up against a man to testify against him with perversity,[15]

17. the two persons who have a judgment[16] shall stand before the Lord, before the priests and judges who will be (in authority) in those days,

18. and the judges shall make a thorough investigation. If the man who testified is a false witness, if he has testified falsely against his fellow-man,

19. you shall do to him as he thought[17] to do to his fellow. Thus you will sweep the evildoer[18] from your midst;

[9] TO renders like Sifre: "if the blood-avenger does not kill him, anyone has the right" (Shefftel, BO). Shefftel may be referring to TO's failure to change "die" to "killed" (like N, M, and Ps-Jon). Thus the latter phrase is independent: "if the blood-avenger does not kill him, he will die at the hands of another."

[10] The Targums add "shedder" and parallel Sifre: "remove the evildoer." See note on 21:9.

[11] TO, like M and Ps-Jon, is clarifying the meaning of the text. MT has a word meaning "turn back" (cf. Isa 42:17 and 59:14): to move the landmark backwards, thereby enlarging one's own field (Rashi). TO unintentionally implies the teachings contained in Sifre; for example, one who *changes* the teaching of the rabbis, to say a thing is pure which is not pure, or the reverse, violates the negative commandment contained in this verse. N has, "You shall not attack."

[12] TO renders "wrongs" or "guilts" in the plural.

[13] MT: "mouth." Wertheimer explains that TO is referring to the Talmudic interpretation that judges must hear oral and not written testimony (b. Gid. 71a; 17:10 is similar).

MT's *ʿl py hdbr* rendered *ʿl mymr ptgmʾ* is understood by Wertheimer as referring to the Oral Torah: there can be a dispute about a rule of the Oral Law, but not

12. וישלחון סבי קרתיה וידברון יתיה מתמן וימסרון יתיה ביד גאיל דמא וימות:
13. לא תחוס עינך עלוהי ותפלי אשדי דם זכי מישראל וייטב לך:
14. לא תשני תחומא דחברך דתחימו קדמאי באחסנתך דתחסין בארעא דיי אלהך דיי יהיב לך למירתה:
15. לא יקום סהיד חד בגבר לכל עוין ולכל חובין בכל חיט דיחטי על מימר תרין סהדין או על מימר תלתה סהדין יתקים פתגמא:
16. ארי יקום סהיד שקר בגבר לאסהדא ביה סטיא:
17. ויקומון תרין גברין דלהון דינא קדם יי קדם כהניא ודיניא דיהון ביומיא האינון:
18. ויתבעון דיניא יאות והא סהיד שיקרא סהדא שקרא אסהיד באחוהי:
19. ותעבדון ליה כמא דחשיב למעבד לאחוהי ותפלי עביד דביש מבינך:

concerning a teaching of the written Torah. Wertheimer is not unique in trying to find special meaning in *ʿl py*, translated by TO as *mymr*, even though this is a characteristic translation. Lowenstein (NH, pp. 7–10) explains TO's translation of *ʿl py ḥrb* as meaning "by the word of prayer"; that is, that Israel's victory is the result of prayer. See note on 13:13. Adler (NL), who preceded Wertheimer, writes that one cannot derive the teaching of b. Git. 71a from TO to v. 15 nor should one understand chapter 17 as referring to the Oral Law. Ps-Jon reads like TO, but N has "mouth."

Ps-Jon drops the second "mouth" and does not add "word." N has "mouth."

[14] MT: "violent." TO is either clarifying the text or informing us that the verse concerns an *ʿd zmm*, a plotting witness. See v. 19. y. Mac. 1:7, Sifre, N, and Ps-Jon have the same interpretation.

[15] MT has a word which literally means "far removed" (Rashi). TO is clarifying the text, as do Sifre and Ps-Jon. N has "false testimony."

[16] MT: "dispute." Again TO is either emphasizing rule of law or stating explicitly what is implied in the MT. N is like TO, but Ps-Jon and M are literal.

[17] MT: *zmm*, a word connoting: plot, device, evil purpose, false testimony. TO: *ḥšb*, meaning: think, intend, consider. TO is simply clarifying the meaning of the Hebrew word; as Malbim indicates: the verb *zmm* always implies "deep thought." This is the same word found in N, M, and Ps-Jon. It is the characteristic rendering, and is found in the Targums to Jer 51:12, Zech 1:6, Prov 31:16, etc.

It is possible, but unlikely, that TO is translating according to the Pharisaic view (found in the Sifre and b. Mac. 5a) and not that of the Sadducees. It is from the word *zmm* (see Rashi, Malbim, and others) that the Pharisees deduced the teaching that *ʿdym zwmmym*, certain witnesses that give false testimony, receive capital punishment when the presentation of the case has been completed, since at that time the witnesses had already expressed their "thought," even though the court had not executed its decision. The Sadducees, on the other hand, derived no lesson from *zmm* and insisted that the witnesses are punished only if and after the

20. the rest will hear and be afraid, and they will not do again such evil things in your midst.

21. Your eye must not have mercy: life for[19] life, eye for eye, tooth for tooth, hand for hand, foot for foot.

Chapter XX

1. When you go out to wage war against your enemies,[1] and see horses and chariots—a nation larger than you—have no fear of them, for the Lord your God, His Memra[2] is your support,[3] brought you from the land of Egypt.

2. Before you draw near to wage war, the priest shall come forward and address the troops.

3. He shall say to them, "Hear,[4] Israel! You are drawing near today to wage battle with your enemies.[5] Let not your hearts be shaken.[6] Do not be afraid, or tremble,[7] or be broken[8] before them.

---

defendant has been executed. The Sadducees relied on "life for life" in verse 21.

[18] TO adds "doer." See note on 13:6. N and Ps-Jon translate similarly.

[19] MT: *npš bnpš*, etc. Whereas in Exod 21:23 f. and Lev 24:18, 20, MT has the additional word *npš tḥt npš*, etc., TO and Ps-Jon render each *npš ḥlp npš*, etc. The Targums generally translate a verse according to what is more clearly stated elsewhere. TO does not reflect the halakhah, that the punishment is monetary, but the plain meaning of the text. N has "life the payment of life," etc.

[1] TO translates here *bʿly dbbk* but *snʾk* in verse 14, probably to avoid a repetition of the same word. This is characteristic. Ps-Jon does the same, but N repeats the word in verse 14.

[2] TO adds Memra. Ps-Jon ends the verse, "for all of them are considered as one horse and one chariot before the Lord your God, whose Memra will be your support, who brought you free from the land of Egypt." N does not add Memra.

[3] MT: "the Lord your God is with you." TO and Ps-Jon add "support," removing the unseemly anthropomorphic image of God marching like a warrior at the head of advancing troops. N is literal.

[4] MT: *šmʿ*, which TO generally renders "accept." No direct object follows *šmʿ* here; hence "accept" would have been inappropriate. It is unlikely that TO retains the Hebrew to refer to the Talmudic teaching (b. Sotah 42a): "Even though you

20. ‏ודישתארון ישמעון וידחלון ולא יוספון למעבד עוד כפתגמא בישא הדין בינך:‏
21. ‏ולא תחוס עינך נפשא חלף נפשא עינא חלף עינא שינא חלף שינא ידא חלף ידא ריגלא חלף ריגלא:‏

XX

1. ‏ארי תיפוק לאגחא קרבא על בעלי דבבך ותיחזי סוסן ורתיכין עם סגי מינך לא תדחל מנהון ארי יי אלהך מימריה בסעדך דאסקך מארעא דמצרים:‏
2. ‏ויהי כמקרבכון לאגחא קרבא ויתקרב כהנא וימליל עם עמא:‏
3. ‏ויימר להון שמע ישראל אתון מתקרבין יומא דין לאגחא קרבא על בעלי דבביכון לא יזוע ליבכון לא תדחלון ולא תתבעתון ולא תיתברון מן קדמיהון:‏

have no other merit than the fulfillment of the command of reading the *šmˁ*, you would deserve that He should help you." N and Ps-Jon have the word in the plural, but most TO texts retain MT's singular form.

⁵ See note 1. It is unlikely that *bˁly dbbk* is used to reflect the teaching in Sifre and the Mishna in b. Sotah 42a: the priest says, as it were: "Remember that these are not your brethren, they will have no pity on you, show yourselves strong for the battle." N and Ps-Jon translate in the same way.

⁶ MT: "soft." TO has *yzwˁ*, "tremble" as in 2:25. Ps-Jon has *yzwḥ*, "tremble." N reads "broken." TO and Ps-Jon render the same word in verse 8 "broken." because: (1) TO avoids repeating the same words (Berkowitz, LV). (2) This word is a verb, while the word in verse 8 is a noun (Adler, NL). (3) Verse 3 refers to the initial, normal fear of even the most courageous when he sees a larger-size troop than his own and hears the noise of their soldiers. This is consistent with the translation in Exod 13:17, II Kings 22:19, Isa 7:4, Jer 51:46, and Sifre (Shefftel, BO). (4) In verse 3, TO renders the word "stronger" because it appears at the beginning of a list but uses "weaker" in verse 8 because the word is at the end of a list (Wertheimer, Or). The difficulty with Wertheimer's interpretation is that *tbyr*, in verse 8, is actually a stronger expression. (5) TO may be referring to the interpretation, also in b. Sotah 42a, that the soldier here is afraid because of his sins, while the reference in verse 8 is to the fear created by a drawn sword. T. Sotah ch. 7 indicates verse 8 speaks of one who is compassionate.

⁷ MT: "and hurry not precipitately." Ps-Jon translates similarly. N has "frightened."

⁸ MT: "frightened." This is a characteristic deviation. However, it is possible that TO, presumably recognizing that fright is normal, is telling us that the verse refers to the degree of fear which causes a person to break. N and Ps-Jon translate similarly, but M is literal.

4. For it is the Lord your God whose Memra[9] leads before you[10] to do battle[11] for you against your enemy,[1] to save you."

5. Then the officers[12] shall speak with[13] the troops, as follows, "Is there anyone who has built a new house[14] but has not dedicated it? Let him go back to his home, lest he be killed[15] in battle and another dedicate it.

6. Is there anyone who has planted a vineyard but has not yet redeemed[16] it? Let him go back to his home, lest he be killed[15] in battle and another redeem[16] it.

7. Is there anyone who has betrothed a wife, but who has not yet taken her? Let him go back to his home, lest he be killed[15] in battle and another take her."

8. The officers[12] shall go on speaking with the troops and say, "Is there anyone afraid and brokenhearted?[17] Let him go back to his home lest his comrades' heart be broken[18] like his heart."

9. When the officers[12] have finished speaking with the troops, they shall appoint army commanders at the head of the troops.

[9] TO adds Memra in some TO texts, Ps-Jon "Shekinah," and N "glory of the Shekinah."

[10] MT: "who goes with you." The Targums avoid the unseemly anthropomorphism of God marching into battle at the head of troops. Similarly 1:30, 33; 31:6.

[11] On 1:30, Lowenstein (NH) writes that when TO speaks of God, it translates "battle" as *'gh'*; but when referring to the Israelites, TO uses *'gh' qrb'*. This verse has the latter words, contrary to his observation. N and Ps-Jon have "arrange your march."

[12] TO renders "officers" here as in Exod 5:6 and not as in Deut 16:18. In 16:18, the verse refers to one who inflicts stern punishment. The reference here is to a considerate official. N and Ps-Jon are like TO.

[13] Some TO texts add "before" here but not in verses 2, 8, and 9. This may have been done to differentiate this speech from the previous ones. N and Ps-Jon do not add "before." Sifre indicates that the officer begins to speak from this verse, not the priest.

[14] While TO translates "build a new house" literally, Ps-Jon adds as a gloss, an interpretation not found in rabbinic literature, "and did not fix a mezuzah on it to finish it" (see Kasher, *Torah Shelemah* XXVI, p. 151, and *Perush Jonathan, loc. cit.*). N does not have a gloss.

4. ארי יי אלהכון מדבר קדמיכון לאגחא לכון קרב עם בעלי דבביכון למיפרק יתכון:

5. וימללון סרכיא עם עמא למימר מן גברא דבנא ביתא חדתא ולא חנכיה יהך ויתוב לביתיה דילמא יתקטיל בקרבא וגבר אוחרן יחנכניה:

6. ומן גברא דנצב כרמא ולא אחליה יהך ויתוב לביתיה דילמא יתקטיל בקרבא וגבר אוחרן יחליניה:

7. ומן גברא דארס איתתא ולא ניסבה יהך ויתוב לביתיה דילמא יתקטיל בקרבא וגבר אוחרן יסבינה:

8. ויוספון סרכיא למללא עם עמא ויימרון מן גברא דדחול ותביר ליביה יהך ויתוב לביתיה ולא יתבר ית ליבא דאחוהי כליביה:

9. ויהי כד ישיצון סרכיא למללא עם עמא וימנון רבני חילא בריש עמא:

---

[15] MT: "die." TO and Ps-Jon are more explicit. N renders literally, as do some TO variant texts.

[16] It is unlikely that TO retains the Hebrew word *ḥl* because of the Talmudic teaching (b. Sotah 43b and y. Sotah 8:4), as Rashi states: "The word means fruit that has not yet been redeemed in the fourth year of its growth. The fruits had either to be eaten in Jerusalem or to be given a non-holy character (*hulin*) by exchanging them for money in Jerusalem." (See 28:30, Lev 19:23–25, and Jer 31:5.)

[17] MT: "fainthearted." Sifre and m. Sotah 8:5 discuss this verse: "R. Akiba says, 'that is fearful and faint-hearted' is to be taken literally, one who is unable to endure when battle is joined or to behold a drawn sword. R. Jose the Galilean (does not give a literal rendering and) says, 'that is fearful and fainthearted', this refers to one who is afraid because of the transgressions he is guilty of, therefore has the Law accounted to him all these (building a house, planting a vineyard, consummating marriage, etc.) that he may return because of them (i.e., his transgressions)" (Translation of Mishna by Philip Blackman).

TO may be translating in line with R. Akiba's view. N and Ps-Jon are like R. Jose or like both of them, for they render "afraid because of transgression, and brokenhearted because of his work." FT reflects R. Jose: "afraid and brokenhearted from transgression." See also v. 3.

[18] MT: "melt." TO evades the more figurative language. However, while doing so, the same word "broken" is used twice in the sentence, something TO generally tries to avoid. Perhaps this is to make the point that the soldier who has a "broken heart" will cause others to have the same condition. Ps-Jon has this idea: "he breaks their hearts as his own." N has "melt" and "broken." TJ generally renders the word like TO; see, for example, Josh 2:9.

10. When you approach a town to fight against it, you shall call to it words[19] of peace.

11. Although it responds peaceably and opens up to you, all the people present there may (still) be tributaries to you and they may (even be required to) serve you.

12. If it does not make peace with you, but wages war with you, you shall lay siege to it;

13. and when the Lord your God delivers it unto your hand, you may smite all its males with the edge of the sword.[20]

14. But the women, the children, and the livestock, and everything in the town, you may (do no more than) take them to yourself as spoil and (you may) eat the spoil of your enemy[1] which the Lord your God gives you.

15. Thus you shall do to all towns that lie very far from you, which do not belong to the towns of these nations.

16. However, in the towns of the latter peoples, which the Lord your god is giving you as a heritage, you (have permission) not (to) let a soul remain alive.

17. Rather, you may utterly destroy them—the Hittites and the Amorites, the Canaanites and the Perizzites, the Hivites and the Jebusites—as the Lord your God has commanded you,

18. so they do not teach you to do all the abhorrent[21] things that they have done for their idols[22] and you stand guilty before[23] the Lord your God.

19. When you besiege a town many days, making war against it, in order to subdue it, you must not destroy its tree, raising[24] the ax against it. You may eat of it, but you must not cut it down; trees of the field are not like a man to come against you during a siege.[25]

20. Only a tree which you know that it is not a tree yielding food, you may destroy it, and cut it down, and construct siegeworks[26] against the city that is waging war with you, until you have subdued it.

---

[19] TO and N add "words" for clarity, but Ps-Jon does not.

[20] TO has *lptgm dḥrb*, which could be considered a literal translation of *lpy ḥrb*, or given an aggadic interpretation as was done by Lowenstein (see note on 19:15). N and Ps-Jon are like TO.

10. ארי תקרב לקרתא לאגחא עלה ותקרי לה מלין דשלם:
11. ויהי אם שלם תעניניך ותיפתח לך ויהי כל עמא דישתכח בה יהון לך מסקי מסין ויפלחונך:
12. ואם לא תשלים עימך ותעביד עימך קרב ותצור עלה:
13. וימסרינה יי אלהך בידך ותמחי ית כל דכורה לפתגם דחרב:
14. לחוד נשיא וטפלא ובעירא וכל דיהי בקרתא כל עדאה תבוז לך ותיכול ית עדי סנאך דיהב יי אלהך לך:
15. כן תעביד לכל קרויא דרחיקן מינך לחדא דלא מקרוי עממיא האילין אינון:
16. לחוד מקרוי עממיא האילין דיי אלהך יהיב לך אחסנא לא תקיים כל נישמא:
17. ארי גמרא תגמרינון חיתאי ואימוראי כנענאי ופרזאי חיואי ויבוסאי כמא דפקדך יי אלהך:
18. בדיל דלא ילפון יתכון למעבד ככל תועבתהון דעבדין לטעותהון ותחובון קדם יי אלהכון:
19. ארי תצור לקרתא יומין סגיאין לאגחא עלה למכבשה לא תחביל ית אילנה לארמא עלוהי ברזלא ארי מיניה תיכול ויתיה לא תקוץ ארי לא כאינשא אילן חקלא למיעל מן קדמך בצירא:
20. לחוד אילן דתידע ארי לא אילן דמיכל הוא יתיה תחביל ותיקוץ ותבני כרקומין על קרתא דהיא עבדא עימך קרב עד דתכבשה:

[21] MT: "abhorrent." Some TO texts (N and Ps-Jon) deviate here and render "remote." The deviation is not appropriate since the emotion is not ascribed to God.

[22] MT: "gods." All the Targums have "idols."

[23] TO, N, and Ps-Jon add "before" instead of MT's *l*, "to."

[24] MT: "press." TO is more explicit. TO does not translate the same word explicitly in verse 19:5. N and Ps-Jon have a similar rendering.

[25] MT has an interrogative: "are trees of the field like a man to come against you during a siege?" TO prefers to avoid interrogatives, see Introduction. The LXX translates: "Does any man wish to have a tree in the field for the purpose of a rampart for you?" N and Ps-Jon render: "for the tree on the face of the field is not as a man to (be hidden, Ps-Jon) (run, N) before you (in the siege, Ps-Jon) (during time of trouble, N)." Ps-Jon has a gloss at the beginning of the verse about the Sabbath (see *Perush Jonathan*).

[26] The Targums place "siegeworks" in the plural although the MT has the singular.

The Aramaic *krqwmyn* is from the Greek *charakoma*. See *Milon Hahadash* by Eben-Shoshan, Jerusalem, 1974, p. 1107.

Chapter XXI

1. If one be found slain in the land that the Lord your God is giving you to possess, cast[1] upon the field, and it is not known[2] who killed him,[3]
2. your elders and magistrates shall go out and measure the towns which are round about him that is slain.
3. And it shall be that the town which is nearest to the corpse, the elders of that town shall take a heifer of the herd which has not been worked, which has not pulled a yoke;
4. and the elders of that town shall bring the heifer down to an uncultivated valley,[4] which is not tilled or sown, and they shall break[5] the heifer's neck there in the valley.
5. The priests, sons of Levi, shall come forward; for the Lord your God has chosen them to minister to Him and to bless in the name of the Lord, and by their words is (decided) every lawsuit and stroke of leprosy.[6]
6. Then all the elders of that town who are nearest to the corpse shall wash their hands over the heifer whose neck was broken in the valley.
7. And they shall answer and say: "Our hands did not shed[7] this blood, nor did our eyes see it (done)."

---

[1] MT: *npl.* TO and N translate here as in 22:4 (and parallel Sifre, b. Sotah 44b, and y. Sotah 89:2) to indicate that the body is lying on the ground and not hanging on a tree or floating in the water. Ps-Jon is more specific: "lying down and not hanged on a tree in the field, nor floating on the face of the water."

[2] Shefftel (BO) notes that TO does not translate *lʾ nwdᶜ* with *ʾytydᶜ* (as in Exod 2:14 and 21:36) but with *ydyᶜ*. Shefftel feels that this reflects the rabbinic interpretation. The language used here by TO implies that if even one person saw what occured, the law of this chapter would not apply. The word *ʾytydᶜ* implies testimony of at least two persons. The rabbis indicate: "even if one at another end of the world knew who killed him, they do not break the heifer's neck" (Sifre and b. Sotah 47b), and "if even a slave or a maid-servant knew who killed him, they do not break the heifer's neck" (y. Sotah 89:1).

N and Ps-Jon have a form of *ʾytydᶜ*. It is also found in the *Biblia Hebraica*, Ixar 1490, TO text.

XXI

1. ‏ארי ישתכח קטילא בארעא דיי אלהך יהיב לך למירתה רמי בחקלא לא ידיע מן קטליה:

2. ‏ויפקון סבך ודינך וימשחון לקרויא דבסחרנות קטילא:

3. ‏ותהי קרתא דקריבא לקטילא ויסבון סבי קרתא ההיא עגלת תורין דלא אתפלח בה דלא נגדת בניר:

4. ‏ויחתון סבי קרתא ההיא ית עגלתא לנחל ביר דלא יתפלח ביה ולא יזדרע ויקפון תמן ית עגלתא בנחלא:

5. ‏ויתקרבון כהניא בני לוי ארי בהון אתרעי יי אלהך לשמשותיה ולברכא בשמא דיי ועל מימרהון יהי כל דין וכל מכתש סגירו:

6. ‏וכל סבי קרתא ההיא דקריבין לקטילא יסחון ית ידיהון על עגלתא דנקיפא בנחלא:

7. ‏ויתיבון ויימרון ידנא לא אשדא ית דמא הדין ועיננא לא חזאה:

---

[3] The Targums change MT's "smote" to "killed" for clarity.

[4] MT: "rough valley." (See also Amos 5:24, TO on Gen 47:19, b. B.M. 104b, and b. Taanit 6b for the translation of the word *ʾytn*.) TO (like N, Ps-Jon, and the Peshitta) translates like the Sifre and b. Sotah 45b. ICC suggests that the true meaning of the word was forgotten and was explained through conjecture. The word in the Arabic means "unfailing." Comp. Exod 14:27, Amos 5:24, and Ps 74:15.

Adler (NL) feels that in using the future tense for "tilled" (literally, "will not be tilled") TO is rendering the verse like to R. Jonathan, who in b. Sotah 46b states that this verse applies to the future; i.e., the field may no longer be tilled. Cf. Sifre and m. Sotah 9:3. Churgin (*Halakhah*, p. 91) points out that there are TO texts which have the past tense. See also *Mene Targuma*. N and Ps-Jon have the future tense.

[5] While TO and Ps-Jon render "break" literally, N has the more specific "kill," as in b. Taan. 7a.

[6] MT: "controversy and stroke." The Targums use "lawsuit." Comp. 17:5.
TO and Ps-Jon add "leprosy" for clarity, but N does not do so. See 17:8.

[7] MT has *špkh* in the *Ketiv* and *špkw* in the *Keri*. (Similarly Ps 73:2 and Jer 2:15, 22:6.) TO as usual follows the *Keri*. N has *špkh*, which M corrects to *špkw*. Ps-Jon has *sdʾ*. This Targum reflects the understanding of m. Sotah 9:6 and Sifre. The elders said, "He came not into our hands that we should have dismissed him without sustenance" (in consequence of which he committed violence resulting in his death).

8. The priests shall say:[8] "Absolve Your people Israel whom You saved Lord, and do not lay guilt[9] for the blood of the innocent among your people Israel." And they will be absolved concerning[10] the blood.

9. Thus you will remove the shedder[11] of innocent blood from your midst, when you will be doing what is right before[12] the Lord.

10. When you go to battle against your enemies, and the Lord your God delivers them[13] into your hands and you take some of them captive,

11. and you see among the captives a beautiful woman[14] and you desire[15] her and would take her[16] to wife,

12. you shall bring her into your house, and she shall trim her hair, let her nails grow long,[17]

13. and discard her captive's garb from her. She shall remain in your house and bewail her father and mother a month's time; after that you may come to her and be her husband, and she shall be your wife.

---

[8] TO (like N and Ps-Jon) adds the gloss "And the priests shall say" probably to clarify that it is the priests who say the following words and not the city elders mentioned in the prior verse (see Rashi). The Targums are using the exact vorlage of m. Sotah 9:5 and Sifre. The priests have to be the ones who say these words since they are involved in ceremonies of atonement. Additionally, unless they say these words, their appearance, indicated in verse 5, would have no purpose.

[9] TO adds *ḥwbt* ("guilt" or "sin") here and *šdy*, "shedder," in the next verse for clarity. Here the concern is about the sin, while the concern in the next verse is about the shedder of the blood (Adler, NL). Ps-Jon has the addition in both verses; N does so in the first verse, but there is a scribal error in the second verse.

[10] TO adds "concerning" for clarity, but N does not. Ps-Jon has a gloss here.

[11] TO and Ps-Jon add "shedder" for clarity paralleling Sifre, b. Sotah 47b, and b. Keth. 37b. B. Keth. 37b, for example, indicates that if the guilty party is found, he is to be killed. The Targums treat verse 19:13 and many other instances similarly. N has a scribal error.

[12] MT: "in the eyes of God," an anthropomorphism which the Targums avoid by substituting "before." See 4:25. N also adds "pleasing."

[13] MT: "delivers him," in the singular. In accordance with its style (see 7:10 and elsewhere), TO (like N and Ps-Jon) recasts the word to the plural since the subject is plural.

[14] MT has the construct *št* and not the absolute *šh*. (See also I Sam 28:7 and Ps 58:9. In Gen 12:11, the construct is not used.) The Targums change the word to its absolute form.

8. כהניא יימרון כפר לעמך ישראל דפרקתא יי ולא תיתין חובת דם זכי בגו עמך
   ישראל ויתכפר להון על דמא:
9. ואת תפלי אשדי דם זכי מבינך ארי תעביד דכשר קדם יי:
10. ארי תיפוק לאגחא קרבא על בעלי דבבך וימסרינון יי אלהך בידך ותשבי שביהון:
11. ותיחזי בשביא איתתא שפירת ריו ותתרעי בה ותיסבה לך לאיתו:
12. ותעלינה לגו ביתך ותגלח ית רישה ותרבי ית טופרהא:
13. ותעדי ית כסות שביה מינה ותיתיב בביתך ותיבכי ית אבוהא וית אמה ירח יומין
    ובתר כן תיעול לותה ותבעלינה ותהי לך לאיתו:

---

[15] TO translates the different words in verses 11 and 14 in the MT by the same Aramaic word. (See 7:7.) N renders like TO, but Ps-Jon paraphrases "you approve of her."

[16] According to Shefftel (BO), *wtysbh* in TO implies a legal marriage. B. Ked. 22a understands the word in the MT as requiring marriage. N and Ps-Jon translate like TO.

[17] MT has a word which literally means "make."

TO's rendering parallels R. Akiba's view in b. Yeb. 48a, and Sifre, and the commentaries of Rashi, Ibn Ezra, Maimonides, and others. N, M, Ps-Jon, and LXX have "cut her nails," which is R. Eliezer's view.

Nachmanides explains that TO may be relying on Lev 25:21, where the word means "growth," but considers that II Samuel 19:25, which suggests a translation of "cutting the nails," to be better proof of the meaning here (see also Job 1:20 and Jer 7:29).

Berkowitz (LV) feels that TO may be translating the verse without reliance on the tannaitic dispute. In Gen 1:7, the word is translated "fix" by Rashi. It is possible that in both Gen and Deut the plain meaning of the word is "fix" and that TO, like Rashi, is informing us that she fixes herself, making her look homely, by letting her nails grow long.

TO does not parallel R. Akiba's interpretation of the following verse (v. 13): "Her father and her mother" refers to idolatry. TO has R. Eliezer's literal interpretation (see Sifre and b. Yeb. 48a). Aberbach and Grossfeld, in a draft of their introduction to *Targum to Genesis*, write: "This does not mean that TO generally agrees with R. Eliezer's line of thinking. It is not the practice of TO to provide homiletical interpretations when the plain meaning is adequate and unquestionable; but where a halakhic problem is involved as in Deut 21:12, TO generally follows R. Akiba's school." The authors cite four instances where TO follows R. Akiba's school in its translation of Deuteronomy. (Comp. Komlosh, *Hamikra*, p. 160, where two instances are cited where TO follows the opinion of R. Ishmael: Exod 21:19 and 22:2. See also the Introduction to this volume on the Targums and halakhah.)

14. Then, should you no longer desire[15] her, you must let her go where she wills. You must surely not sell her for money: you must not trade[18] with her since you afflicted her.

15. If a man has two wives, one loved and the other unloved, and they bear him sons, the loved and the unloved, but the firstborn is the son of the unloved,

16. on the day that he causes his sons to inherit what he has, he does not have the right[19] to treat the son of the loved (wife) as the firstborn, disregarding the son of the unloved (wife) who is (actually) the first-born.

17. Instead, he must separate[20] the firstborn, the son of the unloved one, and give him a double portion[21] of all he has;[22] since he is the beginning of his vigor, the right[23] of the firstborn is his.

18. If a man has a perverse[24] and rebellious son, who does not accept[25] the

[18] The word in the MT only occurs here and in 24:7. It is of doubtful origin and meaning. It is translated "enslave" by Philo (*Spec. Leg.* IV, 115), Sifre Num 2:14, Saadya, Rashi, Rashbam, Kimhi, etc. LXX has a word meaning "set aside" or "disregard." Lowenstein (NH) states that TO uses "trade" here and in 24:7 to let us know that he may not sell her for money, but he may give her as a gift or barter. Thus TO understands the verse like R. Judah in b. Sanh. 85b. If Lowenstein is correct, TO would be rendering the verse not according to the halakhah.

Ps-Jon is like TO, but N is more specific, "you shall surely not sell her for money nor trade her." If TO is understood as being in agreement with N, TO would be translating according to the halakhah. M has, "you shall not do business with her," which parallels R. Judah's teaching.

[19] MT: "he is not able." The Targums render here as in 12:17, 16:5, 17:15, etc. This wording recognizes that although the person has the power to do the act, the Torah prohibits it.

It is possible, but unlikely, that the Targums are interpreting as y. B. Bathra 8:4 and Sifre: "What does 'he is not able' mean? He has no right. When is he able? When he gives it as a gift (and not as an inheritance)."

[20] MT: "recognize." Shefftel (BO) explains that TO is saying: separate the first-born from his brothers by giving him a double portion. Adler (NL) notes that TO does not translate here as in Gen 42:8. He feels that TO wants to exclude the view expressed by R. Judah in b. Ked. 74a, 77b, b. B.B. 142b, and Sifre that the father

14. ויהי אם לא תתרעי בה ותפטרינה לנפשה וזבנא לא תזבנינה בכספא לא תיתגר בה
חלף דעניתה:

15. ארי יהוין לגבר תרתין נשין חדא רחומתא וחדא סנואתא ויילידן ליה בנין רחומתא
וסנואתא ויהי ברא בוכרא לסנואתה:

16. ויהי ביומא דיחסין לבנוהי ית דיהי ליה לית ליה רשו לבכרא ית בר רחומתא על
אפי בר סנואתא בוכרא:

17. ארי ית בוכרא בר סנואתא יפריש למיתן ליה תרין חולקין בכל דישתכח ליה ארי
הוא ריש תוקפיה ליה חזיא בכורותא:

18. ארי יהא לגבר בר סטי ומרוד ליתוהי מקביל למימר אבוהי ולמימר אימיה ומלפין
יתיה ולא מקביל מנהון:

needs to inform others of his son's right. Patshegan and Lowenstein argue the opposite. They note that TO does not render here as in Gen 27:23, 33:32, and elsewhere, and state that "recognize" in these verses implies the person himself sensing or understanding. Here the word implies informing others of the son's right, as is indicated in Sifre, b. Ked. 72a, and b. B.B. 157a. Ps-Jon has this explicitly, "informing everyone." N reads "bring near," and M, "give precedence to" and "recognize."

[21] MT has a phrase which could mean two-thirds. The expression is found also in II Kings 2:9 and Zech 13:8. The Targums (and Peshitta) reflect the halakhah. In Sifre and b. B.B. 122b there is a difference of opinion as to whether the firstborn gets two-thirds or a double portion. TJ to II Kings 2:9 translates differently paralleling a Midrash on the verse.

[22] The word in the Targums may imply that the firstborn receives a double share of material in his father's possession while he is alive, but not from things that come to the father after his death, such as debts and legacies (Sifre and b. Bech. 51b). However, it is a literal rendering.

[23] Some TO texts substitute the MT's *mšpṭ* with two words of similar meaning: *dynʾ* and *ḥzyʾ*. Lowenstein (NH) believes that TO is teaching a lesson contained in the Sifre: "It is proper (one meaning of *ḥzyʾ*) that the court (*dynʾ*) should give the firstborn the double portion if it is denied him." It is more likely, however, that the language in TO is the result of the joining of two TO versions, for N has *dynh* and Ps-Jon has *ḥzyʾ*. Neither B nor Sperber have *dynʾ*.

[24] MT and TO have a word from a root meaning one who deviates from the proper path. The word is also found in TJ to Jer 5:23, Ps 78:3, etc. N and Ps-Jon have "rebellious," and Sifre "foolish."

[25] MT: "hear." Characteristically, TO and Ps-Jon have "accept," and N "hear."

word[26] of his father or the word[26] of his mother, and (though) they instruct[27] him, he does not accept[25] from them,

19. his father and mother shall take hold of him and bring him out before[28] the elders of his town and to the gate of the court[29] of his community.

20. They shall say to[30] the elders of his town, "This son of ours is perverse[24] and rebellious; he does not accept[25] our word.[26] He is a devourer of meat and a wine-bibber.[31]

21. Then all the men of his town shall stone him with stones that he die. Thus you will remove the evildoer[32] from your midst; and all Israel will hear and be afraid.

22. If a man is guilty of a capital offense and is put to death, and you hang him on a gibbet,[33]

23. his corpse shall not remain all night on the gibbet,[33] but you must surely bury him the same day. For he was hanged because he sinned before the Lord.[34] You shall not defile your land that the Lord your God is giving you to possess.

---

[26] MT: "voice." TO and Ps-Jon have "word," but N has "voice."

In verses 18 and 20, TO and Ps-Jon use a form of *memra* for "word." Ps-Jon also has the Memra at the beginning of the verse: "We have transgressed the edict of the Memra of the Lord, therefore has this son been born to us."

[27] MT: "chasten." TO, N, Ps-Jon, LXX, and Peshitta reflect the plain meaning of the text, that the chastening is through exhortation. This is contrary to the rabbinic teaching that he is chastened through bodily punishment (m. Sanh. 8:4, Sifre, and b. Sanh. 71a). M has "punish." TO phrases 22:18 differently, according to the halakhah, because there the verse clearly concerns physical discipline.

Shefftel (BO) feels that although the rabbis deduced from this verse that the court gives the son physical punishment, TO does not inform the general public of all the details of this law because of the rabbinical desire to diminish the possibility that this law would be carried out. Wertheimer (*Or*) explains that TO does not mention physical punishment in this verse because the permission given to the court to punish him physically is derived from another verse. The parents, on the other hand, should not strike him. Komlosh (*Hamikra*, p. 163) suggests that TO may be giving pedagogical advice: warn him before you hit him.

[28] MT: "to." TO and Ps-Jon may have changed the "to" to "before" to emphasize that a hearing is held before the judges or to show respect. N has "to."

19. וייחדון ביה אבוהי ואימיה ויפקון יתיה לקדם סבי קרתיה ולתרע בית דין אתריה:

20. ויימרון לסבי קרתיה ברנא דין סטי ומרוד ליתוהי מקביל למימרנא זליל בסר וסבי חמר:

21. וירגמוניה כל אינשי קרתיה באבניא וימות ותפלי עביד דביש מבינך וכל ישראל ישמעון וידחלון:

22. וארי יהא בגבר חובת דין דקטול ויתקטיל ותיצלוב ותיצלוב יתיה על צליבא:

23. לא תבית נבילתיה על צליבא ארי מיקבר תקברניה ביומא ההוא ארי על דחב קדם יי איצטליב ולא תסאיב ית ארעך דיי אלהך יהיב לך אחסנא:

---

[29] MT: "the gate of his community." The Targums may be explaining the meaning of the idiom, that it refers to the place where the elders sat to administer judgment (see, for example, 22:15, 25:7, and Targums to Esth 2:21, Ruth 4:11 ff.). They may also be emphasizing that the parents may not take justice into their own hands, but must bring their son before a court. The interpretation is also in m. Mac. 10:2.

Typically, N renders MT's "elders" as "wise men."

[30] TO does not add "before" here. See prior verse.

[31] MT: "He is a glutton and a drunkard." The three Targums are more explicit, reflecting the understanding contained in Sifre and b. Sanh. 70a and 71a: "one does not become a perverse and rebellious son until he eats meat and drinks wine" (m. Sanh. 8:2). Comp. also Prov 23:20 f. and Isa 1:22.

[32]The Targums and Sifre add "doer," clarifying the MT.

[33] MT: "hang him on a tree." TO renders the MT's "tree" as "gibbet" as in Gen 40:19, where the context also requires this reading: "Pharaoh will lift up your head and impale you on a gibbet." Both N and Ps-Jon have "tree," *qys'*. See also Targum to Esther 2:23 and elsewhere where *qys'* is used.

Although *ṣlb'*, used here by TO for "hang," is translated in modern Hebrew "crucify," the word does not have this meaning in TO. TO always translates "hang" with this Aramaic word. See, for example, Gen 40:22. N is similar. Ps-Jon is much clearer and paraphrases: "first kill him with stoning and then hang him on a tree." Although Ps-Jon uses the same Aramaic word, it is clear it cannot mean crucifixion. See, however, the Targums on Esther and Ruth, the Qumran scrolls Pesher Nachum and the Temple Scroll 64:8, as well as Ezra 6:11, all of which have been interpreted by some scholars as referring to crucifixion. Sifre also indicates that he is hung after death.

[34] MT: "he that is hanged is a curse of God." The literal meaning could be misunderstood as blasphemy (cursing God); hence the need to reinterpret the phrase. The verse is discussed in m. Sanh. 6:6, where it is given three interpretations, in b. Sanh. 46b, and in Sifre.

Chapter XXII

1. Do not see your fellow's ox or his sheep go astray, and hide yourself from them, you must surely take them back to your fellow.
2. If your fellow is not living near you and you do not know him, you shall bring it into your home and it shall remain with you until your fellow claims[1] it; then you shall give it back to him.
3. You shall do the same with his ass; you shall do the same with his garment; and so shall you do with every lost item of your fellow which he lost and you find: you have no right[2] to hide yourself.[3]
4. Do not see your fellow's ass or his ox fallen on the road and hide yourself from them, you must surely help him raise (them).
5. A woman must not wear a man's armament,[4] nor shall a man put on woman's clothing; for whoever does these things is remote before[5] the Lord your God.
6. If you chance upon a bird's nest along the road, in any tree or on the ground, (with) fledglings or eggs and the mother sitting over the fledglings or on the eggs, do not take the mother with her young.
7. You shall surely send away the mother, and take (only) the young to yourself, in order that it may be well with you, and that you prolong (your) days.
8. When you build a new house, you shall make a parapet[6] for your roof, so that you do not bring a liability of a judgment of death[7] on your house if anyone should fall from it.

Rashbam, Luzzatto, and Elijah Gaon of Vilna feel that Elohim does not refer to God. TO renders Elohim with the Tetragrammaton. Rashi and Ibn Ezra are like TO. Ps-Jon has: "for it is a curse before God (not the Tetragrammaton) to hang a man, except his sins caused it; and because he is made in the image of God (the Tetragrammaton), you shall bury him," etc. N translates literally, with the Tetragrammaton, and adds "before."

Shefftel (BO) states that TO did not indicate the wrong committed so as not to decide between those who argue in the Sifre: one says all who are stoned are hung, and one says only he who curses God. Wertheimer (*Or*) explains that TO may be paralleling the rabbinic comment that you should not abuse this person after he has been hung and paid for his crime. Both interpretations are unlikely.

[1] MT has the constructive infinitive *drš*, but the Targums have the imperfect.

XXII

1. לא תיחזי ית תורא דאחוך או ית אימריה דטען ותיכבוש מנהון אתבא תתיבנון
לאחוך:

2. ואם לא קריב אחוך לותך ולא ידעת ליה ותיכנשניה לגו ביתך ויהי עימך עד דיתבע
אחוך יתיה ותתיבניה ליה:

3. וכן תעביד לחמריה וכן תעביד לכסותיה וכן תעביד לכל אבידתא דאחוך דתיבד
מיניה ותשכחינה לית לך רשו לכסיותה:

4. לא תיחזי ית חמרא דאחוך או תוריה רמן באורחא ותיכבוש מינהון אקמא תקים
עימיה:

5. לא יהי תקון זין דגבר על איתא ולא יתקן גבר בתקוני איתא ארי מרחק קדם יי
אלהך כל עביד אילין:

6. ארי תערע קינא דציפרא קדמך באורחא בכל אילן או על ארעא אפרחין או ביעין
ואימא רביעא על אפרחין או על ביעין לא תיסב אימא על בניא:

7. שלחא תשלח ית אימא וית בניא תיסב לך בדיל דייטב לך ותוריך יומין:

8. ארי תבני ביתא חדתא ותעביד תיקא לאיגרך ולא תשוי חובת קטול בביתך ארי
יפיל דנפיל מיניה:

---

[2] MT: literally, "you are not able." The Targums make a similar deviation in 21:16, 29, and elsewhere, paralleling Sifre.

[3] TO translates *ht'lm* in vv. 1 and 4 differently. Here TO seems to suggest hiding oneself from the owner. The other words seem to imply ignoring the lost item. Lowenstein (NH) writes that TO is phrased according to Raba's view in b. B.M. 26b: one may not hide oneself from the time the item fell until after the owner gives up hope of retrieving it, later taking the item for himself.

TO may not intend something different in this verse but merely uses a synonym for the words in vv. 1 and 4. M and Ps-Jon are like TO, but N uses the same words in all the verses: "cover your eyes."

[4] MT: "apparel." The three Targums can be said to reflect the opinion of R. Eliezer b. Yaakov, in the Sifre and b. Nazir 59a: "a woman may not go to war in armor, nor may she dress as a man generally." See TJ to Judges 5:26 for a similar rendering. However, the Hebrew word is a very general term and is also translated "arms" in Gen 27:3.

[5] MT: "abhorent." The Targums substitute as in 7:25 and add "before."

[6] Ibn Ezra explains the word in the MT as meaning "an enclosure." The top of the typical oriental house was flat and required a parapet for protection. TO therefore has *tyq'*, literally "a case." The fencing is like a case which guards things that are in it. N has "fence," but M and Ps-Jon have "railing."

[7] MT: "do not bring blood on your house." Ps-Jon also adds "judgment," but N and FT do not. TO paraphrases 17:5, 19:10, and Exod 2:1, 2, similarly.

9. You shall not sow your vineyard (with) mixed seed, else the crop from
   the seed you have sown and the yield of the vineyard become unclean.[8]
10. You shall not plow with an ox and an ass together.
11. You shall not wear a mixture of wool and linen joined[9] together.
12. You shall make tassels[10] on the four corners of the garment with which
    you cover yourself.
13. If a man marries[11] a woman and comes unto her, and he takes an
    aversion to her
14. and makes up charges against her and defames her, saying, "I married
    this woman; but (when) I approached[11] her, I did not find in her signs
    of virginity."
15. The girl's father and mother shall take and bring (the evidence of)
    the girl's virginity before[12] the elders of the town at the gate of the
    house of judgment of the place.[13]
16. And the girl's father shall say to the elders, "I gave this man my
    daughter to wife, but he has taken an aversion to her;
17. and he has made up charges, saying, 'I did not find in your daughter
    signs of virginity,' But here is (the evidence of) my daughter's vir-
    ginity!" And they shall spread out the cloth[14] before the elders of the
    town.

[8] MT: "become holy," which usually means, "forfeited to the sanctuary." TO
clarifies the phrase by construing like Sifre and b. Ked. 56b, that the seeds are unfit
for any use. See Isa 65:5. N has "lost," Ps-Jon "lest you become liable to burning
the mixed seed."

[9] TO adds, "joined" which is implied. The addition also precludes us from
thinking that one cannot wear two separate garments of both materials. As indicated in Sifre and b. Yeb. 5b, the prohibition is only when two materials are joined
together. This is not so with the mixture of animals; therefore "joined" is not used
in verse 10. See t. Kilayim chapter 4 and y. Kilayim 8:2. N and Ps-Jon have
"mixed."

[10] TO replaces tassels with a Greek word. The word *tzitzit* is found in three
places in Num, 15, 38, and 39, and TO recasts each with the Greek word used here
for tassel. Ps-Jon has *tzitzit* here, informing the reader that the verse refers to the
commandment to wear *tzitzit*. N has *tnyph*, "borders," to which M adds *tzitzit*.

Komlosh (*Hamikra*) argues that the use of the Greek word is an indication that
at least this part of the Targum existed during the pre-Mishnaic period (p. 28, note

9. לא תזרע כרמך עירובין דילמא תסתאב דמעת זרעא דתזרע ועללת כרמא:
10. לא תירדי בתורא ובחמרא כחדא:
11. לא תלבש שעטניזא עמר וכיתן מחבר כחדא:
12. כרוספדין תעביד לך על ארבע כנפי כסותך דתתכסי בה:
13. ארי יסב גבר איתתא וייעול לותה ויסנינה:
14. וישוי לה תסקופי מלין ויפיק עלה שום ביש ויימר ית איתתא הדא נסיבית ועלית לותה ולא אשכחית לה בתולין:
15. ויסב אבוהא דעולימתא ואימה ויפקון ית בתולי עולימתא לקדם סבי קרתא לתרע בית דין אתרא:
16. ויימר אבוהא דעולימתא לסביא ית ברתי יהבית לגברא הדין לאיתו ויסנה:
17. והא הוא שוי תסקופי מלין למימר לא אשכחית לברתך בתולין ואילין בתולי ברתי ויפירסון שושיפא קדם סבי קרתא:

71, also pp. 252–55). Berliner (*Targum*, p. 104) points out that the Greek word was used in pre-Mishnaic times before *tzitzit* became the accepted term. However, this is not conclusive. Greek words abound in third- and fourth-century rabbinic literature.

[11] Verses 13 and 14 have words in which scholars find different connotations. Regarding verse 13, Adler (NL on Gen 2:23 referring to Rashi on Gen 43:15) indicates that whenever TO uses *nsyb* for a male taking a female, the meaning is marriage. TO has the word in v. 13 in Gen 6:2; 34:4, 9, 16, and elsewhere. TO does not use the word in Gen 34:2, concerning Shechem's taking Dinah, since that taking was rape, not marriage. Other scholars read no special significance in the word.

On verse 14, Shefftel (BO) writes that TO's word does not necessarily imply sexual intercourse, thus not deciding between the rabbinical dispute in Sifre and b. Ket. 46a as to whether sexual intercourse is necessary. Adler disagrees and urges that TO is deciding like R. Eliezer ben Yaakov, who understands that intercourse is required. N is like TO, and Ps-Jon uses a word clearly indicating intercourse.

[12] TO has "before," instead of *ʾl*, "to."

[13] MT: "the elders of the town at the gate." The Targums add "place" and "house of judgment." Sifre states that the case is heard before a court in the locality of her father's house. Shefftel (BO) argues that since "place" is missing in TO to 25:7, the latter verse requires no restriction of jurisdiction of the court to her father's locality. The word is also missing in 17:5. It is in the MT of 21:19 where it appears to be synonymous with "gate" and has no special significance.

Characteristically, N changes "elders" to "wise men."

[14] The three Targums (and the Peshitta) translate this phrase literally. In Sifre and b. Ket. 46a, there is a dispute between R. Akiba and R. Ishmael as to whether the father must spread out the cloth or this language is to be understood only

18. The elders of that town shall take the man and flog[15] him,

19. and they shall fine him a hundred selas[16] of silver and give them to the girl's father; for the man has defamed a virgin in Israel. She shall remain his wife; he does not have the right[2] to divorce her all his days.

20. But if this charge proves true, the girl was found not to have signs of virginity,

21. then the girl shall be brought out to the entrance of her father's house, and the men of her town shall stone her with stones so that she dies; for she did a shameful thing in Israel, committing fornication in her father's house. Thus you will sweep away an evildoer[17] from your midst.

22. If a man is found lying with a woman, another man's wife, both of them shall be killed,[18] the man who lay with the woman and the woman. Thus you will sweep away an evildoer[17] from Israel.

23. If the girl is a virgin who is engaged to a man, and a man comes upon her in town and lies with her,

24. you shall take the two of them out to the gate of that town[19] and stone them with stones and they shall die: the girl because she did not cry out in the town, and the man because he violated his neighbor's wife. Thus you will sweep away an evildoer[17] from your midst.

25. But if the man comes upon the engaged girl in the open country, and the man takes hold of her and lies with her, only the man who lay with her shall be killed.[18]

26. But you shall do nothing to the girl. The girl does not deserve a judgment of killing,[20] for it is like when a man attacks another and murders him, so is this case:

figuratively: the father should make the matter as white (clear) as a sheet. Adler (NL) considers that in rendering the MT literally, TO is deciding that the father must spread out the cloth, in accordance with the opinion of R. Akiba as explained by R. Eliezer ben Yaakov. Conversely, Shefftel (BO) believes that TO is literal so as not to decide. The two also disagree in how to interpret verse 14. Lowenstein (NH) agrees with Adler on verse 17; he does not comment on verse 14. See also Mek. on Exod 22:2, Gen R. LXI, 3, and Eccl R. XI, 6. Ps-Jon to v. 15 has "take out the bed-sheet with the signs of virginity."

In 24:13, TO translates the word "wearing apparel." Here, from the context, the word is more inclusive.

[15] MT: "discipline." The Targums are like Sifre, b. Keth. 46a, Philo (*Spec. Leg.*

18. וידברון סבי קרתא ההיא ית גברא וילקון יתיה:
19. ויגבון מניה מאה סלעין דכסף ויתנון לאבוהא דעולימתא ארי אפיק שום ביש על בתולתא דישראל וליה תהי לאיתו לית ליה רשו למפטרה כל יומוהי:
20. ואם קושטא הוה פתגמא הדין לא אישתכחו בתולין לעולימתא:
21. ויפקון ית עולימתא לתרע בית אבוהא וירגמונה אינשי קרתה באבניא ותמות ארי עבדת קלנא בישראל וזנאה בית אבוהא ותפלי עביד דביש מבינך:
22. ארי ישתכח גבר שכיב עם איתתא איתת גבר ויתקטלון אף תרויהון גברא דשכיב עם איתתא ואיתתא ותפלי עביד דביש מישראל:
23. ארי תהי עולימתא בתולתא דמארסא לגבר וישכחינה גברא בקרתא וישכוב עימה:
24. ותפקון ית תרויהון לתרע קרתא ההיא ותרגמון יתהון באבניא וימותון ית עולימתא על עיסק דלא צוחת בקרתא וית גברא על עיסק דעני ית איתת חבריה ותפלי עביד דביש מבינך:
25. ואם בחקלא ישכח גברא ית עולימתא דמארסא ויתקף בה גברא וישכוב עימה ויתקטיל גברא דשכיב עימה בלחודוהי:
26. ולעולימתא לא תעביד מידעם לית לעולימתא חובת דין דקטול ארי כמא דיקום גברא על חבירה ויקטלניה נפש כן פתגמא הדין:

III, 82), and Josephus (*Antiquities* IV, 8:23) that the discipline is with lashes. LXX has a word meaning "instruct" or "correct." See 21:18 and 25:3.

[16] TO, N, and Ps-Jon add "selas" for clarity; M has "zuzin."

[17] The Targums add "doer," a characteristic change for clarity. The addition is also in Sifre.

[18] MT: "die." TO, M, and Ps-Jon are more specific, but N is literal. See v. 25.

[19] Adler (NL) notes that TO did not add "court" here as in 21:19 and elsewhere because here the text is not referring to the deliberation of the case but its execution. For a similar situation, see b. Ket. 45b. N is like TO, but Ps-Jon has the characteristic "court."

[20] TO adds "judgment" again, clarifying that the judgment must be made by a court. N and Ps-Jon are like TO, and Ps-Jon adds a gloss that the raped girl needs a divorce from her husband. This gloss is apparently not according to the halakhah. *Perush Jonathan* explains that Ps-Jon considers the woman suspect because she may have been a willing participant. Kasher (*Torah Shelemah* XXVI, p. 152) explains that Ps-Jon is referring to a girl who wanted to be caressed by the man who raped her, but did not want intercourse. Possibly, Ps-Jon has the wife of a priest in mind. Perhaps "priest" was originally mentioned and then accidentally omitted.

Kasher (*Torah Shelemah* XVII, p. 287) notes that Rashi does not explain this verse according to the halakhah.

27. since he came upon her in the field, the engaged girl cried out, and there was no one to save her.
28. If a man comes upon a virgin who is not betrothed[21] and he seizes her and lies with her, and they are discovered,
29. the man who lay with her shall give the girl's father fifty selas[16] of silver, and she shall be his wife. Because he has violated her, he does not have the right[21] to divorce her all his days.

Chapter XXIII

1. A man shall not marry his father's (former) wife, and not uncover his father's garment.
2. No one who is cut[1] or injured[1] shall be priviliged[2] to enter into the congregation of the Lord.
3. No mamzer shall be privileged[2] to enter into the congregation of the Lord; even the tenth generation shall not be priviliged[2] to enter into the congregation of the Lord.
4. No Ammonites[3] or Moabites[3] shall be privileged[2] to enter into the congregation of the Lord; even the tenth generation shall not be privileged[2] to enter into the congregation of the Lord forever;

The Targums change MT's *mwt*, "death," to *ktl*, "killing," a characteristic deviation for clarity. Adler, NL to Gen 2:17, argues that the change is made to teach that the death sentence is delivered by the court.

[21] TO translates the MT literally, but Kasher (*Torah Shelemah* XXVI, p. 51) thinks that TO parallels the opinion of R. Akiba and not R. Jose's in Sifre and m. Ket. 3:3: "If a girl were betrothed and then divorced (and afterwards she was seduced or violated), R. Jose the Galilean says, She has no claim to compensation (for the seduction); R. Akiba says, She is entitled to compensation, and her compensation belongs to her (and not to her father as indicated in 22:28)." R. Jose is of the opinion that if she is not engaged, there is no compensation at all. Ps-Jon is like TO, but N has "who was never betrothed," which, according to Kasher, is the opinion of R. Jose.

The problems with this interpretation are (1) TO renders the verse literally, and

27. ארי בחקלא אשכחה צוחת עולימתא דמארסא ולית דפריק לה:
28. ארי ישכח גבר עולימתא בתולתא דלא מארסא ויאחדינה וישכוב עימה וישתכחון:
29. ויתין גברא דשכיב עימה לאבוהא דעולימתא חמשין סלעין דכסף וליה תהי לאיתו חלף דעניא לית ליה רשו למפטרה כל יומוהי:

XXIII

1. לא יסב גבר ית איתת אבוהי ולא יגלי כנפא דאבוהי:
2. לא ידכי דפסיק ודמחבל למיעל בקהלא דיי:
3. לא ידכי ממזירא למיעל בקהלא דיי אף דרא עשיראה לא ידכי ליה למיעל בקהלא דיי:
4. לא ידכון עמונאי ומואבאי למיעל בקהלא דיי אף דרא עשיראה לא ידכי להון למיעל בקהלא דיי עד עלמא:

(2), as Kasher points out, N itself, in Exod 22:16, translates the same words literally, as do TO and Ps-Jon.

[1] MT: "No one whose testes are cut or whose member is injured." This refers to operations resulting in the man becoming a eunuch. TO phrases the verse with delicacy, as do Sifre, b. Yoma 70a, and b. Yeb. 70a, 75a, b, and omits "testes" and "member." The Aramaic word for "cut" is also found in Lev 22:25. N translates "cut" and "castrated." Ps-Jon reverses the order found in TO. E. Z. Melammed (*Bible Commentators*, p. 190) believes that TO has the correct order, for this is how Sifre interprets the verse.

[2] Shefftel believes that TO adds "privileged" frequently in this chapter to emphasize that the individual is only not permitted to marry an Israelite woman (y. Ked. 3:12; y. Yeb. 8:3; b. Ked. 69a, 71a, 73a; b. Yeb. 76a; b. Ber. 28a; Sifre; comp. Ruth 2:10, Lam 1:10, Mal 3:3). He is fit for other purposes. N is literal. Ps-Jon is more specific: "not privileged to take a wife"; and, in v. 3, "an upright wife." Shefftel is not correct. The word does not imply what he suggests. It was added for clarity.

[3] MT has the singular for both nations. TO changes them to the plural since the plural is used later in the passage. In verse 8, in contrast, TO retains the singular because of the singular form used later in the passage. N has the singular in both verses. Ps-Jon translates like TO. Sifre speaks of the nations in the plural in both places.

5. because they did not meet[4] you with food and water on your journey after you left Egypt, and because they hired against you Balaam son of Beor, from Pethor Aram, on the Euphrates,[5] to curse you.—

6. But the Lord your God did not want to accept[6] from Balaam; instead, the Lord your God turned the curses into blessings for you, for the Lord your God loves you.—

7. You shall never seek their welfare or benefit all your days, forever.

8. You shall not reject[7] an Edomite, for he is your kinsman. You shall not reject[7] an Egyptian, for you were a sojourner[8] in his land.

9. Children born to them are privileged[2] to enter into the congregation of the Lord in the third generation.

10. When you go out as a camp against your enemies, be on your guard against anything bad.

11. If there is among you a man who is not clean because of a nocturnal emission, he must leave the camp, he must not enter the camp.

12. Then toward evening, he shall bathe in water, and at sundown he may enter the camp.

13. There shall be a set area[9] for you outside the camp. You shall go there, outside.

14. You shall have a blade upon your weapon,[10] and when you sit on the outside, you shall dig a hole with it and then turn backward and cover up your excrement.

15. Since the Shekinah[11] of the Lord your God moves about in your camp to protect you and to deliver your enemies before you, let your camp be holy; let Him not see anything offensive[12] lest His Memra[13] turn away from doing good[14] for you.

---

[4] MT: literally, "preceded." TO and Ps-Jon translate according to the plain meaning of the text and do not include the teachings in b. Yeb. 73a and b. Sanh. 103b, which are derived from a literal reading. N has the literal reading.

[5] MT: "Naharaim." TO and Ps-Jon explain the name. See also Gen 24:10, Judg 3:8, and Ps 60:2. N is literal. See Gen R. 30.

[6] MT: "hear." TO and Ps-Jon have a characteristic substitution but may also be referring to God's refusal to accept Baalam's curse (Num 24:5). This understanding is in the Sifre. N, as usual, retains MT's "hear."

TO replaces MT's singular "blessing" and "curse" with plurals because of the context.

5. על עיסק דלא ערעו יתכון בלחמא ובמיא באורחא במיפקכון ממצרים ודאגר עלך
   ית בלעם בר בעור מפתור ארם דעל פרת ללטטותך:

6. ולא אבא יי אלהך לקבלא מן בלעם והפך יי אלהך לך ית לוטין לבירכן ארי ריחמך
   יי אלהך:

7. לא תתבע שלמהון וטבתהון כל יומך לעלם:

8. לא תרחיק אידומאה ארי אחוך הוא לא תרחיק מצראה ארי דיר הויתא בארעיה:

9. בנין דיתילדון להון דרא תליתאה ידכי להון למיעל בקהלא דיי:

10. ארי תיפוק משריתא על בעלי דבבך ותסתמר מכל מידעם ביש:

11. ארי יהי בך גבר דלא יהי דכי מקרי ליליא ויפוק למברא למשריתא לא ייעול לגו
    משריתא:

12. ויהי למיפני רמשא יסחי במיא וכמיעל שימשא ייעול לגו משריתא:

13. ואתר מתקן יהי לך מברא למשריתא ותיפוק תמן לברא:

14. וסיכתא תהי לך על זינך ויהי במתבך לברא ותחפר בה ותתוב ותכסי ית מפקתך:

15. ארי יי אלהך שכנתיה מהלכא בגו משריתך לשיזבותך ולמימסר סנאך קדמך ותהי
    משריתך קדישא ולא יחזי בך עבירת פתגם ויתוב מימריה מלאיטבא לך:

---

[7] MT: "abhor."

[8] MT: *ger*, usually translated by the Targums "proselyte," is rendered here "sojourner" since the Israelites were not proselytes.

[9] MT: *yd*; literally, "hand." Comp. 2:37, Num 2:17, Jer 6:13, and elsewhere. The Targums are like Sifre and LXX.

[10] MT: *'znk*, a word found only here. In Aramaic the word means "weapon." The Targums translate like Sifre and Rashi. The LXX has "a paddle in your girdle."

[11] The Targums add Shekinah (N, "glory of His Shekinah") to express God's presence in the camp.

[12] MT has a word which literally means "the nakedness of a thing." See also 24:1. TO can also be translated as "sinful." TO's interpretation is found in Sifre, Maimonides, and others. N is literal. Ps-Jon has "impure."

[13] TO adds Memra. TO mixes Shekinah and Memra in the same verse. Adler thinks this is a scribal error or the mixture of two TO versions. Shekinah is found in b. Sotah 3b and Sifre. N and Ps-Jon have Shekinah twice. It is likely that TO has the Memra turn because unlike the other Targums, TO restricts the use of Shekinah to a depiction of God among the people or in Heaven.

[14] MT: "and turn away from you." Besides joining Memra, TO includes "good," probably to lessen the implication that God will turn away entirely from the people. Ps-Jon has this addition, but not N.

16. You shall not turn over to the hand[15] of his master a slave of the nations[16] who seeks refuge with you from before[17] his master.

17. He shall live with you, among you, in any place he may choose, in a settlement[18] of yours, wherever he pleases; you must not ill-treat him.

18. A woman of the daughters of Israel shall not become the wife of a slave, and no man of Israel shall marry a bondwoman.[19]

19. You shall not bring the fee of a whore or the exchange[20] of a dog into[21] the sanctuary[22] of the Lord your God in fulfillment of any vow, for both are remote before[23] the Lord your God.

20. You shall not deduct interest[24] to your brothers, interest[24] of money, interest[24] of food, interest[24] of anything else that can be deducted as interest.[24]

---

[15] TO and Ps-Jon add "hand" for clarity. N and some TO texts do not.

[16] TO adds "nations" to inform us that the verse refers to an Israelite slave of a non-Israelite who escapes to Israel from another country. This understanding is contained in b. Git. 45a (Shefftel, BO, and Churgin, *Halakhah*, p. 92). Comp. Sifre and Rashi. Ps-Jon includes a non-Israelite slave who escapes to the Land of Israel. N translates literally.

[17] MT: *m'm*, which TO changes to "from before." Patshegen states that TO may be implying that the slave did not escape entirely from his master's control, but only entered Israel. E. Z. Melammed (*Bible Commentators*, p. 197) suggests that "before" is used as a sign of respect, for the same reason that it is often added prior to "the Lord."

[18] MT: "gates."

[19] MT: "No Israelite woman shall be a cult prostitute, nor shall any Israelite man be a cult prostitute." The words *qdšh* and *qdš* in the MT are translated by Ibn Ezra, Radak, and others as an expression of readiness (comp. Isa 13:3, Zeph 1:7, and Jer 6:14), and the word is generally understood as alluding to men and women who prostitute themselves for the pagan sanctuary (see, for example, b. Sanh. 54b). TO alters the plain meaning of the text.

Nachmanides believes that the Biblical prohibition constitutes an admonition addressed to the members of the court that they should not permit an Israelite woman to sit in public soliciting illicit intercourse. He thinks that TO combined with this prohibition the matter of a slave and bondwoman who live with Israelites in common-law marriage to indicate thereby that the betrothal is invalid and it is considered prostitution. This teaching is in b. Kidd. 68a, 69a, and Maimonides, *Laws of Forbidden Intercourse* 2:13.

Aberbach and Grossfeld (in the draft of their introduction to *Targum Onkelos*

16. לא תמסר עבד עממין ליד רבוניה דישתיזב לותך מן קדם ריבוניה:
17. עמך יתיב בינך באתרא דיתרעי בחדא מן קרוך בדייטב ליה לא תוניניה:
18. לא תהי איתתא מבנת ישראל לגבר עבד ולא יסב גברא מבני ישראל איתא אמא:
19. לא תעיל אגר זניתא וחולפן כלבא לבית מקדשא דיי אלהך לכל נדר ארי מרחק
   קדם יי אלהך אף תרויהון:
20. לא תרבי לאחוך רבית כסף רבית עיבור רבית רבית כל מידעם דיתרבי:

to Genesis available to the author) point out that : "TO's interpretation—which may have been influenced by the fact that in Talmudic times there was no conceivable danger of Jewish cult prostitution—agrees with that of R. Akiba who maintained that 'If a heathen or a slave has intercourse with a Jewish woman, the issue is a Mamzer (i.e., legally, a bastard).' R. Ishmael, on the other hand, applies this verse to bestiality." Cf. b. Ker. 3a, b. Sanh. 54b, and Komlosh, *Hamikra*, p. 166, n. 4, where the literature on the subject is cited in full.

Churgin (*Halakhah*, p. 92) suggests that TO did not translate this verse according to its plain meaning, but speaks about the prohibition against marrying a slave, in order to censure the Hasmonean family for marrying into the family of Herod, a descendant of slaves. Melammed (*Bible Commentators*, p. 197) believes TO may be reflecting a lost Midrash.

Shefftel (BO) notes that the language of the MT is subject to several interpretations but since TO was written for popular consumption, it includes a reading that would be most helpful to the people.

Ps-Jon has: "You shall not profane your daughters to make them harlots, nor shall any man of Israel debase himself by fornication." N and LXX are literal, rendering the two words as "female and male prostitute."

20 MT: "price." The Targums are apparently paralleling the understanding in Sifre and b. Tem. 29a, 30a: "if one has exchanged a lamb for a dog."

21 TO, N, and Ps-Jon add "to" for clarity. As *d*, the addition is frequent and generally not noted in this study.

22 MT: "house." TO, N, and Ps-Jon add "sanctuary" for clarity.

23 TO and Ps-Jon change "abhorrent" to "remote" and add "before." This part of the text is missing from N, but M adds it.

24 The word *nšk*, literally "bite," is found five times in this verse and twice in the next verse in the MT. TO (and all sources, such as b. B.M. 75b and Sifre) replaces the metaphor. Comp. Lev 25:36–37, where *nšk* is translated by TO as *ḥbl*, "mutilate," "blemish," or "wound." In Lev, the MT uses two words, one of which clearly means "interest"; hence TO avoids the redundancy there. Here, where only *nšk* is used, TO does not use a metaphor, such as "blemish" or "bite." N and Ps-Jon have "loan."

21. You may deduct interest[24] to foreigners, [25] but do not deduct any interest[24] to your countryman; so that the Lord your God may bless you in all your undertakings in the land which you are about to enter and occupy.

22. When you make a vow before[26] the Lord your God, do not put off fulfilling it, for the Lord your God will surely require it of you, and you will have incurred guilt;

23. whereas you incur no guilt if you refrain from vowing.

24. You must fulfill what has crossed your lips and perform what you have vowed before[26] the Lord your God, having made the promise with your own mouth.

25. When you hire yourself[27] in your neighbor's vineyard, you may eat your fill of the grapes, as many as you want; but you must not put any in your vessel.

26. When you hire yourself[27] into your neighbor's standing grain, you may pluck ears with your hand; but you must not put a sickle to your neighbor's grain.

Chapter XXIV

1. When a man takes a wife and possesses her, and she finds no favor in his eyes because he finds some transgression[1] in her, and he writes her a deed of dismissal,[2] and hands it to her, and dismisses[2] her from his house;

2. she leaves his household and goes and becomes the wife of another man;

[25] MT: "stranger."

[26] TO, N, and Ps-Jon add "before" instead of MT's *l*, "to."

[27] MT: "When you come." The majority view, in Sifre, y. Maas. 2:4, and b. B.M. 87b, is that this verse and the following refer to laborers hired to work in the vineyard and the field. Contrast b. B.M. 92a and Josephus, *Antiquities* IV, 8.21. TO paraphrases here as in 21:14; 24:14, 15. Maimonides (*Commandments*) relies on TO to this verse for the 267th negative command. Ps-Jon is more specific: "When you come to work for hire." N has: "as a field laborer."

[1] MT: "nakedness." TO translates here as in 23:15, avoiding a metaphor.

21. לבר עממין תרבי ולאחוך לא תרבי בדיל דיברכנך יי אלהך בכל אושטות ידך על
ארעא דאת עליל לתמן למירתה:

22. ארי תידר נדר קדם יי אלהך לא תאחר לשלמותיה ארי מתבע יתבעיניה יי אלהך
מינך ויהי בך חובא:

23. וארי תתמנע מלמידר לא יהי בך חובא:

24. אפקות ספותך תיטר ותעביד כמא דנדרתא קדם יי אלהך נדבתא דמלילתא בפומך:

25. ארי תיתגר בכרמא דחברך ותיכול ענבין כנפשך סיבעך ולמנך לא תיתין:

26. ארי תיתגר בקמתא דחברך ותקטוף דמלין בידך ומגלא לא תרים על קמתא דחברך:

XXIV

1. ארי יסב גבר איתתא ויבעלינה ויהי אם לא תשכח רחמין בעינוהי ארי אשכח בה
עבירת פיתגם ויכתוב לה גט פיטורין ויתין בידה ויפטרינה מביתיה:

2. ותיפוק מביתיה ותהך תהי לגבר אוחרן:

In b. Git. 90a and Sifre there is a dispute between the School of Shammai and
the School of Hillel as to what are the grounds for a divorce. The School of Shammai requires something unseemly. The School of Hillel allows any grounds. Thus,
it is possible to argue that TO is like the School of Shammai, not according to the
halakhah. However, Adler (NL), Shefftel (BO), and Kasher (*Torah Shelemah*
XXVI, p. 60) argue that the language in TO is like the School of Hillel. Komlosh
(*Hamikra*, p. 164) thinks that TO found a middle path between both opinions.
Ps-Jon is like TO, but N has "nakedness." Some TO versions also have "nakedness."

² MT: "a writ of separation . . . sends her away." TO renders according to the
intent of the verse and not literally. See Isa 50:1 and Jer 3:8.

Kasher notes that m. Git. 9:3 has the language of the three Targums (TO,
Ps-Jon, and N): "The essential formula of a letter of divorce is: Behold, you are
permitted to any man. R. Judah says, (one should write in Aramaic): Let this be
from me your letter of expulsion (the language of Ps-Jon), and writ of release (N)
and deed of dismissal (TO) that you may be wedded to whatever man you desire."

Kasher explains that R. Judah teaches (and the law is as he teaches) that when
one divorces his wife, each has to understand what it written in the writ of divorce.
Since, as Rashi points out in b. Meg. 21b, the Targum was written for the average
person, who does not understand Hebrew, it contains the language that R. Judah
teaches should be used in the divorce.

Churgin (*Halakhah* pp. 84–85) feels that TO translates "dismissal" because this
was the way the phrase would be understood by the masses, and not to teach a
halakhah. He argues that TO deviates in Exod 13:17 and Lev 23:40 for the same
reason.

3. then this latter man rejects her, writes her a deed of dismissal,[2] hands
   it to her, and dismisses[2] her from his house; or the last man dies,
   who had taken her as a wife;
4. the first husband who dismissed[2] her is not permitted[3] to take her to
   wife again, since she has been defiled[4]—for that would be remote[5]
   before the Lord. You must not bring guilt upon the land which the
   Lord your God is giving you as a heritage.
5. When a man has taken a new bride, he shall not go out with the army
   or be assigned to it for any purpose; he shall be free[6] one year for the
   sake of his household, to give happiness to the woman he has taken.
6. A handmill or an upper millstone shall not be taken in pawn, for he is
   causing with them a loss of food to people.[7]
7. If a man is found to have kidnapped a person, a fellow Israelite, trad-
   ing[8] him or selling him, that kidnapper shall be killed;[9] thus you shall
   sweep out an evildoer[10] from your midst.
8. Take heed in the plague of leprosy that you observe diligently, and do
   all that the priests the levites shall instruct you; as I commanded
   them, so you shall observe to do.
9. Remember[11] what the Lord your God did to Miriam on the journey
   after you left Egypt.
10. When you make a loan of any sort to your neighbor, you must not
    enter his house to take his pledge.
11. You must remain outside, while the man to whom you made the loan
    brings the pledge out to you.

[3] MT: "not able." This is the usual rendering of the three Targums.

Ps-Jon to Num 11:26 indicates that, prior to the promulgation of this command, Moses' mother married a man when Amram, Moses' father, divorced her.
She had two sons with him, Eldad and Medad. Later, she remarried Amram and
bore Moses.

[4] TO translates literally, thereby paralleling the School of Shammai or referring
to the intercourse with the second husband (Adler, NL). N and Ps-Jon use the same
word, but N adds "by another man."

[5] The Targums replace MT's "abhorrent" with "remote."

[6] MT: literally, "clean." See I Kings 15:22. TO and Ps-Jon translate similarly,
but N is literal.

[7] MT: "for he takes a life in pledge." Rashbam points out that TO is explaining

3. ויסנינה גברא בתראה ויכתוב לה גט פיטורין ויתין בידה ויפטרינה מביתיה או ארי
ימות גברא בתראה דניסבה ליה לאיתו:

4. לית ליה רשו לבעלה דפטרה למתב למיסבה למיהוי ליה לאיתו בתר
דאסתאבת ארי מרחקא היא קדם יי ולא תחייב ית ארעא דיי אלהך יהיב לך
אחסנא:

5. ארי יסב גבר איתתא חדתא לא יפוק בחילא ולא יעיבר עלוהי לכל פיתגם פני יהי
לביתיה שתא חדא ויחדי ית איתתיה דנסיב:

6. לא יסב משכונא ריחיא ורכבה ארי בהון מתעביד מזון לכל נפש:

7. ארי ישתכח גבר גניב נפשא מאחוהי מבני ישראל ויתגר בה ויזבנינה ויתקטיל
גנבא ההוא ותפלי עביד דביש מבינך:

8. אסתמר במכתש סגירו למיטר לחדא ולמעבד ככל דילפון יתכון כהניא ליואי כמא
דפקידתנון תטרון למעבד:

9. הוי דכיר ית דעבד יי אלהך למרים באורחא במיפקכון ממצרים:

10. ארי תירשי בחברך רשות מידעם לא תיעול לביתיה למיסב משכוניה:

11. בברא תקום וגברא דאת רשי ביה יפיק לך ית משכונא לברא:

what is implied in the MT—if one demands a pledge through the court for his debt, he may not take as the pledge anything through which food is prepared. See b. B.M. 113a and 115a. A. Geiger (*Jüdische Zeitschrift 9* [1871], p. 92) argues that TO derived its translation from Ps-Jon, which it shortened. The latter Targum has: "A man shall not take the millstones, lower or upper, as a pledge; for they are necessary in making food for everyone." Komlosh (*Hamikra*, p. 205) believes that both TO and Ps-Jon are separate translations based on the same rabbinic tradition. N is phrased similarly: "for the pledge is a necessity of life." There are glosses in N and Ps-Jon which Kasher discusses at length (*Torah Shelemah* XXVI, pp. 152–53).

E. Z. Melammed (*Bible Commentators*, pp. 190–91) states that TO adds "with them" to parallel the teaching in Sifre, "this rule applies to anything that is prepared." More likely the addition was made for clarity. It is implied in the MT.

8 MT: "enslave." See note on 21:14. N and Ps-Jon are like TO. Some say the Targums had a text reading *wtgr* instead of *wtqb*.

9 MT: "die." The Targums are more specific.

10 TO, N, Ps-Jon, and Sifre add "doer" as in 21:21 and elsewhere.

11 MT: *zkwr*. TO: *hwy dkyr*. See note on 5:12, 9:7, 25:17, Exod 20:8 and 13:3. TO reads each as a positive commandment, like Nachmanides: it is "a great admonition to refrain from it (slander) both in public and in private, whether with intent to hurt and to shame or with no intent to harm at all." N translates similarly. Ps-Jon has: "Be careful."

12. If he is a needy man,[12] you shall not go to sleep in his pledge;
13. you must return the pledge to him at sundown, that he may sleep in his cloth and bless you; and it will be to your merit[13] before the Lord your God.
14. You shall not abuse a needy[12] and destitute laborer, whether a fellow countryman or a proselyte,[14] in your land, within your settlement.[15]
15. You must pay him his wages on the same day, before the sun sets, for he is needy[12] and gives[16] his soul for it; else he will cry before[17] the Lord against you and you will incur guilt.
16. Parents shall not be put to death by the mouth of[18] children, nor children be put to death by the mouth of[18] parents; a person shall be put to death (only) for his own crime.
17. You shall not subvert the rights of the proselyte[20] (and the) orphan, and you shall not take a widow's garment in pawn.
18. Remember that you were a slave in Egypt and that the Lord your God redeemed you from there; therefore do I enjoin you to observe this thing.[19]

[12] Adler notes that TO does not translate here (*mskyn*) as in Exod 22:24 and Deut 24:14, 15 (*'ny'*). He suggests that TO may be teaching (like Sifre and b. B.M. 114b) that the law of verse 12 applies even to one who is not destitute. Some TO texts have the same word as the other verses, but N, Ps-Jon, and FT have the same word as TO does, here and in the other verses, except that Ps-Jon has a different word in 24:15.

[13] MT: *ṣdqh*, "right" or "justice." TO: *zkwt'*, "blessing," "merit," "favorable judgment," etc. See 6:25 and Gen 15:6, where the word is translated in the same way. N and Ps-Jon render the word similarly. See the author's *Targumic Studies* for a discussion of the concept of *Zachut*, "merit."

[14] TO, N, and Ps-Jon are like Sifre, indicating that this word refers to a proselyte who embraces the Jewish faith out of conviction. Ps-Jon states this explicitly: "or the proselyte who converts."

[15] MT: "gates."

[16] MT: "lifts." The Hebrew idiom, implying the striving after something, is also found in Jer 22:27, 44:14; Ezek 24:25; Hos 4:8; Ps 24:4, 25:1, and 143:8. TO changes "lifts" to "gives" for the sake of clarity. The word "gives" in this connection is found in b. B.M. 111b, 112a, and Sifre.

TO should be understood literally. Referring to Sifre, Rashi and Rashbam explain that for the sake of payment, the man is exposing his life to the danger of

12. ואם גבר מסכין הוא לא תשכוב במשכוניה:
13. אתבא תתיב ליה ית משכונא כמיעל שימשא וישכוב בכסותיה ויברכינך ולך תהי זכו קדם יי אלהך:
14. לא תיעישוק אגירא עניא ומסכינא מאחך או מגיורך דבארעך בקירוך:
15. ביומיה תתין אגריה ולא תיעול עלוהי שימשא ארי עניא הוא וליה הוא מסר ית נפשיה ולא יקרי עלך קדם יי ויהי בך חובא:
16. לא ימותון אבהן על פום בנין ובנין לא ימותון על פום אבהן אינש בחוביה ימותון:
17. לא תיצלי דין גיור ייתם ולא תיסב משכונא כסות ארמלא:
18. ותידכר ארי עבדא הויתא במצרים ופרקך יי אלהך מתמן על כן אנא מפקיד לך למעבד ית פתגמא הדין:

death. n has this specifically: "for the sake of payment for his work, he gives before you his soul." Ps-Jon has: "he hopes (for the pay) to sustain his soul." Peshitta: "he pays you his soul."

[17] Characteristically, to, n, and Ps-Jon have "before" instead of mt's "to."

[18] mt: *l*, sometimes meaning "for"; as in Jer 15:15; Ps 69:8, 44:23. to has *l pwm*, adding "mouth."

Rashi believes that to is implying "by the evidence of their children" (as in y. Sanh. 3:9 and b. Sanh. 27b); to is teaching that the testimony of relatives may not be accepted in a criminal or civil case. Thus, Rashi would translate to literally, "by the mouth of" as in 25:4. This interpretation is identical with that offered by R. Akiba. Cf. y. Sanh 3:10, 21c; Pnei Moshe, *ad loc.*, also Sifre, where the same interpretation is given anonymously. According to b. Sanh. 86a, the author of the anonymous opinion in Sifre is R. Simeon b. Yohai, a disciple of R. Akiba. Cf. Komlosh, *Hamikra*, p. 263 and Luzzato, OG, p. 24.

This passage is referred to twice in the Hebrew Bible (II Kings 14:6 and II Chron 25:4), and in both instances the meaning is that the family of a criminal is not to be punished for the criminal's crime. See also Exod 34:7, Ps 62:12, b. Yeb. 79a, and b. Ber. 7a.

Churgin (*Halakhah*, p. 93) points out that to has the addition because it is implied in the text and not to inform us of a halakhah. He notes that to can mean that a father cannot be punished for the sin of his children.

Ps-Jon has both ideas: "Fathers shall not die either by the testimony or the crime of the children." n has: "Fathers shall not be put to death because of the crime of children, nor children because of the crime of fathers."

[19] Ps-Jon adds that the Memra redeems.

[20] to, n, and Ps-Jon translate *gr* as "proselyte," like Sifre. See verse 14, 1:16, etc. Some to texts have "sojourner."

19. When you reap your harvest in your field and overlook a sheaf in the field, do not turn back to get it; it shall go to the proselyte,[20] the orphan, and the widow, in order that the Lord your God may bless you in all your undertakings.
20. When you beat down the fruit of your olive trees, do not go over them again; that shall go to the proselyte,[20] the orphan, and the widow.
21. When you gather the grapes of your vineyard, do not pick it over again; that shall go to the proselyte,[20] the orphan, and the widow.
22. Remember that you were a slave in the land of Egypt; therefore do I enjoin you to observe this thing.

Chapter XXV

1. When there is a lawsuit[1] between men and they go to judgment[2] and a decision is rendered finding the innocent not guilty and condemning the guilty,
2. if the guilty one is obliged[3] to be flogged, the judge shall have him lie down and be given lashes in his presence, as his guilt warrants, by count.
3. Give him forty lashes,[4] do not add, lest being flogged more than these, to excess, your brother be degraded before your eyes.
4. You shall not muzzle the mouth[5] of an ox while it is threshing.
5. When brothers dwell together and one of them dies and leaves no son,[6] the wife of the deceased shall not be (married) outside to a stranger. Her husband's brother shall unite with her: take her as his wife and perform the levir's duty.
6. The first son that she bears shall succeed in the name of his brother who is dead, that his name not be blotted out in Israel.[7]

---

[1] MT: "controversy." TO is not phrased as in Gen 13:7 and 8 because there the verses concern a controversy not decided by a court. Here a court must be involved, as indicated in b. Sanh. 10a and Sifre. N is like TO, but Ps-Jon and M are literal.

[2] Some TO texts have "to the judges." N adds "before" here, an example where "before" is added even though it is not in connection with God.

19. ‏ארי תיחצוד חצדך בחקלך ותנשי עומרא בחקלא לא תתוב למיסביה לגיורא‎
‏ליתמא ולארמלתא יהי בדיל דיברכינך יי אלהך בכל עובדי ידך:‎
20. ‏ארי תיחבוט זיתך לא תפלי בתרך לגיורא ליתמא ולארמלתא יהי:‎
21. ‏ארי תקטוף כרמך לא תעליל בתרך לגיורא ליתמא ולארמלתא יהי:‎
22. ‏ותידכר ארי עבדא הויתא בארעא דמצרים על כן אנא מפקיד לך למעבד ית‎
‏פתגמא הדין:‎

XXV

1. ‏ארי יהי דין בין גבריא ויתקרבון לדינא וידיניננון ויזכון ית זכאה ויחייבון ית‎
‏חייבא:‎
2. ‏ויהי אם בר חייב לאלקאה חיבא וירמיניה דינא וילקיניה קדמוהי כמיסת חובתיה‎
‏במנין:‎
3. ‏ארבעין ילקיניה לא יוסיף דילמא יוסיף לאלקיותיה על אלין מחא רבא ויקל אחוך‎
‏לעינך:‎
4. ‏לא תיחוד פום תורא בדישיה:‎
5. ‏ארי יתבון אחין כחדא וימות חד מינהון ובר לית ליה לא תהי איתת מיתנא לברא‎
‏לגבר אוחרן יבמה ייעול עלה ויסבה ליה לאיתו ויבמינה:‎
6. ‏ויהי בוכרא דתליד יקום על שמא דאחוהי מיתנא ולא יתמחי שמיה מישראל:‎

[3] TO and FT add "obliged," but N and Ps-Jon do not. Adler (NL) believes that TO is making the point contained in b. Mac. 2b that not everyone is punished with flogging. It is more likely that TO and FT are (a) simply translating MT's *bn* or (b) emphasizing that flogging can only be administered after a judicial decision.

[4] Although TO, N, and Ps-Jon are literal, Ps-Jon adds the halakhah that only thirty nine lashes are administered (b. Mak. 22a, etc.).

[5] TO and Ps-Jon add "mouth" for clarity. See 24:16. N does not.

[6] TO, N, Ps-Jon, and Peshitta (but not LXX) render "son" literally, although Sifre, b. Yeb. 22b, and Mac. 2b state that the word includes a daughter.

[7] The commentator Ritba (on b. Yeb. 24a) explains that the rabbis interpret this verse to mean that the levir inherits from his dead brother. Contrary to what is indicated in this verse, he need not call his son by the name of his dead brother. TO (like Rashbam, *ad loc.*; Ibn Ezra on Exod 21:8, etc.) renders the verse literally, contrary to the halakhah. Cf. b. Erub. 23b, b. Kid. 80b, b. Hul. 6a and 133a. Although the text of N is somewhat defective, the Targum also appears to be literal. Ps-Jon adds: "shall stand in the inheritance," as b. Yeb. 24a and Sifre.

7. But if the man does not agree[8] to marry his brother's widow, his brother's widow shall go to the court[9] gate before[10] the elders[11] and declare, "My husband's brother does not want[12] to establish a name in Israel for his brother; he does not want[13] to perform the duty of a levir with me."

8. The elders of his town shall summon him and talk to him. If he stands and says, "I do not want[14] to marry her,"

9. his brother's widow shall approach him before[15] the elders, untie[16] the sandal off his foot, spit before him,[17] answer and say: "Thus shall be done to the man who will not build up his brother's house!"

10. And his name shall be called in Israel: "The house of the untied[16] shoe."

11. If two men get into a quarrel with each other, a man and his fellow, and the wife of one comes up to save her husband from the hand of his antagonist and puts out her hand and seizes him by the place[18] of his shame,

---

[8] MT: "does not desire." TO does not read here as in Gen 34:19, Num 20:21, Deut 1:26, or later in verse 8. The Targum may be avoiding redundant usage or it may be paralleling the Mishnaic view (Yeb. 12:4) that the man can refuse to take her as a wife for any reason (for example, because of age differences or because their personalities are not conducive to a happy union, cf. b. Yeb. 44a and 101b). It is also possible that TO chose the Hebrew word contained in 29:9, for as Rashi suggests there, the word implies a "covenant" or "agreement." Thus the Targum does not address the man's feelings, "he does not desire," and points instead to the pertinent point, "he does not agree." Ps-Jon is like TO, but N has the customary word.

[9] TO, N, and Ps-Jon add "the court," as was done several times earlier, to emphasize rule by law court. Cf. 21:19 and 22:15. That a law court is required is explicit in the Sifre and b. Yeb. 101a, b.

The word "gate" is frequently rendered "court" by the Targums. Comp., for example, the Targums to Ruth 3:11, 4:10, 11; Amos 5:10; and Lam 5:14. The word is also frequently rendered "settlement" in Deut.

[10] MT: ʾl, "to."

[11] While TO translates "elders" literally throughout this portion, N and Ps-Jon have "wise men." In fact Ps-Jon indicates "five wise men": three judges and two witnesses (*Perush Jonathan*). Comp. 27:1, where N continues to have "wise men," but Ps-Jon is like TO.

7. ואם לא יצבי גברא למיסב ית יבמתיה ותיסק יבמתיה לתרע בית דינא לקדם סביא
ותימר לא צבי יבמי לאקמא לאחוהי שמא בישראל לא אבי ליבמותי:

8. ויקרון ליה סבי קרתיה וימללון עימיה ויקום ויימר לא רעינא למיסבה:

9. ותתקרב יבמתיה לותיה לקדם סביא ותשרי סיניה מעל ריגלוהי ותרוק באפוהי
ותתיב ותימר כדין יתעביד לגברא דלא יבני ית ביתא דאחוהי:

10. ויתקרי שמיה בישראל בית שרי סינא:

11. ארי יצון גברין כחדא גבר ואחוהי ותתקרב איתת חד לשיזבא ית בעלה מיד מחוהי
ותושיט ידה ותיתקף בבית בהתתיה:

---

[12] MT: "refuses." By its change, TO creates a redundant phrasing because "does not want" is also found at the end of the verse. There is no apparent reason for the deviation, and some TO texts have "refuses."

[13] Some TO texts have the same word *ṭby* discussed in note 8.

[14] Adler (NL) notes that TO is not phrased here as in verse 7 and suggests that the Aramaic *rʿynʾ* may imply a more courteous refusal, since it is being made before the woman. (MT has the perfect tense. TO has the participle in some versions.) Ps-Jon has the same words as TO, but N has the word TO and Ps-Jon use in v. 8 also in v. 7.

[15] MT: "in the eyes of." This metaphor is replaced by TO and Ps-Jon, but not N, which is literal. Comp. 34:12, where TO retains the metaphor.

[16] E. Z. Melammed (*Bible Commentators*, p. 191) posits that TO (and Peshitta) use the word *šry*, "untied," instead of the literal *šlp*, "loosen," "pull," "draw," as it generally does since, as indicated in b. Yeb. 102a, untying the shoe before taking it off is an important aspect of the procedure.

[17] Herskovics ("Halakhah") notes that TO translates MT's *bpnyw*, "in his face," literally, *ʾnpwhy*. The Targum does not use *qdmwy*, "before him," as it does in Num 12:14 and Deut 7:24, for example, or as N and Ps-Jon do here. This is contrary to the halakhah that the spitting is not done in his face but only before him. E. Z. Melammed (*Bible Commentators*, p. 208) suggests that the Aramaic word meaning "face" also means "before." This is true, but had TO wanted to teach halakhah, it would have rendered clearly like N and Ps-Jon.

[18] The three Targums and M add "place" probably because the man is presumably dressed and thus she cannot take hold directly of his genitals, only of the general area. It is unlikely that the Targums are hinting at the lesson which is also in Sifre: "this includes not only the genitals but any *place* of danger." The Targums also add "place" in Gen 1:10, 13:10, 23:6, 42:27, Exod 7:28, 28:38, and Num 32:4.

12. you shall cut off her hand;[19a] show no pity.
13. You shall not have in your pouch a weight and a weight, a larger and a smaller.
14. You shall not have in your house a measure and a measure, a larger and a smaller.
15. Perfect and correct[19] weights[20] you shall have, perfect and correct[19] measures you shall have, if you are to endure long in the land that the Lord your God is giving you.
16. For everyone who does those things, is remote[21] before[22] the Lord your God, everyone who does falsely.[23]
17. Remember[24] what Amalek did to you on your journey when you were delivered from Egypt;
18. how he overtook you on the way, and killed[25] all who were following[26] behind you, and when you were faint and weary, and he was not afraid before[22] the Lord.[27]
19. Therefore, when the Lord your God grants you rest[28] from all your enemies around you, in the land that the Lord your God is giving you as a hereditary portion, you shall blot out the memory of Amalek from under heaven. Do not forget![29]

[19a] Herskovics ("Halakhah"), Melammed (*Bible Commentators*, p. 207), and others note that Sifre and b. B.K. 28a explain that the halakhah is that she has to pay monetary damages but that her hand is not cut off. Thus TO's failure to deviate here seems to be an interpretation contrary to the halakhah. N and Ps-Jon are also literal. As noted in the Introduction, TO is primarily a literal translation and was not intended to teach halakhah. Thus one should not derive an interpretation from TO's failure to deviate.

[19] MT: "just." The Targums replace the word twice in this verse and are more explicit than the MT. In some TO texts (including B and Sperber), TO changes the *vav* twice to a *daleth*. N does not do so. Ps-Jon has the *daleth* because of extra words: "Perfect weights and true balances." Perhaps the TO texts with the *daleth* took the *daleth* from Ps-Jon or a proto-Ps-Jon.

[20] MT: "stone." Again, the Targums are more explicit. TO places this word and "measure" in the plural form although the MT has the singular.

12. ותיקוץ ית ידה לא תחוס עינך:
13. לא יהי לך בכיסך מתקל ומתקל רב וזעיר:
14. לא יהי לך בביתך מכילא ומכילא רבתא וזעירתא:
15. מתקלין שלמין דקשוט יהון לך מכילן שלמן דקשוט יהוין לך בדיל דיורכון יומך על ארעא דיי אלהך יהיב לך:
16. ארי מרחק קדם יי אלהך כל עביד אלין כל עביד שקר:
17. הוי דכיר ית דעבד לך עמלק באורחא במיפקכון ממצרים:
18. דערעך באורחא וקטיל בך כל דהוו מתאחרין בתרך ואת משלהי ולאי ולא דחיל מן קדם יי:
19. ויהי כד יניח יי אלהך לך מכל בעלי דבבך מסחור סחור בארעא דיי אלהך יהיב לך אחסנא למירתה תימחי ית דוכרניה דעמלק מתחות שמיא לא תתנשי:

[21] MT: "abomination." Ps-Jon is like TO, but N has "detestable and remote."

[22] The Targums add "before."

[23] MT: "wickedness." The Targums are more explicit.

[24] TO: *hwy dkyr*. See note on 24:9 for an explanation of this deviation and other citations. TO is like Sifre, b. Meg. 18a, Nachmanides, and others that this verse requires continuous public reading of this section about Amalek. N and Ps-Jon are like TO.

[25] MT has a metaphor, "cut off a tail," which the Targums explain, paralleling Sifre. The word is also in Josh 10:19. It is not rendered "killed" there by TJ because of the context.

[26] MT has a word generally translated "the weak" or "subdued." Again, TO is more explicit. N and Ps-Jon interpret the MT with a gloss: "and slew everyone of those among you who were thinking to go aside from My Memra." Ps-Jon has an aggadah which N refers to briefly: "They were men of the tribe of Dan, who had idols. The cloud abandoned them, and Amalek took them and cut off their sexual organs."

[27] MT: Elohim, which TO characteristically changes to the Tetragrammaton.

[28] MT has the constructive infinitive *bhnyh*. TO and Ps-Jon have *kd* plus the imperfect; N had *dy* and the imperfect.

[29] Ps-Jon adds "until the days of the Messiah, you shall not forget." Cf. Ps-Jon to Exod 17:16 and the author's *Targumic Studies*. TO does not have theological lessons.

Chapter XXVI

1. It shall be when you enter the land that the Lord your God is giving you as a heritage, and you inherit it and settle in it,
2. you shall take some of every first fruit of the soil, which you harvest from the land that the Lord your God is giving you, put it in a basket[1] and go to the place where the Lord your God will choose to make his Shekinah[2] dwell there.
3. You shall come to the priest that shall be at that time and say to him, "I acknowledge this day before[3] the Lord your God that I have entered the land which the Lord confirmed[4] to our fathers to give us."
4. The priest shall take the basket[1] from your hand and set it down before the altar of the Lord your God.
5. You shall speak and say before the Lord your God: "Laban the Aramean sought to destroy my father.[5] He went down to Egypt and sojourned there as a small nation;[6] but there he became a nation, great, mighty and populous.
6. The Egyptians dealt harshly with us and oppressed us; they imposed heavy labor upon us.
7. We prayed[7] before[3] the Lord, the God of our fathers, and the Lord accepted[8] our prayer[9] and there was revealed before Him[10] our plight, our misery, and our oppression.
8. The Lord freed us from Egypt by a mighty hand, by an uplifted arm, and with great visions,[11] and by signs and portents.
9. He brought us to this place and gave us this land, a land producing[12] milk and honey.

---

[1] MT has *ṭnʾ*, a word of doubtful origin, here, verse 4, 28:5 and 17. TO, N, and Ps-Jon translate it "basket," as do the Sifre and y. Bek. 81:7.

[2] MT: "His name." Ps-Jon is like TO, but N has "glory of the Shekinah."

[3] The Targums have "before" instead of MT's *l*, "to."

[4] MT: "swore." FT and M have the Memra confirm.

[5] The first part of the declaration in the MT is obscure and has been variously paraphrased as: "My father was a fugitive Aramean," "My father was a perishing Aramean," and "My father was a straying Aramean."

The LXX has: "My father abandoned Aram." The Peshitta: "My father was led to Aram." The Vulgates: "An Aramean persecuted my father."

XXVI

1. ויהי ארי תיעול לארעא דיי אלהך יהיב לך אחסנא ותירתה ותיתיב בה:
2. ותיסב מריש כל איבא דארעא דתעיל מארעך דיי אלהך יהיב לך ותשוי בסלא ותהך לאתרא דיתרעי יי אלהך לאשראה שכנתיה תמן:
3. ותיתי לות כהנא דיהי ביומיא האינון ותימר ליה חויתי יומא דין קדם יי אלהך ארי עלית לארעא דקיים יי לאבהתנא למיתן לנא:
4. ויסב כהנא סלא מן ידך ויחתניה קדם מדבחא דיי אלהך:
5. ותתיב ותימר קדם יי אלהך לבן ארמאה בעא לאובדא ית אבא ונחת למצרים ודר תמן בעם זעיר והוה תמן לעם רב תקיף וסגי:
6. ואבאישו לנא מצראי ועניונא ויהבו עלנא פולחנא קשיא:
7. וצלינא קדם יי אלהא דאבהתנא וקביל יי צלותנא וגלי קדמוהי עמלנא וליאותנא ודוחקנא:
8. ואפקנא יי ממצרים ביד תקיפא ובדרע מרמם ובחזוונא רבא ובאתין ובמופתין:
9. ואתינא לאתרא הדין ויהב לנא ית ארעא הדא ארע עבדא חלב ודבש:

It is unclear whether "My father" refers to: (1) the three patriarchs, (2) Abraham (Rashbam), (3) Jacob (Ps-Jon, Rashi, Ibn Ezra, Soforno, and others), or (4) to Laban (TO, N, Sifre, the Passover Hagaddah, and elsewhere). (Cf. Jer 50:6, where the prophet speaks of the Israelites being lost sheep: "their shepherds caused them to go astray." Also, Ps 119:176: "I have gone astray like a lost sheep; seek Thy servant; for I have not forgotten Thy Commandments.")

Besides clarifying that the verse refers to Laban, TO and N add "sought to," which is also found in the Passover Hagaddah, making it clear that Laban was not successful.

[6] MT: *mty*, rendered "nation" by the Targums.

[7] MT: "cried." The Targums are more specific.

[8] MT: "heard," a characteristic change for TO and Ps-Jon. N has "heard."

[9] MT: "voice," a usual deviation for the Targums.

[10] MT: "saw." This too is a characteristic change. See, for example, 4:25.

[11] MT: "awesome power," another usual deviation, found in the Sifre. See, for example, 4:34. TO does not remove the anthropomorphic "hand" and "arm," see note on 11:2. MT's "outstretched" is changed to "uplifted." TO renders "visions" in the plural in some versions although the MT has the singular. Sifre has a discussion which includes the plural. TJ to Jer 32:21 has the same reading.

[12] MT: "flowing." A characteristic TO change. See, for example, 6:3, 11:19, 26:15, 27:3, 31:20. N and Ps-Jon have: "a land (producing, N) of fruits; rich (and clean, N) as milk, and sweet (and tasty, N) as honey."

10. Wherefore I now bring the first fruits of the soil which You, O Lord, have given me." You shall leave it before the Lord your God and bow low before the Lord your God.

11. And you shall rejoice in every good thing that the Lord your God has bestowed upon you and the people[13] of your household, you and the levite and the proselyte[14] in your midst.

12. When you finished tithing all the tenth part of your yield—in the third year, the year of the tithe—and have given it to the levite, the proselyte,[14] the orphan, and the widow, that they may eat in your settlement[15] and be satisfied,

13. you shall declare before the Lord your God: "I have cleared out[16] the consecrated tenth[17] from the house; and I have given it to the levite, and the proselyte,[14] the orphan, and the widow, according to all Your commands that You commanded me; I have neither transgressed nor forgotten any of Your commandments.

14. I have not eaten of it while in mourning,[18] I have not exchanged[19] any of it while I was unclean, and I have not given any of it for[20] the dead. I have accepted[21] the Memra[22] of the Lord my God; I have done just as You commanded me.

---

[13] The Targums add "people of" for clarity.

[14] MT: *ger*. The Targums follow their customary practice in translating this word, Cf. b. Mac. 19a.

[15] MT: "gates." TO and Ps-Jon have the singular; N and FT the plural.

[16] Some TO tests and Ps-Jon are like the Sifre: "I did not exchange it even for a ritually clean thing." N has "separated." Sperber's TO text and B are literal.

[17] TO adds "tenth." See b. Sotah 32a. N and Ps-Jon do not do so. Adler (NL) believes the addition is the error of a copyist. It is not found in other verses; as, for example, Lev 22:10. Sifre indicates that *qdš* implies more than *Maaser*, the "tenth." The word is also found in 12:26, but not B or Sperber's text, and there too the addition seems to be an error.

[18] MT: "grief." E. Z. Melammed (*Bible Commentators*, p. 191) notes that TO's rendering parallels Sifre.

[19] See note 16. Here Sperber's TO text and B have "exchanged" but other texts have "cleared out." N and Ps-Jon have "separated."

[20] MT: *lmt*. Some TO texts have *ʾl myt*, while B and Sperber have *lmyt*, a reading preferred by Shefftel (BO).

10. וכען הא איתיתי ית ריש איבא דארעא דיהבת לי יי ותחתיניה קדם יי אלהך
ותיסגוד קדם יי אלהך:
11. ותיחדי בכל טבתא דיהב לך יי אלהך ולאינש ביתך את וליואה וגיורא דבינך:
12. ארי תשיצי לעסרא ית כל מעסר עללתך בשתא תליתיתא שנת מעסרא ותיתין
לליואה לגיורא ליתמא ולארמלתא וייכלון בקרוך ויסבעון:
13. ותימר קדם יי אלהך פליתי קודש מעסרא מן ביתא ואף יהבתיה לליואה ולגיורא
ליתמא ולארמלתא בכל פיקודך דפקידתני לא עברית מפיקודך ולא אתנשיתי:
14. לא אכלית באיבלי מיניה ולא חליפית מניה במסאב ולא יהבית מניה למית קבילית
למימרא דיי אלהי עבדית ככל דפקידתני:

Shefftel writes that if the *ʾl myt* reading is correct, TO could be said to be translating in accordance with R. Akiba's teaching in the Sifre. R. Eliezer is said to
interpret "nor have I given thereof for the dead" as meaning "to prepare a coffin
and shrouds for it." R. Akiba, on the other hand, interprets the words "nor have I
given thereof" as meaning "I have not even used it in exchange for clean, edible
things." (Comp. m. Ma. Sh. 1:1: "Second tithes may not be sold or bartered. Nor
may a man say to his fellow in Jerusalem, 'Here is wine, give me oil (in
exchange).'") Thus, according to R. Akiba, the expression "nor have I given thereof" stands as an independent statement, and the word *lmt* is connected with the
prior statement, "I have not eaten thereof in my mourning—for the dead."

It is also arguable that TO is separating the phrase "the dead" from what pre-
cedes it, to avoid an allusion to the sectarian practice of placing food in the grave
with the dead, for the use of the departed spirit on its journey to the Underworld
(Tob. 4:18, Sir. 30:18, ICC, pp. 291–92).

Both of these interpretations, relying on one word, are probably incorrect. N
and M have *ʾl* and Ps-Jon does not. Yet all of these Targums speak about giving the
second tithes for shrouds, and N adds coffin; thus the PT parallels R. Eliezer's
interpretation of the verse and still uses *ʾl*.

[21] MT: "hear." This is a characteristis deviation.

It is arguable, but unlikely, that TO is referring to a teaching contained in Sifre
and Rashi that this verse refers to the *acceptance* of the prophet Malachi's (3:10)
bidding to bring tithes to the Temple. There is no biblical requirement to do so.
See also Neh 10:39, 40, Rashi on 13:5, and Adler, NL to that verse, who writes that
TO does not parallel Rashi's teaching. N has "hear."

[22] MT: "voice." TO replaces it with Memra, but N and Ps-Jon add Memra. See v.
17.

15. Look down from Your holy abode, from heaven, and bless Your People Israel and the land You have given us, as You confirmed[23] to our fathers, a land producing[12] milk and honey."

16. This day the Lord your God commands you to observe these laws and rules; keep and do them with all your heart and with all your soul.

17. You have made the Lord an object of your love[24] this day, to be for you a God, that you will walk in the ways that are right before Him[25] and keep His statutes, His commandments and His laws, and to accept[21] His Memra.[22]

18. and the Lord has made you an object of His love[24] this day, to be His beloved[26] people, as He told you, keeping all His commandments.

19. And He will set you high above all the nations that He has made in praise, in name and in honor, and that you shall be a holy people before[3] the Lord your God, as He said.

Chapter XXVII

1. Moses and the elders of Israel charged the people, saying: "Observe[1] all the commandments that I enjoin upon you this day.

2. It will be on the day you shall cross the Jordan into the land that the Lord your God is giving you, that you shall set up large stones. Coat them with plaster

3. and inscribe upon them all the words of this Torah when you cross over. That you may enter the land that the Lord your God is giving you, a land producing[2] milk and honey, as the Lord, the God of your fathers, told you.

---

[23] MT: "swore."

[24] MT: *hʾmrt*, the definition of which is not known for certain, but which probably means: "You caused the Lord to say." The word in the Hiphil form occurs only here and in the next verse. TO uses the word, *ḥṭbt*, found in b. Hag. 3a (a word translated by Jastrow as "the only object of your love"; Rashi, "sole or unique object of praise"; Aruch, "a unique concept"; Maharsha, "separation"). The Talmud has: "He further expounded: Thou hast avouched the Lord this day . . . and the Lord has avouched thee this day (Deut 26:17–18). The Holy One, blessed be He, said to Israel: You have made me a unique object of your love in the

15. אִסְתְּכִי מִמְּדוֹר קֻדְשָׁךְ מִן שְׁמַיָּא וּבָרֵךְ יָת עַמָּךְ יָת יִשְׂרָאֵל וְיָת אַרְעָא דִּיהַבְתְּ לָנָא כְּמָא דְקַיֵּימְתָּא לַאֲבָהָתַנָא אֲרַע עָבְדָא חֲלַב וּדְבַשׁ:

16. יוֹמָא הָדֵין יְיָ אֱלָהָךְ מְפַקֵּיד לָךְ לְמֶעְבַּד יָת קְיָמַיָּא הָאִלֵּין וְיָת דִּינַיָּא וְתִטַּר וְתַעְבֵּיד יָתְהוֹן בְּכָל לִבָּךְ וּבְכָל נַפְשָׁךְ:

17. יָת יְיָ חֲטַבְתְּ יוֹמָא דֵין לְמֶהֱוֵי לָךְ לֶאֱלָהּ וּלְמֶהַךְ בְּאוֹרְחָן דְּתַקְנָן קֳדָמוֹהִי וּלְמִטַּר קְיָמוֹהִי וּפִקּוּדוֹהִי וְדִינוֹהִי וּלְקַבָּלָא לְמֵימְרֵיהּ:

18. וַיְיָ חֲטָבָךְ יוֹמָא דֵין לְמֶהֱוֵי לֵיהּ לְעַם חֲבִיב כְּמָא דְמַלִּיל לָךְ וּלְמִטַּר כָּל פִּקּוּדוֹהִי:

19. וּלְמִתְּנָךְ עִלַּי עַל כָּל עַמְמַיָּא דַּעֲבַד לְתוּשְׁבְּחָא וּלְשׁוּם וְלִרְבוּ וּלְמֶהֱוָךְ עַם קַדִּישׁ קֳדָם יְיָ אֱלָהָךְ כְּמָא דְמַלִּיל:

XXVII

1. וּפַקֵּיד מֹשֶׁה וְסָבֵי יִשְׂרָאֵל יָת עַמָּא לְמֵימָר טַרוּ יָת כָּל תַּפְקִדְתָּא דַּאֲנָא מְפַקֵּיד יָתְכוֹן יוֹמָא דֵין:

2. וִיהֵי בְּיוֹמָא דְתֶעֶבְּדוּן יָת יַרְדְּנָא לְאַרְעָא דַּיְיָ אֱלָהָךְ יָהֵיב לָךְ וּתְקִים לָךְ אַבְנִין רַבְרְבָן וּתְסוֹד יָתְהֵין בְּסִידָא:

3. וְתִכְתּוֹב עֲלֵיהֵין יָת כָּל פִּתְגָמֵי אוֹרַיְתָא הָדָא בְּמֶעְבָּרָךְ בְּדִיל דְּתֵיעוֹל לְאַרְעָא דַּיְיָ אֱלָהָךְ יָהֵיב לָךְ אֲרַע עָבְדָא חֲלַב וּדְבַשׁ כְּמָא דְמַלִּיל יְיָ אֱלָהָא דַּאֲבָהָתָךְ לָךְ:

world, and I shall make you a unique object of My love in the world."[2] The LXX has "chosen."

It is possible that the word in the MT is a technical term for parties contracting a covenant. TO, realizing that the technical term would not be understood by the masses, uses a word referring to the goal of the covenant (as described in the Talmud), rather than the preparation of it.

N has: "the Memra of the Lord will be king over you." Ps-Jon uses the same Aramaic word as TO and adds a gloss: "as it is written, Hear, Israel: the Lord our God is one Lord."

[25] MT: "His ways." The Targums add "that are right before Him" to avoid an unseemly anthropomorphism. See 8:6, 10:12, 11:22, 19:9, 28:9, 30:16, and elsewhere.

[26] MT: *segulah*. See 7:6, 14:2, Exod 19:5, and elsewhere. N and FT include two interpretations of the word: the literal *segulah* and "beloved"; "a beloved people as a special possession." Ps-Jon has "unique."

[1] This word is in the singular form in the MT. The Targums recast it in the plural to fit in with the words following, which are plural. Some TO versions have the singular form.

[2] MT: "flowing with." See 26:9.

4. It will be when you cross the Jordan, you shall set up these stones, about which I charge you this day, on Mount Ebal, and coat them with plaster.
5. There you shall build an altar before[3] the Lord your God, an altar of stones. Do not lift (any) iron (tool) upon them;
6. you must build the altar of the Lord your God of perfect stones. You shall offer on it burnt offerings before[3] the Lord your God,
7. and you shall slaughter holy offerings,[4] and eat there, rejoicing before the Lord your God.
8. You shall inscribe on the stones every word of this Torah very plainly."[5]
9. Moses and the levitical priests spoke with all Israel, saying: "Listen![6] Hear, Israel! Today you have become the people before[3] the Lord your God:
10. Accept[7] the Memra[8] of the Lord your God and observe His commandments and His laws, which I enjoin upon you this day."
11. Thereupon Moses charged the people that day, saying:
12. "The following shall stand to bless the people on Mount Gerizim, when you are passed over the Jordan: Simeon, Levi,[9] Judah, Issachar, Joseph and Benjamin.
13. And the following shall stand for the curse on Mount Ebal: Reuben, Gad, Asher, Zebulun, Dan, and Naphthali."
14. The levites shall then respond and say to all the men of Israel in a loud voice:
15. "Cursed be the man who makes a sculptured or molten image, remote before[10] the Lord, a craftsman's handiwork, and sets it up in secret." And all the people shall respond, and say, "Amen."
16. "Cursed (be he) who insults his father or mother." And all the people shall say, "Amen."
17. "Cursed (be he) who changes[11] his neighbor's landmark." And all the people shall say, "Amen."
18. "Cursed (be he) who misdirects a blind person on his way." And all the people shall say, "Amen."

---

[3] The Targums have "before" instead of MT's *l*, "to."

[4] MT: "Shelamim." This is a characteristic change for the three Targums. See, for example, Exod 20:24.

4. ויהי במיעברכון ית ירדנא תקימון ית אבניא האילין דאנא מפקיד יתכון יומא דין בטורא דעיבל ותסוד יתהין בסידא:

5. ותיבני תמן מדבחא קדם יי אלהך מדבח אבנין לא תרים עליהין ברזלא:

6. אבנין שלמן תיבני ית מדבחא דיי אלהך ותסיק עלוהי עלון קדם יי אלהך:

7. ותיכוס ניכסת קודשין ותיכול תמן ותיחדי קדם יי אלהך:

8. ותיכתוב על אבניא ית כל פתגמי אוריתא הדא פריש יאות:

9. ומליל משה וכהניא ליואי עם כל ישראל למימר אצית ושמע ישראל יומא הדין הויתא לעם קדם יי אלהך:

10. ותקביל למימרא דיי אלהך ותעביד ית פיקודוהי וית קימוהי דאנא מפקיד לך יומא דין:

11. ופקיד משה ית עמא ביומא ההוא למימר:

12. אילין יקומון לברכא ית עמא בטורא דגריזין במעיברכון ית ירדנא שמעון ולוי ויהודה ויששכר ויוסף ובנימין:

13. ואילין יקומון על לוטיא בטורא דעיבל ראובן גד ואשר וזבולן דן ונפתלי:

14. ויתיבון ליואי ויימרון לכל איניש ישראל קל רם:

15. ליט גברא דיעביד צילם ומתכא מרחק קדם יי עובד ידי אומנא וישוי בסיתרא ויתיבון כל עמא ויימרון אמן:

16. ליט דיקלי אבוהי ואימיה ויימר כל עמא אמן:

17. ליט דישני תחומא דחבריה ויימר כל עמא אמן:

18. ליט דיטעי עוירא באורחא ויימר כל עמא אמן:

---

[5] N, Ps-Jon, and FT add here authority for Bible translations. Ps-Jon: "read in one language and translated into the seventy languages." Comp. Neh 8:8: "And they read in the book, in the Torah of God, distinctly; and they gave the sense, and caused them to understand the reading." B. Ned. 37a cites Neh 8:8 as proof that Ezra introduced the Aramaic Targum.

[6] MT has a word of uncertain meaning, found only here, which probably signifies "keep silent" (Rashi, b. Ber. 63b, LXX). The Targums render it according to the context of the verse.

[7] MT: "hear," a characteristic deviation for TO and Ps-Jon, but not N. TO and Ps-Jon retain "hear" in the previous verse because of the context.

[8] MT: "voice." TO and Ps-Jon: Memra. N: "voice of the Memra."

[9] The MT adds a *vav*, "and," to most but not all of the names. TO and Ps-Jon are like the MT. N misses one *vav*, but this is probably a scribal error.

[10] The Targums change "abhorrent" to "remote" and add "before."

[11] MT: "turn back," as in Isa 42:17 and 59:14. Ps-Jon and FT are like TO (see also 19:14), but N has "attacks" and LXX "remove." These substitutions avoid the metaphor.

19. "Cursed (be he) who subverts the rights of the proselyte,[12] the orphan, and the widow." And all the people shall say, "Amen."
20. "Cursed (be he) who lies with his father's wife, for he has uncovered his father's garment." And all the people shall say, "Amen."
21. "Cursed (be he) who lies with any beast." And all the people shall say, "Amen."
22. "Cursed (be he) who lies with his sister, daughter of his father or of his mother." And all the people shall say, "Amen."
23. "Cursed (be he) who lies with his mother-in-law." And all the people shall say, "Amen."
24. "Cursed (be he) who strikes down his neighbor in secret." And all the people shall say, "Amen."
25. "Cursed (be he) who accepts a bribe to kill[13] an innocent person." And all the people shall say, "Amen."
26. "Cursed (be he) who will not fulfill[14] the words of this Torah and do them." And all the people shall say, "Amen."

Chapter XXVIII

1. Now, if you surely accept[1] the Memra[2] of the Lord your God to observe and perform all His commandments which I enjoin upon you this day, the Lord your God will set you high above all the nations of the earth.
2. All these blessings shall come upon you and cling to you,[3] if you will but accept[1] the Memra[2] of the Lord your God:
3. Blessed shall you be in the city and blessed shall you be in the country.
4. Blessed shall be the offspring[4] of your womb, the fruit of your soil, and the offspring[4] of your cattle, the calving[5] of your herd and the lambing[6] of your flock.

---

[12] MT: *ger*. See 24:17. N has "proselyte," but Ps-Jon as well as some TO versions have "stranger."

[13] In this and the previous verse, the MT has "strike." The previous verse is understood by some to refer to one who insults his neighbor's honor, and upsets his peace and happiness (*Pirke de Rabbi Eliezer*, chapter 53, Rashi, and others). Here

19. ליט דיצלי דין גיור ייתם וארמלא ויימר כל עמא אמן:
20. ליט דישכוב עם איתת אבוהי ארי כלי כנפא דאבוהי ויימר כל עמא אמן:
21. ליט דישכוב עם כל בעירא ויימר כל עמא אמן:
22. ליט דישכוב עם אחתיה בת אבוהי או בת אימיה ויימר כל עמא אמן:
23. ליט דישכוב עם חמתיה ויימר כל עמא אמן:
24. ליט דימחי חבריה בסיתרא ויימר כל עמא אמן:
25. ליט דיקביל שוחדא למיקטל נפש דם זכי ויימר כל עמא אמן:
26. ליט דלא יקיים ית פתגמי אוריתא הדא למעבד יתהון ויימר כל עמא אמן:

XXVIII

1. ויהי אם קבלא תקביל למימרא דיי אלהך למיטר למעבד ית כל פיקודוהי דאנא
   מפקיד לך יומא דין ויתנינך יי אלהך עילאי על כל עממי ארעא:
2. וייתין עלך כל ברכתא האילין וידבקנך ארי תקביל למימרא דיי אלהך:
3. בריך את בקרתא ובריך את בחקלא:
4. בריך ולדא דמעך ואיבא דארעך וולדא דבעירך בקרי תורך ועדרי ענך:

the Targums have "kill," for that is the plain meaning of the text, as in 19:6 and elsewhere. Cf. Ezek 22:12: "they taken bribes to shed blood." N has "kill" in the prior verse.

[14] MT has a word meaning "to cause to stand up" or "to set firm," which some TO texts render literally. Comp. II Kings 23:3 and 24. Ps-Jon and LXX are literal. The difference between the TO and MT is in the vowels. Since N has no vowels, one cannot tell how it is translating. M adds "fulfill the *praiseworthy* words of this Torah."

[1] MT: "hear."

[2] MT: "voice." TO and Ps-Jon: Memra. N: "voice of the Memra." See 13:5 and elsewhere.

[3] MT: "overtake you." The blessing and curses (see vv. 15 and 45) are pictured as living beings pursuing their objects (ICC, p. 304). TO and Ps-Jon provide a substitute for this gross metaphor; however, N is literal.

[4] MT has the metaphor "fruit" three times in this verse. When the word does not apply to the produce of the soil, TO and Ps-Jon replace it. See 7:13. N does not delete "fruit" here but adds a word to clarify it: "fruit of the offspring of your womb." N makes no change for the next "fruit."

[5] MT has a metaphor meaning "that which is cast out." See 7:13.

[6] See note on 7:13.

5. Blessed shall be your basket[7] and your kneading bowl.[8]
6. Blessed shall you be in your comings and blessed shall you be in your goings.
7. The Lord will cause the enemies that rise against you to be smitten before you; they will come against you by a single road, but flee before you by seven roads.
8. The Lord will command blessings for you upon your storehouses and upon all your undertakings. He will bless you in the land which the Lord your God is giving you.
9. The Lord will establish you before[9] Him as His holy people, as He confirmed[10] to you, if you keep the commandments of the Lord your God and walk in the ways that are right before Him.[11]
10. And all the peoples of the earth shall see that the Lord's name is proclaimed over you, and they shall fear you.
11. The Lord will make you abound in good, in the offspring[4] of your womb, the offspring[12] of your cattle, and the fruit of your soil in the land that the Lord confirmed[10] to your fathers to give you.
12. The Lord will open for you His good store, the heaven, to provide rain for your land in season and to bless all your undertakings. You will be creditor to many nations, but you will not borrow.
13. The Lord will make you strong,[13] not weak;[14] you will only be at the top and never at the bottom, if only you accept[1] the commandments of the Lord your God which I command you this day, to observe and do,
14. and not deviate from any of the words that I command you this day, right or left, and go after the idols of the nations[15] and worship them.
15. But it will be if you do not accept[1] the Memra[2] of the Lord your God to observe and do all His commandments and laws which I command you this day, that all these curses shall come upon you and cling to you.[3, 16]

---

[7] See note on 26:2.

[8] MT has a word of unknown origin which occurs here, v. 17, Exod 7:28 and 12:34. Lowenstein (NH) believes that TO is translating like Rashi: "residue." However, TO uses the same Aramaic word here as was used to translate the Hebrew "kneading trough" in Num 15:20. N and Ps-Jon are like TO. LXX has "stores."

5. בריך סלך ואצותך:
6. בריך את במיעלך ובריך את במיפקך:
7. יתן יי ית בעלי דבבך דקימין עלך תבירין קדמך באורחא חדא יפקון לותך ובשבע אורחן ייעירקון מן קדמך:
8. יפקיד יי לך ית בירכן באוצרך ובכל אושטות ידך ויברכינך בארעא דיי אלהך יהיב לך:
9. יקימינך יי קדמוהי לעם קדיש כמא דקיים לך ארי תיטר ית פיקודיא דיי אלהך ותהך באורחן דתקנן קדמוהי:
10. ויחזון כל עממי ארעא ארי שמא דיי אתקרי עלך וידחלון מינך:
11. ויותרינך יי לטבא בולדא דמעך ובולדא דבעירך ובאיבא דארעך על ארעא דקיים יי לאבהתך למיתן לך:
12. יפתח יי לך ית אוצריה טבא ית שמיא למיתן מטר ארעך בעידניה ולברכא ית כל עובדי ידך ותוזיף לעממין סגיאין ואת לא תזיף:
13. ויתנינך יי תקיף ולא חלש ותהי ברם לעילא ולא תהי לתחתא ארי תקביל לפיקודיא דיי אלהך דאנא מפקיד לך יומא דין למיטר ולמעבד:
14. ולא תסטון מכל פתגמיא דאנא מפקיד יתכון יומא דין לימינא ולסמלא למהך בתר טעות עממיא למפלחהין:
15. ויהי אם לא תקביל למימרא דיי אלהך למיטר למעבד ית כל פיקודוהי וקימוהי דאנא מפקיד לך יומא דין וייתון עלך כל לוטיא האילין וידבקונך:

[9] TO and Ps-Jon use "before" instead of MT's *lw*, "to Him." Ps-Jon has the Memra do the act. N does not have "before" but "to His name," a phrase that N, Ps-Jon and FT resort to frequently instead of "before."

[10] MT: "swore."

[11] MT: "walk in His ways." The three Targums paraphrase characteristically. See, for example, 11:22 and 26:17.

[12] MT: "fruit." See verse 4. Ps-Jon adds Memra here, but the other Targums do not.

[13] MT: "head." TO replaces the metaphor. Adler (NL) points out that this is an example of Luzzatto's observation that TO avoids metaphors because of the likelihood that the general populace would misunderstand them and be misled. Comp. Isa 9:13 and 19:15 for a similar figure of speech. N and Ps-Jon have: "appoint you to be kings and not subjects." Ps-Jon and M have the Memra do the appointing.

[14] MT: "tail." See previous note.

[15] MT: "other gods." The Targums evade any possible thought that other gods exist.

[16] Ps-Jon adds the concept of vicarious *Zachuth*, "merit," in this verse, a con-

16. Cursed shall you be in the city and cursed shall you be in the country.
17. Cursed shall be your basket[7] and your kneading bowl.[8]
18. Cursed shall be the offspring[4] of your womb and the produce of your soil, the calving[5] of your herd and the lambing[6] of your flock.
19. Cursed shall you be in your comings and cursed shall you be in your goings.
20. The Lord will let loose against you the cursing, the terrifying sound,[17] and the rebuke in all the enterprises you undertake, until you are destroyed and until you perish[18] quickly, because of your evildoing in forsaking My fear.[19]
21. The Lord will make the pestilence cling to you, until He has put an end to you in the land which you are coming to occupy.
22. The Lord will strike you with consumption, fever, inflammation, scorching heat, the sword, blasting and mildew; they shall hound you until you perish.
23. The skies above your head shall be as stubborn as brass in withholding rain, and the earth under you shall be as obstinate as iron in producing no fruit.[20]
24. The Lord will make the rain of your land powder and dust, it shall drop on you from the sky, until you are wiped out.
25. The Lord will put you to rout before your enemy;[21] you will come out against him by a single road, but flee before him by seven roads; and you shall become a horror to all the kingdoms of the earth.
26. Your carcasses shall be cast out for food[22] for all the birds of the sky and the beasts of the earth, with none to move[23] them.

cept added on occasions by other Targums, but never by TO. See Israel Drazin's *Targumic Studies.* Ps-Jon has: "The fathers of the world spoke . . . destruction will be vented upon them without our merit to protect them. . . . Then a Bath Qol from the high heaven descended and said . . . even if the merit of all the generations shall cease, yours shall not cease."

[17] There are a number of Hebrew words in this chapter whose meaning is not definitely known. Some of these words are found in chapter 26 of Leviticus.

Rashi explains TO's Aramaic as meaning a terrifying sound. See 7:23. N and Ps-Jon have different words. Ps-Jon and M let the Memra do the act described in this verse and in subsequent verses.

[18] MT has the constructive infinitive *ʾbdk*; TO and Ps-Jon recast it to the imperfect, N does not.

[19] TO adds "My fear," as in 32:15 and elsewhere. Adler (NL) explains the addi-

16. ליט את בקרתא וליט את בחקלא:
17. ליט סלך ואצותך:
18. ליט ולדא דמעך ואיבא דארעך בקרי תורך ועדרי ענך:
19. ליט את במיעלך וליט את במיפקך:
20. ישלח יי בך ית מאירתא ית שיגושיא וית מזופיתא בכל אושטות ידך דתעביד עד דתשתיצי ועד דתיבד בפריע מן קדם בישות עובדך דשבקתא דחלתי:
21. ידביק יי בך ית מותא עד דישיצי יתך מעל ארעא דאת עליל לתמן למירתה:
22. ימחינך יי בשחפתא ובקדחתא ובדליקתא ובחרחורא ובחרבא ובשדפנא ובירקנא וירדפונך עד דתיבד:
23. ויהון שמיא דעילוי רישך חסינין כנחשא מלאחתא מיטרא וארעא דתחותך תקיפא כברזלא מלמעבד פירין:
24. יתין יי ית מטר ארעך אבקא ועפרא מן שמיא ייחות עלך עד דתישתיצי:
25. יתנינך יי תביר קדם סנאך באורחא חדא תיפוק לותיה ובשבע אורחן תיערוק מן קדמוהי ותהי לזיע לכל מלכות ארעא:
26. ותהי נבילתך משגרא למיכל לכל עופא דשמיא ולבעירא דארעא ולית דמניד:

tion as being for the honor of God. Lowenstein (NH) suggests that since it is not possible to forsake God, who is everywhere, TO had to add to the text. Ps-Jon is like TO, but N has: "forsaking the teaching of My Torah."

20 MT: "shall be brass and the earth under you iron." TO adds six Aramaic words to clarify the meaning of the verse. N and Ps-Jon give similar renderings. The paraphrase is the same as the one to Lev 26:19 and parallels the Sifre and b. Meg. 31b. Komlosh (*Hamikra*, p. 230) notes that whereas TO generally deletes metaphors, it frequently leaves similes which the masses can comprehend. Comp. Gen 13:16, 49:9, Deut 32:11 32, 33.

21 TO puts "enemy" in the singular form, although it is generally rendered in the plural, because of the subsequent text in the verse. N and Ps-Jon have the plural, as do some TO texts.

22 MT: "shall be food." TO and Ps-Jon add "cast out," but not N. Lowenstein (NH) suggests that since people generally die in a house, TO clarifies that the body would be cast out of the house. Shefftel (BO) feels that TO is referring to the enemy, who will not bury the dead and will, instead, cast them out for food. In all probability the word was added simply for clarity because it is implied in the text. Comp. TJ to Isa 5:25 and Jer 22:19.

23 MT: "frighten away." TO renders as in Lev 26:6 (see also Isa 17:2 and Jer 7:33) probably to be more explicit. Lowenstein (NH) (evidently connecting TO's *dmnyd* with the Hebrew *nwd*, "lamenting in sympathy") explains that TO is implying that no one will have pity on the carcasses to chase away animals eating them. Ps-Jon is more explicit: "none to move them away from your corpses." N and M have "frighten."

27. The Lord will strike you with the Egyptian inflammation, with dysentery,[24] boil-scars, and dry boil,[25] from which you shall never recover.
28. The Lord will strike you with madness, blindness, and disquietude of heart.
29. You shall grope at noon as a blind man gropes in the dark; you shall not prosper in your ways, but shall be abused and despoiled, all the days, with none to give help.
30. You will betroth a wife, and another man shall lie with[26] her. You will build a house, but not live in it. You will plant a vineyard, but not make it profane.
31. Your ox shall be slaughtered before your eyes, but you shall not eat of it. Your ass shall be seized in front of you, and it shall not be restored to you. Your flock shall be delivered to your enemies, with none to help you.
32. Your sons and daughters shall be delivered to another people, while your eyes look on and long for them all day, but there shall be no power in your hand.[27]
33. The fruit of your land and all your labors shall a nation eat which you do not know; you shall be only abused and downtrodden all the days,
34. and shall become mad by what your eyes behold, from what you see.
35. The Lord will afflict you with a sore boil at the knees and thighs, from which you cannot recover, from the sole of your foot to the crown of your head.
36. The Lord will drive you and the king you will set over you to a nation unknown to you or your fathers; you shall serve there a people who serve idols[28] of wood and stone.
37. You shall be a consternation, a proverb, and a byword[29] among all the peoples to which the Lord will drive you.

---

[24] There are a *Ketiv* and a *Keri* in the MT. The Targums characteristically follow the *Keri*. The *Ketiv* is a word which is generally understood as "hemorrhoids." This is the disease with which the Philistines were smitten after they seized the Ark (I Sam 5:6 ff., 6:4 f.). The word was considered indecent by the Massoretes, so "dysentery" is read in its place. The problems of euphemisms are discussed in b. Meg. 25b and b. Pes. 3a–b.

[25] TO and Ps-Jon add "dry," clarifying like Rashi: "this is a boil as dry as a

27. יִמְחִינָךְ יְיָ בְּשַׁחֲפָן מִצְרִים וּבְטַחֲרִין וּבְגַרְבָא וּבַחֲרַס יְבִישׁ דְּלָא תִיכּוֹל לְאִיתַּסָּאָה:

28. יִמְחִינָךְ יְיָ בְּטַפְשׁוּתָא וּבְסַמְיוּתָא וּבְשַׁעֲמָמוּת לִיבָּא:

29. וּתְהֵי מְמַשֵׁשׁ בְּטִיהֲרָא כְּמָא דִּמְמַשֵׁשׁ עִוִירָא בְּקַבְלָא וְלָא תַצְלַח יָת אוֹרְחָתָךְ וּתְהֵי בְּרַם עֲשִׁיק וַאֲנִיס כָּל יוֹמַיָּא וְלֵית דְּפָרִיק:

30. אִיתְּתָא תֵירוֹס וּגְבַר אָחֳרָן יִשְׁכְּבִנַהּ בֵּיתָא תִיבְנֵי וְלָא תִיתִּיב בֵּיהּ כַּרְמָא תִיצּוֹב וְלָא תַחְלִינֵיהּ:

31. תּוֹרָךְ יְהֵי נְכִיס לְעֵינָךְ וְלָא תֵיכוֹל מִנֵּיהּ חֲמָרָךְ יְהֵי אֲנִיס מִן קֳדָמָךְ וְלָא יְתוּב לָךְ עָנָךְ מְסִירִין לְבַעֲלֵי דְּבָבָךְ וְלֵית לָךְ פָּרִיק:

32. בְּנָךְ וּבְנָתָךְ מְסִירִין לְעַם אָחֳרָן וְעֵינָךְ חָזְיָן וְיָסוֹפָן בְּגִלְלְהוֹן כָּל יוֹמָא וְלֵית חֵילָא בִּידָךְ:

33. אִיבָּא דְּאַרְעָךְ וְכָל לֵיאוּתָךְ יֵיכוֹל עַם דְּלָא יְדַעְתָּא וּתְהֵי בְּרַם עֲשִׁיק וּרְעִיעַ כָּל יוֹמַיָּא:

34. וּתְהֵי מְשַׁתְּטֵי מֵחֵיזוּ עֵינָךְ דְּתֶחֱזֵי:

35. יִמְחִינָךְ יְיָ בְּשִׁיחֲנָא בִישָׁא עַל רְכוּבִין וְעַל שָׁקִין דְּלָא תִיכּוֹל לְאִיתַּסָּאָה מִפַּרְסַת רַגְלָךְ וְעַד מוֹחָךְ:

36. יַגְלֵי יְיָ יָתָךְ וְיָת מַלְכָּךְ דִּתְקִים עֲלָךְ לְעַם דְּלָא יְדַעְתָּא אַתְּ וַאֲבָהָתָךְ וְתִפְלַח תַּמָּן לְעַמְמַיָּא פָּלְחֵי טָעֲוָתָא אָעָא וְאַבְנָא:

37. וּתְהֵי לְצָדוּ לִמְתַל וּלְשׁוֹעֵי בְּכָל עַמְמַיָּא דִּידַבְּרִינָךְ יְיָ לְתַמָּן:

---

potsherd." Cf. Rashi on Lev 21:20. See b. Bek.40a. N translates similarly, with a word meaning "rough" or "scaly."

[26] MT has one word in the *Ketiv* and another in the *Keri*. As usual, the Targums follow the *Keri*. The *Ketiv* is "concubine" (see Isa 13:16, Jer 3:2, Zech 14:2, and Ps 45:10) which was considered indecent by the Massoretes, who initiated the practice of reading instead "lie with her." Cf. Rashi on Gen 18:22.

[27] MT: *w'yn l'l ydk*, "and (there) shall be nought in the power of your hand." This idiom, implying helplessness, is found in Neh 5:5. A positive version of it is found in Gen 31:29, Mic 2:1, and Prov 3:27. TO explains the phrase. N, M, and Ps-Jon have similar substitutions. Ps-Jon adds: "in your hand there will be no good work by which you prevail in prayer before the Lord," another instance where the Targum introduces prayer into the text and implies the merit concept; see note on v. 15 and the Introduction. N has: "no god will be at hand to redeem you."

[28] MT: "where you shall serve other gods." See note on 4:28 and below v. 64. N does not add "people," implying that the Israelites will serve the idols. Ps-Jon has: "and you will carry tribute to idolaters" indicating, like TO, that the Israelites will not serve idols.

[29] Rashi points out that TO is explaining the meaning of the Hebrew word, that the people will become a topic of conversation. N and Ps-Jon are like TO.

38. You will take much seed out to the field, but gather in little, for the locust shall consume it.
39. You will plant vineyards and till (them), but have no wine to drink or store, for the worm shall devour them.
40. You will have olive trees throughout your border, but have no oil for anointment, for your olives shall drop off.[30]
41. You will beget sons and daughters; they shall not remain with you, for they shall go into captivity.
42. All the trees and produce of your land shall the locust[31] possess.
43. The uncircumcised stranger[32] in your midst shall rise above you higher and higher, while you sink lower and lower:
44. he shall lend to you, but you shall not lend to him; he will be strong[13] and you weak.[14]
45. All these curses shall befall you; they shall pursue you and cling[3] to you, until you are wiped out, because you did not accept[1] the Memra[2] of the Lord your God and keep His commandments and laws that He commanded you.
46. They shall serve as a sign and proof against you and your offspring for all time.
47. Because you would not serve before[33] the Lord your God in joy and elegance[34] of heart because of the abundance of everything,
48. you shall have to serve the enemies whom the Lord will send[35] against you, in hunger and thirst, naked and lacking everything. He will put an iron yoke upon your neck until He has wiped you out.
49. The Lord will bring a nation against you from afar, from the end of the earth, which will shoot[36] like the eagle—a nation whose language you did not hear,[37]
50. a ruthless nation, that will show the old no regard and the young no mercy.

---

[30] The Targums render here, as in 7:1, like y. Mac. 1:2: "What is *yšl* (drop off)? It is *yšr* (drop off)." Comp. 19:5, "and the iron will drop off (*wnšl*)."

[31] In discussing whether a word in the Mishna (b. B.K. 116b) should have a *sade* (and be read *maṣikin*) or a *samech* (and be read *masikin*), the Talmud shows that a variation of the word is found in the MT (Deut 28:57) with a *ṣade* and in a Targum (*sakah*) with a *samech*. This is one of the four times a Targum of Deut is

38. בר זרע סגי תפיק לחקלא וזעיר תכנוש ארי יחסליניה גובא:
39. כרמין תיצוב ותפלח וחמרא לא תישתי ולא תכנוש ארי תיכלניה תולעתא:
40. זיתין יהון לך בכל תחומך ומשחא לא תשוף ארי יתרון זיתך:
41. בנין ובנן תוליד ולא יהון לך ארי יהבון בשביא:
42. כל אילנך ואיבא דארעך יחסניניה סקאה:
43. תותב ערל דבינך יהי סליק עיל מינך לעילא לעילא ואת תהי נחית לתחתא לתחתא:
44. הוא יוזפינך ואת לא תוזפיניה הוא יהי תקיף ואת תהי חלש:
45. וייתון עלך כל לוטיא האילין וירדפונך וידבקונך עד דתישתיצי ארי לא קבילתא למימרא דיי אלהך למיטר פיקודוהי וקימוהי דפקדך:
46. ויהון בך לאת ולמופת ובבנך עד עלמא:
47. חלף דלא פלחתא קדם יי אלהך בחדוא ובשפירות ליבא מסגי כולא:
48. ותיפלח ית בעלי דבבך דיגרינון יי בך בכפנא ובצחותא ובערטיליותא ובחסירות כולא ויתין ניר דברזל על צורך עד דישיצי יתך:
49. ייתי יי עלך עם מרחיק מסיפי ארעא כמא דמשתדי נישרא עמא דלא תשמע לישניה:
50. עם תקיף אפין דלא נסיב אפי סבא ועל ינקא לא מרחים:

mentioned in the Babylonian Talmud. All the Targums have the *samech*. See note on 14:5.

Jastrow translates *sakah* as "locust" or "beetle" (see b. Taan. 6a). R. Tam maintains that it refers to the enemy.

Ps-Jon is like TO. N has two translations: "locust" and "worm."

Rashi indicates that MT's *yrš* means "impoverish," probably having a TO text indicating *ytryk*. N and Ps-Jon render similarly "destroy." FT has *yrt*, which is either the same word as the MT (the *s* and *t* interchanging) or it means "possess."

[32] MT: *ger*. TO and Ps-Jon read "stranger" and add "uncircumcised" probably to make it emphatically clear that, in contrast to the stranger, one does not need to fear proselytes. N has *ger*, "proselyte."

[33] The Targums use "before" instead of MT's *'t*.

[34] MT: "good." TO and Ps-Jon are more explicit, perhaps implying to the concept of *hiddur mitzva*, observing every command in the most elegant manner. N has "good."

[35] TO and Ps-Jon change the MT's singular form to the plural because of the remainder of the verse. N retains the singular.

[36] MT: "fly fast," a word found in Ps 18:11. TO translates as in Exod 19:13. N and Ps-Jon have "fly."

[37] This is one of the instances where TO and Ps-Jon do not replace "hear" with "accept" because of the context. Some TO texts read "accept."

51. It shall devour the offspring[4] of your cattle and the produce of your soil, until you have been wiped out, leaving you nothing of grain, wine, and oil, or the calving[5] of your herds and the lambing[6] of your flocks, until it has ruined you.

52. It shall shut you up in all your settlement[38] until every high, fortified wall in which you trust to be saved[39] has come down throughout your land. And it will besiege you in all your settlement[38] throughout your land that the Lord your God has given you.

53. You shall eat the offspring[4] of your womb, the flesh of your sons and daughters that the Lord your God has given you, in the siege and during the distress with which your enemy shall distress you.

54. The man who is tender among you and very delicate, his eye shall be evil against his brother and the wife of his covenant[40] and the remaining children who remain,

55. not sharing with any of them the flesh of his children that he eats, because he has nothing else left as a result of the siege and distress which your enemy shall distress you in all your settlement.[38]

56. And she who is most tender and delicate among you, who would not venture to set the sole of her foot on the ground for delicateness and tenderness shall begrudge the husband of her covenant[40] and her son and her daughter,

57. the smallest of her children[41] which issues from her[42] and the babies she bears; she shall eat them because of utter want, secretly, in the siege and distress with which your enemy shall distress you in your settlement.[38]

58. If you fail to observe and perform all the words of this Torah that are written in this book, to fear[43] this honored and fearful name, the Lord your God,

59. the Lord will distinguish[44] your plagues and the plagues of your offspring, great and lasting plagues,[45] malignant and lasting sicknesses.

---

[38] MT: "gates."

[39] TO and Ps-Jon add "to be saved," which is implied in the MT, to explain the meaning of the text, that the Israelites are hoping to be saved by the walls. N does not make the addition.

[40] MT: "bosom." TO is more delicate and clarifies that the reference is to the

51. וייכול ולדא דבעירך ואיבא דארעך עד דתשתיצי דלא ישאר לך עיבורא חמרא ומשחא בקרי תורך ועדרי ענך עד דיוביד יתך:

52. ויעיק לך בכל קרוך עד דיכביש שורך רמיא וכריכיא דאת רחיץ לאישתיזבא בהון בכל ארעך ויעיק לך בכל קרוך בכל ארעך דיהב יי אלהך לך:

53. ותיכול ולדא דמעך בסר בנך ובנתך דיהב לך יי אלהך בציארא ובעקתא דייעיק לך סנאך:

54. גברא דרכיך בך ודמפנק לחדא תבאש עיניה באחוהי ובאיתת קימיה ובשאר בנוהי דישאר:

55. מלמיתן לחד מינהון מבסר בנוהי דייכול מדלא אשתאר ליה כולא בצירא ובעקתא דייעיק לך סנאך בכל קרוך:

56. דרכיכא בך ודמפנקא דלא נסיאת פרסת ריגלה לאחתא על ארעא ממפנקו ומרכיכו תבאש עינה בגבר קימה ובברה ובברתה:

57. ובזעיר בנהא דיפקון מינה ובבנהא דתליד ארי תיכולינון בחסירות כולא בסיתרא בצירא ובעקתא דייעיק לך סנאך בקירוך:

58. אם לא תיטר למעבד ית כל פתגמי אוריתא הדא דכתיבין בסיפרא הדין למידחל ית שמא יקירא ודחילא הדין ית יי אלהך:

59. ויפריש יי ית מחתך וית מחת בנך מחן רברבן ומהימנן ומכתשין בישין ומהימנין:

marriage contract. See note on 13:7. Ps-Jon and N are literal. See also v. 57, where N and Ps-Jon do not use delicate language.

[41] MT has a word which occurs only here in the Hebrew Bible. In Talmudic literature the word means "afterbirth." TO uses delicate language. Like Rashi, TO understands the verse to refer to the smallest, most recently born children. N and Ps-Jon retain the word. See also Ps-Jon to Gen 49:10. The LXX translates: "the female infant she bore, or the male child which she may bring forth."

[42] MT: "between her legs." Again, TO is written with delicacy. N renders the phrase literally. Ps-Jon has: "that exits from the place of shame at the time of birth."

[43] Lowenstein (NH, Introduction to Lev, p. 3) explains that TO does not add "before" here since the MT has the "name," and not Elohim or the Tetragrammaton. B. Tem. 3b indicates that the verse refers to one who swears, using God's name in vain. Ps-Jon is like TO, but N adds "before."

[44] MT: "make the plagues extraordinary." TO interprets like Rashi: "He will afflict you with plagues exceptional and quite different from other plagues." N is like TO. Ps-Jon changes the meaning: "the Memra of the Lord will hide the Holy Spirit from you, when the plagues come upon you."

[45] TO uses the same word for plague in the next verse, in 7:15 and 32:24. The other Targums do not.

60. He will bring back upon you all the plagues[46] of Egypt which you feared so, and they shall cling to you.

61. Moreover, every sickness[46] and every plague[46] that are not written in the book of this Torah, the Lord will bring upon you until you are wiped out.

62. You shall be left a small people,[47] after having been as numerous as the stars in the heaven, because you did not accept[1] the Memra[2] of the Lord your God.

63. And as the Lord delighted over you, to do you good and to multiply you, so will the Lord delight over you to cause you to perish and to destroy you; you shall be plucked from the land which you are about to enter and inherit.

64. The Lord will scatter you among all the peoples from one end of the earth to the other, and there you shall serve nations who serve idols,[48] whom neither you nor your fathers have known, of wood and stone,

65. yet among those nations you shall find no rest, nor shall the sole of your foot find a place to rest. The Lord will give you there a fearful[49] heart and eyes that fail and a despondent spirit.

66. The life you face shall hang in doubt before you; you shall be in terror, night and day, with no assurance of survival.

67. In the morning you shall say, "If only it were evening!" and in the evening you shall say, "If only it were morning!"—because of the fear of your heart which you dread and for the sight of your eyes which you see.

68. The Lord will send you back to Egypt in ships, by the route which I told you, you should not see again. There you shall sell yourselves to your enemies as male and female slaves, but none will buy.

69. These are the words of the covenant which the Lord commanded Moses to conclude with the Israelites in the land of Moab, in addition to the covenant which He had made with them at Horeb.

Chapter XXIX

1. Moses summoned all Israel[1a] and said to them: You have seen all that the Lord did before your eyes in the land of Egypt, to Pharaoh and to all his servants and to his whole country:

60. ויתיב בך ית כל מכתשי מצרים דדחילתא מן קדמיהון וידבקון בך:
61. אף כל מרע וכל מחא דלא כתיבין בספר אוריתא הדא ייתינון יי עלך עד דתשתיצי:
62. ותשתארון בעם זעיר חלף דהויתון ככוכבי שמיא ליסגי ארי לא קבילתא למימרא
    דיי אלהך:
63. ויהי כמא דחדי יי עליכון לאיטבא לכון ולאסגאה יתכון כן יחדי יי עליכון לאובדא
    יתכון ולשיציאה יתכון ותטלטלון מעל ארעא דאת עליל לתמן למירתה:
64. ויבדרינך יי בכל עממיא מסיפי ארעא ועד סיפי ארעא ותפלח תמן לעממיא פלחי
    טעותא דלא ידעת את ואבהתך אעא ואבנא:
65. ובעממיא האינון לא תנוח ולא יהי מנח לפרסת ריגלך ויתין יי לך תמן לב דחול
    וחשכות עינין ומפחת נפש:
66. ויהון חיך תלן לך מקבל ותהי תוה בליליא וביממא ולא תהימין בחיך:
67. בצפרא תימר מן יתן רמשא וברמשא תימר מן יתן צפרא מתוהות ליבך דתהי תוה
    ומחיזו עינך דתהי חזי:
68. ויתיבנך יי מצרים בספינן באורחא דאמרית לך לא תוסיף עוד למחזיה ותזדבנון
    תמן לבעלי דבביכון לעבדין ולאמהן ולית דקני:
69. אילין פתגמי קימא דפקיד יי ית משה למגזר עם בני ישראל בארעא דמואב בר
    מקימא דגזר עמהון בחורב:

XXIX

1. וקרא משה לכל זקני ישראל ואמר להון אתון חזיתון ית כל דעבד יי לעיניכון
   בארעא דמצרים לפרעה ולכל עבדוהי ולכל ארעיה:

---

[46] The words for "sicknesses" and "plagues" in the next two passages are in the singular in the MT. TO has the plural in verse 60, and some TO texts have it in verse 61.

[47] MT: *bmty m̂ṣ*. See note on 4:27.

[48] MT: "serve other gods." The Targums rephrase here as in v. 36 and 4:28. Rashi explains that the Israelites will not have to serve idols, but will pay tribute to the priests of the idols.

[49] MT: "trembling." TO and Ps-Jon are more explicit. Comp. Exod 15:14, Lev 26:36, Isa 14:19, and II Sam 22:8. N is literal.

[1a] B adds "(all) elders of (Israel)."

2. the great miracles[1] that your eyes saw, the signs and those great marvels.
3. Yet the Lord has not given you a heart to understand or eyes to see or ears to hear to this day.
4. I led you for forty years through the wilderness; your clothes[2] are not worn out, nor are your sandals worn away[3] from off your feet;
5. you have not eaten bread, nor drunk wine, new or old[4]—that you might know that I the Lord am your God.
6. When you came to this place, Sihon king of Heshbon and Og king of Mathnan[5] came out against us to engage us in battle, but we defeated them.
7. We took their land and gave it as a heritage to the tribe[6] of Reuben and to the tribe[6] of Gad, and to the half-tribe of Manassah.
8. Therefore, keep all the words of this covenant and do them, that you may succeed[7] in all that you undertake.
9. You stand[8] this day, all of you, before the Lord your God—your heads,[9] your tribes, your elders and your officials,[10] all the men of Israel,

---

[1] MT: "trials." The Targums explain the meaning of the MT. See 4:34 and 7:19.

[2] TO and Ps-Jon change the MT's plural for "clothes" to the singular form because of the latter part of the verse, which is in the singular form (Adler, NL). N retains the plural.

[3] The MT has the same Hebrew word for "wear away" for both clothes and sandals. TO uses a synonym for sandals to avoid a redundancy (Shefftel, BO) or because the first word is appropriate for clothes but not for sandals (Adler, NL). See 8:4 for a similar expression. Ps-Jon varies the text like TO, but N repeats the same word twice.

[4] MT: "strong drink." TO does not translate here as in Lev 10:19, where it is clear that the priest may drink neither wine nor any strong drink. N is like TO, but Ps-Jon renders literally.

[5] MT: "Bashan." The Targums change the name here as in 3:1 and elsewhere.

[6] The Targums add the explanatory word "tribe" twice. Some TO texts and Ps-Jon have "conquered their land," but not N.

[7] MT: *tśkylw*, from a root meaning "good sense." The Targums: *dṣlḥwn*. The Hebrew word is found in prophetic literature meaning "success" (see Jos 1:7, 8; I Sam 18:14; I Kings 2:3; and elsewhere). In b. Ab. Zar. 19b, the Talmud refers to

2. נסין רברבין דחזאה עינך אתיא ומופתיא רברביא האינון:
3. ולא יהב יי לכון ליבא למידע ועינין למחזי ואודנין למשמע עד יומא הדין:
4. ודברית יתכון ארבעין שנין במדברא לא בליאת כסותכון מנכון ומסנך לא עדו מעל רגלך:
5. לחמא לא אכלתון וחמר חדת ועתיק לא שתיתון בדיל דתדעון ארי אנא יי אלהכון:
6. ואתיתון לאתרא הדין ונפק סיחון מלכא דחשבון ועוג מלכא דמתנן לקדמותנא לאגחא קרבא ומחיננון:
7. ונסיבנא ית ארעהון ויהבנה לאחסנא לשיבט ראובן ולשיבט גד ולפלגות שיבטא דמשנה:
8. ותיטרון ית פתגמי קימא הדין ותעבדון יתהון בדיל דתצלחון ית כל דתעבדון:
9. אתון קימין יומא דין כולכון קדם יי אלהכון רישיכון שבטיכון סביכון וסרביכון כל אינש ישראל:

this verse in Deuteronomy and uses the word "success": R. Joshua ben Levi said, whoever engages in Torah, his property (others read "his ways," see *Torah Temimah*) bring him success, *mṣlyḥyn lw*, as it is said: "Therefore keep all the terms of this covenant and do them, that you may succeed in all that you undertake." The LXX translates "comprehend."

[8] The MT, like TO, uses a word connoting "standing firm" or "enduring." TO has *qym*. Midrash Lam R. notes: "the Israelites were strong enough to endure the curses."

This is one of the seventeen times that a Targum to the Pentateuch is mentioned in the Midrash (Reifmann, *Sedeh*, pp. 12 ff.). See also 32:14, 24, the other two times that a Targum to Deuteronomy is mentioned in a Midrash.

Ps-Jon has *ʿd* here and N has both words.

Rashi understands that the verse refers to the covenant about to be made, probably because TO uses the same word found in verse 12. See 31:14, where *ʿd* is used by the Targum.

[9] Adler (NL) points out that since TO does not use *lšbṭykwn* but *šbṭykwn*, it is interpreting like Nachmanides that two separate groups are referred to (heads and tribes) and not like Rashi, who renders the two words as one phrase: "tribal heads." However, TO is merely translating the MT literally. N is like TO, but Ps-Jon has: "the heads of your sanhedrin, the chiefs of your tribes."

TO and Ps-Jon renders "elders" literally, but N has "wise men."

[10] TO translates here differently than in 16:18 but the same as in Exod 5:6. See the note on 16:18. N and Ps-Jon are like TO.

10. your children, your wives, even your proselyte[11] within your camp, from wood-gatherers[12] to the filler[13] of water—
11. to enter into the covenant of the Lord your God and into His oath, which the Lord your God is concluding[14] with you this day;
12. to the end that He may stand[8] you this day before Him[15] as His people and He will be your God,[16] as He told you and as He affirmed[17] to your fathers, to Abraham, to Isaac, and to Jacob.
13. Not with you alone did I conclude[14] this covenant and this oath,
14. but[17a] with those who are standing here with us this day before the Lord our God and with those who are not with us here this day.
15. For you know that we dwelt in the land of Egypt and that we passed through the midst of nations which you inhabited.[18]
16. And you have seen their detestable things and their idols[21] of wood and stone, silver and gold, that they keep.
17. Perchance there is among you some man or some woman, or some family or tribe, whose heart is turning away today from the fear[19] of the Lord our God to worship[20] the idols[21] of those nations—perchance there is among you a man who reflects on sins of inadvertence or a sin of presumption.[22]

[11] MT: *ger*, which can be construed as "stranger" or "proselyte." The Targums generally prefer the latter. The MT, N, Ps-Jon, FT, and some TO texts have "your *ger*." This may refer to Canaanites who became proselytes and performed work for the people, see Rashi. More likely, it is a characteristic MT idiom which the Targums render literally.

[12] MT: "hewers." TO is like TJ to Josh 9:23. Comp.19:5, where TO renders differently because of the context of the verse. N and Ps-Jon are literal. Reifmann (*Sedeh*, p. 44) suggest that TO should read *mqṭl*, meaning "cut," rather than *mlqṭ*, "gather," and he is probably correct.

[13] MT: "drawers." While the MT speaks of the initial act, the drawing of the water from wells and brooks, the Targums refer to the final act, filling the pitcher.

[14] MT: *krt*, a Hebrew idiom for establishing covenants, which TO and Ps-Jon render *gzr* and N *mqyym*.

[15] MT: "to Him." TO has "before." Ps-Jon is literal, and N has "to the name of the Lord."

[16] MT: Elohim, which the Targums replace with the singular *'lh*.

[17] MT: "swore." MT and TO literally have "curse" in vv. 11, 13, and 18, but FT has "oath" in v. 11, ignoring the characteristic deviation.

[17a] B adds the Tetragrammaton here incorrrectly.

10. טפלכון נשיכון וגיורך דבגו משריתך מלקיט אעך עד מלי מך:
11. לאעלותך בקימא דיי אלהך ובמומתיה דיי אלהך גזר עימך יומא דין:
12. בדיל לאקמא יתך יומא דין קדמוהי לעם והוא יהוי לך לאילה כמא דמליל לך וכמא
    דקיים לאבהתך לאברהם ליצחק וליעקב:
13. לא עימכון בלחודיכון אנא גזר ית קימא הדין וית מומתא הדא:
14. ארי יי ית מן דאיתוהי הכא עימנא קאים יומא דין קדם יי אלהנא וית מן דליתוהי
    הכא עימנא יומא דין:
15. ארי אתון ידעתון ית דיתיבנא בארעא דמצרים וית דעברנא ביני עממיא דעברתון:
16. וחזיתון ית שיקוציהון וית טעותהון אעא ואבנא כספא ודהבא דעימהון:
17. דילמא אית בכון גבר או איתא או זרעי או שיבטא דליביה דליביה פני יומא דין מדחלתא
    דיי אלהנא למפלח ית טעות עממיא האינון דילמא אית בכון גבר מהרהר חטאין
    או זדון:

[18] MT: "which you passed by." Some TO texts (also N and Ps-Jon) parallel the MT, but not Sperber's text. The literal rendering is probably correct because the deviation is unnecessary and indeed confusing. B is literal.

[19] TO adds "fear," probably to remove the thought that one would turn entirely from God. Ps-Jon is like TO, but N adds "Memra" and FT "before."

[20] Some TO texts (including Sperber's and B) and Ps-Jon drop MT's "to go (to worship)." N and FT do not.

[21] MT: "gods of the nations." Characteristically, the Targums avoid the possible idea that other gods exist.

[22] MT has a metaphor which TO explains: "a root that is fruitful in poisonous herb and wormword." Rashi explains that the MT means: "perhaps there be a man or woman or family or tribe that produces and spreads wickedness in your midst." Adler (NL) notes that TO uses a plural form for sins of inadvertence and the singular for sins of presumption and admits he cannot explain this. The singular form "sin of inadvertence" is found in some TO texts, but not sperber's or B. N and Ps-Jon have the singular. The full wording in N is: "perchance there is among you a man whose heart reflects on sin, which is like a root stuck into the earth, for its beginning may be as sweet as honey, but its end will be bitter as the deadly wormwood." Ps-Jon has: "perchance there is among you the error which strikes root (in those) whose heart reflects on his sin, for the beginning of sin may be sweet, but its end is bitter as the deadly wormword." LXX has: "Is there any such root among you, springing up for gall and bitterness." W. Bacher (*Jewish Encyclopedia*, s.v. "Targum") cites this verse as an example where TO's paraphrase appears to be a curtailed form of the earlier and longer one found in its entirety in Ps-Jon. Cf. Gen 4:7, 10; 49:3, 22; Exod 14:15; and Num 24:4 for other instances cited by Bacher. It is clear from this study that although TO often differs from N and Ps-Jon, it can be understood better by reference to the expansive renderings in the other Targums.

18. When he hears the words of this oath, he may consider[23] in his heart, saying, "I shall be safe, though I follow the reflections[24] of my heart, as a result[25] I may add negligent sins of inadvertence to those of presumption."[26]

19. The Lord will not want to forgive him; rather will the Lord's anger and passion rage[27] against that man, until all the curses[28] written in this book cleave[29] to him, and the Lord blots out his name from under heaven.

20. The Lord will separate him for misfortune from all the tribes of Israel, in accordance with all the curses of the covenant written in this book of the Torah.

21. And later generations will say—the children who succeed you, and nations[30] who come from distant lands and see the plagues of that land and diseases that the Lord has inflicted upon it,

22. all its soil devastated by sulfur and salt, beyond sowing and producing, no grass growing in it, just like the upheaval of Sodom and Gomorrah, Admah and Zeboiim, which the Lord overthrew in His anger and indignation—

23. all nations will say, "Why did the Lord do thus to this land? Wherefore that great, passionate wrath?"

24. They will be told, "Because they forsook the covenant that the Lord, God of their fathers, made with them when He freed them from the land of Egypt;

25. they went[31] and served the idols of the nations[32] and worshipped

---

[23] MT: "bless himself in his heart," a metaphor TO replaces. N has "appease the thoughts of his heart," Ps-Jon has "become reprobate in his heart."

[24] MT: *šrrwt*. Rashi explains the word as meaning "according to my point of view." TO is like TJ to Jer 7:24 and 9:13. N has *qšt*, "to go in a straight line," "strong" (Jastrow, 1429b), as if the root in the MT were *yšr*. Ps-Jon has: "strength of the evil desire of my heart." The LXX has: "error of my own heart."

[25] Nachmanides explains the word *lmʿn* as meaning: "as a result." Comp. Ez 6:6, 21:20, and Hos 8:4. N and Ps-Jon are similar.

[26] MT has a metaphor which is variously translated. Some render it: "to add drunkenness to the thirst," others, "to the utter ruin of moist and dry alike." Rashi explains the words as follows: "I may add punishment for him even for the sins he has committed until now inadvertently." According to Rashi, the word "drunken-

18. ויהי במשמעיה ית פתגמי מומתא הדא ויחשיב בליביה למימר שלמא יהי לי ארי
בהרהור לבי אנא אזיל בדיל לאוספא ליה חטאי שלותא על זידנותא:

19. לא ייבי יי למשבק ליה ארי בכין יתקף רוגזא דיי וחימתיה בגברא ההוא וידבקון
ביה כל לוטיא דכתיבין בספרא הדין וימחי יי ית שמיה מתחות שמיא:

20. ויפרשיניה יי לבישא מכל שיבטיא דישראל ככל לוטי קימא דכתיבין בספר
אוריתא הדין:

21. ויימר דרא בתראה בניכון דיקומון מבתריכון ובר עממין דייתי מארע רחיקא
ויחזון ית מחתא דארעא ההיא וית מרעהא דאמרע יי בה:

22. גופריתא ומילחא יקרא כל ארעה לא תזדרע ולא תצמח ולא יסק בה כל עסב
כהפיכתא דסדום ועמרה אדמה וצבואים דהפך יי ברוגזיה ובחימתיה:

23. ויימרון כל עממיא על מה עבד יי כדין לארעא הדא מא תקוף רוגזא רבא הדין:

24. ויימרון על דשבקו ית קימא דיי אלהא דיי אלהא דאבהתהון דגזר עימהון באפקותיה יתהון
מארעא דמצרים:

25. ואזלו ופלחו לטעות עממיא וסגידו להין דחלן דלא ידעונין ולא איטיבא להון:

---

ness" implies "inadvertence." Thirst implies a witting act. The Targums interpret
this phrase in the same way. The LXX has: "involve the guiltless in ruin with himself."

27 MT: "smoke," a metaphor which the Targums replace. The same Aramaic
word is found in vv. 23, 26, 27, and elsewhere. There is no attempt to separate
anger from God.

28 MT: "curse," in the singular. The Targums render the word in the plural
probably because the chapter is speaking of many curses.

29 MT has a word meaning "crouch" or "lie down." See note on 28:2 as well as
vv. 21 and 60. N and the LXX are like TO; however, Ps-Jon is literal.

30 MT: "stranger": the Targums take the word from verse 23.

31 TO uses three words for "walk": (1) *hlk*, when God leads the people, when
the word is used symbolically for pursuing good thoughts or actions, and for
describing those who follow the divine path. See TJ to Isa 50:10, for example,
where the word defines MT's: "though he walks in darkness . . . let him trust in the
name of the Lord." (2) *'zl*, as a symbol for bad action, for distances, and important
undertakings. See TJ to Isa 50:11, for example, where the word is in the Aramaic of:
"walk in the flame of your fire" (i.e., plan destruction). (3) *'t'*, for short distances
and a normal walk. TO uses the first word in 13:5: "After the service of the Lord
your God shall you walk." The second term is in this verse in all the Targums.

32 MT: "other gods." TO evades the polytheistic idea. Ps-Jon is like TO, but N has
"other idols."

them: fearful things[33] which they had not known and which had not done them any good.[34]

26. So the Lord was incensed at that land and brought upon it all the curses written in this book.

27. The Lord cast them away[35] from their soil in anger, fury, and great wrath, and dispersed them into another land, as today."

28. Secret things are before the Lord our God;[36] but revealed things are for us and our children forever, to do all the words of this Torah.

Chapter XXX

1. When all these things befall you—the blessing and the curse that I have set before you—and you take them to heart amidst all the nations to which the Lord your God has banished you,

2. and you return to the fear[1] of the Lord your God, and you accept[2] His Memra,[3] just as I command upon you this day, you and your children, with all your heart and with all your soul;

---

[33] MT: "gods." See above note. Rather than being redundant and repeating "idol," TO and Ps-Jon have "fearful things." N has "idol." See the Introduction for other instances where TO uses "fear" in reference to idols.

[34] MT: "He had not apportioned to them." See 4:19. Rashi explains that the MT means: "Idols in whom they had never seen divine power." Rashi points out that TO interprets the singular form of the word "apportioned" as meaning that the idols the Israelites chose never gave them an inheritance, or portion, or even one good thing. N has "did not bless them." Ps-Jon has "did not give them a portion (in Israel)."

[35] MT: *wytšm* a word found only here in the Pentateuch. Rashi notes that TO is explaining the Hebrew word as meaning, "and He cast them out." Jer 12:14 is similar: "Behold, I cast them out from their land," and TJ renders as here. B. Sanh. 110b explains the word in the same way. Ps-Jon is like TO, but N, LXX, and Ibn Ezra translate the word "uproot" as in Jer 24:6, 42:10, and Amos 9:15.

[36] The Targums have "before" instead of MT's *l*, "to." As noted repeatedly, this is a characteristic deviation. The Targums include the word as a mark of respect when reference is made to something near to God or a high official.

26. ותקיף רוגזא דיי בארעא ההיא לאיתאה עלה ית כל לוטיא דכתיבין בסיפרא הדין:
27. וטלטילנון יי מעל ארעהון ברגז ובחמא ובתקוף רב ואגלינון לארע אוחרי כיומא הדין:
28. דמטמרן קדם יי אלהנא ודגלין לנא ולבנא עד עלמא למעבד ית כל פתגמי אוריתא הדא:

XXX

1. ויהי ארי ייתון עלך כל פתגמיא האילין בירכן ולוטין דיהבית קדמך ותתיב לליבך בכל עממיא דאגליך יי אלהך לתמן:
2. ותתוב לדחלתא דיי אלהך ותקביל למימריה ככל דאנא מפקיד לך יומא דין את ובנך בכל ליבך ובכל נפשך:

Nachmanides, however, argues that the deviation teaches a theological lesson. He writes that "before" shows that TO agrees with the commentators who interpret this verse as teaching that we are not punished for sins committed unknowingly: secret things (unconscious acts) belong *before* God, we bear no guilt for them. We are only guilty for revealed things; i.e., conscious acts. TO, according to Nachmanides, is not interpreting the verse like Rashi and others who refer to v. 16 and state: "It is for the Lord our God to execute judgment upon those who worship idols secretly, for all hidden things are revealed before Him, we only have a duty to smite idol worshippers who openly violate God's will." See b. Sanh. 43b.

Besides the fact that this is a characteristic deviation, it seems forced to conclude that one can derive the lesson from "before," or that "before," in this respect, is more explicit than "to." Nachmanides also derives a theological lesson from the typical deviation "name" in Lev 16:8. See Introduction for a discussion of "before" and "name."

N and Ps-Jon add to the beginning of the verse: "Secret things (they, N) are revealed before the Lord our God." While N phrases the remaining part of the verse like TO, Ps-Jon continues: "and He will take vengeance for them. And the revealed things are given over to us and to our children forever, to make judgments concerning them."

[1] TO adds "fear." See Introduction and notes on 1:36 and vv. 20, 10:20, 11:22, 13:5, and elsewhere. N has "teachings of the Torah" and Ps-Jon "throne of glory."
[2] MT: "hear."
[3] MT: "voice."

3. then the Lord your God, will turn your outcasts[4] and have mercy on you, and will return[5] and gather you from all the peoples where the Lord your God has scattered you.

4. Even if your outcasts are at the ends of the heaven, from there the Lord your God will gather you, from there He will bring you near.[5a]

5. And the Lord your God will bring you to the land which your fathers occupied, and you shall occupy it; and He will do you good and make you more numerous than your fathers.

6. Then the Lord your God will remove[6] the foolishness[7] of your heart and the foolishness[7] of the hearts of your offspring (to cause you) to love the Lord your God with all your heart and with all your soul, in order that you may live.

7. The Lord your God will inflict all those curses upon your enemies and your foes who persecuted you.

8. You will return and accept[2] the Memra[3] of the Lord and do all the commandments which I command you this day.

9. And the Lord your God will make you overabundant in all your undertakings, in the issue[8] of your womb, the offspring[8] of your cattle, and the produce of your soil for good. For the Lord will again rejoice in you for good, as He rejoiced over your fathers,

10. since you will be accepting[2] the Memra[3] of the Lord your God and keeping His commandments and laws that are written in this book of the Torah—once you return to the fear[9] of the Lord your God with all your heart and soul.

11. Surely, this command which I command you this day is not separated[10] from you, nor is it far away.

12. It is not in heaven, that you should say, "Who among us can go up to heaven and get it for us and impart it to us, that we may do it?"

13. Neither is it beyond the sea, that you should say, "Who among us can cross to the other side of the sea and get it for us and impart it to us, that we may do it?"

---

[4] Many moderns translate the first part of the verse literally "will turn your turnings"; that is, change a person's fortune. Peshitta, Vulgate, Saadya, and the early commentators are like TO. Comp. Amos 9:14; Jer 29:14; 30:3, 18; 31:23; 33:26; 49:6, 39; Ezek 16:53, 29:14; Hos 6:11; Job 42:10; etc. N and Ps-Jon speak of the Memra receiving Israelite repentance.

[5] Adler (NL) believes, because of the Kal form found in many TO texts, that TO

3. ויתיב יי אלהך ית גלותך וירחים עלך ויתוב ויכנשנך מכל עממיא דבדרך יי אלהך
לתמן:

4. אם יהוין גלותך בסיפי שמיא מתמן יכנשנך יי אלהך ומתמן יקרבינך:

5. ויעלינך יי אלהך לארעא דיריתו אבהתך ותירתה ויוטיב לך ויסגינך מאבהתך:

6. ויעדי יי אלהך ית טפשות ליבך וית טפשות ליבא דבנך למירחם ית יי אלהך בכל
ליבך ובכל נפשך בדיל חיך:

7. ויתין יי אלהך ית כל לוטיא האילין על בעלי דבבך ועל סנאך דרדפוך:

8. ואת תתוב ותקביל למימרא דיי ותעביד ית כל פיקודוהי דאנא מפקיד לך יומא דין:

9. ויותרינך יי אלהך בכל עובדי ידך בולדא דמעך ובולדא דבעירך ובאיבא דארעך
כטבא ארי יתוב יי למיחדי עלך לטב כמא דחדי על אבהתך:

10. ארי תקביל למימרא דיי אלהך למיטר פקודוהי וקימוהי דכתיבין בספר אוריתא
הדין ארי תתוב לדחלתא דיי אלהך בכל ליבך ובכל נפשך:

11. ארי תפקידתא הדא דאנא מפקיד לך יומא דין לא מפרשא היא מנך ולא רחיקא
היא:

12. לא בשמיא היא למימר מן יסק לנא לשמיא ויסבה לנא וישמעיננא יתה ונעבדינה:

13. ולא מעיברא לימא היא למימר מן יעבר לנא לעיבר ימא ויסבה לנא וישמעיננא
יתה ונעבדינה:

is hinting at the teachings contained in the Sifre on Num 35:34 and b. Meg. 29a: "God goes into exile with Israel and dwells with them in their misery. When He speaks in this verse of their being redeemed, He makes Scripture write of redemption as if He Himself is redeemed and returns with them." The MT, however, also has the Kal (see Rashi) and TO is literal.

Ps-Jon has the same word as TO, but N has "will bring you back."

5a Sperber's text and B but not all TO texts deviate here to soften the anthropomorphism (MT's "fetch"), or, more likely, to incorporate a word from Ps-Jon, which reads: "from there He will bring you near by the hand of the king messiah." N has "take you."

6 MT: "circumcise." TO and Ps-Jon replace the metaphor. N does not. See note on 10:16.

7 TO and Ps-Jon add "foolishness," thereby explaining the metaphor "uncircumcised heart." They are informing us that men do not do wrong unless foolishness enters their hearts. See note on 10:16. Thus, an uncircumcised heart is one from which foolishness has not been excised. N does not deviate here.

8 MT: "fruit." See note on 28:11.

9 TO and Ps-Jon add "fear" to remove the implication of close proximity to God. See note on v. 2. N adds "before" like some TO texts.

10 MT: "too wonderful for you." TO translates as in Exod 34:10. N and Ps-Jon have "is not hidden from you."

14. Rather, the thing is very close to you, in your mouth and in your heart, to do it.
15. See, I set before you this day life and good, death and evil.
16. For I command you this day, to love the Lord your God, to walk in the ways that are right before Him,[11] and to keep His commandments, His laws, and His rules, that you may live and increase, and that the Lord your God may bless you in the land which you are about to enter and possess.
17. But if your heart turns away and you do not accept[2] and go astray and serve the idols of the nations[12] and worship them,
18. I told you today that you shall certainly perish; you shall not long endure in the land which you are crossing the Jordan to enter and occupy.
19. I call heaven and earth to witness against you this day: I have put before you life and death, blessing and curse. Choose life—so you and your offspring may live—
20. by loving the Lord your God, accepting[2] His Memra[3] and keeping close[13] to His fear[14]—He is your life and the length of your days—and dwell upon the land that the Lord your God confirmed[15] to Abraham, Isaac, and Jacob to give to them.

Chapter XXXI

1. Moses went and spoke these words with all Israel.
2. He said to them: "I am one hundred and twenty years old today. I am no longer able[1] to go out and come in. Moreover, the Lord has said to me, 'You shall not go across this Jordan.'
3. The Lord your God, He[2] will cross over before you; He will wipe out those nations from before you and you shall dispossess them. (Joshua is the one who shall cross before you, as the Lord has spoken.)

---

[11] MT: "to walk in His ways." This is a characteristic Targumic deviation. See note on 26:17.

[12] MT: "other gods." The Targums reject the implication of polytheism.

[13] MT: "cleave." In b. Ket. 111b, the Talmud states that it is not possible to cleave to God. Why, then, does the Torah mention this word? To teach that the fol-

14. אֲרֵי קָרִיב לָךְ פִּתְגָמָא לַחְדָא בְּפוּמָךְ וּבְלִבָּךְ לְמֶעְבְּדֵיהּ:
15. חֲזִי דִיהַבִית קְדָמָךְ יוֹמָא דֵין יָת חַיֵי וְיָת טָבְתָא וְיָת מוֹתָא וְיָת בִּישְׁתָא:
16. דַאֲנָא מְפַקֵּיד לָךְ יוֹמָא דֵין לְמִרְחַם יָת יְיָ אֱלָהָךְ לִמְהָךְ בְּאוֹרְחָן דְתָקְנָן קֳדָמוֹהִי וּלְמִטַּר פִּיקוּדוֹהִי וּקְיָמוֹהִי וְדִינוֹהִי וְתִיחֵי וְתִסְגֵּי וִיבָרְכִינָךְ יְיָ אֱלָהָךְ בְּאַרְעָא דְאַתְּ עָלֵיל לְתַמָּן לְמֵירְתַהּ:
17. וְאִם יִתְפְּנֵי לִבָּךְ וְלָא תְקַבֵּיל וְתִיטְעֵי וְתִסְגּוֹד לְטָעֲוָת עַמְמַיָא וְתִפְלְחִינּוּן:
18. חַוֵּיתִי לְכוֹן יוֹמָא דֵין אֲרֵי מֵיבַד תֵּיבְדוּן לָא תוֹרְכוּן יוֹמִין עַל אַרְעָא דְאַתְּ עָבַר יָת יַרְדְּנָא לְמֵיעַל לְתַמָּן לְמֵירְתַהּ:
19. אַסְהֵידִית בְּכוֹן יוֹמָא דֵין יָת שְׁמַיָא וְיָת אַרְעָא חַיֵי וּמוֹתָא יְהָבִית קֳדָמָךְ בִּירְכָן וְלוֹטִין וְתִתְרְעֵי בְּחַיֵי בְּדִיל דְתֵיחֵי אַתְּ וּבְנָךְ:
20. לְמִרְחַם יָת יְיָ אֱלָהָךְ לְקַבָּלָא לְמֵימְרֵיהּ וּלְאִתְקָרָבָא לְדַחְלְתֵיהּ אֲרֵי הוּא חַיָּךְ וְאוֹרְכוּת יוֹמָךְ לְמֵיתַב עַל אַרְעָא דְקַיֵים יְיָ לַאֲבָהָתָךְ לְאַבְרָהָם לְיִצְחָק וּלְיַעֲקֹב לְמִיתַּן לְהוֹן:

XXXI

1. וַאֲזַל מֹשֶׁה וּמַלֵּיל יָת פִּתְגָמַיָא הָאִלֵּין עִם כָּל יִשְׂרָאֵל:
2. וַאֲמַר לְהוֹן בַּר מְאָה וְעַסְרִין שְׁנִין אֲנָא יוֹמָא דֵין לֵית אֲנָא יָכֵיל עוֹד לְמִיפַּק וּלְמֵיעַל וַייָ אֲמַר לִי לָא תְעִיבַּר יָת יַרְדְּנָא הָדֵין:
3. יְיָ אֱלָהָךְ הוּא עָבַר קֳדָמָךְ הוּא יְשֵׁיצֵי יָת עַמְמַיָא הָאִלֵּין מִן קֳדָמָךְ וְתֵירְתִנּוּן יְהוֹשֻׁעַ הוּא עָבַר קֳדָמָךְ כְּמָא דְמַלֵּיל יְיָ:

lowing are considered "as if" they are cleaving to God: one who marries his daughter to a scholar and one who helps scholars. Ps-Jon is like TO, but N is literal.

[14] MT: "to Him." TO and Ps-Jon add "fear" as in vv. 1, 1:36, 10:20, 11:22, 13:5, and elsewhere. N is literal.

[15] MT: "swore."

[1] The Targums render "not able" literally and do not have the characteristic "does not have permission" (comp., for example, 12:12 and 24:4). The Targums may have understood the verse like Rashi, either that he was not able to perform because the leadership was taken from him, or that he could not think as well as before, because the sources of wisdom had been sealed to him (comp. b. Sotah 13b).

[2] Some TO versions, including Sperber's, do not add Memra here. Ps-Jon adds Shekinah, and N has "glory of the Shekinah."

TO does not add Shekinah because the Targumist restricts Shekinah to verses that speak of God's presence in heaven or among the Israelites. Perhaps Memra is absent because the word implies God's "command," "instruction," "inspiration,"

4. The Lord will do to them as He did to Sihon and Og, kings of the Amorites, and to their countries, when He wiped them out.
5. The Lord will deliver them up before you, and you shall deal with them in accordance with the command that I commanded you.
6. Be strong and resolute, be not in fear or break[2a] before them; for the Lord your God, His Memra[3] goes before[4] you: He will not fail you or forsake you."
7. Then Moses called Joshua and said to him in the sight of all Israel: "Be strong and resolute, for it is you who shall go[5] with this people into the land that the Lord affirmed[6] to their fathers to give them, and it is you who shall cause them to inherit it.
8. And the Lord, He[2] will go before you. His Memra[7] will be your helper;[8] He will not fail you or forsake you. Fear not and do not break!"[2a]
9. Moses wrote down this Torah and gave it to the priests, sons of Levi, who carried the Ark of the Lord's Covenant, and to all the elders of Israel.
10. And Moses instructed them as follows: "At the end of seven years, the year set for remission, at the Feast of Booths,
11. when all Israel comes to appear before[9] the Lord your God in the place which He will choose, you shall read this Torah before all Israel and make them hear.[9]
12. Gather the people—men, women, children, and your proselyte[10] in

---

etc. In this verse, Moses is speaking of something more than that. Perhaps, also, Memra is not used here because TO does not like to make repetitions and Memra is in vv. 6 and 8. See note on v. 8.

[2a] MT: "in dread."

[3] MT: "He." TO substitutes Memra. See v. 8. Ps-Jon has Shekinah, and N has "glory of Shekinah." Here Memra could mean "inspiration."

[4] MT: "with you." The Targums replace the gross anthropomorphic association of God and man marching into battle.

[5] Reider (*Deuteronomy*) notes that TO parallels the MT's "you shall go" (as do N, Ps-Jon, and the LXX) and does not have the reading contained in v. 23, "you shall bring," which the Samaritan Targum, Peshitta, and Vulgate read here. The difference in Hebrew is one letter: either a *yud* or a *vav*. See b. Sanh. 8a. M. Klein (*JBL* 92 [1973]: 584–85) discusses this matter from the perspective of N and shows that the vorlage in N does not support a variant MT reading.

4. ויעביד יי להון כמא דעבד לסיחון ולעוג מלכי אימוראה ולארעהון דשיצי יתהון:

5. וימסרינון יי קדמיכון ותעבדון להון ככל תפקידתא דפקידית יתכון:

6. תקפו ועילמו לא תידחלון ולא תיתברון מן קדמיהון ארי יי אלהך מימריה מדבר קדמך לא ישבקינך ולא ירחקינך:

7. וקרא משה ליהושע ואמר ליה לעיני כל ישראל תקף ועילם ארי את תיעול עם עמא הדין לארעא דקיים יי לאבהתהון למיתן להון ואת תחסנינה להון:

8. ויי הוא מדבר קדמך מימריה יהא בסעדך לא ישבקינך ולא ירחקינך לא תידחל ולא תיתבר:

9. וכתב משה ית אוריתא הדא ויהבה לכהניא בני לוי דנטלין ית ארון קימא דיי ולכל סבי ישראל:

10. ופקיד משה יתהון למימר מסוף שבע שנין בזמן שתא דשמטתא בחגא דמטליא:

11. במיתי כל ישראל לאתחזאה קדם יי אלהך באתרא דיתרעי תיקרי ית אוריתא הדא קדם כל ישראל ותשמעינון:

12. כנוש ית עמא גבריא ונשיא טפליא וגיורך דבקירוך בדיל דישמעון ובדיל דיילפון וידחלון קדם יי אלהכון ויטרון למעבד ית כל פגתמי אוריתא הדא:

---

[6] MT: "swore."

[7] MT: "He." As in v. 6, TO again substitutes Memra. Although here there is an opportunity for using Memra at least twice (N has Memra once and "glory of Shekinah" once, Ps-Jon has Memra twice and Shekinah once), it is characteristic of TO to restrict the use of Memra. See notes on vv. 3 and 6.

[8] MT: "with you." See note on v. 6. In v. 6, TO uses "before," which is appropriate in that verse. "Before" is not used here since it is in the prior phrase and TO prefers to avoid repetitions. Ps-Jon does not have "before," but N does .

[9] MT: literally, "the face of the Lord your God . . . in their ears." The Targums evade the anthropomorphism by substituting "before" and the metaphor by rendering according to the context.

Shefftel (BO) notes that TO generally replaces "ears" with "before" (comp. vv. 28 and 30); however, since "before" is already in the verse, TO avoids the redundancy.

Lowenstein (NH) writes that TO replaces "ears" so as not to decide between those who dispute whether a person deaf in one or two ears is exempt from the commandment of appearing at the Temple (b. Hag. 3a). Had TO used the plural "ears," one might have thought that the Targum was deciding that one who is deaf in one ear is exempt from this command. This interpretation is unlikely since TO characteristically avoids metaphors. N and Ps-Jon also do not add "before" here.

[10] MT: *ger*, which can be translated "stranger" or "proselyte" and for which the Targums generally prefer the latter. Some TO texts have "the proselyte."

your settlement[11]—that they may hear and so learn to fear before[12] the Lord your God and to observe to perform every word of this Torah.

13. Their children, too, who have not known, shall hear and learn to fear before[13] the Lord your God all the days which they live in the land which you are crossing the Jordan to possess it."

14. The lord said to Moses: "The time is drawing near for you to die. Call Joshua and let him make ready[14] in the Tent of Meeting, that I may command him." Moses and Joshua went and made ready[14] in the Tent of Meeting.

15. The Lord was revealed in the Tent, in a pillar of cloud, and the pillar of cloud stood at the entrance of the Tent.

16. The Lord said to Moses: "You are to lie with your fathers. This people will rise and go astray[15] after idols of the people of the land[16] which they are about to enter (to be) among them; they will forsake my fear[17] and change[18] My covenant which I made with them.

17. My anger will flare up against them at that time, and I will drive them far away[19] and remove[20] My Shekinah[21] from them. They shall be ready prey; and many evils and troubles shall befall them. And they shall say on that day, 'Surely it is because the Shekinah[22] of our God is not in our midst that these evils have befallen us.'

---

[11] MT: "gates."

[12] TO and N have "before" instead of MT's *'t*. Ps-Jon adds both "before" and Memra.

[13] The Targums have "before" instead of MT's *'t*.

[14] MT has a word, repeated twice, which literally means: "draw yourself erect." The Targums render it according to the context. Comp. Num 11:16, etc., where TO translates in the same way, but 29:9 and elsewhere are contrary. TO may be referring to the idea in the Sifre: Joshua should study and prepare himself while Moses is still alive. N and Ps-Jon have the same word as TO here.

[15] MT: "prostitute themselves." The Targums soften the criticism for the honor of the Israelites, as in Exod 34:15, 16; Lev 17:7, 20:5; Num 15:39.

The Targums cast the beginning of the verse in the singular form and virtually all of the remaining verses in this section (verses 16, 17, 18, except for the second half of v. 17) in the plural, even though the MT is singular. Luzzatto (OG) explains

13. וּבְנֵיהוֹן דְּלָא יְדַעוּ יִשְׁמְעוּן וְיֵילְפוּן לְמִדְחַל קֳדָם יְיָ אֱלָהֲכוֹן כָּל יוֹמַיָּא דְּאַתּוּן קַיָּמִין
עַל אַרְעָא דְּאַתּוּן עָבְרִין יָת יַרְדְּנָא לְתַמָּן לְמֵירְתַהּ:

14. וַאֲמַר יְיָ לְמֹשֶׁה הָא קָרִיבוּ יוֹמָךְ לִמְמָת קְרִי יָת יְהוֹשֻׁעַ וְאִתְעַתַּדוּ בְּמַשְׁכַּן זִמְנָא
וַאֲפַקֵּדִינֵּיהּ וַאֲזַל מֹשֶׁה וִיהוֹשֻׁעַ וְאִתְעַתַּדוּ בְּמַשְׁכַּן זִמְנָא:

15. וְאִתְגְּלִי יְיָ בְּמַשְׁכְּנָא בְּעַמּוּדָא דַּעֲנָנָא וְקָם עַמּוּדָא דַּעֲנָנָא עַל תְּרַע מַשְׁכְּנָא:

16. וַאֲמַר יְיָ לְמֹשֶׁה הָא אַתְּ שָׁכֵיב עִם אֲבָהָתָךְ וִיקוּם עַמָּא הָדֵין וְיִטְעֵי בָּתַר טָעֲוָת עַמְמֵי
אַרְעָא דְּהוּא עָלֵיל לְתַמָּן בֵּינֵיהוֹן וְיִשְׁבְּקוּן דַּחַלְתִּי וִישַׁנּוֹן יָת קְיָמִי דִּגְזָרִית עִמְּהוֹן:

17. וְיִתְקַף רוּגְזִי בְהוֹן בְּעִידְנָא הַהוּא וְאֵירַחֵיקִינּוּן וְאֵיסַלֵּיק שְׁכִנְתִּי מִנְּהוֹן וִיהוֹן לְמֵיבַז
וִיעַרְעָן יָתְהוֹן בִּישָׁן סַגִּיאָן וְעָקָן וְיֵימַר בְּעִידְנָא הַהוּא הֲלָא מִדְּלֵית שְׁכִינַת אֱלָהִי בֵּינִי
עַרְעָנִי בִישָׁתָא הָאִילֵּין:

---

that the singular refers to the entire nation as a unit, while the plural addresses each individual separately. Shefftel (BO) questions this interpretation. The MT seems to frequently vary grammatical usages without this purpose. However, when commenting on the MT of Deuteronomy generally, the Sifre and some moderns, such as S. R. Hirsch, repeatedly note this difficulty and explain the use of the singular and plural forms like Luzzatto.

[16] MT: *ʾlhy nkr hʾrṣ*. Rashi applies the word *nkr* to the people: "the gods (or idols) of foreign peoples." Nachmanides disagrees and contends that the term applies to the gods (idols). TO translates like Rashi, probably to avoid the thought that there are "other gods." N, characteristically, does not bother to deviate here and reads "other" or "strange gods." Ps-Jon drops the word.

[17] TO and Ps-Jon add "fear," a usual addition for the honor of God. These Targums do not want to leave the impression that one forsakes God completely. The next verse has a similar reading. N, characteristically, does not make the addition.

[18] MT: "break." The deviation is probably for the honor of the people. TO, N, and Ps-Jon do not want to imply that the people will break the entire covenant so they state that they will only change it. TO here is as in vv. 20, Lev 26:15, 44, and elsewhere.

[19] MT: "I will abandon them." Again, the Targums do not want to have the implication that God will leave the people entirely. See note on v. 16.

[20] MT: "hide." TO deviates to remove the unseemly anthropomorphism. See vv. 18 and 32:20 and Isa 5:5. Ps-Jon is like TO, but N has "turn away."

[21] MT: "My face." TO and Ps-Jon avoid the anthropomorphism by adding Shekinah, which denotes God's presence. N does not.

[22] MT: "because our God is not in our midst." The three Targums add Shekinah.

18. Yet I will surely remove[23] My Shekinah[21] from them[24] on that day, because of all the evil they have done in turning to the idols of the nations.[25]

19. Therefore, write down this poem and teach it to the people of Israel; put it in their mouths, in order that this poem may be before[26] Me a witness against the people of Israel.

20. When I bring them into the land I affirmed[27] to their fathers, producing[28] milk and honey, and they eat, are full, satisfied and luxurious[29] and turn to idols of the nations[25] and serve them, causing anger before Me[30] and changing[18] My covenant,

21. and when the many evils and troubles befall them—then this poem shall confront them as a witness, since it will never be lost from the mouth of their offspring. For their inclination is revealed before Me[31] what they are doing today, before I bring them into the land that I affirmed."[27]

22. Moses wrote down this poem that day and taught it to the Israelites.

23. And He commanded Joshua son of Nun and said: "Be strong and resolute: for you shall bring the Israelites into the land which I affirmed[27] to them, and My Memra[32] will help you."[33]

24. When Moses had finished writing the words of this Torah in a book to the very end,

25. Moses charged the levites who carried the Ark of the Covenant of the Lord, saying:

26. "Take[34] this book of the Torah and place it beside the Ark of the Covenant of the Lord your God, and let it remain there as a witness against you.

27. Well I know how defiant and stiff-necked you are: even now, while I am still alive in your midst, you have been defiant before[35] the Lord; how much more, then, when I am dead!

28. Gather to me all the elders of your tribes and your officials, that I may speak all these words before[36] them and that I may call heaven and earth to witness against them.

---

[23] MT: "hide." See note 18. Ps-Jon reads like TO, but N has: "I with My Memra will surely hide My face."

[24] TO and Ps-Jon add "from them" for clarity. N does not.

[25] MT: "other gods," a characteristic change for TO and Ps-Jon to reject the concept of polytheism. N, as usual, takes only a halfway measure, "other idols."

18. ואנא סלקא איסליק שכנתי מנהון בעידנא ההוא על כל בישתא דעבדו ארי אתפניאו בתר טעות עממיא:

19. וכען כתובו לכון ית תושבחתא הדא ואליפה לבני ישראל שויה בפומהון בדיל דתהי קדמי תושבתחא הדא לסהיד בבני ישראל:

20. ארי אעיילינון לארעא דקיימית לאבהתהון עבדא חלב ודבש וייכלון ויסבעון ויתפנקון ויתפנון בתר טעות עממיא ויפלחון להין וירגזון קדמי וישנון ית קימי:

21. ויהי ארי יערען יתהון בישן סגיאן ועקן ותתיב תושבחתא הדא קדמוהי לסהיד ארי לא תתנשי מפום בניהון ארי גלי קדמי יצרהון דאינון עבדין יומא דין עד לא אעלינון לארעא דקיימית:

22. וכתב משה ית תושבחתא הדא ביומא ההוא ואלפה לבני ישראל:

23. ופקיד ית יהושע בר נון ואמר תקף ועילם ארי את תעיל ית בני ישראל לארעא דקיימית להון ומימרי יהי בסעדך:

24. והוה כד שיצי משה למיכתב ית פתגמי אוריתא הדא על סיפרא עד דשלימו:

25. ופקיד משה ית ליואי נטלי ארון קימא דיי למימר:

26. סבו ית סיפרא דאוריתא הדין ותשוון יתיה מסטר ארון קימא דיי אלהכון ויהי תמן בך לסהיד:

27. ארי אנא ידענא ית סרבנותך וית קדלך קשיא הא עד דאנא קים עימכון יומא דין מסרבין הויתון קדם יי ואף בתר דאימות:

28. כנושו לותי ית כל סבי שבטיכון וסרכיכון ואימליל קדמיכון ית פתגמיא האילין ואסהיד בהון ית שמיא וית ארעא:

---

[26] TO and Ps-Jon have "before Me" instead of MT's "to Me." N does not.

[27] MT: "swore."

[28] MT: "flowing," a characteristic change. See, for example, 6:3.

[29] MT: "grow fat." TO and N deviate out of respect for the Israelites. Ps-Jon renders literally.

[30] The Targums add "before."

[31] MT: "I know." This is a characteristic substitution for the Targums, to remove any idea that it is possible for God not to know. However, see v. 27, where there is no deviation in TO or N, but there is in Ps-Jon.

[32] MT: "I." This is a typical change for the three Targums.

[33] MT: "with you." This, like the prior deviation, is characteristic. It removes an unseemly anthropomorphism by explaining it.

[34] Some TO texts render MT's *lqḥ*, which is in the infinitive, in the imperative, as do N and Ps-Jon.

[35] MT: "with." TO and Ps-Jon change it to "before." N adds Memra.

[36] MT: "in their ears." TO drops the metaphor. N and Ps-Jon have "in their hearing."

29. For I know that, after I am dead, you will surely act wickedly and turn
away from the path which I commanded you, and that in time to
come misfortune will befall you for having done evil before³⁷ the Lord
and having caused anger before³⁸ Him by the work of your hands."

30. Then Moses recited before³⁶ the whole congregation of Israel the
words of this poem until the very end:

Chapter XXXII

1. Listen, heaven, and I will speak; let the earth hear the words of my
mouth.¹.

2. (Let) my teaching² be sweet³ as rain, my word be received⁴ as the
dew; as the breath of rain that blows⁵ upon the young growth, and as
the showers of the latter rain⁶ upon the grass.

---

³⁷ MT: "in the sight." The Targums replace the anthropomorphism.
³⁸ TO and Ps-Jon add "before." N does not.

¹ Chapters 32 and 33 are poetic and are instances where TO deviates to a con-
siderable extent from the MT. Extensive paraphrases are also contained in Gen 49,
Exod 15, and Num 23 and 24.
² MT: lkḥy. Lowenstein (NH) points out that TO has the same Aramaic here as
in 4:5 and 8:5, a word he feels implies moral teaching, and not Torah. However,
Malbim believes that this verse extols the value of the entire Torah, not only its
moral teachings, whose value is readily apparent. N, Ps-Jon, Saadya, and LXX are
as vague as TO. FT is more specific, "teaching of my Torah."
That the Hebrew word refers to Torah or its moral teachings can be seen in
Prov 1:5, 4:2, 7:21, 9:9, 16:21, 23; Isa 29:24; Job 11:4; b. Taanit 7a; and Sifre.
The Targum to Songs 1:4 indicates that the Torah was stored in God's treasure-
house of heaven.
³ MT: yʿrp, "smite." Adler (NL) and Lowenstein (NH) note that TO may be
based on an MT text reading yʿrb, "sweet." See TO to Exod 15:25 and Ps 119:122
for the Aramaic word. The Hebrew word is found in 21:4 and 33:28, but TO renders it differently there. Lowenstein feels that the Targum parallels the teaching of
R. Eliezer in b. Taanit 31a: "just as rain is sweet, so are my lessons." Sifre also contains this interpretation: "although it is only one thing, rain has the power to give

29. ארי ידענא בתר דאימות ארי חבלא תחבלון ותסטון מן ארחא דפקידית יתכון
ותערע יתכון בישתא בסוף יומיא ארי תעבדון ית דביש קדם יי לארגזא קדמוהי
בעובדי ידיכון:

30. ומליל משה קדם כל קהלא דישראל ית פיתגמי תושבחתא הדא עד דשלימו:

XXXII

1. אציתו שמיא ואימליל ותשמע ארעא מימרי פומי:

2. יבסם כמיטרא אולפני תתקבל כטלא מימרי כרוחי מיטרא דנשבין על דתאה
וכרסיסי מלקושא על עיסבא:

each tree its distinct sweetness; Torah is similar, each person derives his own sweetness from it." While Adler and Lowenstein understand TO correctly, it is possible that TO is not reading *yᶜrb* but is evading the MT's metaphor by rendering according to the general context. TO is using a characteristic rabbinic method of interpretation: reading a word as if it were written differently. Ps-Jon is literal, "break the neck," a meaning also found in the Sifre. N is like TO.

[4] MT has a poetic phrase expressing a downward flow. The Targums interpret the Hebrew simile as referring to the effects the Torah has upon those who receive it. Malbim explains: "just as rain affects the dust and the worms in the dust, so Torah should be received by and affect all parts of the body and all its inclinations." Comp. TJ to Isa 5:6 and Mic 2:6, where rain is interpreted as prophecy.

TO renders MT's *ʾmrty*, "my word," as *mymry*, literally, "My Memra" or "my word," and is not careful to distinguish the Aramaic vorlage from the *nomen regens*. TO does this also at the end of verse 1. N is like TO in verse 1 and has *mymr pwmy*, "the word of my mouth," here. Ps-Jon uses *mmll* for "word" in both verses. FT has *mmlyl* in the first and *mymr*, in the second.

[5] MT: *śᶜyrym*, a term found only here. Ibn Ezra writes that it means "hair." Rashi, referring to TO, explains it as "storm": just as a rain storm strengthens the grass and helps it improve and grow, so Torah matures those who learn it. This understanding is in the Sifre and b. Taan. 3b. N and Ps-Jon are like TO. Saadya understands *śᶜyrym* as "much rain," and *rbybym* as "soft rain," the opposite of what is understood by most commentators.

[6] MT: *rbybym*, a word whose root means "much"; here "copious showers" (Ibn Ezra). See Mic 5:6 and Ps 72:6. N and Ps-Jon speak of the rains of Nissan. Malbim explains: "each person should receive Torah according to his inclination, some learn better with a soft approach (*śᶜyrym*), others need stronger measures (*rbybym*)."

3. For in[7] the name of the Lord do I pray,[8] ascribe greatness[9] before[10] our God,

4. the Mighty One[11] whose deeds are perfect, for all His ways are just, the faithful God, before whom[12] no iniquity proceeds[13] because[14] He is just and true.

5. Corruption is theirs, not His;[15] children who worship idols,[16] a generation that changes its work, and has itself become changed.[17]

---

[7] MT: *šm*. TO: *bšm*, adding "in." *bšm* is in Exod 34:5, 39:19, and elsewhere. N, FT, and Ps-Jon have a long gloss here, and all have *bšm*.

[8] MT: "call." When "call" is used in reference to God, the Targums frequently understand it as "prayer." See Introduction for a discussion of prayer. N and Ps-Jon also have Moses praying.

[9] MT: *gwdl*. Lowenstein (NH) notes that the Targum usually has *sgy* for *gwdl*. See, for example, Num 14:19. Here *rbwtʾ* is used. Lowenstein suggests that the latter term implies something larger than what preceded it. He feels that TO is alluding to the teaching contained in the Talmud and the Sifre. The Talmud indicates in b. Ber. 21a and b. Yoma 37a: "How do we know that the Torah requires that a blessing be made before fulfilling a command?" The Talmud responds by referring to this verse. "Moses said, 'I will precede the song with a blessing; you, Israel, respond by saying Amen.'" In b. Ber. 53b, the Talmud teaches that one who responds with Amen has done more than the person who made the blessing. This, Lowenstein points out, is TO's teaching: "when you respond to my blessing by answering Amen, you will do something larger, *rbwtʾ*, than I have done." See also Mek. on Exod 13:3, b. Ber. 11b, b. Taan. 16b, and y. Ber. 7:1.

There is some difficulty with Lowenstein's premise since the Aramaic translation of 3:24, 5:21, and 11:2 is like here. In verse 9:26, another word is used. Ps-Jon and N do not have this teaching any clearer. Moses says: "I will pray and you people of Israel bring honor and praise and extol God greatly." Saadya has: "and therefore ascribe greatness to God."

The tendency to understand an introductory verse as a benediction is also found in the Targum to Songs 1:1: "Bless the name of the Lord, who gave us a law by the hand of Moses the great scribe." Also, it was the ancient practice to recite a benediction prior to the recitation of a teaching. Such a benediction is found in Sifre Deut 305, b. Shab. 88a, and elsewhere. The practice continues today with the customary benediction preceding the public reading of the Torah in the synagogue.

[10] TO and Ps-Jon recast MT's *l* as "before." N does not.

[11] MT: "the Rock." TO rejects the metaphor for God and reads like Sifre and b.

3. ארי בשמא דיי אנא מצלי הבו רבותא קדם אלהנא:
4. תקיפא דשלמין עובדוהי ארי כל ארחתיה דינא אלהא מהימנא מן קדמוהי עולה
לא נפיק מן קדם זכאי וקשיט הוא:
5. חבילו להון לא ליה בניא דפלחו לטעותא דרא דאשני עובדוהי ואשתניו:

Ber. 6b. A rock is an earthy, inanimate object and may have been considered an inappropriate term for God. Maimonides (*Guide* 1:16) explains that "Rock" implies that God is the quarry, the origin and the *causa efficiens* of all things besides Himself. Perhaps TO understands the word in the same way: "God is the source of strength." The word is repeated eight times in the song, see also vv. 13, 15, 18, 30, 31 (twice), 37. N and Ps-Jon have long glosses, but Ps-Jon includes "Mighty One." Saadya has "the creator." The Targums change "a faithful God" to "the faithful God" so as not to imply plurality. The Targums and Saadya add "whose" for clarity.

[12] MT: "He is not iniquitous." TO and Ps-Jon add "before whom" and "proceeds" to remove any possible idea that God can be iniquitous. N has: "a faithful and true God; falsehood is not before Him; He is just and true in judgment."

[13] See note 12.

[14] TO adds *mn qdm*; literally, "from before." Ps-Jon does not make this addition although this Targum has the other words contained in TO. N also lacks the addition but probably because of a scribal error.

[15] MT has an obscure passage which is variously translated: "They have dealt corruptly, not towards Him, children of blemish" (Samaritan, LXX, Peshitta), "His no-sons have dealt corruptly towards Him" (Symmachus, Saadya, Ibn Ezra), "They who are not His children, their blemish is corruption unto Him" (Nachmanides, Luzzatto), etc. TO changes the MT's singular form to plural (theirs) and explains that in this verse Moses is reminding the people of the first of the Ten Commandments and is chastising them for their first sin, worshipping the golden calf. Moses chastised the Israelites in the same spirit in 31:27–29. By its reading, TO avoids applying the corruption to God. N has: "The beloved children have done corruption before Him, and not (only) before Him, but the blemish which is found in them is theirs." FT: "The children have corrupted their works; and not (only) before Me, but also to themselves." Ps-Jon: "The beloved children have corrupted their good works."

[16] MT is variously translated. Rashi explains (like Sifre) the MT as meaning: it was the fault of His children, not His fault. This is part of the difficult passage (see above note) that TO is interpreting. TO drops the pronoun "His" because when the Israelites sin, it is not to the honor of God to call them His children, see v. 19

[17] MT: "a perverse and crooked generation." TO softens the criticism of the Israelites and explains the metaphor. N and Ps-Jon are similar.

6. Behold,[18] do you requite this before[19] the Lord, O people who have received the Torah,[20] but have not become wise?[21] Is He not your Father, and you are His,[22] who fashioned you with rules?[23]

7. Remember the days of old, consider[24] the years of generation and generation; ask your father, and he will inform you, your elders and they will tell you.

8. When the Most High gave nations their inheritance, and separated the sons of man, He fixed the boundaries of the nations according to the number of the sons of Israel.

9. For the Lord's portion is His people, Jacob is the lot[25] of His inheritance.

10. He satisfied their needs in the land of the wilderness, in the dry place where there was no water;[26] He placed them round about His Sheki-

---

[18] MT has an additional letter *h*, which is treated as a separate one-letter word by the Massorah (y. Meg. 1:9). TO and FT read it as an exclamation, translating the letter like the Hebrew word *hn*. Comp. Gen 15:3, 29:7, 47:23, and elsewhere. It is possible that the Targums are not translating the *h* separately but are rendering according to the context of the entire verse. N has: "Is it not." Ps-Jon: "Is it possible."

[19] TO and N add "before" instead of MT's *l*, "to." Ps-Jon uses Memra.

[20] MT: "foolish" (in deeds, Ibn Ezra). Sifre explains: "who but yourself caused you to be so stupid as to fail to study and becomes wise from the Torah?" TO implies this understanding. Ps-Jon is like TO, but N is literal.

N. H. Tur-Sinai (*Halashon Vehasefer*, pp. 94–101), who feels that TO is an abbreviated version of an earlier, more extensive Targum like Ps-Jon, argues that this verse is an example of a truncated Targum: too much was deleted. MT's "foolish" is missing from TO, but it is in Ps-Jon. As indicated above, it is arguable that it is not "missing," but interpreted.

Perush Jonathan states that TO's deviation resulted from the need to explain "foolish." Without TO and Ps-Jon we would have asked: Surely if a person is dull, he is not wise; therefore why do we need the latter word? Thus, the Targums explain: "although you received the Torah, it has not made you wise."

[21] MT: "and not wise." Rashi and Nachmanides construe the MT as meaning the people did not consider the results of their actions. TO's understanding is similar. Comp. v. 21 and Exod 18:18.

A. Y. Zaslenski ("Perushey Hatargumim," *Sinai* 56–57 [1965]: 262) interprets MT's and TO's "wise" as "Oral Torah." He understands TO to be criticizing people who accept the Written Torah but deny the Oral Law. This interpretation of the MT is in b. B.M. 33a and b. Nidd. 19a. It is really not possible to say for certain that

6. .הא קדם יי אתון גמלין דא עמא דקבילו אוריתא ולא חכימו הלא הוא אבוך ואת
דיליה הוא עבדך ואתקנך:
7. אידכר יומין דמן עלמא אסתכל בשני דר ודר שאל לאבוך ויחוי לך סבך ויימרון
לך:
8. באחסנא עילאה עממיא בפרשותיה בני אינשא קיים תחומי עממיא למנין בני
ישראל:
9. ארי חולקיה דיי עמיה יעקב עדב אחסנתיה:
10. סופיק צורכיהון בארע מדברא ובית צחונא אתר דלית מיא אשרינון סחור סחור
לשכנתיה אליפינון פתגמי אוריתיה נטרינון כבבת עיניהון:

the Targumist had this teaching in mind since the word is rendered literally.

[22] MT: *qnk*. Rashi understands this word as meaning either "who acquired you" or "who placed you in a protective nest" or "who fitted you out with everything that will benefit you." This is in Sifre. TO may agree. TO does not translate the word as in Gen 4:1, 14:19, and elsewhere. TO elevates the relationship: God does not perform acts of acquisition, the Israelites are His. N and Ps-Jon are literal.

[23] MT: *wyknnk*. TO: *wᵓtqnk*. Rashi feels the Hebrew term is derived from a word meaning "base" or "foundation," and which can be translated, "and establish you." The word is also found in Ps 119:73. Our translation of TO follows Lowenstein (NH), that TO is referring back to the laws. N, FT, and Ps-Jon have "and perfected you."

[24] MT is plural. TO is in the singular because of the remainder of the verse. N, Ps-Jon, and some TO texts have the plural. The plural reflects Sifre's teaching on the phrase: "each person is judged by his deeds."

[25] MT: "measuring cord." Similarly Ps 105:11. The Targums drop the metaphor and render as in Num 23:54, but not 3:4. The Targums parallel the Sifre, which refers to Ps 15:6 and Josh 14 and 19.

[26] MT: "He found him in a desert land, in an empty howling waste." TO avoids the unseemly anthropomorphism of God "finding" and the historical problem that God was involved with the Israelites before they were in the desert. N and Ps-Jon render the phrase literally. TO changes this verse, paraphrasing the latter part according to the context. Cf. Jer 2:2: "I remember thee the loving-kindness of thy youth, the love of thine espousals, when thou wentest after me into the wilderness, into a land that was not sown." See also Hos 9:10 and Ps 107: 35, where the Hebrew word *mṣᵓ*, "found," is used in reference to water.

Rashi points out that TO treats the Hebrew *mṣᵓ* as in Num 11:22 and Josh 17:16, where the word means "to supply the needs" and "gave enough." Sifre, among other interpretations, indicates that God prepared much for the Israelites in the desert: "a well, meat, and clouds of glory."

The second half of the first phrase in TO parallels 8:15.

nah; He taught them the words of His Torah; He guarded them as the apple of their[27] eye;

11. as an eagle which broods over[28] her nest, hovering over her young ones, stretching out her wings, taking them, bearing them, on the strength[29] of her pinions.

12. The Lord alone will in the future make them to dwell in the land which He will renew in the future, and the worship of idols shall not exist before Him.[30]

13. He made them to dwell on the strong places of the earth; He made them eat the spoil of their enemies. He gave them the spoil of the

[27] MT: "He surrounded him, He instructed him, He guarded him as the apple of His eye." TO adds Shekinah in the first part of this pharse. Sifre, among other interpretations, has: "He compassed them at the bottom of Mount Sinai." The word *ṣbb*, found here in the MT, is also in Exod 19:12 in regard to the giving of the Torah at Sinai. N and Ps-Jon parallel another interpretation in the Sifre: "He surrounded them with clouds of glory." See note 26.

TO and Ps-Jon add "Torah" to the next phrase for clarity. This is similar to Sifre and N's: "Ten Commandments."

MT has "apple of His eye" for the third pharse, which TO changes to "their eye," meaning man's eye, replacing the anthropomorphism. Soforno understands the MT as referring to man's eye, but Sifre is contrary. N and Ps-Jon have : "His eye."

The Targums convert the words from the singular to the plural because the text was given to the people mentioned in the previous verses. See also note 24.

[28] MT: "stirs up." TO clarifies the simile and interprets like Sifre: "He guides them with mercy and pity like the eagle, which is full of pity towards its young and does not enter its nest suddenly—first it beats and flaps with its wings above its young, passing between tree and tree, between branch and branch, in order that its young may awake and have enough strength to receive it." It is also possible that TO is translating the word as if it were Syriac and means "hover" or "brood over." The LXX has "defend."

Komlosh (*Hamikra*, p. 230) notes that whereas TO generally replaces metaphors which are difficult for the masses to understand, the Targum frequently does not do so for similes, where the word "as" or "like" shows that the phrase is a figure of speech. Comp. Gen 13:16, 49:9; Deut 28:23, 32:32, 33.

N has "stirs up" like the MT. Ps-Jon has both words: "stirs up and broods over."

[29] TO, Ps-Jon, and N add "strength."

[30] MT: "The Lord alone did guide him, and there was no alien god with him."

11. כנשרא דמחיש לקיניה על בנוהי מתחופף פריס גדפוהי מקבילהון מנטילהון על תקוף איברוהי:
12. יי בלחודיהון עתיד לאשריותהון בעלמא דהוא עתיד לאתחדתא ולא יתקים קדמוהי פולחן טעון:
13. אשרינון על תוקפי ארעא ואוכילינון ביזת סנאיהון יהב להון ביזת שליטי קרוין וניכסי יתבי כרכין תקיפין:

Lowenstein (NH) believes that TO deviates here and has Moses speak of the rewards of the world-to-come as encouragement to the people, who would later hear him tell them about the tragic realities of this world. Sifre has: "The Holy One, blessed be He, said to Israel: You dwelt alone in this world and derived no benefit from the nations; so I will place you in the world-to-come alone, and none of the nations will benefit from you at all." One could also compare this Targum to Num 23:9, where TO adds, "it is a people that shall inherit a land alone in the future."

There is little support for Lowenstein's position. One can question both the originality of the TO vorlage and the meaning given to it.

Regarding Num 23:9, TO's language is not in N, FT or Ps-Jon, and it is clear from Rashi's commentary that he had another TO text before him. Thus, the language appears to be a scribal addition. Furthermore, even if the language is original, the context of the verse shows that "land" refers simply to the Israelites' conquest of Canaan. No theological lesson should be derived from the word "alone" since it is a literal rendering of the MT.

Similarly, TO's gloss in Deuteronomy appears to be a scribal addition. N, FT, and Ps-Jon who frequently reflect the same general interpretation contained in TO, and who are inclined toward theological speculations, do not mention a future world. These Targums connect this verse with the next one and speak of God (FT) or His Memra (N and Ps-Jon) settling the Israelites (in His Land, N and Ps-Jon) without the presence of those who engage in strange worship. Rashi had a TO vorlage before him speaking about the future, which may (although this is by no means certain) have been the language in front of us, and he objects that it is out of context with the plain meaning of the text.

Compare 32:34 and 33:6, where there are similar glosses concerning "the day of judgment," "the second death," and "everlasting life," other phrases that could suggest a belief in life after death. These may not have existed in the original TO text. The additions are contrary to TO's style of deviating only when necessary in a manner consistent with the plain meaning of the text. A full discussion of the world-to-come in TO and the manner in which N and Ps-Jon treat the subject is contained in Israel Drazin's *Targumic Studies*.

rulers of cities, and the possessions of them who dwelt in strong defenses.[31]

14. He[32] gave them the spoil of their kings and rulers[33] with the riches of their princes, and the strength of the people of their lands, their possessions, with the booty of their hosts and camps, and the blood of their heroes was poured out like water.

15. (But) Israel[34] waxed fat and kicked, he prospered,[35] grew strong and acquired possessions,[36] (and) forgot the worship of God who made him, and provoked before the Almighty who redeemed him.[37]

16. They provoked before[38] Him by the worship of idols,[39] by abominations they made anger before[40] Him.

17. They sacrificed to demons for whom there is no need,[41] fearful things

---

[31] MT: "He set him atop the highlands and he did eat of the yield of the earth. He fed him honey from the crag and oil from the flinty rock."

TO interprets this and the next verse as referring to the land of Israel, and is more explicit than the MT.

Commentators generally agree that the MT relates to Israel since Israel was regarded as the most elevated country on earth (Sifre, b. Sanh. 88a, etc., see also Am 4:13 and Mic 1:3). However, Sifre, N, and Ps-Jon understand this verse to allude to the fruits of the land of Israel, which are quicker to bud and ripen than the fruits of other lands. TO interprets this and the next verse as referring to the Israelites' victories.

TO (like Samaritan, LXX, Peshitta, N, and Ps-Jon) has "and He made them eat," in agreement with the preceding and following Hiphil verbs, and not "and he did eat" as in the MT.

[32] MT: "Curd of kine and milk of flocks; with the fat of lambs, and rams, bulls of Bashan and he-goats; with the kidney fat of wheat—and foaming grape-blood was your drink." TO paraphrases the entire passage, further developing the idea introduced in the previous verse. N and Ps-Jon have a different interpretation, and speak about the rewards for observing the law. The reward in N is that "from one bunch of grapes they will drink a _kor_ of wine," and in Ps-Jon that "their grain kernels will be like ox kidneys and one grape will produce a _kor_ of red wine." Sifre also speaks of rewards.

[33] The two words "kings" and "rulers" are apparently redundant, the language is a virtual repetition of a phrase in the previous verse, with the addition of the word "kings." Num R. 13:13, quoting the Targum, has only "He gave them the spoil of kings." (This is one of the three times that a Targum to Deut is mentioned in a Midrash. See also 29:9 and 32:24.) It is possible that TO is a shortened version

14. יהב להון ביזת מלכיהון ושליטיהון עם עותר רברבנהון ותקיפיהון עמא דארעהון אחסנתהון עם ביזת חיליהון ומשריתהון ודם גיבריהון יתאשד כמיא:

15. ועתר ישראל ובעט אצלח תקוף קנא ניכסין ושבק פולחן אלהא דעבדיה וארגיז קדם תקיפה דפרקיה:

16. אקניאו קדמוהי בפולחן טעון בתועיבתא ארגיזו קדמוהי:

17. דבחו לשידין דלית בהון צרוך דחלן דלא ידעונין חדתן דמקריב אתעבידא דלא איתעסקו בהין אבהתכון:

of Ps-Jon: "He gave them rich butter of kine from the spoil of their kings, and the fat of the firstlings of the sheep from the prey of their rulers." N explains this metaphor differently than TO and Ps-Jon and phrases the beginning of the verse literally.

[34] MT: "Jeshurun," a poetical name for Israel found here and in 33:5, 26, and Isa 44:2. Both have the element *yšr*, "upright" (Ibn Ezra). MT uses the word with irony, but TO, N, and Ps-Jon avoid this. FT retains the word "Jeshurun."

[35] MT: "grew fat." The idea of prosperity may have been derived from "Jeshurun," also meaning *wšr*. This understanding is in Saadya. Comp. Gen 30:13. MT, N, and Ps-Jon have the second-person "you," which TO and LXX change to the third-person "he" because of the context.

[36] MT: "fat, gross and coarse." TO, like N and Ps-Jon, changes the three synonyms for the sake of the honor of the Israelites. The Targums understand the verse like the Sifre: they rebelled against God because of food, drink, and being at ease. Sifre also mentions possessions of silver and gold. See also b. Sanh. 108, 109.

[37] MT: "forsook the God who made him and spurned the Rock of his support." TO and Ps-Jon make a typical substitution: not allowing people to believe they can forget God completely and making metaphors concrete. N has: "forsook the Memra of the God who created them and refused to worship (or, denied the fear of) the Almighty who redeemed them at the time of their trouble."

[38] TO and FT add "before." N and Ps-Jon do not.

[39] MT: "alien things."

[40] TO and Ps-Jon add "before." N and FT do not.

[41] TO, like M and some FT texts, renders "demons" literally. N has "idols of the demons" and Ps-Jon "idols that are like demons."

MT: "not being God." TO characteristically deviates to remove the thought that there are other gods. This is the only instance where TO uses the phrase "there is no need." However, comp. TJ to Judges 6:31, I Kings 18:21, II Kings 19:18, and Jer 2:11. N has "no substance" and Ps-Jon is like TO. Sifre explains: "Had they worshipped the sun and the moon . . . things the world needs and which produce delight, this would not have increased God's anger; but they worshipped things that do not benefit them, and which harm them."

they had not known,[42] new things that were recently made,[43] with which your fathers had no dealings.[44]

18. The fear of[45] the Mighty One[46] who created you, you forgot; you have forsaken[47] the worship of[48] the God who made you.[49]

19. And it was revealed before the Lord,[50] and His anger was kindled[51] because of the provocation before Him[52] of sons and daughters.[53]

20. And He said: "I will take away My Shekinah from among them;[54] there is revealed before Me[55] what their end will be, for they are a generation that changes,[56] children with no loyalty in them.[57]

[42] MT: "to gods whom they knew not." Again, TO rejects the reference to polytheism. See 11:28. N and Ps-Jon have "idols." The use of "fear" here is contrary to TO's style. See Introduction. It may have been influenced by one interpretation of *š'r*, see note 44, meaning "fear."

[43] MT: "that came from near." TO is explaining the phrase. N and Ps-Jon are similar.

[44] MT is uncertain, but can be translated, as in the LXX (based on the Arabic *sha'ara*): "whom your fathers did not know." Comp. Gen 4:5 and Exod 5:9. TO may be interpreting the verse in this way, or may understand the Hebrew as *š'r*, meaning "estimate," "suppose," "know," etc., as Saadya, and may be typically counteracting the possible thought that the Israelites would have no knowledge of God at all. N and Ps-Jon render the phrase similarly. Rashi, Ibn Ezra, etc., understand the MT as "which your fathers dreaded not." Sifre translates the word as "fear" and "regard." FT has "remembrance."

[45] TO and Ps-Jon apparently add *dḥl*, "fear," to prevent the thought that one can forget God Himself. N does not. This is the only instance where "fear" is added to "Mighty One," and this may be a doublet, the former term explaining the latter.

[46] MT: "Rock," a metaphor found frequently in the song. See v. 4.

[47] MT: "forgot." TO and FT deviate to oppose the idea that one can forget God, see note 45. TO may have changed "forgotten" to "forsaken" to avoid repeating a word twice in the verse (Lowenstein NH). N reverses the order, putting "forsake" before "forgot." Ps-Jon repeats "forgot."

[48] TO adds "the worship of" to remove the thought that one can entirely forget or forsake God, see note 45. The other Targums add Memra.

[49] MT: "who gave you birth" (or, "brought you forth"), see Ps 90:2. The Targums replace the metaphor with concrete language.

[50] MT: "the Lord saw." The Targums remove the anthropomorphism.

18. דחלת תקיפא דברך אתנשיתא שבקתא פולחן אלהא דעבדך:
19. וגלי קדם יי ותקיף רוגזיה מדארגיזו קדמוהי בנין ובנן:
20. ואמר איסליק שכנתי מנהון גלי קדמי מא יהי בסופהון ארי דרא דאשני אינון בניא
דלית בהון הימנו:

[51] MT: "He scorned them." See Jer 14:21. Cf. Lam 2:6. The Targums deviate for the honor of Israel and alter an anthropomorphism. Ps-Jon repeats "before" here, but it is characteristic of TO not to have repetitions. N does not use "before."

[52] TO and Ps-Jon add "before Him." N does not.

[53] MT: "His sons and His daughters." The Targums drop the possessive adjectives because when Israel does wrong, it is not to the honor of God to call them His children (Luzzatto, Adler, etc.), or, it is not proper to call sinners children of God (Lowenstein, etc.). See also v. 5. The latter interpretation parallels the opinion of R. Judah in b. Ked. 36b: when you behave like children, you are called children, when you do not behave like children, you are not called children. However, R. Meir differed and said that the Israelites are always called children. See also Sifre. The PT indicate clearly that the Israelites are God's children. N reads: "they who were beloved by Him like sons and daughters." Ps-Jon has : "those called sons and daughters by His name."

[54] MT: "I will hide My countenance from them." TO replaces the anthropomorphism like Sifre. See also 31:17, 18, and the antithesis in Lev 26:9. Ps-Jon is like TO, but N has "turn away." Neither N nor Ps-Jon renders "countenance" as Shekinah, although Ps-Jon does so in 31:17, 18. See also Targums to Isa 1:15, 8:17; Jer 33:5; Ez 39:23, 24, 29; Mic 3:9; Ps 22:25, 27:9, 30:8, 69:18, 102:3, 104:29, 143:7. Contrary is the Targum to Ps 10:11, 88:15. Saadya has: "I will hide My mercy."

[55] MT: "I will see what their end will be." TO adds words rejecting the anthropomorphism.The past tense is also substituted for the future since this section (as well as basic theology) implies that God already knew what will occur (comp. 8:2 and 13:14). Ps-Jon changes the wording to: "it will be seen." N is literal. Saadya has: "I will show them."

[56] MT: "a perverse generation," or, "a generation that turns things upside down." TO changes the metaphor to a concrete statement. N and Ps-Jon do not.

[57] MT has a word found only here. It can be translated "training" or "loyalty." The Targums prefer the latter. Rashi, mentioning both renderings, explains the latter with a quote from Sifre. It refers to Sinai, when the Israelites said, "We will do and will hearken," but after a short time they broke their promise and made the golden calf.

21. They have caused jealousy before Me[58] with that which is not fear-ful,[59] they have caused anger before Me[60] with their idols,[61] and I will make them jealous with that which is not a people, I will vex them with a nation of fools.
22. For a wind strong as fire, shall go forth before Me in fury[62] destroying[63] unto the lowest Sheol, to make an end[64] of the earth and its produce, and to destroy[65] the last mountains.[66]
23. I will join[67] evils to them, My plagues will destroy among them;[68]
24. they shall be swollen with hunger,[69] be eaten by the fowl,[70] and be plagued with evil spirits;[71] and the teeth of wild beasts[72] will I let loose among them with the fury of serpents [73] that crawl in the dust.
25. Without shall the sword bereave them, and in the chambers is fear of death,[74] to youths and maidens alike, sucklings with the aged.[75]

[58] TO and Ps-Jon add "before Me." N does not.

[59] MT: "with no-gods." TO rejects the reference to other gods. N and Ps-Jon do not. FT has "idols." TO generally restricts its use of *dhl*, "fear," for idols, but uses it here. See Introduction. This may be the error of a copyist, as evidenced by its absence in the other Targums. It is possible that the term refers the reader back to verse 17, implying that the images give no benefit, see notes 41 and 42. It is also possible that TO has *dhl* instead of idol, since the latter word is at the end of the verse, to avoid redundancy.

[60] TO , FT, and Ps-Jon add "before Me." N does not.

[61] MT: "futilities." TO is more explicit. N has "remote things (abominations)," Saadya "rebellions," and Ps-Jon is literal.

[62] MT: "For a fire has flared in My fury." TO deviates and removes the unseemly anthropomorphism for the honor of God. N has "fire" but Ps-Jon is like TO. Comp. Exod 10:13, 14:21, and Num 21:28.

[63] MT: "burning." TO is continuing its more concrete metaphor. The other Targums are literal.

[64] MT: "consume." See note 63.

[65] MT: "set on fire." See note 63.

[66] MT: "the base of the mountains." TO parallels the rabbinic interpretation, that the verse refers to Jerusalem which is surrounded by mountains. See Ps 18:8, 125:2, and Sifre. N and Ps-Jon are literal.

[67] MT has a word of uncertain meaning. See Mic 4:6, Isa 29:1, Jer 7:21, Ezek

21. אינון אקניאו קדמי בלא דחלא ארגיזו קדמי בטעותהון ואנא אקנינון בלא עם
בעמא טפשא ארגיזינון:
22. ארי קידום תקיף כאישא נפק מן קדמי ברגז שיצי עד שאול ארעיתא אסיף ארעא
ועללתה שיצי עד סיפי טוריא:
23. אסיף עליהון בישן מכתשי אישיצי בהון:
24. נפיחי כפן ואכילי עוף וכתישי רוחין בישין ושן חית ברא איגרי בהון עם חמת
תניניא דזחלין בעפרא:
25. מברא תכיל חרבא ומתוניא חרגת מותא אף עולימיהון אף עולימתהון ינקיהון
עם סביהון:

5:16, etc. It may also mean "use up," see Rashi. TO translates as in 29:18 and like
Sifre, Saadya, and the LXX. N and Ps-Jon have the Memra bring the evil.

[68] MT: "I will spend my arrows on them." TO removes the unseemly anthropomorphic portrayal of God shooting arrows. Ps-Jon is similar, but N has God send
the arrows. The Sifre has "arrows of hunger."

[69] MT has words of uncertain meaning. TO translates like N, Ps-Jon, Saadya,
Rashi, and Rashbam. The Targum is mentioned in Num Rabba 9, one of three
times a Targum to Deut is mentioned in a Midrash. See also 29:9 and 32:14. Comp.
b. Hul. 45b and the Aramaic terms in Dan 3:19.

[70] Again, the words in the MT are of uncertain meaning. Rashi explains:
"demons fight with them." While Rashi understands *lhm* as "fighting," TO, N, and
Ps-Jon interpret it as "food" (see Prov 4:17 and elsewhere) contrary to b. Ber. 5a.
The Targums translate *ršp*, a poetic word defined as "a pointed, darting flame"
(Cant 8:6, Job 5:7, Ps 76:4, 78:48), in accordance with its meaning in Job 5:7,
"birds."

[71] Rashi, following the Sifre, explains the ambiguous Hebrew words: "the
destruction caused by the demon Meriri." TO, like N and Ps-Jon, understands
"Meriri" as meaning "evil." TO parallels the Genesis Apocryphon 20:16. See *The
Genesis Apocryphon of Qumran Cave 1*, by J. A. Fitzmyer, Rome 1966, pp.
116–17, for a discussion of whether the second word means "wind" or "spirit." See
also note on 7:15.

[72] MT: "animals." TO, N, and Ps-Jon render according to the context.

[73] TO adds "serpents," like N, Ps-Jon, and the Sifre.

[74] TO, like N and Ps-Jon, adds "of death." Rashi explains TO as interpreting the
verse: "in the house there will be fear of pestilence, as it says (Jer 9:20): 'For the
death came up to our windows.'" Cf. b. B.K. 60b, Sifre, and Ibn Ezra.

[75] The Targums change the nouns in the verse, from "youth" on, to the plural.

26. I said: I would make My anger to fall upon them[76] and consume them;[77] I will abolish their memory from among the children of men;

27. were it not that the wrath of the enemy is gathered[78] (to destroy the Israelites); lest the adversary (after prevailing over them) make himself great[79] and say: 'Our own hand has prevailed[80] and all this is not from before[81] the Lord.'

28. For they are a people void of counsel[82] and there is no understanding in them.

29. If they were wise, they would understand this, they would consider what will be in their end:

30. How should one have pursued a thousand, or two put ten thousand to flight, unless the Mighty One[83] had delivered them up,[84] and the Lord delivered them.[85]

[76] MT: *p'yhm*, the meaning of which is unclear. TO seems to understand the word as being from the root *p*, and may be following the interpretation also found in Sifre, which divides the word into three *p 'y hm*, which means, "I said in My anger I will make them as though they were not existent." The Arabic *fa'a* means "to cleave" or "split," and it is possible that TO understands the Hebrew in this sense and is explaining the metaphor. Sam. and Sam. Targum have "they are my anger." Rashi (like N, Ps-Jon, and the LXX) understands the word as meaning "remainder" or "corner" and explains why he believes TO is incorrect. These sources construe the verse as meaning, "I will spread them out to the corners of the world." Komlosh (*Hamikra*, p. 152) suggests that TO may also derive its meaning from "remainder," and it was for this reason that it adds "and consume them." The Peshitta is like TO.

N and Ps-Jon add the Memra concept here.

[77] Adler (NL) notes that Rashi does not mention the Aramaic word which means "and consume them." He wonders whether it is added to our text from a variant TO version. He seems to be correct: the word is redundant and is not found in N or Ps-Jon. The entire phrase is found in Exod 32:10, from where it may have been taken. In Exodus, there is a Hebrew word in the MT for "and consume them." TO and Ps-Jon add "children," and N "the number of the family."

[78] MT: *'gwr*. Ibn Ezra and the LXX explain the Hebrew as "fear." TO is like Sifre (quoting Ps 55). N has "become strong," Ps-Jon is literal, and Peshitta has "inflamed."

[79] Rashi interprets the MT as meaning: "he will attribute the greatness to himself and to his gods, but not to Me." Thus, *nkr* in the MT is understood as: "attrib-

26. אמרית ייחול רוגזי עליהון ואישיצינון אבטיל מבני אינשא דוכרנהון:
27. אילו לא פון רוגזא דסנאה כניש דילמא יתרברב בעיל דבבא דילמא יימרון ידנא
    תקיפת לנא ולא מן קדם יי הות כל דא:
28. ארי עם מאבדי עיצא אינון ולית בהון סוכלתנו:
29. אילו חכימו אסתכלו בדא סברו מא יהי בסופהון:
30. איכדין ירדוף חד לאלפא ותרין יערקון לריבותא אילהין תקיפיהון מסרינון ויי
    אשלימינון:

uting power to a stranger to whom the greatness does not belong." Comp. Jer
19:14 and Job 21:29. TO renders as in Gen 42:7. It changes the phrase to the singular because the beginning of the verse is in the singular. Ps-Jon has the plural. N
has a different interpretation for this verse, see note 82.

[80] MT: "our hand is exalted." Similarly Isa 26:11. Berkowitz (LV) argues that
the word *ln'* is unnecessary; however, a form of the word is in the other Targums.

[81] MT: "this was not wrought by God." TO deletes "wrought" and adds
"before," changing the anthropomorphic active, "God wrought," to the passive,
the act happening before Him. The other Targums are similar.

[82] Ibn Ezra and Komlosh (*Hamikra*, p. 238) note that TO's language is as
ambiguous as the MT's, not informing us whether verses 28–38 apply to Israel or its
enemy. The dispute is described in the Sifre. R. Judah interprets the verses as
referring to the Israelites, who abandoned the Torah and lost their ability to understand that they were no longer successful in battles becuase God had forsaken
them. R. Nehemiah relates the verses to the Babylonians, who abandoned the
seven Noachide commandments and were no longer able to realize that their mili-
tary successes were due to God forsaking the Israelites. See note on v. 35, where
Adler argues that TO assigns these verses, or at least some of them, to the Israelites.
Komlosh notes that N and Ps-Jon to v. 29 concern the Israelites, but the other
verses speak of their enemies.

[83] MT: "their Rock." See note on verse 4.

[84] MT: "sold them." TO, Ps-Jon, and Saadya deviate in the same way for the
honor of God. Comp. Judg 2:14, 3:8, 4:2, etc. N has: "because they sinned and
caused anger before the Mighty one, He abandoned them."

[85] MT: "shut them up." Rashi translates the word in the MT as "deliver," and
Shefftel (BO) understands TO to be similar. Lowenstein (NH) translates TO as
"assented," which parallels I Kings 1:4. The same word is understood in v. 32 as
"retribution." Ps-Jon renders like TO; N has: "and the Memra of the Lord delivered them into the hand of their enemies." The word in N clearly means "deliver."
The LXX has "deliver."

31. For their strength[86] is not as our strength,[86] and our enemies are judges.

32. For their punishment[87] is the punishment[87] of the people[88] of Sodom, and their chastisement[89] like the people[90] of Gomorrah; their plagues will be bad as the (bite from the) poison of serpents,[91] the retribution for their behavior being like their venom.[92]

33. Behold,[93] as the poison of serpents is the cup of their punishment,[94] and as the poison[95] of the cruel asps.

34. Are not all their doings revealed before Me,[96] laid up in My treasures against the day of judgment.[97]

---

[86] MT: "Rock." Shefftel and others note that the spelling in TO is *twqpn'* and not *tqypn'* as elsewhere. They explain the change as a desire not to compare God to idols, something TO always rejects. The verse compares the laws and practices of Israel and its enemies. TO is interpreting, therefore, like Sifre (which apparently understands MT's "rock" as a metaphor for "strength" and not "God") and similar to N ("For the confidence of the nations is not like our confidence"), but Ps-Jon compares God with idols.

[87] MT: "vine." TO clarifies the metaphor. Comp. Jer 2:21. N and Ps-Jon have "work" instead of "punishment."

[88] The Targums add "people."

[89] Rashi explains the MT as meaning: "and of the fields of grain." Comp. Isa 19:8 and Hab 3:17. TO clarifies the metaphor in the first part by adding a word meaning "the punishment of lashes"; hence, "their fields will be struck like that of Gomorrah." However, instead of the innocent earth being punished, TO has the punishment descend upon the people. See next note. N has "thoughts," and Ps-Jon "evil counsels."

[90] The Targums add "people."

[91] MT: "their grapes are grapes of gall." TO seems to be interpreting the metaphor in the MT that the punishment will be like the bite of serpents. Adler (NL) and Berkowitz (LV) explain that TO took "serpents" from the next verse since the verses go together. Komlosh notes (*Hamikra*, p. 230) that whereas TO generally avoids metaphors, the Targum uses similes, which are more comprehensible to the masses because of the word "as" or "like." Comp. Gen 13:16, 49:9; Deut 28:23, 32:11, 33. FT has: "their evil deeds make them desolate." N: "their deeds do bad." Ps-Jon: "their wicked thoughts are as serpents' heads."

[92] MT: "their clusters are bitter." Comp. 29:17. TO explains the metaphor. FT has: "and become bitter to them." N: "and they receive retribution for their bad deeds." Ps-Jon: "therefore is their punishment desolate and bitter to them."

[93] The Targums add this word. TO also adds "as" twice by means of an addi-

31. אֲרֵי לָא כְתוּקְפָּנָא תוּקְפְּהוֹן וּבַעֲלֵי דְבָבָא הֲווֹ דַיָּינָא:
32. אֲרֵי כְפוּרְעֲנוּת עַמָּא דִסְדוֹם פּוּרְעֲנוּתְהוֹן וְלִקְוָתְהוֹן כְעַם עֲמֹרָה מַחְתְהוֹן בִּישָׁן כְּרֵישֵׁי חִיוְיָן וְתוּשְׁלֶמֶת עוֹבָדֵיהוֹן כִּמְרָרַתְהוֹן:
33. הָא כְמָרַת תַנִינַיָא כַּס פּוּרְעֲנוּתְהוֹן וּכְרֵישׁ פִּתְנִין חִיוְיָן אַכְזְרָאִין:
34. הֲלָא כָל עוֹבָדֵיהוֹן גְּלָן קֳדָמַי גְּנִיזִין לְיוֹם דִּינָא בְּאוֹצְרַי:

tional letter for clarity, and to create a simile instead of the metaphor. N and Ps-Jon are similar.

94 MT: "in their wine." TO clarifies the metaphor. N and Ps-Jon have a different interpretation.

95 All three Targums have *ryš* in this verse and the preceding one, which can be translated as "poison" or "head." The latter is preferred by Lowenstein (NH):"head" includes the thought that the enemy acts with a revealed face; openly and presumptuously; so the punishment will be open for all to see. This would be in accordance with the teaching of R. Jochanan ben Beroka: whoever desecrates God in secret will be punished openly (m. Ab. 4:4). It is unlikely that Lowenstein is correct: he is reading too much into a single, ambiguous word. Besides, TO is literal. Even if "head" is correct, it is possible that the Targums are referring to the ability of the serpents' head both to poison and to charm. Cf. Ps 58:5 and Jer 8:17. The Sifre understands the word as "head," but gives the two verses an aggadic interpretation: "head" refers to "Adam and Eve" in one interpretation and "chiefs" in another. Saadya has "poison," which is also the preferable Targumic meaning.

96 MT: "Is not this laid up in store with Me." TO avoids the anthropomorphism and explains the metaphor; i.e., they believe that I have forgotten their bad acts, but actually they are all laid up and kept with Me (Rashi). N and Ps-Jon also replace the anthropomorphism.

97 MT: "sealed up among My treasures." TO adds "against the day of judgment," which Adler (NL) feels is one of several references in TO to Deut to life after death. See also 32:12 and 33:6 and Israel Drazin's *Targumic Studies*, where the suggestion is made that TO does not deviate to teach theological lessons.

There is no indication that the Targum intends to imply the final judgment day. TO is alluding simply to a day of judgment during the malefactors' lifetime. (Cf. b. Sanh. 8a, where the Talmud calls a regular court day *ywm ddyn*, "day of judgment.") The word "day" is in the MT and TO of verse 35, and TO adds "judgment" to verse 36. Both of these words clearly refer to "the time when they will go into exile," which is in verse 35.

Ps-Jon is literal. N and FT have "the day of great judgment," cf. b. R.H. 21a, where the Day of Atonement is called "the great day." Sifre understands the MT to refer to the world-to-come.

35. Their punishment[98] is before[99] Me, and I will pay,[100] in the time when they will go into exile from their land;[101] for the day of their calamity is near, and the things that shall come upon them are hurrying.

36. When the Lord shall execute the judgment of[102] His people, and the punishment of His righteous servants will be carried out[103]—for it is revealed before Him,[104] that in the time when the chastisement of their enemies will be heavy upon them,[105] they will be scattered and forsaken[106]—

37. then he will say: 'where is their fear,[107] the mighty thing,[108] in whom[109] they trusted,

38. who ate the fat of their sacrifices, and drank[110] the wine of their libations? Let them now[111] rise up and help you, let them[112] be a protection for you.'

---

[98] MT: "To Me (belongs) vengeance." TO changes "vengeance" to "punishment" and adds "before" to explain the metaphor, removing the unseemly anthropopathic concept that God feels vengeful and desires revenge. N has "vengeance is Mine," but Ps-Jon is like TO.

[99] TO and Ps-Jon add "before" instead of MT's *l*, "to," but not N.

[100] MT: "and payment." The Targums make this into a separate phrase by adding the subject "I" and changing the noun "payment" into a verb. The Targumic form of the phrase is also in the LXX, Peshitta, Heb 10:30, and Rom 12:19. Sifre notes that "I" is not in the MT but is implied.

[101] MT: "in time when their foot shall totter." TO explains the metaphor, a frequent image for a reversal of fortune; comp. Ps 38:17, 94:18, etc. Adler (NL) notes that this paraphrase by TO, implying the exile of the Israelites, shows that the Targum is reflecting the view of R. Judah that these verses (28–38) apply to the Israelites and not their enemies, as taught by R. Nehemiah. See v. 28. N has "I am He who repays, in the time when the feet of the righteous are moved." Ps-Jon reads: "in the time when their feet shall move to the captivity."

N adds the world-to-come at the end of the verse: "the fire of Gehenna is prepared for them, and retribution hastens and comes upon them in the world-to-come."

[102] The Targums add "the judgment of" for clarity. See note 97.

[103] MT: "and repent Himself of His servants." This means "changing one's mind" (Rashi). TO deviates to prevent the thought that God changes His mind, to explain the metaphor, and to clarify that it is the righteous that will be rewarded. N has: "and comfort His righteous servants." Ps-Jon: "and for the evil He appointed upon His servants there shall be repentance before Him."

[104] MT: "when He sees." The Targums rephrase the anthropomorphism.

35. קדמי פורענותא ואנא אישלים לעידן דיגלון מארעהון ארי קריב יום תברהון ומבע
    דעתיד להון:

36. ארי ידין יי דינא דעמיה ופורענות עבדוהי צדיקיא יתפרע ארי גלי קדמוהי דבעידן
    דתיתקף עליהון מחת סנאה יהון מטלטלין ושביקין:

37. ויימר אן דחלתהון תקיפא דהוו רחיצין ביה:

38. דתרב נכסתהון הוו אכלין שתן חמר נסכיהון יקומון כען ויסעדונכון יהון עליכון
    למגין:

---

[105] MT: literally, "hand (meaning, power or support) is gone." TO explains the metaphor in the MT as Israel's enemies causing Israel to weaken, and overpowering them. Ps-Jon is more specific: "the chastisement of their enemies will be heavy upon them, and help will have passed away from their hands, and the faithful will have failed in their works and be scattered and forsaken." N has: "for it is revealed before Him that the hand of the righteous will waiver, and that they will be forsaken and cast down, with none to help or support them." It is clear that N and TO are shortened versions of the explanation in Ps-Jon, an explanation also in Sifre and the Peshitta.

[106] MT: "and that neither restrained nor checked remains." The MT is difficult and numerous interpretations are proposed. Rashi explains "there is not left one who is restrained (by an Israelite ruler who would restrain them) and one who is checked (by an Israelite ruler who keeps the people from scattering)." TO clarifies the metaphor by changing the passive to the active. Ps-Jon is like TO, and N renders similarly.

[107] MT: "gods." Since the respectful *dḥl* is used, TO seems to understand that the enemy is speaking, as N, Ps-Jon, Saadya, Ibn Ezra, Rashbam, etc. but not as Rashi, Soforno, etc. Otherwise, TO would have read *ṭʿwt*, "idol." See dispute in Sifre. The LXX has specifically: "Then the Lord said."

[108] MT: "Rock." TO, N and Ps-Jon read as in v. 4.

[109] The Targums add "in whom" for clarity.

[110] MT has the word in the present form, as does N, but TO and Ps-Jon have the past. TO has the enemy say: "where are the idols you served so well with fat and wine? They are not here to help you now when we are harming you."

[111] TO, N, Ps-Jon, and Saadya add "now" for clarity.

[112] MT has "it" in the singular (probably referring back to the "Rock" in v. 37), which TO, LXX, and Peshitta render in the plural because of the content of this verse. N and Ps-Jon have the singular. Ibn Ezra, who also understands the two verses as being the words of the enemy, interprets our verse as reflecting the enemy's conception that the Israelites have polytheism like them. Therefore, God replies in the next verse that He is one. N and Ps-Jon understand vv. 37 and 38 as the non-Jews referring to God.

39. See now that I, even I, am He, and there is no god beside Me.[113] I kill and make alive. I wound but I heal. And there is none who can deliver out of My hand.
40. For I have established in the heaven the abode of My Shekinah,[114] and have said, 'I live forever.'
41. My sword will be revealed as double the flashing of lightning from one end of heaven to another,[115] and My hand[116] will seize hold[117] with judgment, I will render punishment[118] on My enemies, and I will pay My adversaries,[119]
42. I will make My arrows drunk with blood, and My sword shall slay the peoples;[120] because of the blood of the slain and the captives, I will remove the crowns[121] from the head of the foe and the enemy."[122]

---

[113] MT: literally, "with Me." TO, N, and Ps-Jon reject the implication of an idol being close to God and being His equal. Cf. 4:35, 39, and Exod 15:11.

[114] MT: "For I lift up My hand to heaven." TO replaces the anthropomorphism. The MT means: "I lift up My hand in an oath" (Rashi and Saadya). TO apparently sees no need for God to swear and changes the meaning of the verse. However, in Exod 6:8, 17:16, and Num 14:30, TO does not remove God's oath. Adler (NL) notes the difficulty and argues that the final part of the verse here is an oath, so there is no need to mention it at the beginning of the verse. Shefftel (BO) explains that TO only retains God's oath when it would be clear to the masses that it is a metaphor, but this verse may be understood literally. Churgin (*AJSL 50*, p. 59) feels that our TO passage is the result of tampering by a copyist who wanted to add a theological lesson. N and Ps-Jon have the oath.

By its rendition, TO seems to imply that God is restricted to heaven. Lowenstein (NH) states that TO is referring to the lesson in Psalms (115:16), a verse well known to the masses: "The heaven is the heaven of the Lord, but the earth He gave to the children of men." That verse teaches that God made both heaven and earth. The former symbolizes the place from which God promulgated His Torah; the latter is assigned to man as the stage on which he plays his part. Thus, God is reminding the Israelites here that He gave them the Torah.

TO could be understood as follows: God says, even if I remove the hand of punishment from the earth, I need not hurry the penalty, for I live forever. If I do not claim punishment for your misdeeds now, I will get it later. This understanding of the verse is in the Sifre.

[115] MT: "If I whet the lightning of My sword." God is represented as a mighty warrior preparing for combat against His enemies, who are also Israel's enemies. TO is explaining the metaphor, by removing an unseemly anthropomorphism and adding a gloss. God's sword will be seen like repeated flashes of lightning, lighting

39. חזו כען דאנא אנא הוא ולית אילה בר מיני אנא ממית ומיחי מחינא ואף מסינא
ולית מן ידי משיזיב:

40. ארי אתקינית בשמיא בית שכנתי ואמרית קים אנא לעלמין:

41. אם על חד תרין כחיזו ברקא מסוף שמיא ועד סוף שמיא תתגלי חרבי ותתקף
בדינא ידי אתיב פורענותא לסנאי ולבעלי דבבי אישלים:

42. אירוי גיררי מדמא וחרבי תקטיל בעממיא מדם קטילין ושכן לאעדאה כתרין
מריש סנאה ובעיל דבבא:

up the sky from one end to another. Reifman cites this Targum as one of several which is difficult to comprehend (*Sedeh*, p. 23). N and Ps-Jon are literal.

Compare Ezek 21:19: "Thou therefore, son of man, prophesy, and smite thy hands together; and let the sword be doubled the third time, the sword of those to be slain; it is the sword of the great one that is to be slain, which compasseth them about." See also Ezek 21:15, Neh 3:8, Hab 3:11. For God described as warrior, see Exod 15:3, Isa 42:13, 59:17, and elsewhere.

[116] TO does not remove the anthropomorphism here as in Exod 16:3 and Num 11:23. The Mekilta, on Exod 16:3, comments that God's nature is not like that of human beings: When human beings shoot an arrow, they cannot bring it back; when God shoots His arrows, He can bring them back as though He is still holding them in hand. Perhaps TO retains the metaphor here so that this interpretation can be inferred; or, more likely, because it is clear to all that the phrase is a metaphor and not an anthropomorphic belief about God. Some TO texts do not have "hand." N and Ps-Jon have the word.

[117] The Targums, like the MT, use a term that implies holding with strength.

[118] MT: "vengeance." TO and Ps-Jon replace the anthropopathism and use a less harsh word for the sake of God's honor. See also v. 35. N does not.

[119] MT: "them that hate Me." TO and N soften this for God's honor. Ps-Jon does not

[120] MT: "and My sword shall devour flesh." TO explains the metaphor. N and Ps-Jon are literal.

[121] MT: "from the head of loose (or flowing) locks of the enemy." In construing the metaphor, TO apparently understands the word pr'wt in the MT as "loose locks" (Comp. Num 5:18, 6:5, and Ezek 44:20); i.e., removing the adornment of a victorious warrior; or as "leaders" (from the Arabic root *fara'a*, denoting "to surpass, excel"), i.e., removing their leaders; or, simply, leaving the defeated enemy in a state of disarray (with loose locks). N and FT relate the phrase to the enemy leaders; Ps-Jon does not.

The Talmud interprets the word in some instances as "bareheaded" and in others as "disheveled." See "Studies in the Septuagint of Leviticus" in *Bar-Ilan Annual* (1972): 98–101.

[122] MT has only "of the enemy." The conflation in TO is apparently from two

43. Give praise[123] nations to His people, for there will be retribution for the punishment[124] of His righteous servants;[125] punishment will be rendered to those who hate Him, and it will atone for[126] His land and for[126] His people.

44. Moses came and recited all the words of this poem before[127] the people, he and Hosea[128] son of Nun.

45. And (when) Moses finished reciting all these words with all Israel,

46. he said to them: "Take to heart all the words with which I have testified among you this day. Command your children, that they may observe to do all the words of this Torah.

47. For this is not a trifling thing for you: it is your life; through these words you shall long endure on the land which you are crossing the Jordan to possess."

48. And the Lord spoke with Moses that very day, [129] saying:

49. "Ascend this Mount Abarim, Mount Nebo, which is in the land of Moab facing Jericho, and view the land of Canaan which I am giving the children of Israel as their holding.

50. You shall die on the mountain that you are about to ascend, and shall be gathered to your people, as your brother Aaron died on Mount Hor and was gathered to his people;

51. for you both broke faith with My Memra[130] among the children of Israel, at the Waters of Mazut Rekem[131] in the wilderness of Zin, by not sanctifying Me among the children of Israel.

52. You may view the land before you, but you shall not go there, to the land that I am giving to the children of Israel."

---

different TO texts that are combined here (Berkowitz, LV). N, FT, and Ps-Jon do not have the conflation. N has "enemy"; Ps-Jon, "foe"; FT, neither.

[123] MT: "Cause to shout." Comp. Ps 65:9, Job 29:13. TO is like N, Ps-Jon, LXX, Vulgate, Peshitta, Rashi, Saadya, etc.

[124] MT: "for He will avenge the blood of His servants." N: "avenge the insult of His righteous servants." Ps-Jon has "blood."

[125] TO and N add "righteous" as in v. 36. Ps-Jon does not.

[126] Ibn Ezra notes that some say that the MT is missing a *vav*, "and." The Tar-

‏43. שבחו עממיא עמיה ארי פורענות עבדוהי צדיקיא מתפרע ופורענותא יתיב
לסנאוהי ויכפר על ארעיה ועל עמיה:

‏44. ואתא משה ומליל ית כל פיתגמי תושבחתא הדא קדם עמא הוא והושע בר נון:

‏45. ושיצי משה למללא ית כל פתגמיא האילין עם כל ישראל:

‏46. ואמר להון שוו ליבכון לכל פתגמיא דאנא מסהיד בכון יומא דין דתפקדינון ית
בניכון למיטר למעבד ית כל פתגמי אוריתא הדא:

‏47. ארי לא פתגם ריקן הוא מינכון ארי הוא חייכון ובפתגמא הדין תורכון יומין על
ארעא דאתון עברין ית ירדנא לתמן למירתה:

‏48. ומליל יי עם משה בכרן יומא הדין למימר:

‏49. סק לטורא דעבראי הדין לטורא דנבו דבארעא דמואב דעל אפי ירחו וחזי ית
ארעא דכנען דאנא יהיב לבני ישראל לאחסנא:

‏50. ומות בטורא דאת סליק לתמן ואתכניש לעמך כמא דמית אהרן אחוך בהור טורא
ואתכניש לעמיה:

‏51. על דשקרתון במימרי בגו בני ישראל במי מצות רקם מדברא דצין על דלא
קדישתון יתי בגו בני ישראל:

‏52. ארי מקביל תיחזי ית ארעא ולתמן לא תעול לארעא דאנא יהיב לבני ישראל:

gums have the *vav*, "and it will atone," but "and" may have been added for clarity, not because it was in the text before the translators.

Similarly, TO, N, and Saadya add "for" and later "and for." Ps-Jon reads only "for his land and people." LXX has "his people's land."

[127] MT: "in the ears." TO replaces the metaphor. N and Ps-Jon have: "in the hearing."

[128] Generally the MT has Joshua except here and in Num 13:8 and 16. TO and Ps-Jon follow the MT in all three instances. N, Samaritan, LXX, Vulgate, and Peshitta read "Joshua."

[129] The words *'tm hywm* are found twelve times in the Torah. TO translates each as *bkrn ywm' hdyn*, the first word being Greek, meaning "time." N translates each with the Hebrew word for "time." Ps-Jon is eleven times like TO and uses both the Hebrew and the Greek words once.

[130] The Targums add Memra. *dhl*, "fear" or "service," is probably not used since Moses did not forsake God's "service" but His "command," "word," to speak to the rock. The use of Memra softens the criticism of Moses, because *dhl* implies a broader transgression.

[131] MT: "Meribath Kadesh." This incident is related in Num 20:1 ff. Comp. also 33:8, and Ps 81:8 and 106:32. TO reads like N and Ps-Jon.

Chapter XXXIII

1. And this is the blessing which Moses, the prophet of the Lord,[1] blessed the children of Israel before he died.
2. And he said: "The Lord was revealed[2] at Sinai and the brightness of His glory[3] appeared[4] to us[5] from Seir. He was revealed in His power on Mount Paran,[6] and with Him[7] were[8] ten thousand holy ones. The writing of His right hand,[9] the Torah, he gave to us from the fire.[10]

---

[1] MT: "the man of God." N and Ps-Jon render like TO. There are many instances where the Bible has "man of God" and the Targums recast each as "prophet of God." Saadya has "messenger of God."

[2] MT: "The Lord came from Sinai." The Targums remove the anthropomorphic "came." Revealed, on the other hand, is not usually considered a corporeal appearance by TO. Cf. Gen 12:7, 26:2, 35:9, 48:3, and elsewhere. Sifre and b. Zeb. 116a mention "revealed" regarding this phrase and explain it as the revelation of the Torah. Saadya also has "revealed."

[3] MT: "He shone upon them from Seir." The word "glory" is a substitute for the anthropomorphism. TO uses it five times in Genesis (17:22, 18:33, 28:13, 28:16, and 35:13), avoiding the idea of God departing, standing, and ascending. N has "glory" like TO, but Ps-Jon reads "glory of His Shekinah." Saadya also adds "glory."

[4] TO has "appeared" for clarity. N and Ps-Jon retain the metaphor "shone."

[5] MT: "unto them." TO renders like LXX and Vulgate. TO interprets the verse as Moses speaking directly to the people about "us" rather than the indirect "them." H. S. Nyberg (in "Deuteronomy 33, 2-3," *ZDMG* 92 [1938]: 320–344) suggests that some commentators might argue that TO had a pre-Massoretic text for verses 2 and 3, and that it read *lnw* here rather than *lmw*. Nyberg's article refutes this view. TO is following a rabbinical method of interpretation: translating a word as if it were written differently.

N and Ps-Jon have a long aggada about offering the Torah to the sons of Esau.

[6] MT: "He beamed from Mount Paran." TO explains the metaphor "beamed" by changing it with two words: "revealed" and "power." Some TO texts, including Sperber's and B, have "on Mount Paran," instead of "from" like the MT, a reading that perplexed commentators (see Shefftel). The wording is probably from a longer Targum. N and Ps-Jon speak about the attempt by God to give the Torah to the sons of Ishmael "on" these mountains.

Sifre understands "beamed" as the revelation of the Torah, and this could explain the second use by TO of "revealed."

XXXIII

1. ‏ודא ברכתא דבריך משה נביא דיי ית בני ישראל קדם מותיה:‏
2. ‏ואמר יי מסיני אתגלי וזיהור יקריה מסעיר אתחזי לנא אתגלי בגבורתיה על טורא‏
‏דפרן ועמיה רבות קדישין כתב ימיניה מגו אישתא אוריתא ויהב לנא:‏

N, FT, and Ps-Jon have a reference to Edom and Ishmael (Byzantium and Christian Europe) as world powers, arguably dating this part of the Targums no earlier than the seventh century. See also 33:11.

Saadya explains the three mountains as various names for Sinai. Thus he denies the Muslim claim that this verse supports a Biblical expectation of an Arabian prophet.

[7] MT: "He came." TO replaces the anthropomorphism. Comp. v. 1, Isa 21:12, Jer 3:22, etc. N, Ps-Jon, LXX, Peshitta, and Vulgate render similarly, leaving some to think that the MT originally had "with him" (Komlosh, *Hamikra*, p. 138, and Nyberg). The difference is one letter; *wʾth* and *wʾtw*. Saadya: "and He brought to the ten thousand holy ones the Torah of light from His hand to them."

[8] MT: "from." TO does not include Rashi's *derash* that God brought some of His angels. Nevertheless, TO (like N, Ps-Jon, Aquila, Peshitta, Vulgate, Rashi, Ibn Ezra, etc.) may understand the MT as indicating that God came from heaven, where He is surrounded by hosts of angels. LXX has "kadesh," and some read "from Meribath Kadesh."

[9] MT: "from His right hand." TO explains the metaphor. See y. Shek. 9:1 on the writing of his right hand. TO, N, and Ps-Jon do not replace the anthropomorphism. See note on 9:10, "written with the finger of God." Comp. Targum to Eccl 10:2, b. Shab. 63a, and the Midrashim Num R. 22, Soḥer Tov 18:28, PRK on this verse, and Tanḥuma Beracha 3.

Nyberg suggests that TO may have read the *š* of *qdš* twice applying one to the next word, which is then broken in two, *šm ymynw*. Nyberg translates this TO phrase: "His right hand wrote."

[10] MT: *ʾšdt lmw*. Following the massoretic note, TO, N, Ps-Jon, Sifre, Aquila, etc., read *ʾšdt* as two words, "fire" and "law." Nyberg suggests that TO read the word as *mʾš dt*. He also notes that *lnw* is read instead of *lmw*. TO is explaining: God gave us the Torah, the writing of His right hand, which he secured from the fire. Symmachus, Vulgate, Saadya, etc., read *ʾšdt* as one word: "a fiery law."

Sperber and B have the reading "and He gave to us," adding a *vav*, and making this phrase a separate clause at the end of the verse. Not all TO texts have the *vav*. We follow the reading without the *vav* since N and Ps-Jon do not have it, and this suggests that our rendering is correct. N has: "gave the law to his people." Ps-Jon: "gave commands to them." FT has the *vav*, and it is appropriate in this Targum because of the context.

3. Yea, He loved[11] the tribes,[12] all the holy ones, the house of Israel;[13] with power He led them out of Egypt.[14] And they were conducted under the cover of Your cloud,[15] journeying by Your words."[16]

4. Moses gave us[17] Torah, (and) delivered it[18] as an inheritance to[19] the congregation of Jacob.

5. And he was the king in Israel,[20] when the heads of the people were gathered with the tribes of Israel.

[11] MT: "loves." TO, like LXX, Peshitta, and Vulgate, has the perfect. N, FT, and Ps-Jon have long glosses on this verse.

[12] MT: "peoples." TO understands the word to refer to the tribes, because of MT's plural. Comp. Gen 28:3, 48:4, Judg 5:14, etc. Shefftel (BO) explains that had TO written "peoples," it would have appeared to allude to non-Israelites. N and Ps-Jon, who retain "peoples," clarify that it is Israelite people.

[13] MT: "all His holy ones." TO clarifies the phrase with the addition "the house of Israel," like the Sifre. Ps-Jon is like TO, but N and FT speak of angels.

[14] MT: "they are in Your hand." TO removes the anthropomorphism and ellucidates the metaphor with a gloss. Comp. Exod 3:20. N refers to "chastisements." Ps-Jon understands "hand" to imply that the Israelites are called to the Temple.

[15] MT: "and they sit at Your feet." "Feet" is converted to "conducted." Comp. TO to Exod 24:10 and TJ on Hos 11:3. The metaphor "sit at Your feet" is explained as "under God's protection." The meaning of the word tkw in the MT can only be guessed at. Rashi connects it with twk, "midst," rendering: "they placed themselves in the midst of the lower part of Mount Sinai." The LXX has: "immediately under You." Adler (NL) feels that TO may derive the word from hkw, "beaten"; i.e., they fall to earth under the cloud of glory (comp. Nachmanides). Berkowitz (LV) understands the word as being derived from dwkw, "crushed." Nyberg states that MT's tkw lrglk was read as mtht lrglk and yśᵓa as yśᵓu. N has the people resting under the cloud, and Ps-Jon has them resting and encamped there. In Isa 1:5, TJ has qynᵓ, "established." Saadya: "and they follow Your steps."

[16] MT: "receiving Your words." TO may understand the verse as the Sifre: "they bore upon themselves the yoke of the law." It is also possible that TO is focusing on the ultimate objective; that is, they received God's words, which were used as guidance for their journey. Shefftel (BO) suggests that the MT also means "journeying by Your words." Rashi states that TO is interpreting MT's m. N and Ps-Jon are similar to TO. Saadya has "and deliver to each other Your words." The MT has the singular in this phrase, which the Targums render in the plural to fit in with the context. TO has mymrk, "your words," which can also be translated "Your Memra." N, FT, and Ps-Jon have a different word based on the root dbr.

[17] MT: "commands us." Berkowitz (LV) believes that TO is deviating to include

3. אַף חֲבִיבִינוּן לְשִׁבְטַיָּא כָּל קַדִּישׁוֹהִי בֵּית יִשְׂרָאֵל בִּגְבוּרָא אַפֵּיק מִמִּצְרַיִם וְאִינוּן
מְדַבְּרִין תְּחוֹת עֲנָנָךְ נָטְלִין עַל מֵימְרָךְ:
4. אוֹרַיְתָא יְהַב לַנָא מֹשֶׁה מְסַרַהּ יְרוּתָא לִכְנִשְׁתָּא יַעֲקֹב:
5. וַהֲוָה בְיִשְׂרָאֵל מַלְכָּא בְּאִיתְכַּנָּשׁוּת רֵישֵׁי עַמָּא כַּחֲדָא שִׁבְטַיָּא דְּיִשְׂרָאֵל:

the Oral Law as part of what Moses received for the Israelites from God. The Oral Law was not "commanded," because of its large size, but "given." He cites m. Aboth 1:1: "Moses received the Torah (meaning, Oral Law) from Sinai and *gave it* to Joshua." Berkowitz's interpretation is unlikely. It is more probable that TO has "gave" because it is an appropriate parallel to "delivered," which is added in the next phrase. Also, TO may have softened MT's word for the honor of the Israelites: implying no need for a command because the Israelites readily accepted the Torah. Even more likely, TO has "gave" because the word is generally used in Rabbinic literature with Torah. It is found in the Targum to Songs 1:1: "God who gave us a law through Moses." It is also in the Targum to Ps 68:19: "You learned the words of the law, you gave them as gifts to the sons of man." Gen R. 6 has: "R. Yochanan said, three things were given to the world as a gift: Torah, heavenly bodies, and rain." See also Sifre 305; Sheeltot, ed. Dyhernfurth, 2a; Tanhuma; ed. Buber V 16; Seder Eliyahu R., ed. Friedmann, 79. See also b. Shab. 88a and many other places. Furthermore, Berkowitz's thesis is refuted by the Talmud, b. Mac. 23b, which understands the verse to allude to the Pentateuch: "Moses commanded 611 commandments; the first two of the Ten Commandments were heard at Sinai directly from God." N and Ps-Jon retain "commanded us."

[18] TO adds "delivered it" for the sake of clarity. N, FT, and Ps-Jon add "gave it," which TO used in the prior phrase. Again, the commentators read more into the one word than is warranted. Berkowitz explains the addition in TO as appropriate for the Oral Law, as in m. Aboth 1:1: "*delivered* (or gave it over) to Joshua." Lowenstein (NH) feels that the deviation refers to the teaching in the Sifre: "We do not keep the Torah only because of Moses; our ancestors also upheld it and delivered it to us." B. Yoma 28a and 108b, as well as Exod R. 1, indicate that the patriarchs learned Torah and "delivered it" to their children. Shefftel (BO) believes that the addition emphasizes that Moses delivered the Torah during his lifetime and gave it to the Israelites to pass on as an inheritance. Saadya also has "and delivered it."

[19] TO,N, FT, and Ps-Jon, add "to" for clarity.

[20] MT: "Jeshurun." Jeshurun is used, according to Ibn Ezra, as a poetical name for Israel, both words containing the element *yšr*, "upright." See 32:15. Saadya and Ibn Ezra feel the reference is to Moses, who was king over Israel. Sifre and Rashi understand the verse to relate to God. TO, like the MT and Ps-Jon, is not clear on this point. N seems to speak of the Messiah, who will be king in the future.

6. "Let Reuben live in this world,[21] and not die the second death,[22] and let his children receive their inheritance in their numbers."[23]

[21] The words *ḥyy ʿlmʿ* are a TO gloss. They mean either "life eternal" or "life of this world." We translated as we did because N and Ps-Jon indicate clearly "this world" and because Rashi, probably explaining TO, also states this.

In Lev 18:5, the same phrase is found in TO, and Sifra, Ps-Jon, Rashi, Ibn Ezra, and others understand the MT to refer to "life eternal." However, the originality of the TO vorlage in Lev is questionable. B. Yoma 88b derives another lesson from the MT: danger to life overrules the Sabbath. Thus it is arguable that, if the Targumist wanted to teach about the after-life, it would have been more proper for TO to include the lesson elsewhere, such as Exod 20:12 and Deut 22:17. More importantly, it seems that if TO deviates here to combat the Sadducee belief (as argued by Adler, NL), it should have done so more clearly, with language that is not subject to contrary interpretations, and in other verses as well. See the author's *Targumic Studies* for a full discussion of this issue.

Saadya adds "house of" and uses the plural (as in v. 18 for Zebulun), clarifying that the verse refers to the entire tribe.

[22] MT: "and not die." Adler (NL) argues that TO is referring to the teaching in the Sifre: "Let Reuben live in this world and let him not die in the world to come, that the incident of Bilhah not be remembered to him." The Talmud, b. Sanh. 92a, derives the belief in the revival of the dead from this verse. See also y. Sanh. 10:1.

Berkowitz (LV) counters that it is inconceivable that Moses would only bless Reuben with life in the world-to-come, and not the other tribes. He explains that in context "the second death" refers to Reuben's descendants. Since a person "lives on" through his descendants, Moses is praying that the tribe should not be diminished through war (see next note).

It is possible that "the second death" is a scribal addition or the modification by a copyist of another phrase in the original TO text. Compare 32:12 and 24 for other phrases which may have been added by scribes because of a desire to have TO hint at life after death. Support for this view is twofold. First, the expression "the second death" is not found elsewhere in TO, and its use is restricted to only several other sources. Second, of all the Targums to this verse, only some of the fragmented Targums have the phrase, and its placement in these texts could easily have been influenced by the Sifre and Talmuds.

"The second death" is found five other times in a Targum (other than the fragmented Targums to this verse) and four times in the New Testament. In each instance the phrase implies either exclusion from resurrection or some event following resurrection (such as a punishment).

6. יחי ראובן בחיי עלמא ומותא תנינא לא ימות ויקבלון בנוהי אחסנתהון במנינהון:

TJ to Jer 51:39	"they shall die the second death and shall not live in the world-to-come"
TJ to Jer 51:57	"They shall die the second death and shall not come to the world-to-come"
TJ to Isa 22:14	"This sin shall not be forgiven you until you die the second death"
TJ to Isa 65:6	"Their punishment shall be in Gehenna where the fire burns all day . . . I . . . will give them the punishment for their transgressions and deliver their bodies to the second death"
TJ to Isa 65:15	"the Lord will slay you with the second death"
Ap 2:11	"he who conquers shall not be hurt by the second death"
Ap 20:6	"Over such the second death has no power"
Ap 20:14	"This is the second death, the lake of fire"
Ap 21:8	"their lot shall be in the lake that burns with fire and brimstone, which is the second death"

The Bomberg fragmented Targum and Targums Paris MS 110 and Leipzig MS No. 1 have: "Let Reuben live in this world and not die the second death in which death the wicked die in the world-to-come." N and FT have *mwtn*, "plague," instead of *mwt*, "death," which may be a copyist's error, or may mean in context a malignant death. Ps-Jon has the same text as Paris 110 but omits the word "second"; this may also be the mistake of a scribe, or it might be the original version.

23 MT: "and let his men be a number." This is an obscure phrase. LXX renders the end as "numerous." Rashi explains: let the tribe of Reuben be counted among the other tribes; that is, that Reuben should not be excluded because he lay with Bilhah. Adler suggests that the text may direct attention to the tribe's role as vanguard; Moses is praying that their battles do not diminish them. Lowenstein believes that our passage alludes to Gen 49:3, 4, that Reuben, being the firstborn, should receive a double inheritance of the birthright; "But now you have sinned, the birthright has been given to Joseph (Gen R. 93, 4, p. 1253). It is also possible that the TO vorlage here is incorrect and should read: *wyhy bnwhy mtmnyn bmnynhwn*, "let his children be counted in their number."

N has: "and let his youth be with the men in number." Ps-Jon has: "and let his youth be numbered with the young men of his Israelite brethren."

7. And this for Judah, and he said: "Accept,²⁴ Lord, the prayer²⁵ of Judah when he goes forth to battle²⁶ and bring him back to his people in peace.²⁷ Let his hands do vengeance upon his enemies²⁸ and be to him a help²⁹ against his foes."

8. And of Levi he said: "The Thumim and Urim You put on the man who was found holy before You,³⁰ whom You tested with trials³¹ and he was upright,³² and whom You put to the test³³ at the waters of contention,³⁴ and he was found faithful.³⁵

9. Who has no compassion on his father and his mother when they are proved guilty by law, ³⁶ and regards not the persons of his brothers

---

²⁴ MT: "hear." This is a typical change.

²⁵ MT: "voice." Again, a characteristic deviation. The Targums frequently change "call" to "pray." See Introduction. The substitution is made here both to elevate Judah's action and to be more specific.

²⁶ "when he goes forth to battle" is a gloss, also in Ps-Jon, but not N. Rashi writes: "hear the prayer of Judah's descendants, David and Solomon, and of Asa because of the Ethiopians, of Jehoshaphat because of the Ammonites, and of Hezekiah because of Sannacherib." Saadya interprets the verse similarly: "return him from his wars."

²⁷ TO and Ps-Jon add "in peace." See prior note. N adds "from battle" here.

²⁸ MT: "let his hands be numerous for him." TO, N, and Ps-Jon clarify the phrase in accordance with their understanding of the first part of the verse. As Rashi explains: "let his hands successfully strive for him and avenge his wrongs." TO translates *rb* as "strive," as does the LXX.

²⁹ Uncharacteristically, neither TO nor Ps-Jon add Memra here. N has Memra at the beginning of the verse.

³⁰ MT: "Your Thumim and your Urim (belong) to Your pious man." Rashi understands the phrase to be addressed to God, not Levi. Hence, TO drops the pronouns "your" three times and adds "before" once. TO adds words for clarity. The "man" referred to in the verse is Aaron according to N and Ps-Jon. See Exod 28:30, Lev 8:8, Ezr 2:63, and Neh 7:65 regarding the Thumim and Urim, generally rendered "lights and perfections."

³¹ MT: "at Massah." TO (like N, Ps-Jon, and the Sifre) does not treat Massah as a noun. Moses is referring to the tribe of Levi (Adler, NL). Nachmanides believes that this phrase also concerns Aaron, the high priest. N and Ps-Jon mention Aaron. See Exod 17:1 ff., Num 20:2 ff., and Deut 6:16, 9:22, and 32:51. TO renders the name here as in Exod 17:7, Num 20:13, etc.

7. ודא ליהודה ואמר קביל יי צלותיה דיהודה במיפקיה לקרבא ולעמיה תתיבניה
בשלם ידוהי יעבדן ליה פורענותא בסנאוהי וסעיד מבעיל דבבא הוי ליה:

8. וללוי אמר תומיא ואוריא אלבישתא לגבר דאשתכח חסיד קדמך דניסיתהי
בניסיתא והוה שלים בחנתהי על מי מצותא ואשתכח מהימן:

9. דעל אבוהי ועל אימיה לא רחים כד חבו מן דינא אפי אחוהי ובנוהי לא נסיב ארי
נטרו מטרת מימרך וקימך לא אשניאו:

[32] This phrase is a TO and Ps-Jon gloss. The word translated here as "upright" literally means "complete." N has "and he withstood the test."

[33] MT: "and with whom You strived." TO, N, and Ps-Jon avoid the unseemly anthropomorphism by substituting "strive" with "test."

[34] MT: "at the waters of Meribah." TO does not view "Meribah" as a noun. See note on Massah, above, for citations. N and Ps-Jon have: "waters of contention of Rekem."

[35] This last phrase is a TO, N, and Ps-Jon gloss for clarity. It is also in the Sifre. It is possible that the Targums add "he was upright" and "he was faithful" to emphasize that despite Aaron's involvement in the episode of the golden calf, he was "faithful" and "upright." Comp. the approximately 100 times in Genesis where TO deviates for the honor of Israel's ancestors, in Israel Drazin's *Targumic Studies*.

[36] MT: "Who said to his father and to his mother, I have not seen him." TO explains the intention of MT's poetical statement. TO alludes either (a) to the incident of the golden calf (Exod 32:26, 27), when the tribe of Levi showed zeal for God in slaying their own relatives who were guilty of worshipping the calf (Sifre), or (b) to the restraint practiced by the tribe in not worshipping idols in Egypt (b. Yoma 66b), or (c) to the tribe's judicial function mentioned in the next verse (Adler, NL). See also the explanation of Berkowitz and Lowenstein below. N and Ps-Jon list other reasons.

FT indicates, among other things: "Who had no compassion on his father and mother in the judgment of Tamar." This bothered the commentators (see *Perush Jerushalmi*) because Levi is not mentioned in the story of Tamar, Gen 38. Various explanations have been given, including that the word "Tamar" should be "Dinah." It is so in some manuscripts.

It is possible that the words "proved guilty by law" were added to emphasize that the tribe only killed those who were found guilty by a court of law. Cf. TO on Gen 9:6.

and sons;[37] for they kept the charge of Your word[38] and did not alter Your covenant.[39]

10. These are worthy to teach Your laws to Jacob[40] and Your Torah to Israel. They shall set smoking incense before You,[41] and the whole[42] for favor[43] on Your altar.

11. Bless, O Lord, his possessions,[44] and the sacrifices of his hands[45] receive with favor;[46] break the loins of his foes[47] and his enemies[48] that they rise no more."[49]

[37] MT: "neither did he acknowledge his brothers nor know his sons." Again, as above, TO explains the MT. TO may not repeat the verbs "acknowledge" and "know" to avoid redundancy, or our text is faulty.

[38] TO adds "the charge of" for clarity. It is implied in the MT. The language is from Num 9:23. N and Ps-Jon do not. The Targums render "Your word," *mymrk*; which could be confused with "Your Memra."

[39] MT: "and guarded Your covenant." Uncharacteristically, TO changes a positive statement to a negative. Adler (NL) and Reifmann (*Sedeh*, p. 45) explain that this is done to avoid a redundancy with the previous statement. Berkowitz (LV) and Lowenstein (NH) feel that TO is suggesting that the tribe of Levi performed the covenant of circumcision in the desert even though the "fathers" who were ordinary Israelites did not do so. Thus, the tribe of Levi "did not alter" the covenant of circumcision (see b. Yeb. 72a and Sifre). Other possible explanations are: perhaps a positive affirmation would contradict Moses' prediction in chapter 32 that the people would sin. People may sin and fail without altering the covenant. Additionally, the wording "did not alter" is appropriate for circumcision and is found in TO to Exod 34:27 and m. Aboth 3:11. Also negative statements do appear in TO, comp. Exod 15:11 and v. 15. Both N and Ps-Jon have positive statements. N: "and were careful with the decrees of Your law." Ps-Jon: "and they kept the matters of the holy service."

[40] MT: "They shall teach Jacob Your laws." TO adds "worthy" which is implied. It is also arguable, but unlikely, that rather than have the verse only indicate the two primary functions of the priests: to instruct and offer sacrifices, TO, N, and Ps-Jon add "worthy" to connect this verse with the preceding verse. The tribe of Levi is rewarded with the prerogative of the priesthood (comp. 10:8 and see b. Yoma 26a) because of their prior deeds. Shefftel (BO) feels that TO may be referring to the teaching, which is also in Sifre, that the tribe of Levi are fit by nature for their task.

[41] MT: "in Your nostril." Comp. Gen 8:21, Lev 26:31, Am 5:21, Ps 18:9, etc. TO avoids the gross anthropomorphism. N and Ps-Jon understand "nostril" as "anger" and translate accordingly, N: "restrain Your anger." Saadya also has "before You."

10. כשרין אילין דילפון דינך ליעקב ואוריתך לישראל ישוון קטורת בוסמין קדמך
וגמיר לרעוא על מדבחך:
11. בריך יי ניכסוהי וקורבן ידוהי קביל ברעוא תבר חרצא דסנאוהי ודבעלי דבבוהי
דלא יקומון:

[42] TO is literal. Sifre and the Talmud (b. Yoma 26a) explain that the MT is referring to the whole-offering; i.e., the holocaust offering. TO does not deviate here to
clarify what the verse is referring to. Adler (NL) points out that TO could be understood to refer to the coals under the holocaust (Lev 16:12), or the priestly Minhah
sacrifice (Lev 6:16). Lowenstein (NH) feels it is only the latter. He explains that TO
does not read "the holocaust offering" because the Targumist found it hard to
understand why Moses would want to restrict his blessing. The Targumist chose to
imply that Moses meant the Minhah offering since it was brought daily and the
priest shared in the meat. N and Ps-Jon translate similarly, only adding the word
"sacrifice." The LXX renders; "let them lay incense continually."

[43] The Targums add "for favor," implied in the MT. Shefftel (BO) argues that
these words clarify that the verse is speaking of the holocaust offering because
these words are used for that offering (see Lev 1:13).

[44] MT has a word meaning "strength" or "might" (translated so by LXX, Vulgate, and others), or "hosts" or "ranks" (N, Nachmanides, and others). TO (like b.
Yoma 26a, Ps-Jon, Sifre, Ibn Ezra, Soforno, etc.) has the word imply material possessions; for example, that the Levites have no material cares and are able to spend
their time teaching (Soforno), or that they receive many levitical gifts (Ibn Ezra).
TO translates here as in 8:17 and Num 24:18.

[45] MT: "the work of his hands." TO clarifies the meaning of the words, like N,
Ps-Jon, and Ibn Ezra. Soforno explains "levitical duties."

[46] MT: "accept." TO, N, and Ps-Jon are more specific.

[47] MT: "smite the loins, those who rise against him." Again TO and N clarify the
meaning of the text by being more specific: "fight against those who object to the
Levites" (Adler, NL).

Ps-Jon lists the enemies, and mentions the high priest Johanan. This addition
may date this part of Ps-Jon to the first century B.C.E. The priest John Hyrcanus
reigned from 135 to 104 B.C.E. There is also evidence of late material in Ps-Jon:
Gen 15:4 (calendar), 21:21 (Adisha and Fatima; the wife and daughter of
Mohammed), Exod 14:2 (an interpolation from Mek. Bešalaḥ 2:4), 26:9, 36:16 (six
orders of the Mishna), Num 24:24 (Constantinople), Deut 33:2 (Byzantium and
Christian Europe), etc.

Ps-Jon also speaks of "Elijah the priest" who made offerings on Mount Carmel.

[48] MT: "them that hate him." The Targums are more specific.

[49] MT: "from rising." The MT lacks a relative particle before the verb. N: "that
his enemies may not be able to stand up before him." The other Targums also lack
"from rising."

12. Of Benjamin he said: "Beloved of the Lord, he rests securely beside Him; let the shield be over him all the days,[50] and the Shekinah dwell in his land."[51]

13. And of Joseph he said: "Blessed be his land from before the Lord,[52] it makes sweet things by the dew of the heaven from above,[53] and from the fountain springs and the deep[54] that flow out of the depths of the earth below.[55]

14. Let it make sweet things and produce from the bounty of the sun.[56] Let it make sweet things at the beginning of every month (literally, month after month),[57]

15. and from the top of the ancient[58] mountains, and from the goodly[59] hills that never fail,[60]

---

[50] MT: "He covers him all the day." The Targums remove the gross anthropomorphism, God serving as a blanket, by having the shield do the act rather than God.

[51] MT: "and He dwells between his shoulders." The Targums add "Shekinah" (N has "glory of His Shekinah"), removing the anthropomorphism of God "dwelling," and explain "between his shoulders" as an allusion to the site of the Temple within the rocky border of Benjamin. Sifre states that a strip of land in the shape of the head of an ox projected from Benjamin's territory into Judah's, and the Temple was built upon the shoulders, where the Shekinah dwelt. See also b. Zeb. 54b, 118a, b. Yoma 12a, 31a, and b. Meg. 26b.

TO's interpretation of the final phrase of this verse parallels its explanation of Gen 49:27. The MT's "Benjamin is a ravenous wolf. In the morning, he devours the prey, and at evening-time, he divides the spoil" is rendered by TO: "Benjamin: in his land the Shekinah will dwell, and in his possession the Temple will be built. In the morning and afternoon the priests will offer the sacrifice, and at evening-time they will divide the remaining portions of other holy things."

[52] MT: "Blessed of the Lord be his land." The Targums add "from before."

[53] MT: "from the precious things of heaven, from the dew." TO and Ps-Jon explain the phrase: "precious things" as sweet things. N has "treasures." The words "from above" are also in N and Ps-Jon, being implied in the MT. A similar expression is found in the MT of Gen 49:25: "with blessings of heaven above." The word "makes" is added for clarity, as in 8:8.

[54] This phrase "springs and the deep" is not in the MT of Gen, the MT of Deut, or TO to Gen. N and Ps-Jon also lack the phrase. It is possible that there is a conflation here, the word "deep" being rendered in two ways.

[55] MT: "and from the deep that crouches below." This phrase is very similar to one contained in Gen 49:25. Aberbach and Grossfeld (*Targum Onkelos to Genesis*)

12. לבנימין אמר רחימא דיי ישרי לרוחצן עלוהי יהי מגין עלוהי כל יומא ובארעיה
תשרי שכינתא:
13. וליוסף אמר מברכא מן קדם יי ארעיה עבדא מגדנין מטלא דשמיא מלעילא
וממבועי עינוון ותהומין דנגדין ממעמקי ארעא מלרע:
14. ועבדא מגדנין ועללן מיבול שימשא עבדא מגדנין מריש ירח בירח:
15. ומריש טוריא בכיריא ומטוב ראמן דלא פסקן:

explain TO's deviation as follows: MT is a poetical metaphor which TO is trying to interpret in more prosaic terms. Since MT *rbṣt*, "crouches," is derived from the root *rbṣ*, which is used in Mishnaic Hebrew as well as in Aramaic in the sense of "sprinkle," "irrigate," TO explains *rbṣt* in a similar sense: "flowing."

The same tendency to clarify the poetry of the text by turning it into sober prose is apparent in TO's rendering of "deep." Instead of the abstract noun, TO paraphrases "out of the depths of the earth." It is also possible that "the deep," *thwm*, and "crouches" might suggest the mythical Tiamat, an idea TO prefers to avoid.

Ps-Jon has: "that rise out and flow to water the herbage from below." N is similar.

[56] MT: "And from the precious things of the revenue of the sun." As in the previous verse, "precious things" is interpreted as "sweet things" by TO. N and Ps-Jon have "fruits." *tbwʾ* is understood as "income," "revenue," or "produce" by TO and Ps-Jon. N has "it will yield." TO adds "Let it make." The Targums understand the phrase like the Sifre: "Joseph's land lay exposed to the sun and it therefore produced sweet fruit."

[57] MT: "and from the precious things put forth by the moons." The word *yrḥym* can be defined as "moons," as does the LXX, or "months." Accepting the latter interpretation (since the earth's moon is singular, not plural), TO explains the poetry as referring to fruits which the earth yields from month to month (Rashi). N and Ps-Jon understand the word like TO. Comp. Isa 66:23.

Shefftel (BO) explains that TO adds "at the beginning" because the early part of the month is a better time for growth. It is also possible that it was added for clarity since "at the beginning" is implied. It is also in N and Ps-Jon.

[58] TO evidently interprets *qdm*, also translated "priority," as "ancient." N, Ps-Jon, and FT understand the mountains to allude to the patriarchs and the hills to the matriarchs, and translate accordingly. Sifre has TO's interpretation.

N and FT state explicitly that the good fruits are produced because of the *Zachuth*, "merit," of the patriarchs and matriarchs. Ps-Jon implies this interpretation. There are many references to vicarious *Zachuth* in the PT, but TO ignores the concept. See the author's *Targumic Studies*.

[59] MT: "precious." Since TO had already translated "precious" as "sweet

16. from the goodness[61] of the earth and its fullness, the favor of Him whose Shekinah is in heaven"[62]—and who was revealed to Moses at the bush.[63] "Let all these come[64] upon the head of Joseph, upon the man who was separated from his brothers.[65]

17. The great one of his sons will be his beauty (lit. possess radiance).[66] The mighty works done by him through his power and dominance are

things" twice in the previous verse, and once before that, TO is different here to avoid redundancy (Adler, NL).

[60] MT: "everlasting hills." This is another instance where TO uncharacteristically renders a positive statement negatively. The Targum may be stating that nature, *per se*, is not "everlasting," but God's blessing never fails. Rashi, apparently explaining TO, writes, "hills which everlastingly produce fruit, and do not fail to do so through restraint of rain." It is also possible that TO deviates here from its usual practice to prevent a redundancy with the prior phrase "ancient mountains," which is similar to "everlasting" (comp. v. 9). N does not have an adjective for the "hills." Ps-Jon is like TO.

[61] MT: "precious things." Again, as in the previous verse, "precious things" is replaced by "good" rather than "sweet things." Lowenstein (NH) suggests that TO has "good" because of "fullness" which follows. The latter word, according to Lowenstein, implies more than fruits; see also Nachmanides, who interprets the verse in this way without reference to TO. N and Ps-Jon speak of "good fruits."

N and FT may imply that even inanimate objects can produce *Zachuth*, "merit" (see note 58), which is stored for the use of the Israelites. N has: "(trees) producing good fruits by the *Zachuth* of the land and its fullness, and which do the will of Him who made the glory of His Shekinah dwell in the thorn bush."

[62] MT: "and the favor of Him that dwelt in the bush." Evading the gross anthropomorphism, TO divides the phrase into two. God is not described as dwelling in the bush, but His Shekinah is in heaven. Neither N nor Ps-Jon break up this phrase. A text of Saadya has "heaven" instead of the "bush." Ibn Ezra also has "heaven."

[63] TO adds a gloss to the word "bush" to remove the anthropomorphism. N and FT have the "glory of the Shekinah" dwell in the bush. Ps-Jon has it revealed to Moses in the bush.

[64] MT has a difficult word which TO and N construe like Rashi: "let (the blessings) come." Ps-Jon has "gather."

[65] MT: "and upon the crown of the head of him that is separated from his brothers." This verse may refer to the sale of Joseph by his brothers (Rashi), or to

16. ומטוב ארעא ומלאה רעי ליה דשכנתיה בשמיא ועל משה אתגלי באסנא ייתין כל
אילין לרישא דיוסף גברא פרישא דאחוהי:
17. רבא דבנוהי זיוא ליה גבורן איתעבידא ליה מן קדם דתוקפא ורומא דיליה
בגבורתיה עממיא יקטיל כחדא עד סיפי ארעא ואינון רבותא דבית אפרים ואינון
אלפיא דבית מנשה:

the tribe's ability to separate itself from its neighbors and develop better character traits (Adler, NL).

TO recasts the poetic "crown of the head" with the prose "man."

In their commentary *Targum Onkelos to Genesis*, on 49:66 (the draft was made available to the author by Dr. Aberbach), Aberbach and Grossfeld take issue with those who understand TO's rendering of the MT's *qdqd*, "crown of the head," as "man." The authors find no "valid evidence that the two nouns have anything in common." Although they note that Rashi, Sifre (on Deut 33:16), Gen R., and Midrash Aggadah disagree with their view, they consider that the word in the MT implies distinction and that "man" is a gloss. Thus TO should be rendered, "a man distinguished among his brothers." Deut 33:20 is cited in support, as the same word in the MT is rendered "kings" by TO. Actually, TO is replacing a synecdoche (a figure of speech by which a part is put for the whole). In 49:66 and here, the poetic "crown," referring to part of a man, is converted to the prose "man," designating the whole. Similarly, in context, the word "crown" in 33:20 is a synecdoche for "kings."

Both N and Ps-Jon have *qdqd*, add "man," and speak of Joseph's high position: "and for the crown of the head of the man who was chief (and ruler, Ps-Jon) in the land of Egypt, and was careful about the honor of his brothers." The Targums probably derived both Joseph's position and his relation to his brothers from the word *nzyr*, translated by TO as "separated," a word implying both high position and distinctive care over his brothers. The LXX has: "come upon the head of Joseph. He indeed is glorified in being the chief over brothers."

Joseph's blessing is more difficult to understand than the other verses in this chapter. The author translated TO to verses 13–15 as essentially one blessing: fruitfulness. Verse 16 is a kind of invocation: for the sake of two reasons, the good of the earth and the favor of God, Moses prays that his prayer by accepted. Interpreting verse 16 as a prayer makes it parallel Gen 49:18 ("I wait for Your deliverance, O Lord") and helps us understand that verse better.

66 MT: "The firstborn of his oxen is comeliness to him." TO clarifies the metaphor. N, Ps-Jon, Sifre, Rashi, etc., explain that the reference is to Joshua of the tribe of Ephraim, whose strength will be as mighty as an ox, helping him subdue many kings.

his.[67] By his might nations will be slain as one[68] until the ends of the earth.[69] Now they are the ten thousands of the house of[70] Ephraim, and they are the thousands of the house of[71] Manasseh."

18. And of Zebulun he said: "Rejoice Zebulun when you go out to war against your adversaries,[72] and Issachar, when you go out to set the time of the festivals in Jerusalem.[73]

19. The tribes of Israel shall assemble at the mountain of the sanctuary;[74] there shall they offer holy sacrifices for favor,[75] for they will eat the

---

[67] MT: "and his horns are the horns of the wild ox." Sifre, Rashi, etc., elucidate the metaphor: "the ox is strong but its horns are not beautiful, a wild ox has beautiful horns but its strength is not mighty; therefore the verse ascribes to Joshua both the strength of an ox and the beauty of the wild ox's horns." N and Ps-Jon have a simpler explanation which is also probably the intention of TO; it is through its horns that the ox wins victories, so shall Joshua thrust forth into victory.

Several of the words in TO can be interpreted as "works done for him from before the Omnipotent and Most High are His." Shefftel (BO) believes they direct attention to the acts done for Joseph in Egypt. Adler (NL) writes that the phrase does not relate to God, but to Joseph, as we translated. Adler is probably correct since both N and Ps-Jon speak about the strength and dominance of the tribe achieved through the victories of Joshua and Gideon.

[68] MT: "with them he shall gore the peoples together." Evading the metaphor of the ox, TO presents the meaning of the phrase in specific language. N and Ps-Jon paraphrase this and the next phrase at length.

[69] MT: "the ends of the earth." TO adds "until" which is implied.

[70] TO and Ps-Jon add "house of" for clarity, N and FT add "tribe of." N, Ps-Jon, Rashi, etc., explain: "those who are gored (killed) are the ten thousands whom Joshua, a descendant of Ephraim, slew."

[71] TO and Ps-Jon include "house of" for clarity, N and FT add "tribe of." N, Ps-Jon, Rashi, etc., explain: "they are the ten thousands whom Gideon, a descendant of Manasseh, slew."

[72] MT: "Rejoice, Zebulun, in your going out." N, Ps-Jon, FT, Sifre, Rashi, and Nachmanides clarify the MT: "be successful when you go out to trade." TO interprets like the Talmud, b. Meg. 6a, and Ibn Ezra, that the allusion is to war. Cf. TO on Gen 49:13: "Zebulun shall dwell by the seashore, and he shall conquer coastal districts with ships, and the best of the sea he shall consume, and his border shall

18. ולזבולן אמר חדי זבולן במיפקך לאגחא קרבא על בעלי דבבך וישׁשׂכר במהכך
למעבד זימני מועדיא בירושלם:

19. שׁיבטיא דישׂראל לטור בית מקדשׁא יתכנשׁון תמן יכסון ניכסת קודשׁין לרעוא ארי
ניכסי עממיא ייכלון וסימן דמטמרן בחלא יתגלין להון:

reach as far as Sidon." Cf. also I Chron 12:33: "Of Zebulun, such as were able to go
out in the host, that could set the battle in array, with all manner of instruments of
war, fifty thousand; and that could order the battle array, and were not of double
heart." For other references to "going out" implying battle, see, e.g., I Sam 18:13,
16, 30; II Sam 5:2.

[73] MT: "and Issachar, in your tents." TO (like N, Ps-Jon, and Sifre) treats
"tents" as referring to study, as in Gen 25:27, "Jacob dwelt in tents." Moses
blessed Issachar that they be successful in this enterprise: sitting in the Sanhedrin
and intercalating the years and fixing the day of the new moon. Comp. I Chron
12:32: "And the children of Issachar, men that had understanding of the times, to
know what Israel ought to do; the heads of them were two hundred; and all their
brethren were at their commandment." See the Targum on this verse and on Esth
1:13. Comp. the Targum to Songs 7:5, the scribes intercalate the years in the gate
of the great Sanhedrin.

Adler (NL) feels that TO uses "go" like b. Sanh. 11b: until the destruction of
the second Temple, the intercalating was only done in Jerusalem; thus, the tribe of
Issachar had to go to that city.

TO's "go," *bmhk*, is also found in Exod 18:23: "If you do this (seek the
advice of judges)—and God so commands you—you (Moses) will be able to bear
up; and all these people too will go home unwearied."

The PT is not as specific as TO: "when you are seated in your schoolhouses."

[74] MT: "They shall call peoples unto the mountain." TO and Rashi construe
"peoples," in the plural, to mean the tribes of Israel, as in v. 3, and the mountain as
Mount Moriah, as in Exod 15:17. Since Issachar calculated the festivals, they summoned the tribes on the festivals. N has "peoples" refer to the tribe of Zebulun,
Ps-Jon and Sifre have "many peoples." Each speaks of the mountain of the
sanctuary.

[75] MT: "there shall they offer sacrifices of righteousness." TO transposes the latter word to "holy" for clarity and adds a gloss "for favor." It is possible that
"holy" is applied by TO to the tribes and not the sacrifice, as in Ps 51:21.
N and Ps-Jon translate "righteousness" as "truth" and do not have "for favor."

property of the nations,[76] and the treasure hidden in the sand shall be disclosed for them."[77]

20. And of Gad he said: "Blessed is He who enlarges Gad. He dwells like a lioness. He will kill[78] sultans[79] with[80] kings."[81]

21. And he shall receive[82] his own at the beginning,[83] for there, in his inheritance,[84] Moses the great scribe of Israel[85] is (to be) buried.[86] He

[76] MT: "for they shall suck the abundance of the seas." TO and N change "suck" to the more refined "eat." Rashi explains the verse: "they" refers to Zebulun and Issachar, who will obtain wealth in abundance from the sea (which belongs to all nations). Reifmann (*Sedeh*, p. 45) and others point out that TO should read "seas," like the MT; this would require the change of only one Aramaic letter. They are probably correct since while all TO texts have "nations," the other Targum texts have "seas." However, the possibility that TO is based on texts which had *'mym* instead of *ymym* is not to be lightly dismissed. See note on 5:19 concerning the use by Targums of pre-Massoretic texts.

[77] MT: "and the hidden treasures of the sand." Rashi, in his commentary on b. Meg. 6a, states that this refers to a kind of fish, the *hilazon*, from which a purple dye was obtained, and white glass which comes out of the sea and the sand. Both were valuable articles of commerce, difficult to find. The Talmud (*ibid.*) and Sifre state that Zebulun complained about its territory being inferior. God replied that He would give them the "treasures hidden in the sand" and the other tribes would be in need of them. Ibn Ezra explains the verse: "they will have so much riches that they will need to hide some in the sand, and because of their wealth most of them will travel to the Temple mount to offer thanksgiving sacrifices to God." N renders like TO, and Ps-Jon is similar.

[78] MT: "tears." TO, N, and Ps-Jon are more explicit. Although TO always translates *lby'* as "lioness" (comp. Gen 49:9, Num 23:24, 24:9), TJ renders it *'ry'*, "lion," a word that does not connote gender (comp. TJ to Isa 5:29, and see Radak on Judges 14:5).

[79] MT: "arm." this is a synecdoche, which TO replaces. Rulers have power, like an arm. Comp. TO to Gen 49:4, 10, and 26. N has: "his slaughtered are recognized among the slain by the head being cut away with the arm." Ps-Jon has both ideas.

[80] MT: *'p*, "also," "though," "even"; a poetic use avoided by TO and Ps-Jon, who prefer the prosaic "with." For N, see note 79.

[81] MT: "crown of the head," a synecdoche changed by TO and Ps-Jon. Kings rule, like the head. For N, see note 79. Comp. TJ to Isa 3:17, where the word is ren-

20. וְלִגָד אֲמַר בְּרִיךְ דְּאַפְתֵי לְגָד כְּלִיתָא שֵׁרִי וְקַטִּיל שִׁלְטוֹנִין עִם מַלְכִין:

21. וְיִתְקַבַּל בְּקַדְמֵיתָא דִּילֵיהּ אֲרֵי תַמָּן בְּאַחְסַנְתֵּיהּ מֹשֶׁה סָפְרָא רַבָּא דְיִשְׂרָאֵל קְבִיר הוּא נְפַק וְעַל בְּרֵישׁ עַמָּא זָכוּן קֳדָם יְיָ עֲבַד וְדִינוֹהִי עִם יִשְׂרָאֵל:

dered "the glory"; there it connotes something honorable. See also 33:16.

[82] MT: "And he saw." "Saw" can suggest "chose." TO goes a step further and understands the word as implying a taking of land before most of the tribes, as Rashi explains: "he saw good to take for himself territory in the land of Sihon and Og." Comp. I Chron 12:37: "And on the other side of the Jordan, of the Reubenites, and the Gadites, and of the half-tribe of Manasseh." N has "saw." Ps-Jon has both words.

[83] The MT can be understood as meaning either the "best part" of the newly acquired territory or that it was the "first to be conquered." TO seems to prefer the latter sense, as Sifre explains: "the subjugation of Gad's portion was the beginning of the conquest of the land." N is like TO, and Ps-Jon renders it in both senses.

[84] MT: "for there was the portion of." TO makes it clear that the allusion is to Gad and not Moses. *Sifte Hachamim,* explaining Rashi, notes that the MT seems to imply that Moses was already buried. TO's deviation heightens this difficulty. N removes it: "a place had been prepared there for a sepulcher." Ps-Jon, which has a long gloss, retains the difficulty.

[85] MT: "the lawgiver." TO is more explicit. N has: "the prophet, the scribe." Ps-Jon: "the scribe." The epithet "great scribe" appended to the name of Moses is used in the Targums to Songs 1:2, 2:4, 3:3; Ps 62:12; Ps-Jon to Gen 5:24, where Enoch is identified with the angel Metatron (see Ginzberg, VI, p. 325, n. 40, and p. 446, n. 50); and FT to Num 11:26, "the prophet Moses, scribe of Israel." It is also found in Sifre and b. Sotah 13b (see Ginzberg, VI, p. 165, n. 955).

[86] MT: "is hidden." TO construes the verse, like N, Ps-Jon, Sifre, Rashi, etc., as an allusion to Moses' burial place, which was hidden from mankind (see 34:6). Since Moses was apparently buried on Mount Nebo (32:49, 50), which is believed to have been in the territory of Reuben, modern commentators (Driver, etc.) explain the MT as a reference to the tribe of Gad, which obtained in the conquered territory a portion worthy of its martial character. Deut R. 2 indicates Moses was buried outside of Israel because he did not say "I am a Hebrew" when he was called an Egyptian (Exod. 2:19). However, the Talmud, b. Suc. 13b, and Sifre indicate that Moses died in the territory of Reuben but was buried in the territory of Gad.

came out and went up at the head of the people.[87] He executed righteousness before[88] the Lord and His judgments with Israel.

22. And of Dan he said: "Dan is strong as a lion's whelp,[89] his land is watered by the rivers that flow[90] from Matnan."[91]

23. And of Naphtali he said: "Naphtali is satisfied with favor and full of blessings[92] from before[93] the Lord: the west, the Sea of Ginosar, and its south,[94] you will possess."

24. And of Asher he said: "Blessed be Asher with the blessings[95] of children: that he be acceptable to his brethren, and be nourished with the dainties of kings.[96]

---

[87] MT: "and there came the heads of the people." This phrase is obscure, some even thinking that the MT is corrupt. According to Rashi and Ibn Ezra, TO explains that it calls attention to the pioneering role played by the tribe of Gad (Reuben and half the tribe of Manasseh) when the Israelites conquered Canaan (cf. Gen 49:19, Num 32:16–32, Jos 1:12 ff., 4:12 ff., 22:1 ff.). Adler (NL) believes that TO is referring to Moses, who came out from the people and went up to the Tabernacle, comp. m. Aboth 5:18. N and Ps-Jon have the interpretation of the Sifre that the verses speak of Moses' leadership: as he went in and out at the head of the people in this world, so he will do in the next because he did righteousness and taught judgment. TO generally avoids referring to the world-to-come. See the author's *Targumic Studies*.

[88] TO and Ps-Jon add "before" but N does not.

[89] MT: "Dan is a lion's whelp." The Targums change the metaphor, which is subject to misunderstanding by the masses, to a simile. The Targums may be referring to the exploits of Samson, a judge from the tribe of Dan; cf. Judg 13:12 ff. TO to Gen 49:16, 17, speaks of Samson more explicitly.

[90] MT: "that leaps." In the Syriac, the word in the MT is understood as "squirt, sputter, eject with force." Rather than describing the tribe as unseemingly leaping, the Targums understand the phrase to concern to the land, using the sense implied in the Syriac: that the water is leaping; that is, gushing forth. Cf. b. Bech. 55a. The Peshitta is the same as the Targums, leading some to believe that these translators had a text that read *yynq* rather than *yznq*, the *y* and the *z* being easily confused. This conclusion is unwarranted since the Targumists are following a characteristic Targumic method of translation, avoiding metaphors. See note to 5:19.

[91] MT: "Bashan." TO uses the name that existed during the Talmudic age. See 3:1, etc. N has Batanea. Ps-Jon has both names.

[92] MT has the singular, which the Targums change to the plural as required by the context, since Naphtali receives possessions both in the west and the south. Sifre and y. Ber. 7:5 comment on this verse: "the blessing containing three parts."

22. וּלְדָן אֲמַר דָּן תַּקִּיף כְּגוֹר אַרְיָון אַרְעֵיהּ שַׁתְיָא מִן נַחֲלַיָּא דְּנַגְדִּין מִן מַתְנָן:
23. וּלְנַפְתָּלִי אֲמַר נַפְתָּלִי סְבַע רְעוּא וּמְלֵי בִּירְכַן מִן קֳדָם יְיָ מַעְרַב יַם גְּנֵיסַר וְדָרוֹמִי יֵירַת:
24. וּלְאָשֵׁר אֲמַר בְּרִיךְ מִבִּרְכַת בְּנַיָּא אֲשֵׁר יְהֵי רְעוּא לַאֲחוֹהִי וְיִתְרְבָא בְּתַפְנוּקֵי מַלְכִין:

The Targums may be referring to this interpretation." Some TO texts retain the singular.

[93] The Targums add "from before."

[94] MT: "you will possess the west and the south." The Targums explain the intention of the MT; as Rashi states: "The sea of Chinnereth (Ginosar) fell to the portion of Naphtali, and he received on its south a rope's length of fishing-coast for spreading out his nets and meshes." Cf. b. B.K. 81b and Sifre.

The Midrash on Psalms (92) also refers to the sea of Chinnereth in a comment on this verse. God says that He is more satisfied with this sea than the rest of creation, for concerning the Chinnereth the Torah says: "satisfied with favor and full of blessing."

TO has the two senses of the word *yam*, i.e., "west" and "sea," and this may be a conflation. N and Ps-Jon do not do so. Some TO texts have "the south," like the MT, rather than "its south," which seems to imply the southern part of the Chinnereth.

[95] MT: "blessed be Asher among (or, on account of) sons." TO disassociates the *mem* (among) from "sons" and attaches it to "blessings," which TO adds for clarity. N and Ps-Jon do not do so, and add a gloss here. TO may be explaining the verse like Sifre: "You will find none of the tribes who was so blessed with children as Asher." However, a comparison of the figures in Num 1 with those in Num 26 shows that Asher's increase was not larger than other tribes. Rashi comments: "I do not know how this (the greatest increase) was so." TO may also be referring to the idea (found in Tanhuma, Vayechi, 13; Gen R. 99:12) that no tribe was so blessed by the men of Israel as Asher because of the beauty of its women. It is also possible that the word was added simply because it is implied in the text. N states that Asher is blessed for "he shall make reconciliation between his brothers and their Father who is in heaven." Ps-Jon has: "He will provide for his brothers, supplying them with provisions in the years of release."

[96] MT: "and let him dip his foot in oil." TO is explaining the metaphor by using the language of Gen 49:20, "Asher, his bread is fat; and he yields a king's dainties." In accordance with the interpretation given above, that the verse concerns the beautiful daughters of Asher, TO may be implying that these daughters will marry kings. Cf. I Chron 7:31 and Gen R. 71. TO may also be addressing Asher's use of the oil, using the more acceptable "nourishment" instead of "foot dipping," a practice that was unnessary during the non-nomadic period of the composition of the Targum. N has: "and he shall bathe his feet in oil," and Ps-Jon: "yielding oil, enough for him to immerse his legs."

25. Strong shall you be as iron and brass,[97] and as the days of your youth[98] shall be your strength.[99]

26. There is no God but the God of Israel,[100] whose Shekinah in the heaven is your help,[101] and whose strength is in the heaven of heavens.[102]

27. The dwelling place of God is from eternity,[103] the world was made by His Memra.[104] And He will drive out the enemy from before you, and will say, destroy.

28. And Israel shall dwell securely by themselves according to the blessing with which Jacob their father blessed them[105] upon the land producing[106] corn and wine; also the heaven above them[107] shall drop down dew.

---

[97] MT: "Your door-locks shall be iron and brass." TO explains the metaphor "door-locks" as either the land being as strong as iron and brass, or that it is locked against the enemy like a door made of iron and brass (Adler, NL). Rashi states that Moses has now begun to address all Israel. Strong men used to live in the border cities and, as it were, locked the country against invading enemies. N and Ps-Jon indicate clearly that Moses is addressing the tribe of Asher, who are as sound as iron and as strong as brass. Ps-Jon translates *n'l*, "door-locks," also as "feet." The LXX has: "His shoes shall be iron and brass."

[98] MT: "and as your days." The Targums add "your youth," which is implied. Rashi explains: "the days that are your best, the days of your youth, shall continue until old age."

[99] The word in the MT is obscure. TO renders like LXX, Peshitta, Ps-Jon, Saadya, Ibn Ezra, etc. N, FT, Vulgate, Rashi, etc., have "old age." Reifmann (*Sedeh*, p. 45) suggests that TO's "strength" means old age, as in Ps 90:10, "and with strength, eighty years." Thus, TO would be saying, you shall be as strong in your old age as you were in your youth. There are other suggested renderings, such as "rest" and "security."

[100] MT: "There is none like God, Jeshurun." See verse 5 for an explanation of Jeshurun. Some TO versions have "There is no God like the God of Israel," but as pointed out by Adler (NL) and Lowenstein (NH), this would be an uncharacteristic TO rendering. Adler and Lowenstein prefer "There is no God but the God of Israel." Comp. Exod 18:11, 20:3. N and Ps-Jon also have negative statements.

[101] MT: "who rides upon the heaven is your help." TO avoids the unseemly anthropomorphism by substituting "whose Shekinah" for "who rides." The same

25. תְּקִיף כְּבַרְזְלָא וּכְנַחְשָׁא וְכִיּוֹמֵי עוֹלֵימוֹתָךְ תּוּקְפָּךְ:
26. לֵית אֵילָה אֶלָא אֱלָהָא דְיִשְׂרָאֵל דִּשְׁכִנְתֵּיהּ בִּשְׁמַיָּא בְּסַעֲדָךְ וְתוּקְפֵּיהּ בִּשְׁמֵי שְׁמַיָּא:
27. מְדוֹר אֱלָהָא דְמִלְּקַדְמִין דִּבְמֵימְרֵיהּ אִתְעֲבִיד עָלְמָא וְיִתְרִיךְ מִן קֳדָם סָנְאָה וַאֲמַר שֵׁיצִי:
28. וְיִשְׁרֵי יִשְׂרָאֵל לְרוֹחֲצָן בִּלְחוֹדוֹהִי כְּעֵין בִּרְכָתָא דְבָרִיכִנּוּן יַעֲקֹב אֲבוּהוֹן בְּאַרַע עַבְדָא עִיבּוּר וַחֲמַר אַף שְׁמַיָּא דְעֵילָּוֵיהוֹן יְשַׁמְּשׁוּנִנּוּן בְּטַלָּא:

figure of speech is found in Ps 68:34. Comp. Isa 19:1, Hab 3:8, Ps 18:11 ff. Ps-Jon has the Shekinah and chariot dwell in heaven. N has the glory of the Shekinah dwell in heaven.

[102] MT: "and in His excellency on the sky." "Excellency," implying loftiness and grandeur (similarly Ps 68:35), is rendered in a more concrete manner, referring back to verse 25. Neither N nor Ps-Jon has the change.

[103] MT: "The God of eternity is a dwelling place." TO removes the unseemly anthropomorphism of God being Israel's dwelling place. Rashi explains that this verse must be connected with the preceding verse: "Heaven serves as God's dwelling place." Ps-Jon translates like TO; N, FT, and Saadya are similar.

[104] MT: "and beneath are the arms of the world." TO explains the phrase as a continuation of the previous idea: God's dwelling place exists forever, He made the earth, the world is under His control, and mankind does not have more power over it than God. N mentions "arm"; "beneath the arm of whose might the tribes of the children of Israel are led." Ps-Jon is more anthropomorphic: "and He carries the world under His mighty arm." FT is like N, but does not have the anthropomorphic "arm."

It is highly likely that Memra was erroneously copied here from the end of Ps-Jon, or a proto-Ps-Jon. A copyist then substituted "made" for what existed in the Targum so as to have an understandable phrase. Among other reasons for this conclusion: It is not clear how the phrase fits into the context without explanation. None of the other Targums use Memra here. TO never includes Memra elsewhere with creation. None of the medieval commentators mention this reading.

[105] MT: "like Jacob." Rashi states that the Hebrew word *'yn* here is translated as in Num 11:7 and means "as" or "like." Accordingly, the Targums explain that "like Jacob" implies the blessing given to them by Jacob, Gen 48:21. The interpretation is also in Sifre and Saadya.

[106] The Targums typically add "producing" for clarity. Sperber's text (but not B) has "like" the land, but this is an obvious error of a copyist confusing a *b* with a *k*.

[107] The Targums add "above them" for clarity, as in Lev 26:21 and Isa 45:8.

29. Happy are you, Israel; none is like you,[108] a people whose salvation is from before [109] the Lord, who is the strength[110] of your help, and before whom is the might of your victory;[111] your enemies shall be found to be liars to you, and you shall tread on the necks of their kings."[112]

Chapter XXXIV

1. Moses went up from the plains of Moab to Mount Nebo, to the heights of the slopes,[1] which is opposite Jericho, and the Lord showed him the whole land: Gilead as far as Dan;
2. all of Naphtali; the land of Ephraim and Manasseh; the whole land of Judah as far as the Western[2] Sea;
3. the south;[3] and the Plain—the valley of Jericho, the city of palm trees—as far as Zoar.
4. And the Lord said to him, "This is the land of which I confirmed[4] to Abraham, Isaac, and Jacob, saying, 'I will give it to your offspring.' I have let you see it with your own eyes, but you shall not cross there."
5. So Moses, the servant of the Lord, died there, in the land of Moab, by the Memra[5] of the Lord.
6. He buried him in the valley of Moab, opposite Beth-peor; and no man knows his burial place to this day.

---

[108] MT: "who is like unto you." Characteristically, TO replaces a rhetorical question and makes a positive statement. N and Ps-Jon do not.

[109] MT: *b*, "with." TO and N have "before," evading a depiction of a close proximity to God. Ps-Jon adds "name" and "Memra."

[110] MT: "the shield of your help." TO explains the anthropomorphic metaphor as in Gen 15:1. N and Ps-Jon retain the metaphor.

[111] MT: "and who is the sword of your excellency." TO clarifies the metaphor like Ibn Ezra: "God fights for you against your enemies to maintain your superiority over them." The PT retain the metaphor and explain it as "strength."

[112] MT: "and you shall tread upon their high places." The Targums interpret the figure of speech—to march over them triumphantly—probably thinking of Josh 10:24: "Put your feet upon the necks of those kings," and Gen 27:40, where the words *prq* and *ṣw'r* are found in the MT. Comp. b. Meg. 16a. The LXX has: "and you shall tread on their neck."

29. טובך ישראל לית דכותך עמא דפורקניה מן קדם יי תקוף בסעדך ודמן קדמוהי
נצחן גיברותך ויתכדבון סנאך לך ואת על פירקת צורי מלכיהון תדרוך:

XXXIV

1. וסליק משה ממשריא דמואב לטורא דנבו ריש רמתא דעל אפי ירחו ואחזייה יי ית
כל ארעא ית גלעד עד דן:
2. וית כל נפתלי וית ארע אפרים ומנשה וית כל ארע יהודה עד ימא בתראה:
3. וית דרומא וית מישרא בקעת ירחו קרית דקליא עד צער:
4. ואמר יי ליה דא ארעא דקיימית לאברהם ליצחק ולייעקב למימר לבנך אתנינה
אחזיתך בעינך ולתמן לא תיעיבר:
5. ומית תמן משה עבדא דיי בארעא דמואב על מימרא דיי:
6. וקבר יתיה בחילתא בארעא דמואב לקביל בית פעור ולא ידע אינש ית קבורתיה
עד יומא הדין:

N and FT add that all of this is conditional upon the Israelites studying the Torah and observing the commandments. Study of Torah is a frequent Targumic theme. The rabbis considered Israel's special privilege to be the study and observance of the Torah: this distinguished them from non-Jews. See, for example, Exod R. 30:9, where Aquila, who translated the Torah into Greek, states that he wanted to become a proselyte so he could study Torah.

[1] MT: "Pisgah." The Targums render here as in 3:17, 27, and Num 21:20, 27:12. N and FT add "Caesarea" at the end of the verse: "Dan of Caesarea."
[2] MT: "hindmost sea." TO and Saadya translate here as in 11:24. N and some TO texts (including B) render literally. Ps-Jon has a long gloss.
[3] MT: "Negeb." The Targums substitute here as in 1:7.
[4] MT: "swore."
[5] MT has a word which literally means "according to the mouth of" from which rabbinical tradition derives the belief that Moses died by the kiss of God (Tanhuma). The Targums avoid the anthropomorphism by adding "Memra." Ps-Jon has the story of the kiss: "So Moses, the servant of the Lord, was gathered there, in the land of Moab, by a kiss of the Memra of the Lord."
Ps-Jon speaks of Moses politely. He does not "die" (as in the MT, TO, FT, and N), but is "gathered from the world." N and FT have "gathered" in verse 7, where Ps-Jon has "lie" and TO is literal. Comp. Ps-Jon to 31:16, where the Targum erroneously renders MT's "you will lie with your fathers" as "you will lie in the earth with your fathers" even though Moses did not do so.

7. Moses was a hundred and twenty years old when he died; his eyes[6] were undimmed and the splendor of the glory of his countenance[7] was unchanged.
8. And the Israelites bewailed Moses in the plains of Moab for thirty days. The period of wailing and mourning for Moses came to an end.
9. Then Joshua son of Nun was filled with the spirit of wisdom because Moses had laid his hands upon him; and the Israelites accepted[9] him; and did as the Lord had commanded Moses.
10. Never again did there arise in Israel a prophet like Moses to whom the Lord revealed Himself,[10] face to face,[11]

[6] The MT has the singular for "eye." Some TO versions have the singular and others have the plural." N, FT, and Ps-Jon have "eyes."

[7] MT: "nor had his sap fled." TO: "and the *zyb yqr' d'pwhy* was unchanged." It is uncertain exactly what the three Aramaic words refer to, but it is clear that TO (and N and FT) are deviating for Moses' honor.

TO may be alluding to the ray of light on Moses' face. This story is in the MT of Exod 34:29, 30, and 35. Exod 34:29 has: "Moses did not know that the skin of his face shone because he had been talking with God." TO, N, and Ps-Jon use the same three Aramaic words in Exod used by TO here.

Secondly, the wording here is similar to Ps-Jon to Num 27:20, where Moses is told by God to invest Joshua with authority: "And you shall give from the splendor of your glory to him." TO may be informing us that this glory also remained with Moses until his death.

However, as a third possibility, it should be noted that the Aramaic word translated "glory" also means "features." See, for example, Ps-Jon to Gen 4:5, 25:49, 37:3; Exod 34:29, 30, 33, 34, 35. Thus, TO may be explaining MT's metaphor, saying, in effect, that Moses continued to look well until his death. Indeed, N and FT, which also use delicate language, read "the splendor of his countenance," without the word "glory."

In view of the absence of the word in N and FT, a fourth possibility is that *yqr'*, "glory" or "features," is a doublet for *d'pwhy*, "countenance."

Ps-Jon fails to deviate for Moses' honor, rendering: "his molar teeth had not fallen out." LXX has: "natural moistness of the body," understanding *lḥ* as "moistness."

Both words are found in the Targum to Songs 1:5 and 5:10 where the Targumist speaks of the face of those who repent being like that of angels and God's face, respectively. Ps-Jon to Exod. 33:11, however, states that Moses did not see the *zyw 'pyn* of God.

7. ומשה בר מאה ועסרין שנין כד מית לא כהת עיניה ולא שנא זיו יקרא דאפוהי:
8. ובכו בני ישראל ית משה במישריא דמואב תלתין יומין ושלימו יומי בכיתא אבלא דמשה:
9. ויהושע בר נון אתמלי רוח חוכמתא ארי סמך משה ית ידוהי עלוהי וקבילו מניה בני ישראל ועבדו כמא דפקיד יי ית משה:
10. ולא קם נביא עוד בישראל כמשה דאיתגלי ליה יי אפין באפין:

---

[8] MT: *nws*, "fled." In an article in *Zeitschrift für Die Alttestamentliche Wissenschaft* 91 (1979): 107–123, B. Grossfeld points out that of the thirty-three uses of *nws* in the MT, TO consistently translates *ʿrq*, except for Exod 9:20, where *knyš*, "gather," is used, and Deut 34:7, where *šnʾ*, "change," is the rendering. None of the versions render our verse by *ʿrq*. The Peshitta has "shrink." LXX "destroyed." FT and Ps-Jon "fallen out." N agrees with TO. Grossfeld does not explain the differences. However, P. Churgin ("The Targum and the Septuagint," pp. 41–44) explains such divergences as either showing respect for Israelite ancestors, reflecting rabbinic interpretations, or the result of different recensions; i.e., changes made in the translation at a later date. Actually there is no complex rationale needed for our substitution: it replaces a metaphor.

[9] MT: "heard." TO and Ps-Jon make a typical change. N, characteristically, is literal.

[10] MT: "knew," a word which implies a close attachment (see Rashi on Gen 18:19 and Ruth 2:3). (Comp. Ps 144:3, where the word means "bestowing honor by giving heed to the person.") TO captures the plain meaning of the text. Nachmanides understands the MT as giving a mystical teaching: God knew Moses face to face to a degree that it was possible to cleave to Him whenever the spirit came upon Moses. This is the kind of teaching TO tries to avoid.

N and Ps-Jon retain the word "knew," but it is the Memra that knows and speaks to Moses word to word, rather than face to face.

[11] TO retains the anthropomorphism of the MT, as in Gen 32:31, although deviating in 5:4, Exod 33:11, 23, and Num 12:8. N, FT, and Ps-Jon change the wording. Adler (NL) argues that TO did not deviate to teach Maimonides' principle that Moses was the greatest of the prophets, having a clearer revelation. This argument, based solely on TO's literal rendering, is unconvincing since TO makes no addition to highlight the teaching. There are many instances where TO fails to avoid anthropomorphisms without teaching a theological lesson, and no clear evidence exists that there is a desire on the part of the author(s) of TO to teach theological principles. Furthermore, a rather simple explanation can be given for this failure to deviate. The words "face to face" do not refer to God but to the "signs and wonders that the Lord sent him to display in the land of Egypt" (v.

11. with the various signs and wonders that the Lord sent him to display in the land of Egypt, against Pharaoh and all his courtiers and his whole country,

12. and with all that mighty hand, and with all that great vision[12] that Moses wrought in the sight of all Israel.

11). This understanding also clarifies the use of the word "revealed" (in this verse): "the Lord revealed Himself" to Moses by a clear manifestation of the various signs and wonders.

12 MT: "terror." TO and N interpret "great terror" here, as elsewhere, as a divine revelation. See, for example, 4:34, 26:8, and Exod 3:3. Sifre explains that the

11. לכל אתיא ומופתיא דשלחיה יי למעבד בארעא דמצרים לפרעה לכל עבדוהי ולכל
ארעיה:

12. ולכל ידא תקיפתא ולכל חיזוונא רבא דעבד משה לעיני כל ישראל:

חזק

"great terror" here refers to the division of the Red Sea or the revelation at Mount
Sinai. Ps-Jon speaks of the revelation at Sinai. Compare Rashi to Exod. 18:1:
Jethro heard of the division of the Red Sea and the victory over Amalek and joined
the Israelites (b. Zeb. 116).

SELECTED BIBLIOGRAPHY

A complete bibliography on the Targums will be found in: Bernard Grossfeld, A *Bibliography of Targum Literature*, 2 vols. (Cincinnati: Hebrew Union College Press, 1972; New York: KTAV, 1977).

Abelson, J. *The Immanence of God in Rabbinic Literature*. London: 1912.
Aberbach, Moses. "Patriotic Tendencies in Targum Onkelos." *JHS* 1, 1969, pp. 13–24.
———. "Patriotic Tendencies in Targum Jonathan to the Prophets." *HA* 15, 1974, pp. 89–90.
Aberbach, Moses, and Grossfeld, Bernard. *Targum Onkelos on Genesis 49*. Montana: 1979.
———. *Targum Onkelos to Genesis*. New York: 1981.
Adler, Nathan. *Netina Lager*. Wilna: 1886.
Ahana, M. "Agneau Pascal et Circoncision." *VT* 23, 1974, pp. 385–389.
Albeck, H. "Apocryphal Halakhah in the Palestinian Targums and the Aggadah." *Jubilee Volume to B. M. Lewin*, pp. 93–104. Jerusalem 1940.
———. "Mekoroth Ha-Bereshit Rabba." *Einleitung und Register zu Bereshit Rabba*, Vol. 1. Jerusalem: 1965.
———. Bacher, W. "Targum." *Jewish Encyclopeia* XII. 1906, pp. 57–63.
Bamberger, B. J. "Halakic Elements in the Neofiti Targum: A Preliminary Statement." *JQR* 66, 1975, pp. 27–38.
Ben Elijah, Abraham. *Targum Abraham*. Jerusalem: 1896.
Berkowitz, B. Z. J. *Oteh Or*. Wilna: 1843.
———. *Lechem Vesimla*. Wilna: 1843.
———. *Chalifot Semalot*. Wilna: 1874.
———. *Abne Tziyon*. Wilna: 1877.
Berlin, Isaiah B. *Mini Targuma*. Breslau: 1831.
Berliner, A. *The Massorah to Targum Onkelos*. Leipzig: 1877.
———. *Targum Onkelos*. 2 vols. Berlin: 1884.
Black, M. *An Aramaic Approach to the Gospels and Acts*. Oxford: 1954.

Bloch, R. "Note methodologique pour l'étude de la littérature rabbinique." *RSR* XLIII, 1955, pp. 194–227.
———. *Revue des Études Juives* XIV, 1955, pp. 5–35.
Bowker, J. W. "Haggadah in the Targum Onkelos." *JSS* 12, 1967, pp. 51–65.
———. *The Targums and Rabbinic Literature.* Cambridge: 1969.
Brauer, M. M. "Studies on Targum Jonathan ben Uzziel." Unpublished Ph.D. thesis, Yeshiva University, 1950.
Churgin, P. *Targum Jonathan to the Prophets.* New Haven: 1907.
———. "The Targum and the Septuagint." *AJSL* 50, 1933, pp. 41–65.
———. "The Origin of Targumic Formulas." *Horeb* 7, 1943, pp. 103–109.
———. *The Targum to Hagiographa.* New York: 1945.
———. "The Halakhah in Targum Onkelos." *Horeb* 9, 1946, pp. 79–93.
Cowling, Geoffery J. "The Palestinian Targum: Textual and Linguistic Investigations in Codex Neofiti and Allied Manuscripts." Unpublished Ph.D. thesis, University of Aberdeen, 1968.
Dalman, G. *Grammatik des Jüdisch-Palästinischen Aramäisch.* Leipzig: 1905.
Davies, W. D. *Torah in the Messianic Age and/or the Age to Come.* Philadelphia: 1952.
Diez Macho A. "The Recently Discovered Palestinian Targum: Its Antiquity, and Relationship with the Other Targums." *VT Supp.* 7, 1959, pp. 222 ff.
——— *Mélanges Eugene Tisserant,* vol. I. Vatican, 1964.
——— *Neophyti I. Targum Palestinense,* vols. 1–5. Madrid: 1968–78.
Drazin, Israel. "Targumic Studies." Unpublished Ph.D. thesis, St. Mary's University, 1980.
Drazin, Nathan. *History of Jewish Education from 515 B.C.E. to 200 C. E.* Baltimore: 1940.
Etheridge, John W. *The Targum of Onkelos and Jonathan Ben Uzziel on the Pentateuch.* New York: 1968.
Faur, José. "The Massorah of Targum Onkelos." *Sinai* 60–61, 1966–67, pp. 14–27.
———. "The Targumim and Halakhah." *JQR* 66, 1975–76, pp. 19–26.
Fitzmyer, Joseph A. *The Genesis Apocryphon of Qumram Cave I.* Rome: 1966.
Foster, Julia A. "The Languages and Text of Codex Neofiti I in the Light of other Palestinian Sources." Unpublished Ph.D. thesis, Boston University, 1969.

Frankel, Z. *Vorstudien zur Septuaginta,* Leipzig: 1841.
———. "Notizen zu Onkelos Deuteron. 23, 11." *MGWJ* 2, 1853, p. 40.
Friedmann, M. ed. *Sifre.* Vienna: 1864 (reprinted Tel Aviv: 1968).
———. *Onkelos und Akylas.* Vienna: 1896.
Geiger, Abraham. *Hamikra Vetargumov.* Jerusalem: 1948.
Ginsburger, M. *Die Anthropomorphism in den Thargumim.* Braun-
schwieg: 1891.
———. *Das Fragmententhargum.* Berlin: 1899.
———. *Targum Jonathan ben Usiel zum Pentateuch.* Berlin: 1903.
Goshen-Gottstein, Moshe H. *Aramaic Bible Versions.* Jerusalem: 1963.
———. *The Third Targum on Esther and Ms Neofiti I.* Ramat Gan:
1973.
Grossfeld, B. "A Commentary on the Text of a New Palestinian Targum
(Codex Neofiti I) on Genesis 1–XXV." Unpublished Ph.D. thesis,
Johns Hopkins University, 1968.
Heinemann, J. "The Targum of Ex. 22:4 and the Ancient Halakhah." *Tar-
biz* 38, 1968–69, pp. 294–296.
Herskovics, Meir. "Halakah and Aggadah in Targum Onkelos." Unpub-
lished Ph.D. thesis, Yeshiva University, 1950.
———. "Rabbinic Relations to Targum Onkelos." *Joshua Finkel Fest-
schrift,* pp. 169–176. New York: 1974.
Horowitz, H. S., and Rabin T. A., eds. *Mechilta.* Jerusalem: 1970.
Isenberg, Sheldon R. "Studies in the Jewish Aramaic Translations of the
Pentateuch." Unpublished Ph.D. thesis, Harvard University, 1969.
Jastrow, M. *A Dictionary of the Targumim, the Talmud Babli and Yeru-
shalmi, and the Midrashic Literature,* 2 vols. 1886–1903.
Jurgrau, Moshe. "Targumim Method." *Bar Ilan* 12, 1974, pp. 179–199.
Kadushin, Max. "Anthropomorphism and Targum Onkelos." *The Rab-
binic Mind,* pp. 325–336. New York: 1952.
Kahle, Paul. *The Cairo Geniza.* Oxford: 1959.
———. *Masoreten des Westerns II.* Stuttgart: 1930.
Kasher, M. M. *Torah Shelemah,* vol. 17 and vol. 24. Jerusalem: 1956,
1974.
Kasovsky, H. J. *Elim Ledugma.* Jerusalem: 1933.
Klein, M. L. "Converse Translation: A Targumic Technique." *Biblica* 57,
1976, pp. 525–537.
———. "The Preposition *Qdm* (Before): A Pseudo-Anthropomorphism in
the Targums." *JTS,* 1979, pp. 502–507.
Knobel, Peter S. "Targum Qoheleth: A Linguistic and Exegetical

Inquiry." Unpublished Ph.D. thesis, Yale University, 1976.

Komlosh, Yehudah. "Targumic Manuscript." *Sinai Jubilee Volume*, 1948, pp. 466–481.

————. "The Ten Commandments in the Jerusalem Targums." *Sinai*, 1962–63, pp. 289–295.

————. "Haagada Betargume Berchat Yaakov." *Annual of Bar Ilan University, Studies in Judaica and Humanities I. Pinkhos Churgin Memorial Volume*. Jerusalem: 1963.

————. *Hamikra Beor HaTargum*. Tel Aviv: 1973.

Kuiper, Gerard Johannes. *The Pseudo-Jonathan Targum and Its Relationship to Targum Onkelos*. Rome: 1972.

Kutscher, E. Y. "Aspects of the Dead Sea Scrolls." *Scripta Hierosolymitana*. Jerusalem: 1957.

————. "The Language of the Genesis Apocryphon." *Scripta Hierosolymitana*. Jerusalem, 1958.

LeDeaut, Roger. "La Nuit Pascale: Essai sur la significacion de la Pâque juive à partir due Targum d'Exode XII 42." *Analecta Biblica 42*. Rome: 1963.

————. *Introduction a la Literature Targumique I*. Rome: 1966.

Lehman, George I. "Anthropomorphisms in the Former Prophets of the Hebrew Bible as Compared with the Septuagint and Targum Jonathan." Unpublished Ph.D. thesis, New York Univesity, 1964.

Levey S. H. "The Date of Targum Jonathan to the Prophets." *VT* 21, 1971, pp. 186 ff.

————. *The Messiah: An Aramaic Interpretation: The Messianic Exegesis of the Targum*. Cincinnati-New York: 1974.

Levine, Etan. "Aggadic Elements in Targum Jonathan ben Uzziel to Genesis." *Neophyti I*, vol 2 (1973) through Vol. 5 (1978).

Liver, J. "The Doctrine of the Two Messiahs in Sectarian Literature in the Time of the Second Commonwealth." *HTR* 52, 1959, pp. 149 ff.

Lowenstein, M. *Nefesh Hager*. Pietrokov: 1906.

Lund, Shirley, and Foster, Julia. *Variant Versions of Targumic Traditions within Codex Neofiti I*. Montana: 1977.

Luzzatto, S. D. *Oheb Ger*. Vienna: 1830; second edition, Krakow: 1895.

————. *Briefen*. Przemysl: 1882.

McNamara, Martin. *The New Testament and the Palestinian Targum to the Pentateuch*. Rome: 1966.

————. "Targumic Studies." *CBQ* 28. 1966, pp. 1–19.

———. "Some Early Rabbinic Citations and the Palestinian Targum to the Pentateuch." *RSO* 41, 1966 pp. 1–15.

———. *Targum and Testament.* Shannon: 1972.

Maimonides, Moses. *The Guide for the Perplexed.* Written about 1190.

Marmorstein, A. *The Doctrine of Merits in Old Rabbinic Literature.* London: 1920.

———. *The Old Rabbinic Doctrine of God.* London: 1937.

———. *Studies in Jewish Theology.* London: 1950.

———. "Participation in Eternal Life in Rabbinic Theology and Legend." *REJ* 89, 1930, pp. 305 ff.

Masorah al Hatargum. Found in Netina Lager, Wilna: 1886.

Maybaum, S. *Die Anthropomorphism und Anthropopathien bei Onkelos und späteren Targumim.* Breslau: 1870.

Melammed, E. Z. *Bible Commentators.* Jerusalem: 1978.

Miller, Merril P. "Targum, Midrash and the Use of the Old Testament in the New Testament." *JSJ* 2, 1971, pp. 29–92.

Moore, George F. "Intermediaries in Jewish Theology." *HTR* 15, 1922, pp. 41 ff.

Nickels, Peter. *Targum and New Testament.* Rome: 1967.

Nöldeke, Theodor. *Die Alttestamentliche Literatur in einer Reihe von Aufsätzen dargestellt von Theodor Nöldeke.* Leipzig: 1868.

Nyberg, H. S. "Deuteronomion 33, 2–3." *ZDMG* 92, 1938, pp. 320–344.

Orlinsky, Harry M. "Studies in the Septuagint of the Book of Job." *HUCA* 30, 1959.

———. "The Treatment of Anthropomorphisms and Anthropopathisms in the Septuagint of Isaiah." *HUCA* 27, 1956.

Patshegen. Found in Netina Lager, Wilna: 1886.

Rasmussen, Ellis T. "Relationships of God and Man According to a Text and Targum of Deuteronomy." Unpublished Ph.D. thesis, Brigham Young University, 1967.

Reider, David. "On the Targum Yerushalmi Ms Neofiti I." *Tarbiz* 38, 1958, pp. 81–86.

———. "On the Targum Yerushalmi known as the Fragmentary Targum." *Tarbiz* 39, 1969, pp. 83–85.

Reifmann, J. *Sedeh Aram.* Berlin: 1875.

Sabourin, L. "The Memra of God in the Targums." *BTB*, 1966, pp. 79–85.

Schefftel, S. B. *Biure Onkelos.* Munich: 1888.

Schmerler, B. *Ahavath Jehonothan.* Bilgoraj: 1932.

Schneekloth, Larry G. "The Targum of the Song of Songs: A Study in Rabbinic Biblical Interpretation." Unpublished Ph.D. thesis, University of Wisconsin, Madison: 1977.

Seligsohn, Hermann. *Die Duabus Hierosolymitana Pentateuchi Paraphrasibus.* Breslau: 1858.

Shmidman, Joshua. "Zekhut Abot." *EJ* vol. 16, col. 976. Jerusalem: 1972.

Shunary, Jonathan. "Avoidance of Anthropomorphisms in the Targum of Psalms." *Textus* 5, 1966, 133 ff.

Silverstone, A. E. *Aquila and Onkelos.* Manchester University Press, 1931.

Soffer, Arthur. "The Treatment of Anthropomorphisms and Anthropopathisms in the Septuagint of Psalms." *HUCA* 28, 1957.

Sperber, Alexander, ed. *The Bible in Aramaic, vol. 1: The Pentateuch According to Targum Onkelos.* Leiden: 1959.

——. "The Targum Onkelos in Its Relation to the Massoretic Hebrew Text." *PAAJR* 6, 1934–35, pp. 309–351.

Szebrczyn, David. *Perush Jonathan and Yerushalmi.* Prague: 1609.

Tur-Sinai, N. H. *Halashon Vehasefer.* Jerusalem: 1960, pp. 94–101.

Vermes, Pamela. "Buber's Understanding of the Divine Names Related to Bible, Targum and Midrash." *JJS*, 1973, pp. 147–166.

Vermez, Geza. *Scripture and Tradition in Judaism: Haggadic Studies.* Leiden: 1961.

——. *The Annual of Leeds University Oriental Society,* pp. 81–114. Leiden: 1963.

——. "Haggadah in the Onkelos Targum." *JSS* 8, 1963, pp. 159 ff.

——. *In Memoriam Paul Kahle,* pp. 236 ff. Berlin: 1968.

Waldberg, Samuel. *Lashon Hachamim.* Found in Netina Lager, Wilna: 1886.

Weinberg, J. "LeToldoth HaTargumim." *The Abraham Weiss Jubilee Volume,* 1964, pp. 361–376.

Weinfeld, Moshe. *Deuteronomy and the Deuteronomic School.* London: 1972.

Wernberg-Møller, Preben. "An Inquiry into the Validity of the Text-Critical Argument for an Early Dating of the Recently Discovered Palestinian Targum." *VT* 12, 1962, pp. 312–330.

——. "Prolegomena to a Re-examination of the Palestinian Targum Fragments of the Book of Genesis Published by P. Kahle, and Their Relationship to the Peshitta." *JSS* 7, 1962, pp. 253–266.

Wertheimer, S. A. *Or Hatargum.* Jerusalem: 1935.

Wieder, N. "The Doctrine of the Two Messiahs among the Karaites." *JJS* 6, 1955, pp. 14 ff.

Wine, Alter. *Yayin Tob.* Rehovot: 1976.

Zaslenski, A. Y. "Perushey Hatargumim." *Sinai* 56–57, 1965, p. 262.

Zimels, Abraham. "The Palestinian Targum: MS Neofiti I on Genesis and Noah in Comparison with Pseudo-Jonathan and Targum Onkelos." Unpublished Ph.D. thesis, Yeshiva University, 1972.

Zunz, Leopold. *Die Gottesdienstlichen Vorträge der Juden.* Berlin: 1832.

INDEX

BIBLICAL

TARGUMIM

TOSEFTA, MISHNA, TALMUDS

POST-BIBLICAL LITERATURE

AUTHORS

N.M. Adler, B.Z.J. Berkowitz, M. Lowenstein and S.B. Schefftel are not indexed since they are mentioned frequently in the notes.

About the Author

Israel Drazin, M.Ed., M.A., J.D., Ph.D., was born in Baltimore, Maryland, on December 5, 1935.

He was ordained as a rabbi in 1957 and entered the army as the youngest U.S. chaplain ever to serve on active duty. He presently holds the rank of colonel, the highest rank achieved by a Jewish army chaplain, and serves in the army reserves as a senior instructor at the U.S. Army Chaplains School. He has officiated as a weekend rabbi at several synagogues, including being the first Orthodox rabbi in Randallstown, Maryland, and the first rabbi in the planned city of Columbia, Maryland.

Dr. Drazin has a master's degree in psychology and was an Equal Employment Opportunity consultant for five years with the Social Security Administration.

As a lawyer, he is presently acting as deputy director of the Regulations staff of the Health Care Financing Administration responsible for Medicare, Medicaid, and other federal health-care regulations. He also has a private law practice.

He is the author of *Targumic Studies* and about 200 articles on various subjects.